CRIME, PRISONS, AND JAILS

ISSN 1938-890X

CRIME, PRISONS, AND JAILS

Kim Masters Evans

INFORMATION PLUS® REFERENCE SERIES
Formerly Published by Information Plus, Wylie, Texas

GALE
CENGAGE Learning™

Detroit • New York • San Francisco • New Haven, Conn • Waterville, Maine • London

GALE
CENGAGE Learning·

Crime, Prisons, and Jails

Kim Masters Evans
Paula Kepos, Series Editor

Project Editors: Kathleen J. Edgar, Elizabeth Manar

Rights Acquisition and Management: Margaret Adendroth, Jacqueline Flowers

Composition: Evi Abou-El-Seoud, Mary Beth Trimper

Manufacturing: Cynde Lentz

For product information and technology assistance, contact us at
Gale Customer Support, 1-800-877-4253.
For permission to use material from this text or product,
submit all requests online at **www.cengage.com/permissions.**
Further permissions questions can be e-mailed to
permissionrequest@cengage.com

Gale
27500 Drake Rd.
Farmington Hills, MI 48331-3535

ISBN-13: 978-0-7876-5103-9 (set)   ISBN-10: 0-7876-5103-6 (set)
ISBN-13: 978-1-4144-3381-3   ISBN-10: 1-4144-3381-6

ISSN 1938-890X

This title is also available as an e-book.
ISBN-13: 978-1-4144-5765-9 (set)
ISBN-10: 1-4144-5765-0 (set)
Contact your Gale sales representative for ordering information.

Printed in the United States of America
1 2 3 4 5 6 7 13 12 11 10 09

TABLE OF CONTENTS

PREFACE

Crime, Prisons, and Jails is part of the *Information Plus Reference Series*. The purpose of each volume of the series is to present the latest facts on a topic of pressing concern in modern American life. These topics include the most controversial and studied social issues in the twenty-first century: abortion, capital punishment, care of senior citizens, the environment, health care, immigration, minorities, national security, social welfare, women, youth, and many more. Even though this series is written especially for high school and undergraduate students, it is an excellent resource for anyone in need of factual information on current affairs.

By presenting the facts, it is the intention of Gale, Cengage Learning, to provide its readers with everything they need to reach an informed opinion on current issues. To that end, there is a particular emphasis in this series on the presentation of scientific studies, surveys, and statistics. These data are generally presented in the form of tables, charts, and other graphics placed within the text of each book. Every graphic is directly referred to and carefully explained in the text. The source of each graphic is presented within the graphic itself. The data used in these graphics are drawn from the most reputable and reliable sources, such as from the various branches of the U.S. government and from major independent polling organizations. Every effort has been made to secure the most recent information available. Readers should bear in mind that many major studies take years to conduct and that additional years often pass before the data from these studies are made available to the public. Therefore, in many cases the most recent information available in 2009 is dated from 2006 or 2007. Older statistics are sometimes presented as well if they are of particular interest and no more-recent information exists.

Even though statistics are a major focus of the *Information Plus Reference Series*, they are by no means its only content. Each book also presents the widely held positions and important ideas that shape how the book's subject is discussed in the United States. These positions are explained in detail and, where possible, in the words of their proponents. Some of the other material to be found in these books includes historical background, descriptions of major events related to the subject, relevant laws and court cases, and examples of how these issues play out in American life. Some books also feature primary documents or have pro and con debate sections that provide the words and opinions of prominent Americans on both sides of a controversial topic. All material is presented in an even-handed and unbiased manner; readers will never be encouraged to accept one view of an issue over another.

HOW TO USE THIS BOOK

In general, crime has been on the decline in recent years. Some crimes, however, are increasing in number among different segments of the population. For example, violent crime has decreased since the 1990s, whereas identity theft has increased. Besides exploring crime in the United States, this volume examines the U.S. penal system as well as its inmates. Prisons and jails are an important and controversial part of the effort to control crime in the United States. Much public funding is spent on the construction of new prisons and jails and the maintenance of old facilities, but many people question the effectiveness of prisons and jails as a deterrent to crime. Who is locked up in U.S. prisons, what crimes have they committed, and how effective is the prison system? These and other basic questions are discussed in this volume.

Crime, Prisons, and Jails consists of ten chapters and three appendixes. Each chapter is devoted to a particular aspect of crime, prisons, and jails in the United States. For a summary of the information covered in each chapter, please see the synopses provided in the Table of Contents at the front of the book. Chapters generally begin with an overview of the basic facts and background information on the chapter's topic, then proceed to examine subtopics of particular interest. For example, Chapter 6, Controlling Crime, begins with a brief discussion of the types of law enforcement agencies and the numbers of employees that fill the ranks of these agencies. Next, various aspects of these agencies are discussed, such as their key components for controlling modern crime and the numbers and types of arrests that are made. The chapter then addresses the legal system by highlighting the rights of the people who are arrested and the role of prosecutors. The judiciary system is examined by addressing topics such as sentences, truth-in-sentencing, federal sentencing guidelines, three-strikes laws, alternative sentences, and the death penalty. The chapter concludes with a look at the corrections system. Readers can find their way through a chapter by looking for the section and subsection headings, which are clearly set off from the text. They can also refer to the book's extensive Index, if they already know what they are looking for.

Statistical Information

The tables and figures featured throughout *Crime, Prisons, and Jails* will be of particular use to readers in learning about this topic. These tables and figures represent an extensive collection of the most recent and valuable statistics on prisons and jails, as well as related issues—for example, graphics cover the number of people in jail or prison in the United States; the characteristics of those incarcerated; and the amount of money spent on the prison system. Gale, Cengage Learning, believes that making this information available to readers is the most important way to fulfill the goal of this book: to help readers understand the issues and controversies surrounding crime, prisons, and jails in the United States and to reach their own conclusions.

Each table or figure has a unique identifier appearing above it for ease of identification and reference. Titles for the tables and figures explain their purpose. At the end of each table or figure, the original source of the data is provided.

To help readers understand these often complicated statistics, all tables and figures are explained in the text. References in the text direct readers to the relevant statistics. Furthermore, the contents of all tables and figures are fully indexed. Please see the opening section of the Index at the back of this volume for a description of how to find tables and figures within it.

Appendixes

Besides the main body text and images, *Crime, Prisons, and Jails* has three appendixes. The first is the Important Names and Addresses directory. Here, readers will find contact information for a number of government and private organizations that can provide further information on aspects of crime and the U.S. prison and jail system. The second appendix is the Resources section, which can also assist readers in conducting their own research. In this section, the editors of *Crime, Prisons, and Jails* describe some of the sources that were most useful during the compilation of this book. The final appendix is the Index.

ADVISORY BOARD CONTRIBUTIONS

The staff of Information Plus would like to extend its heartfelt appreciation to the Information Plus Advisory Board. This dedicated group of media professionals provides feedback on the series on an ongoing basis. Their comments allow the editorial staff who work on the project to make the series better and more user-friendly. The staff's top priorities are to produce the highest-quality and most useful books possible, and the Advisory Board's contributions to this process are invaluable.

The members of the Information Plus Advisory Board are:

- Kathleen R. Bonn, Librarian, Newbury Park High School, Newbury Park, California

- Madelyn Garner, Librarian, San Jacinto College, North Campus, Houston, Texas

- Anne Oxenrider, Media Specialist, Dundee High School, Dundee, Michigan

- Charles R. Rodgers, Director of Libraries, Pasco-Hernando Community College, Dade City, Florida

- James N. Zitzelsberger, Library Media Department Chairman, Oshkosh West High School, Oshkosh, Wisconsin

COMMENTS AND SUGGESTIONS

The editors of the *Information Plus Reference Series* welcome your feedback on *Crime, Prisons, and Jails*. Please direct all correspondence to:

Editors
Information Plus Reference Series
27500 Drake Rd.
Farmington Hills, MI 48331-3535

CHAPTER 1
AN OVERVIEW OF CRIME

A crime occurs when a person commits an act prohibited by law or fails to act where there is a legal responsibility to do so. Crime has both legal and moral components. Federal, state, and local laws define criminal behavior and specify corresponding punishments. These laws are designed to protect the public good and are based, in some part, on the moral beliefs held by that society about the relative rightness and wrongness of various human actions. Americans consider crime to be a serious problem. They worry about the level of criminal behavior in their neighborhoods and in the country as a whole.

CATEGORIZING CRIME
Morality and Mental State
At a basic level, crime is divided into two categories based on whether the behavior violates the moral standards of a society or simply the administrative policies of its government. The Latin term *mala in se* means "morally wrong" or "inherently wrong." *Mala in se* crimes are those condemned universally as wrong or evil because the criminal action is inherently bad. These are crimes that offend the moral beliefs of people. Crimes such as murder and stealing have been considered wrong since ancient times. Some societal morals change with time. For example, slavery was once accepted as a legal practice in the United States. Eventually, it became so morally repugnant that it was considered a *mala in se* crime. In recent decades such actions as driving under the influence or using certain drugs have become *mala in se*. By contrast, other crimes are considered *mala prohibita* (wrongs prohibited). These are behaviors that are not inherently bad in themselves, but are prohibited by government policy. Many traffic laws are *mala prohibita*. For example, speeding is criminal not because it is morally evil, but because it is deemed criminal by government authorities.

Governments' decisions about how to define and punish certain crimes are based, in part, on the moral beliefs of the society in which the crimes occur. Even though *mala in se* behaviors are universally condemned as wrong, punishments for these crimes can vary significantly between societies and between governments. During the colonial period in U.S. history the death penalty was commonly meted out for crimes such as horse stealing and robbery. Over time, societal morals demanded less harsh punishments for these crimes.

An important element in how crimes are categorized and punished is called *mens rea*, which translates from Latin as "guilty mind," or more commonly, "criminal intent." The U.S. justice system seeks to determine the mental state of a perpetrator at the time the criminal act was committed and assign punishment accordingly. Intentional criminal acts that are planned in advance are considered much more serious than unintentional criminal acts or crimes committed in the "heat of passion."

Punishment Categories

From a punishment standpoint, crimes are divided into three broad categories: felonies, misdemeanors, and infractions. Felonies are considered the most serious crimes and are punished the most severely. The word *felony* is believed to be derived from a Latin word meaning "evil doer." Crimes that inflict death or serious injury or the threat of death or serious injury are considered felonies. Many property crimes that involve large economic losses to the victim are also classified as felonies. In general, people convicted of felonies are punished with prison terms at least a year in length and are sometimes assessed a fine of many thousands of dollars. Convicted felons may also lose some of their constitutional rights, such as the right to vote in elections. The most serious felony is the intentional murder of another human being. This crime is considered so heinous that capital punishment (execution) is sometimes the penalty for committing murder.

Misdemeanors are less serious crimes than felonies. They involve less personal harm and lower economic losses than felonies. These "lesser" crimes are typically punished with jail sentences of less than one year and fines of up to a few thousand dollars. People convicted of misdemeanors do not typically lose any of their constitutional rights once their sentences are served.

States divide felonies and misdemeanors into levels or classes to indicate their relative seriousness. For example, the Virginia Department of Alcoholic Beverage Control indicates in "Punishment for Criminal Offenses" (2009, http://www.abc.state.va.us/facts/punish.html) that Virginia has six classes of felonies and four classes of misdemeanors. In both categories Class 1 crimes are the most serious and punished the most severely. Other states use a letter system in which Class A felonies or misdemeanors are considered the most serious in their category.

Finally, the least serious crimes are called infractions (or petty offenses). These include minor traffic and parking violations and violations of local ordinances. The punishment for an infraction is usually only a fine of up to a few hundred dollars.

DEFINING THE TYPES OF CRIMES

Crimes are defined and punished differently by different jurisdictions within the United States. Sorting out all the various and complicated legal definitions for particular crimes can be complicated. This section will present some general and widely used definitions for the most common crimes. The American Bar Association (ABA) is a private organization for legal professionals, such as lawyers and judges. The ABA maintains an online glossary (http://www.abanet.org/publiced/glossary.html) of legal terms that includes general definitions of various crimes. This glossary is the source for many of the crime definitions presented in the following section.

Killing Crimes

Killing crimes are defined and punished at various levels depending on the mental state of the killer and the circumstances under which the killing took place. Criminal intent (or lack thereof) plays a major role in how these crimes are categorized. Killing with criminal intent is typically called murder. There are various degrees (or levels) of murder in criminal law. First-degree murder is the most serious charge and means the killer planned the crime and deliberately carried it out. First-degree murder is often described as deliberate killing with "malice aforethought." Malice is the desire or intent to cause great harm. Aforethought means "previously in mind." In other words, murder committed with aforethought is premeditated (considered and thought through before being committed).

Second-degree murder is a lesser charge that is applied to a killing that may or may not be intentional but is not premeditated. A person who gets into a fistfight and ultimately kills his or her opponent might be charged with second-degree murder. This crime might also be called manslaughter. There are two levels of manslaughter: voluntary manslaughter and involuntary manslaughter. Voluntary manslaughter is a killing believed to be intentional but not premeditated. It occurs on a sudden impulse, as in the fistfight example. Involuntary manslaughter is an unintentional killing that occurs as a consequence of reckless behavior or extreme negligence. The reckless behavior is typically some minor unlawful action that is not ordinarily expected to result in a death. An example is a driver who runs a red light and inadvertently strikes and kills a pedestrian crossing the street. Ordinarily, running a red light is a minor crime. The accidental taking of life elevates the crime to the level of manslaughter. Involuntary manslaughter involving extreme negligence may also be called criminally negligent homicide. Involuntary manslaughter involving recklessness, rather than negligence, is often called nonnegligent homicide.

An accidental killing that occurs as a result of a felony is a much more serious crime in the eyes of the law. Some states define a crime called felony murder. It can be charged against any willing participant in a serious felony (such as a bank robbery) if a person is inadvertently killed as a result of the felonious act. These laws apply even to criminals who are not actually in the victim's presence at the time of the accidental death (e.g., getaway drivers at bank robberies). As a result, these laws are highly controversial.

There are some homicides that are not considered criminal. These include killings performed in self-defense and accidental killings that occur during noncriminal actions. Intent and circumstances are the primary elements that influence whether criminal charges are filed and the extent of any resulting punishments.

Bodily Harm Crimes

Bodily harm crimes are crimes that are intended to cause or do cause personal injury to another person. The primary example is assault, which is an attempted or completed attack on a victim by a perpetrator who intends to inflict or recklessly inflicts bodily harm.

AGGRAVATED AND SIMPLE ASSAULT. In general, there are two levels of assault: aggravated assault and simple assault. Aggravated assault charges are typically filed if the attacker uses a deadly weapon and/or intends to inflict or does inflict serous injury to the victim. Aggravated assault can also result from reckless behavior. Simple assault is a lesser crime that does not include the more serious circumstances or consequences to the victim. In *Crime in the United States, 2007* (September 2008, http://www.fbi.gov/ucr/cius2007/index.html), the Federal Bureau of Investigation (FBI) includes such crimes as intimidation, stalking, and hazing in its definition of simple assault.

Simple assault can also be charged when a person's extreme negligence causes bodily harm to another person. Some state laws define a crime called assault and battery that includes both threat (assault) and bodily attack (battery).

In most jurisdictions the penalties for assault (or assault and battery) are more severe when the victim is a public official, such as a law enforcement officer, firefighter, social worker, judge, school teacher, and so on, who is attacked while on duty.

Sex Crimes

Sexually based offenses are crimes that involve some type of sexual activity that is deemed illegal. The most serious sexual offenses are those in which force or the threat of force is used by the perpetrator and those in which the victims are children.

RAPE. Rape, or sexual assault as it is called in some states, is a crime. In *Crime in the United States, 2007*, the FBI defines forcible rape as "the carnal knowledge of a female forcibly and against her will." State laws typically classify rapes at different felony levels depending on the circumstances of the crime. For example, the Office of Code Revision Indiana Legislative Services Agency (2008, http://www.in.gov/legislative/ic/code/title35/ar42/ch4.html) indicates that Indiana classifies rape as a Class A felony if the rape includes the threat or use of deadly force, the perpetrator has a deadly weapon (such as a firearm), the victim is seriously injured in the attack, or the victim is unknowingly drugged by the perpetrator. Otherwise, rape is a Class B felony in Indiana.

Use (or threat) of force and lack of consent are common elements that define rape when the victim is an adult with full mental and physical capacities. Statutory rape is a separately defined crime in which the victim is either younger than a legally set age of consent or the victim is an adult with a debilitating mental or physical condition. In these cases a crime occurs even if the victim consents to the sexual activity and no force or threat of force is used.

There are many other offenses besides rape that may be considered sexually based crimes under the law. Typical examples include offenses related to prostitution or pornography. Depending on the circumstances, these crimes might be deemed felonies or less serious misdemeanors.

Theft Crimes

Theft crimes cover a very broad spectrum of offenses. The most serious theft crime is called robbery. In *Crime in the United States, 2007*, the FBI defines robbery as "the taking or attempting to take anything of value from the care, custody, or control of a person or persons by force or threat of force or violence and/or by putting the victim in fear." An important distinction between robbery and other theft crimes is that robbery involves an element of personal force or the threat of personal force and harm to the victim.

Thus, robberies are typically face-to-face crimes in which the victim is personally menaced by the perpetrator. This can occur on the street (e.g., a mugging or car jacking) or in a business or residence (e.g., a bank robbery or home invasion). Because of the danger to the victims posed by these personal encounters, the penalties for robbery are severe.

Burglary is a different crime from robbery. The FBI defines burglary as "the unlawful entry of a structure to commit a felony or a theft." Burglary is also known as breaking and entering, although the actual act of "breaking in" is not always required. In general, any entry made without the owner's permission, for example, through an unlocked door, may legally be considered burglary.

Theft (or larceny) is a broad category that includes many different offenses. The Legislative Counsel of California (2008, http://www.leginfo.ca.gov/cgi-bin/displaycode?section=pen&group=00001-01000&file=484-502.9) defines theft as:

> Every person who shall feloniously steal, take, carry, lead, or drive away the personal property of another, or who shall fraudulently appropriate property which has been entrusted to him or her, or who shall knowingly and designedly, by any false or fraudulent representation or pretense, defraud any other person of money, labor or real or personal property, or who causes or procures others to report falsely of his or her wealth or mercantile character and by thus imposing upon any person, obtains credit and thereby fraudulently gets or obtains possession of money, or property or obtains the labor or service of another, is guilty of theft.

The FBI states in *Crime in the United States, 2007* that larceny-theft is "the unlawful taking, carrying, leading, or riding away of property from the possession or constructive possession of another," and includes offenses such as stealing bicycles, shoplifting, pocket picking, and other theft crimes in which force or violence is not used.

There are many other theft-type offenses defined by law. Examples include forgery, counterfeiting, fraud, identity theft, confidence games, writing bad checks, and embezzlement. In all these cases, the intent of the perpetrator is to obtain something of value through illegal means.

Theft crimes are generally classified into levels or degrees of seriousness based on the particular circumstances of the crime. These classifications often take into account the economic losses to the victim. In other words, a large value theft is treated more severely than a low value theft.

WHITE-COLLAR CRIMES. White-collar crimes are a subset of theft crimes. They differ from crimes such as burglary and robbery in that white-collar crimes are typically conducted without the threat or use of violence and without physical labor (e.g., breaking into a building) on the part of the perpetrator. Examples include fraud, counterfeiting, and embezzlement. White-collar crimes will be discussed in detail in Chapter 5.

Alcohol and Drug Crimes

Alcohol and drugs are substances that can impair judgment and inflame passions. People under the influence of these substances may engage in reckless or violent behavior that seriously harms others. Societal concerns about alcohol and drug use have varied dramatically throughout U.S. history.

ALCOHOL CRIMES. During the late 1880s and early 1900s a Progressive movement swept the nation in which many people believed that laws could "socially engineer" Americans out of immoral and destructive behaviors—such as drinking alcohol. Some states passed laws intended to restrict its consumption. By 1918 alcohol was considered such a menace to the public good that its manufacture and sales were outlawed by Congress via the Eighteenth Amendment to the U.S. Constitution. Prohibition, as it was called, proved to be unworkable and was abandoned at the federal level in 1933. Nevertheless, states and local jurisdictions have passed laws criminalizing certain alcohol-related actions, particularly public drunkenness and driving under the influence of alcohol.

DRUG CRIMES. The history of drug criminalization has also been checkered. Drugs such as cocaine and heroin were once common ingredients in popular products that Americans bought and consumed. Over time, growing awareness about the physical, psychological, and social harm associated with use of these drugs spurred laws against them. Modern drug laws are complex and sometimes controversial as Americans continue to debate how best to control human behaviors considered undesirable to the public good. A detailed discussion of drug crimes is presented in Chapter 4.

Hate Crimes

Laws against some crimes, such as murder and stealing, have their roots in the ancient past. Other behaviors are deemed illegal, because of social mores that have developed more recently, such as prohibitions against drug and alcohol offenses. Hate crimes are criminal offenses motivated by the offender's personal prejudice or bias against the victim. Even though no single, comprehensive legal definition is available for hate crimes, the FBI defines it in *Hate Crime Statistics, 2007* (October 2008, http://www.fbi.gov/ucr/hc2007/index.html) as "criminal offenses that are motivated, in whole or in part, by the offender's bias against a race, religion, sexual orientation, ethnicity/national origin, or disability and are committed against persons, property, or society."

The first federal anticrime hate legislation was passed in 1969. In 1990 Congress passed the Hate Crime Statistics Act, which required the U.S. attorney general to "acquire data ... about crimes that manifest evidence of prejudice

based on race, religion, disability, sexual orientation, or ethnicity" and to publish a summary of the data. The Hate Crimes Statistics Act was amended by the Violent Crime and Law Enforcement Act of 1994 to include bias-motivated acts against disabled people. Further amendments in the Church Arsons Prevention Act of 1996 directed the FBI to track bias-related church arsons as a permanent part of its duties.

The Anti-Defamation League, an organization that fights anti-Semitism and bigotry, states in "Anti-Defamation League State Hate Crime Statutory Provisions" (http://www.adl.org/99hatecrime/state_hate_crime_laws.pdf) that as of 2008, 45 states and the District of Columbia had adopted some form of penalty-enhancement hate crime statute. The states that had not criminalized bias-motivated violence and intimidation were Arkansas, Georgia, Indiana, South Carolina, and Wyoming. The District of Columbia and 44 states included race, religion, and ethnicity in their hate crime laws, and 30 states plus the District of Columbia included sexual orientation. In addition, 26 states plus the District of Columbia included gender, and 30 states plus the District of Columbia included disability.

TEXAS HATE CRIME LEGISLATION. The nation was shocked and outraged by the brutal killing of an African-American man, James Byrd Jr. (1949–1998), near the small town of Jasper, Texas, in June 1998. Two white men convicted of the murder, John William King (1975–) and Lawrence Russell Brewer (1967–), were suspected of ties to white supremacy organizations. A third man, Shawn Allen Berry (1975–), was also convicted. These men beat and kicked Byrd and then chained him to the back of a pickup truck and dragged him until his body was torn apart.

In the aftermath of the murder, members of the Ku Klux Klan gathered in Jasper, saying that they were there to protect whites from African-Americans. In response, African-American activist groups, including the Black Muslims and the New Black Panthers, assembled in Jasper to protect African-Americans from whites. Jasper residents repeatedly expressed their sorrow for the murder and begged outsiders to go away and let them try to cope with the crime and its consequences. The Byrd family issued a written statement asking the public not to use the murder as an excuse for further hatred and retribution. They asked that Americans view the incident as a wake-up call and expressed the hope that it would lead to self-examination and reflection. Eventually, the murder led to state legislation that intensifies penalties for crimes motivated by the victim's race, religion, sex, disability, sexual orientation, age, or national origin. The James Byrd Jr. Hate Crimes Act was signed into law by Texas governor Rick Perry (1950–) in May 2001.

THE CONSTITUTIONALITY OF HATE CRIME LEGISLATION. The constitutionality of hate crime legislation has been challenged on the grounds that these laws punish free thought. In 1992 the U.S. Supreme Court, in *R.A.V. v. City* *of St. Paul* (505 U.S. 377), found a Minnesota law outlawing certain "fighting words" to be unconstitutional. In this case, the defendant had burned a cross "inside the fenced yard of a black family."

A law limiting pure speech or symbolic speech can only be upheld if it meets the "clear and present danger" standard of *Brandenburg v. Ohio* (395 U.S. 444 [1969]). This standard means that speech may be outlawed if it incites or produces "imminent lawless action."

However, in *Wisconsin v. Mitchell* (508 U.S. 476 [1993]), the Supreme Court upheld laws that impose harsher prison sentences and greater fines for criminals who are motivated by bigotry. The court found that statutes such as the Wisconsin law do not illegally restrict free speech and are not so general as to restrict constitutional behavior.

Terrorism

Terrorism is difficult to define legally. In *2007 Report on Terrorism* (April 30, 2008, http://wits.nctc.gov/reports/crot2007nctcannexfinal.pdf), the National Counterterrorism Center defines terrorism as "premeditated, politically motivated violence perpetrated against noncombatant targets by subnational groups or clandestine agents." In general terms the word *terrorism* is associated with violent actions perpetrated by people with a certain mind-set against other people. The perpetrators of terrorist acts typically justify their behavior as appropriate because it is waged against people they consider to be enemies for various political, social, and/or religious reasons. Thus, terrorism is the ultimate hate crime and is motivated by bias. Much modern terrorism is international in nature, meaning that it involves perpetrators and victims of different nationalities. Some horrifying acts of international terrorism have taken place, including the September 11, 2001, attacks on the United States. Such acts are criminal under U.S. law, and the perpetrators can be tried and convicted of criminal offenses. The scope of international terrorism places it squarely under the jurisdiction of federal authorities. However, capturing and trying foreign nationals can be difficult, particularly when they are in countries unfriendly to the United States. In some cases, the U.S. armed forces may become involved, as they have in the war in Afghanistan, to capture alleged terrorists for prosecution under U.S. law.

Incidents of Domestic Terrorism

Terrorism is domestic when it involves the citizens or residents of the country where the terrorist incident takes place, for example, a terrorist attack carried out on U.S. soil by Americans. According to James F. Jarboe of the FBI, in "The Threat of Eco-Terrorism" (February 12, 2002, http://www.fbi.gov/congress/congress02/jarboe021202.htm), the FBI defines domestic terrorism as "the unlawful use, or threatened use, of violence by a group or individual based

and operating entirely within the United States (or its territories) without foreign direction, committed against persons or property to intimidate or coerce a government, the civilian population, or any segment thereof, in furtherance of political or social objectives." Thus, the distinction between acts of domestic terrorism and other domestic crimes hinges on motive.

It can be difficult to determine whether a particular crime is committed for social/political reasons, personal reasons (e.g., revenge), or a mixture of these motives. For example, in January 1998 Theodore Kaczynski (1942–) was sentenced to life imprisonment with no possibility of parole for his actions as the "Unabomber." Over a 17-year period Kaczynski committed 16 bombings in several states. Three people were killed, and 23 people injured in the attacks. Kaczynski has given varying reasons for his crimes, including personal revenge and a deep hatred against the use of high-technology in American society. In October 2002 two men dubbed "the Beltway snipers" terrorized people in the District of Columbia area with a killing spree that left 10 people dead and three people wounded. One of the perpetrators, John Allen Muhammad (1960–), has been described in the media as committing the killings for a mixture of personal and social/political reasons. He reportedly hoped to extract revenge on his former wife and extort money from the government to fund a terrorist training camp. These cases highlight the difficulties in branding particular crimes as terrorist incidents. However, there have been a number of crimes committed in the United States since the mid-1990s that are widely considered to be incidents of domestic terrorism.

OKLAHOMA CITY BOMBING. On April 19, 1995, one of the most deadly acts of domestic terrorism occurred in Oklahoma City, Oklahoma, when a 2-ton (1.8-tonne) truck bomb exploded just outside the Alfred P. Murrah Federal Building, killing 168 people and injuring more than 800. The attack was perpetrated by Timothy McVeigh (1968–2001), a 27-year-old military veteran with ties to antigovernment militia groups. McVeigh was executed by lethal injection in June 2001. Terry Nichols (1955–), an accomplice who helped McVeigh plan the attack and construct the bomb, was sentenced to life in prison without parole.

OLYMPIC PARK BOMBING. In July 1996, during the Olympic Games in Atlanta, Georgia, a nail-packed pipe bomb exploded in a large common area. One person was killed and more than 100 victims were injured. Even though authorities had no leads at the time, similar explosive devices were later used in bomb attacks on a nightclub favored by homosexuals and two abortion clinics. These incidents led investigators to Eric Robert Rudolph (1967–), a Christian extremist whose views combined antigovernment political sentiments with opposition to abortion and antihomosexual bigotry. Rudolph eluded capture for five years before he surrendered to authorities in May 2003.

Confessing to the Olympic bombing, he said he was motivated by antigovernment and antisocialist beliefs. He is serving life imprisonment without possibility of parole.

ANTHRAX ATTACKS. On September 25, 2001, a letter containing a white powdery substance was handled by an assistant to the NBC News anchor Tom Brokaw (1940–). After complaining of a rash, the assistant consulted a physician and tested positive for exposure to the anthrax bacterium (*Bacillus anthracis*), an infectious agent that, if inhaled into the lungs, can lead to death. Over the next two months, envelopes testing positive for anthrax were received by various news organizations in the United States and by government offices, including the offices of the U.S. Senate majority leader Tom A. Daschle (1947–; D-SD) and of the New York governor George Pataki (1945–). As a result of exposure to anthrax sent via the U.S. mail, five people died, including two postal workers who handled letters carrying the anthrax spores. Hundreds more who were exposed were placed on antibiotics as a preventive measure.

The FBI eventually traced the source of the anthrax to the U.S. Army Medical Research Institute of Infectious Diseases, a bioweapons laboratory at Fort Detrick, Maryland. At first, authorities focused on a civilian researcher at that facility, Steven J. Hatfill (1953–). He was later cleared of the attacks. In August 2008 another researcher from the same laboratory, Bruce E. Ivins (1946–2008), committed suicide before he could be arrested and charged with the crime. The FBI has expressed confidence that Ivins was the perpetrator of the 2001 anthrax attacks. However, because he will never stand trial, some doubts remain about the strength of the government's case against Ivins.

MIDWEST PIPE BOMBER. In a spree that began on May 3, 2002, 18 pipe bombs were found in rural mailboxes in Illinois, Iowa, Nebraska, Colorado, and Texas, injuring five people. Four days after the first bomb exploded, the FBI arrested Luke J. Helder (1981–), a 21-year-old college student, in connection with the bombings. Helder was charged by federal prosecutors with using an explosive device to maliciously destroy property affecting interstate commerce and with using a destructive device to commit a crime of violence, punishable by up to life imprisonment. The pipe bombs, some of which did not detonate, were accompanied by letters warning of excessive government control over individual behavior. In 2004 a federal judge ruled that Helder was not mentally fit to stand trial and ordered that he be held for psychological evaluation. As of April 2009 Helder remained in federal custody.

ATTACKS SINCE 2004. Between January 2004 and June 2008 the National Counterterrorism Center (2008, http://wits.nctc.gov/RunSearchCountry.do?countryId=174) recorded 20 domestic terrorism incidents in the United States. None of these incidents resulted in fatalities or involved hostages. Most of these events did not result in any injuries, but nine people were injured in March 2006 when a man drove a sport utility vehicle through a crowd of students at the University of North Carolina, Chapel Hill. Other domestic terrorism incidents included arson attacks on several residences and bomb attacks on schools and the British consulate in New York City. Several attacks are believed to have been carried out by ecoterrorist groups, including the destruction of several multimillion-dollar homes in Woodinville, Washington, in March 2008. These are extremist groups that support causes, such as environmentalism or animal rights, and use criminal violence to promote their ideas and attack their perceived enemies. Radical animal rights activists are believed to be behind bombs that exploded outside the homes of two University of California, Santa Cruz, biomedical researchers in August 2008. The scientists were allegedly targeted due to the use of animals in university research—research that the university claims was conducted using the highest humane standards.

GOVERNMENT JURISDICTION AND SPENDING

As noted throughout this chapter, criminal legislation and law enforcement are carried out by federal, state, and local governments. Sometimes government entities have overlapping responsibilities. State and local governments have always played a central role in controlling crime. They operate police and law enforcement agencies, court systems, and correctional facilities, such as prisons and jails. The federal government enforces laws that fall within its jurisdiction. Examples include mail fraud, bank robbery, gun laws, counterfeiting, forgery, espionage, immigration violations, child pornography, drug trafficking, and money laundering. The federal government also operates the federal court system and has its own prisons for people convicted of federal crimes. In addition, the federal government provides funding for some state and local crime-control programs.

Figure 1.1 shows direct expenditures on criminal justice by local and state governments and the federal government from 1982 to 2006. Over this period local expenditures increased by 422%, state expenditures increased by 548%, and federal expenditures increased by 749%. In 2006 local governments spent $109.2 billion on criminal justice, and state governments spent $69 billion. The federal government spent $36.2 billion on criminal justice in 2006.

Figure 1.2 provides a breakdown of criminal justice expenditures by major function (police, judicial, and corrections) for all three levels of government from 1982 to 2006. Corrections refers to the system of prisons, jails, and other facilities operated to house arrested and convicted individuals, and to the programs for the oversight of these and other individuals under the supervision of the criminal justice system. From 1982 to 2006 police expenditures increased by 420%, corrections expenditures increased by 660%, and judicial expenditures increased by 503%. In 2006 police expenditures totaled $98.9 billion, corrections

FIGURE 1.1

Direct government expenditures on criminal justice, by level of government, 1982–2006

SOURCE: "Direct Expenditure by Level of Government, 1982–2006," in *Expenditure Facts at a Glance*, U.S. Department of Justice, Office of Justice Programs, Bureau of Justice Statistics, December 18, 2008, http://www.ojp.usdoj.gov/bjs/glance/expgov.htm (accessed April 3, 2009)

FIGURE 1.2

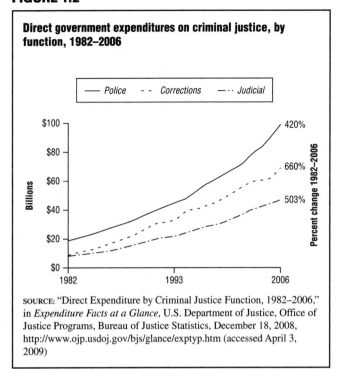

Direct government expenditures on criminal justice, by function, 1982–2006

SOURCE: "Direct Expenditure by Criminal Justice Function, 1982–2006," in *Expenditure Facts at a Glance*, U.S. Department of Justice, Office of Justice Programs, Bureau of Justice Statistics, December 18, 2008, http://www.ojp.usdoj.gov/bjs/glance/exptyp.htm (accessed April 3, 2009)

expenses totaled $68.7 billion, and judicial expenditures totaled $46.9 billion.

PUBLIC OPINION ABOUT CRIME

The Gallup Organization conducts annual polls on American concerns and viewpoints about crime. Results from the October 2008 survey and earlier crime polls are reported in *Gallup's Pulse of Democracy: Crime* (2008, http://www.gallup.com/poll/1603/Crime.aspx).

How Serious Is the Crime Problem?

Figure 1.3 shows the ratings given by respondents during the 2008 poll when they were asked to describe the crime problem in the area where they live and in the United States overall. The national crime problem was rated as "extremely serious" by 16% of poll participants. Another 35% thought it was "very serious," and 43% said it was "moderately serious." A small percentage (5%) thought the crime problem was "not too serious" and less than 0.5% said it was "not serious at all."

The poll participants expressed a far more optimistic viewpoint about crime in their own area. Only 3% of those asked said the crime problem was "extremely serious" in their area. A slightly larger percentage (8%) thought the problem was very serious. Nearly a third (32%) indicated the crime problem was "moderately serious" in their area. A larger percentage (35%) said the problem was "not too serious." About one-fifth (22%) thought the crime problem was "not serious at all" in their area.

More Crime or Less Crime Today?

In crime polls dating back to 1972, Gallup has asked poll participants whether they believe there is more or less crime in their area than there was the previous year. Less than half of respondents (44%) thought there was more crime in their area in 2008 than there had been the year before. (See Table 1.1.) About a third (31%) believed there was less crime in their area, and 19% thought there had been no change in the crime level over the previous year. The percentage of respondents expressing the belief that crime had risen in their area in the past year varied from a low of 26% in 2001 to a high of 54% in 1981 and 1992.

Table 1.2 shows the results when poll participants were asked about the national level of crime and its change over the previous year. In 2008 two-thirds (67%) of respondents said crime had increased in the United States in the past year, 15% thought national crime had decreased, and 9% indicated that crime levels had not changed over the previous year. Gallup presents results for this question dating back to 1989. At that time, and throughout the early 1990s, more than 80% of respondents said crime had increased in the United States during the previous year.

Crime Victims?

Figure 1.4 provides the percentages of poll participants indicating that they or another member in their household had been the victim of a specific crime in the 12 months leading up to the 2008 survey. The largest percentage (14%) had money or property stolen. Other categories included 13% who said their home, car, or other property

FIGURE 1.3

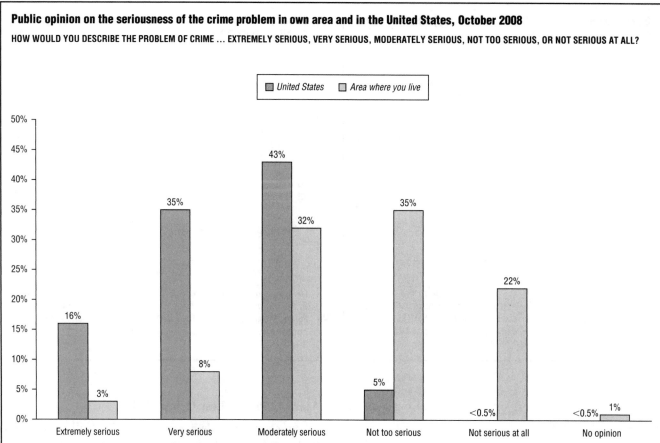

Public opinion on the seriousness of the crime problem in own area and in the United States, October 2008

HOW WOULD YOU DESCRIBE THE PROBLEM OF CRIME ... EXTREMELY SERIOUS, VERY SERIOUS, MODERATELY SERIOUS, NOT TOO SERIOUS, OR NOT SERIOUS AT ALL?

SOURCE: Adapted from "Overall, How Would You Describe the Problem of Crime [ROTATED: In the United States/in the Area Where You Live] —Is It Extremely Serious, Very Serious, Moderately Serious, Not Too Serious, or Not Serious at All?" in *Gallup's Pulse of Democracy: Crime*, The Gallup Organization, 2008, http://www.gallup.com/poll/1603/Crime.aspx (accessed November 27, 2008). Copyright © 2008 by The Gallup Organization. Reproduced by permission of The Gallup Organization.

had been vandalized, 8% who had been victims of a computer or Internet-based crime, and 5% whose house or apartment had been broken into within the previous year. Smaller percentages had been mugged (3%), physically assaulted (3%), had a car stolen (3%), had money or property stolen by an assailant using force or the threat of force (2%), or had been sexually assaulted (1%).

Worry about Being Victimized by Crime

In 2008 Gallup asked participants how often they worried about being victimized by particular crimes. Figure 1.5 shows the percentage of respondents indicating they "frequently" or "occasionally" worried about being victimized. Nearly half (46%) worried frequently or occasionally about their home being burglarized while they are not home. Nearly as many (43%) worried about their car being stolen or broken into by criminals. Smaller percentages admitted worrying frequently or occasionally about being a victim of terrorism (31%), getting mugged (29%), having their home burglarized while they are at home (28%), or being attacked while driving their car (21%). Nearly one-fifth of respondents (19%) worried frequently or occasionally about being sexually assaulted, 17% worried about

being murdered, and 16% worried about becoming the victim of a hate crime. A smaller group of poll participants (6%) worried frequently or occasionally about being assaulted or killed by a coworker or other employee at their workplace.

Crime Protection Methods

In October 2007 Gallup pollsters asked Americans whether they use (or have used) various crime protection methods. Concern about crime kept nearly half (48%) of the respondents from going to certain places or neighborhoods they might otherwise have visited. (See Figure 1.6.) Nearly one-third (31%) each kept a dog for protection or had a burglar alarm installed in their home. Nearly one-quarter (23%) of those asked had bought a gun for self-protection or protection of their home, 14% carried mace or pepper spray, and 12% each carried a knife or gun for defense purposes.

Confidence in the Police

In 2006 Gallup pollsters found that 20% of respondents had "a great deal" of confidence in the police to protect them from violent crime, and 41% expressed "quite a lot"

TABLE 1.1

TABLE 1.2

Public opinion on level of crime in own area, selected years 1972–2008

IS THERE MORE CRIME IN YOUR AREA THAN THERE WAS A YEAR AGO, OR LESS?

	More	Less	Same (vol.)	No opinion
	%	%	%	%
2008 Oct 3–5	44	31	19	5
2007 Oct 4–7	51	29	17	4
2006 Oct 9–12	51	30	15	4
2005 Oct 13–16	47	33	18	2
2004 Oct 11–14	37	37	22	4
2003 Oct 6–8	40	39	19	2
2002 Oct 14–17	37	34	24	5
2001 Oct 11–14	26	52	18	4
2000 Aug 29–Sep 5	34	46	15	5
1998 Oct 23–25	31	48	16	5
1997 Aug 22–25	46	32	20	2
1996 Jul 25–28	46	24	25	5
1992 Feb 28–Mar 1	54	19	23	4
1990 Sep 10–11	51	18	24	8
1989 Jun 8–11	53	18	22	7
1989 Jan 24–28	47	21	27	5
1983 Jan 28–31	37	17	36	10
1981 Jan 9–12	54	8	29	9
1977 Nov 18–21	43	17	32	8
1975 Jun 27–30	50	12	29	9
1972 Dec 8–11	51	10	27	12

(vol.) = Volunteered response.

SOURCE: "Is There More Crime in Your Area Than There Was a Year Ago, or Less?" in *Gallup's Pulse of Democracy: Crime*, The Gallup Organization, 2008, http://www.gallup.com/poll/1603/Crime.aspx (accessed November 27, 2008). Copyright © 2008 by The Gallup Organization. Reproduced by permission of The Gallup Organization.

Public opinion on level of crime in the United States, selected years 1989–2008

IS THERE MORE CRIME IN THE U.S. THAN THERE WAS A YEAR AGO, OR LESS?

	More	Less	Same (vol.)	No opinion
	%	%	%	%
2008 Oct 3–5	67	15	9	9
2007 Oct 4–7	71	14	8	6
2006 Oct 9–12	68	16	8	8
2005 Oct 13–16	67	21	9	3
2004 Oct 11–14	53	28	14	5
2003 Oct 6–8	60	25	11	4
2002 Oct 14–17	62	21	11	6
2001 Oct 11–14	41	43	10	6
2000 Aug 29–Sep 5	47	41	7	5
1998 Oct 23–25	52	35	8	5
1997 Aug 22–25	64	25	6	5
1996 Jul 25–28	71	15	8	6
1993 Oct 13–18	87	4	5	4
1992 Feb 28–Mar 1	89	3	4	4
1990 Sep 10	84	3	7	6
1989 Jan 24–28	84	5	5	6

(vol.) = Volunteered response

SOURCE: "Is There More Crime in the U.S. Than There Was a Year Ago, or Less?" in *Gallup's Pulse of Democracy: Crime*, The Gallup Organization, 2008, http://www.gallup.com/poll/1603/Crime.aspx (accessed November 27, 2008). Copyright © 2008 by The Gallup Organization. Reproduced by permission of The Gallup Organization.

of confidence. (See Table 1.3.) Nearly a third (32%) said they had "not very much" confidence, and 6% had "none at all." Gallup had asked this same question in polls dating back to 1981. In the earliest poll, 15% of the respondents expressed "a great deal" of confidence, and 34% had "quite a lot" of confidence in the ability of the police to protect them from violent crime. In general, subsequent polls reveal that the level of confidence in the police has risen slightly over time.

Approaches to the Crime Problem

Table 1.4 shows the results of Gallup polls in which participants were asked to choose one of two approaches to lowering the U.S. crime rate: "attacking the social and economic problems that lead to crime through better education and job training" or providing "more money and effort" to "deterring crime by improving law enforcement with more prisons, police, and judges." When this question was asked in 2006, nearly two-thirds (65%) of the respondents preferred attacking social problems as a way to combat crime, compared with 31% who thought that more law enforcement was needed. Gallup first asked this question in 1989. At that time, 61% of respondents chose attacking social problems, whereas 32% chose improving law enforcement. The breakdown between these two choices has varied somewhat in subsequent polls; however, most respondents have consistently favored attacking social problems over improving law enforcement.

FIGURE 1.4

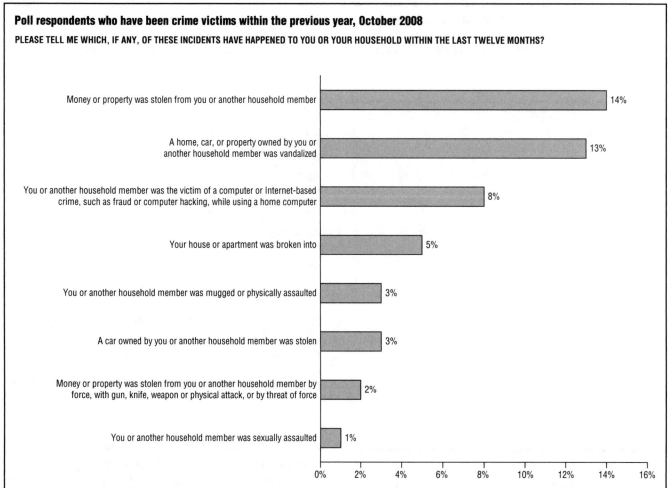

Poll respondents who have been crime victims within the previous year, October 2008

PLEASE TELL ME WHICH, IF ANY, OF THESE INCIDENTS HAVE HAPPENED TO YOU OR YOUR HOUSEHOLD WITHIN THE LAST TWELVE MONTHS?

SOURCE: Adapted from "Please Tell Me Which, If Any, of These Incidents Have Happened to You or Your Household within the Last Twelve Months?" in *Gallup's Pulse of Democracy: Crime*, The Gallup Organization, 2008, http://www.gallup.com/poll/1603/Crime.aspx (accessed November 27, 2008). Copyright © 2008 by The Gallup Organization. Reproduced by permission of The Gallup Organization.

FIGURE 1.5

Poll respondents indicating that they worry frequently or occasionally about particular crimes happening to them or their household, October 2008

HOW OFTEN DO YOU, YOURSELF, WORRY ABOUT THE FOLLOWING THINGS—FREQUENTLY, OCCASIONALLY, RARELY OR NEVER?

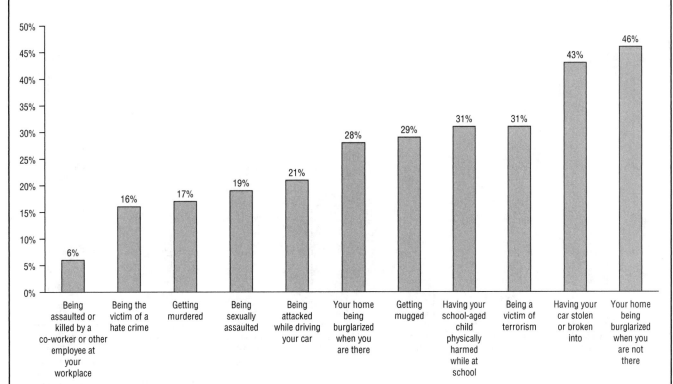

Note: Percent of respondents saying "frequently" or "occasionally."

SOURCE: Adapted from "How Often Do You, Yourself, Worry about the Following Things—Frequently, Occasionally, Rarely or Never? How about—?" in *Gallup's Pulse of Democracy: Crime*, The Gallup Organization, 2008, http://www.gallup.com/poll/1603/Crime.aspx (accessed November 27, 2008). Copyright © 2008 by The Gallup Organization. Reproduced by permission of The Gallup Organization.

FIGURE 1.6

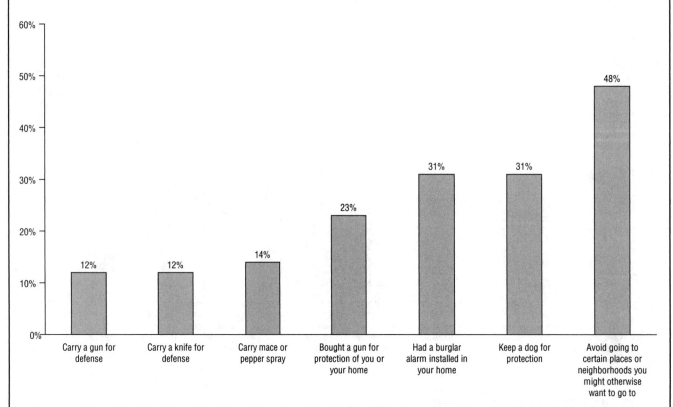

Poll respondents who have taken or are taking specific crime prevention measures, October 2007

NEXT, I'M GOING TO READ SOME THINGS PEOPLE DO BECAUSE OF THEIR CONCERN OVER CRIME. PLEASE TELL ME WHICH, IF ANY, OF THESE THINGS YOU, YOURSELF, DO OR HAVE DONE.

SOURCE: Adapted from "Next, I'm Going to Read Some Things People Do Because of Their Concern over Crime. Please Tell Me Which, If Any, of These Things You, Yourself, Do or Have Done," in *Gallup's Pulse of Democracy: Crime*, The Gallup Organization, 2008, http://www.gallup.com/poll/1603/ Crime.aspx (accessed November 27, 2008). Copyright © 2008 by The Gallup Organization. Reproduced by permission of The Gallup Organization.

TABLE 1.3

Poll respondents' confidence in the ability of the police to protect them from violent crime, selected years 1981–2006

HOW MUCH CONFIDENCE DO YOU HAVE IN THE ABILITY OF THE POLICE TO PROTECT YOU FROM VIOLENT CRIME—A GREAT DEAL, QUITE A LOT, NOT VERY MUCH, OR NONE AT ALL?

	A great deal	Quite a lot	Not very much	None at all	No opinion
	%	%	%	%	%
2006 Oct 9–12	20	41	32	6	1
2005 Oct 13–16	18	35	39	7	1
2004 Oct 11–14	21	40	28	10	1
2003 Oct 6–8	20	40	31	8	1
2002 Oct 14–17	19	39	31	9	2
2001 Oct 11–14	25	41	27	6	1
2000 Aug 29–Sep 5	20	42	31	6	1
1999 Mar 5–7	29	41	25	4	1
1998 Oct 23–25	19	36	37	8	*
1995 Sep 22–24	20	30	39	9	2
1993 Oct 13–18	14	31	45	9	1
1989 Jun 8–11	14	34	42	8	2
1985 Feb 28–Mar 1	15	37	39	6	3
1981 Jan 16–23	15	34	42	8	1

SOURCE: "How Much Confidence Do You Have in the Ability of the Police to Protect You from Violent Crime—a Great Deal, Quite a Lot, Not Very Much, or None at All?" in *Gallup's Pulse of Democracy: Crime*, The Gallup Organization, 2008, http://www.gallup.com/poll/1603/Crime.aspx (accessed November 27, 2008). Copyright © 2008 by The Gallup Organization. Reproduced by permission of The Gallup Organization.

TABLE 1.4

Public opinion on approaches for lowering the crime rate in the United States, selected years 1989–2006

WHICH OF THE FOLLOWING APPROACHES TO LOWERING THE CRIME RATE IN THE UNITED STATES COMES CLOSER TO YOUR OWN VIEW—DO YOU THINK MORE MONEY AND EFFORT SHOULD GO TO ATTACKING THE SOCIAL AND ECONOMIC PROBLEMS THAT LEAD TO CRIME THROUGH BETTER EDUCATION AND JOB TRAINING (OR) MORE MONEY AND EFFORT SHOULD GO TO DETERRING CRIME BY IMPROVING LAW ENFORCEMENT WITH MORE PRISONS, POLICE, AND JUDGES?

	Attack social problems	More law enforcement	No opinion
	%	%	%
2006 Oct 9–12	65	31	4
2003 Oct 6–8	69	29	2
2000 Aug 29–Sep 5	68	27	5
1994 Aug 15–16*	51	42	7
1994 Feb 26–28*	57	39	4
1992 Aug 28–Sep 2*	67	25	8
1992 Mar 30–Apr 5*	64	27	9
1990 Sep 10–11*	57	36	2
1989 Jun 8–11*	61	32	7

*WORDING: "To lower the crime rate in the United States, some people think additional money and effort should go to attacking the social and economic problems that lead to crime through better education and job training. Others feel more money and effort should go to deterring crime by improving law enforcement with more prisons, police, and judges. Which comes closer to your view?"

SOURCE: "Which of the Following Approaches to Lowering the Crime Rate in the United States Comes Closer to Your Own View—Do You Think [Rotated: More Money and Effort Should Go to Attacking the Social and Economic Problems That Lead to Crime through Better Education and Job Training (or) More Money and Effort Should Go to Deterring Crime by Improving Law Enforcement with More Prisons, Police, and Judges]?" in *Gallup's Pulse of Democracy: Crime*, The Gallup Organization, 2008, http://www.gallup.com/poll/1603/Crime.aspx (accessed November 27, 2008). Copyright © 2008 by The Gallup Organization. Reproduced by permission of The Gallup Organization.

CHAPTER 2
CRIME STATISTICS

The Federal Bureau of Investigation (FBI) is the primary federal government source for crime statistics. The FBI's Uniform Crime Reporting (UCR) Program gathers crime data from law enforcement agencies around the country and publishes selected data in the annual *Crime in the United States*. The most recent edition, *Crime in the United States, 2007* (http://www.fbi.gov/ucr/cius2007/index.html), was published in September 2008. According to the FBI, in 2007 more than 17,700 agencies participated in the program, representing 94.6% of the U.S. population. However, the FBI notes in "A Word about UCR Data" (2008, http://www.fbi.gov/ucr/word.htm) that not every agency contributed data for every crime tracked by the UCR Program due to "computer problems, changes in record management systems, personnel shortages, or a number of other reasons." In other words, the tables and figures in *Crime in the United States, 2007* provide crime statistics on only those crimes reported to the UCR Program and do not reflect the total number of crimes committed or processed by local agencies.

The FBI compiles two main sets of crime statistics: crimes reported to agencies and crimes cleared by agencies. Reported crimes do not necessarily result in arrests or convictions. Cleared offenses are of two types. The first type of cleared offenses consists of crimes for which agencies report that at least one person has been arrested, charged, and turned over to the court for prosecution. This does not necessarily mean the person arrested was guilty or convicted of the crime. The second type of cleared offenses includes those cleared by "extraordinary means," that is, offenses for which there can be no arrest. Such cases include, for example, a murder-suicide, when the perpetrator is known to be deceased.

The FBI collects data for dozens of specifically defined crimes. Some of these crimes are categorized as violent crimes or property crimes. In *Crime in the United States, 2007*, the FBI defines violent crimes as those that "involve force or threat of force." These include murder and nonnegli-gent manslaughter, forcible rape, robbery, and aggravated assault. The FBI defines murder and nonnegligent manslaughter as "the willful (nonnegligent) killing of one human being by another." The murder statistics do not include suicides, accidents, or justifiable homicides by either citizens or law enforcement officers. The FBI considers four crimes to be property crimes: burglary, larceny-theft, motor vehicle theft, and arson. The FBI explains that "the object of the theft-type offenses is the taking of money or property, but there is no force or threat of force against the victims."

REPORTED CRIMES

Table 2.1 lists the number of certain crimes reported by law enforcement agencies from 1988 to 2007 and the rates of these crimes per 100,000 U.S. inhabitants. In 2007, 1.4 million violent crimes were reported, including 16,929 murders and nonnegligent manslaughters, 90,427 forcible rapes, 445,125 robberies, and 855,856 aggravated assaults. The overall rate for violent crime in 2007 was 466.9 per 100,000 inhabitants. The rates for different types of violent crime varied. For example, the rate for murder and nonnegligent manslaughters was 5.6 per 100,000 inhabitants; for forcible rape, 30 per 100,000; for robbery, 147.6 per 100,000; and for aggravated assault, 283.8 per 100,000. All these rates are down dramatically from rates dating back to 1988.

Murder and Nonnegligent Manslaughter

The total number of reported murders and nonnegligent manslaughters in 2007 was 16,929 for a rate of 5.6 per 100,000 U.S. inhabitants. (See Table 2.1.) During the late 1980s and early 1990s the murder rate was much higher, often more than 9 murders per 100,000 inhabitants. The rate began dropping in the mid-1990s and has leveled off since 2001. It should be noted that Table 2.1 does not include the thousands of people killed as a result of the September 11, 2001, terrorist attacks in the United States.

TABLE 2.1

Violent crimes and property crimes by volume and rate per 100,000 inhabitants, 1988–2007

Year	Population[a]	Violent crime	Violent crime rate	Murder and non-negligent man-slaughter	Murder and non-negligent man-slaughter rate	Forcible rape	Forcible rape rate	Robbery	Robbery rate	Aggravated assault	Aggravated assault rate	Property crime	Property crime rate	Burglary	Burglary rate	Larceny-theft	Larceny-theft rate	Motor vehicle theft	Motor vehicle theft rate
1988	244,498,982	1,566,221	640.6	20,675	8.5	92,486	37.8	542,968	222.1	910,092	372.2	12,356,865	5,054.0	3,218,077	1,316.2	7,705,872	3,151.7	1,432,916	586.1
1989	246,819,230	1,646,037	666.9	21,500	8.7	94,504	38.3	578,326	234.3	951,707	385.6	12,605,412	5,107.1	3,168,170	1,283.6	7,872,442	3,189.6	1,564,800	634.0
1990	249,464,396	1,820,127	729.6	23,438	9.4	102,555	41.1	639,271	256.3	1,054,863	422.9	12,655,486	5,073.1	3,073,909	1,232.2	7,945,670	3,185.1	1,635,907	655.8
1991	252,153,092	1,911,767	758.2	24,703	9.8	106,593	42.3	687,732	272.7	1,092,739	433.4	12,961,116	5,140.2	3,157,150	1,252.1	8,142,228	3,229.1	1,661,738	659.0
1992	255,029,699	1,932,274	757.7	23,760	9.3	109,062	42.8	672,478	263.7	1,126,974	441.9	12,505,917	4,903.7	2,979,884	1,168.4	7,915,199	3,103.6	1,610,834	631.6
1993	257,782,608	1,926,017	747.1	24,526	9.5	106,014	41.1	659,870	256.0	1,135,607	440.5	12,218,777	4,740.0	2,834,808	1,099.7	7,820,909	3,033.9	1,563,060	606.3
1994	260,327,021	1,857,670	713.6	23,326	9.0	102,216	39.3	618,949	237.8	1,113,179	427.6	12,131,873	4,660.2	2,712,774	1,042.1	7,879,812	3,026.9	1,539,287	591.3
1995	262,803,276	1,798,792	684.5	21,606	8.2	97,470	37.1	580,509	220.9	1,099,207	418.3	12,063,935	4,590.5	2,593,784	987.0	7,997,710	3,043.2	1,472,441	560.3
1996	265,228,572	1,688,540	636.6	19,645	7.4	96,252	36.3	535,594	201.9	1,037,049	391.0	11,805,323	4,451.0	2,506,400	945.0	7,904,685	2,980.3	1,394,238	525.7
1997	267,783,607	1,636,096	611.0	18,208	6.8	96,153	35.9	498,534	186.2	1,023,201	382.1	11,558,475	4,316.3	2,460,526	918.8	7,743,760	2,891.8	1,354,189	505.7
1998	270,248,003	1,533,887	567.6	16,974	6.3	93,144	34.5	447,186	165.5	976,583	361.4	10,951,827	4,052.5	2,332,735	863.2	7,376,311	2,729.5	1,242,781	459.9
1999	272,690,813	1,426,044	523.0	15,522	5.7	89,411	32.8	409,371	150.1	911,740	334.3	10,208,334	3,743.6	2,100,739	770.4	6,955,520	2,550.7	1,152,075	422.5
2000	281,421,906	1,425,486	506.5	15,586	5.5	90,178	32.0	408,016	145.0	911,706	324.0	10,182,584	3,618.3	2,050,992	728.8	6,971,590	2,477.3	1,160,002	412.2
2001[b]	285,317,559	1,439,480	504.5	16,037	5.6	90,863	31.8	423,557	148.5	909,023	318.6	10,437,189	3,658.1	2,116,531	741.8	7,092,267	2,485.7	1,228,391	430.5
2002	287,973,924	1,423,677	494.4	16,229	5.6	95,235	33.1	420,806	146.1	891,407	309.5	10,455,277	3,630.6	2,151,252	747.0	7,057,379	2,450.7	1,246,646	432.9
2003	290,788,976	1,383,676	475.8	16,528	5.7	93,883	32.3	414,235	142.5	859,030	295.4	10,442,862	3,591.2	2,154,834	741.0	7,026,802	2,416.5	1,261,226	433.7
2004	293,656,842	1,360,088	463.2	16,148	5.5	95,089	32.4	401,470	136.7	847,381	288.6	10,319,386	3,514.1	2,144,446	730.3	6,937,089	2,362.3	1,237,851	421.5
2005	296,507,061	1,390,745	469.0	16,740	5.6	94,347	31.8	417,438	140.8	862,220	290.8	10,174,754	3,431.5	2,155,448	726.9	6,783,447	2,287.8	1,235,859	416.8
2006[c]	299,398,484	1,418,043	473.6	17,030	5.7	92,757	31.0	447,403	149.4	860,853	287.5	9,983,568	3,334.5	2,183,746	729.4	6,607,013	2,206.8	1,192,809	398.4
2007	301,621,157	1,408,337	466.9	16,929	5.6	90,427	30.0	445,125	147.6	855,856	283.8	9,843,481	3,263.5	2,179,140	722.5	6,568,572	2,177.8	1,095,769	363.3

[a]Population figures are U.S. Census Bureau provisional estimates as of July 1 for each year except 1990 and 2000, which are decennial census counts.

[b]The murder and nonnegligent manslaughters that occurred as a result of the events of September 11, 2001, are not included in this table.

[c]The 2006 figures have been adjusted since publication of *Crime in the United States, 2006.*

Note: Although arson data are included in the trend and clearance tables, sufficient data are not available to estimate totals for this offense. Therefore, no arson data are published in this table.

SOURCE: "Table 1. Crime in the United States, by Volume and Rate per 100,000 Inhabitants, 1988–2007," in *Crime in the United States, 2007,* U.S. Department of Justice, Federal Bureau of Investigation, September 2008, http://www.fbi.gov/ucr/cius2007/data/table_01.html (accessed October 2, 2008)

The FBI collects detailed homicide data in the UCR Program's Supplementary Homicide Report (SHR). SHR data include the age, sex, and race of murder offenders and victims, the relationships between offenders and victims, the circumstances surrounding murders, and the types of weapons used in murders. It should be noted that not all these statistics are reported by all agencies for every reported murder, offender, and victim.

MURDER OFFENDERS AND VICTIMS. SHR data for 2007 include age, sex, and race data for 17,040 murder offenders. These data are reported by the FBI in *Crime in the United States, 2007*. Because offender data are based on reported crimes not actual arrests, SHR tables classify the age, sex, or race of some offenders as "unknown." SHR categorizations for 2007 murder offenders by sex are:

- Male offenders—10,975 (64.4%)

- Female offenders—1,206 (7.1%)

- Unknown—4,859 (28.5%)

SHR categorizations for 2007 murder offenders by race are:

- African-American offenders—6,463 (37.9%)

- White offenders—5,278 (31%)

- Other offenders—245 (1.4%)

- Unknown—5,054 (29.7%)

SHR data for 2007 murder victims include age, sex, and race data for 14,831 victims. The vast majority of these murder victims (11,618 or 78.3%) were male, whereas 3,177 (21.4%) were female. Another 36 victims (0.2%) were of unknown sex. African-Americans accounted for 7,316 (49.3%) of the victims, and whites accounted for 6,948 (46.8%) of the victims. Another 345 victims (2.3%) were of other races, and 222 victims (1.5%) were of unknown race.

Figure 2.1 shows a breakdown by age of the 11,209 murder offenders and 14,567 murder victims for which age was known in 2007. Large numbers of offenders and victims were between the ages of 17 and 34.

FIGURE 2.1

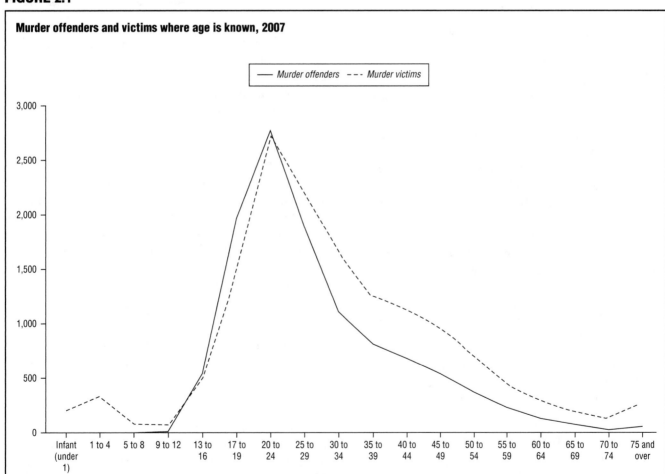

Murder offenders and victims where age is known, 2007

— Murder offenders   - - - Murder victims

SOURCE: Adapted from "Expanded Homicide Data Table 3. Murder Offenders, by Age, Sex, and Race, 2007," in *Crime in the United States, 2007*, U.S. Department of Justice, Federal Bureau of Investigation, September 2008, http://www.fbi.gov/ucr/cius2007/offenses/expanded_information/data/shrtable_03.html (accessed October 3, 2008), and "Expanded Homicide Data Table 2. Murder Victims by Age, Sex, and Race, 2007," in *Crime in the United States, 2007*, U.S. Department of Justice, Federal Bureau of Investigation, September 2008, http://www.fbi.gov/ucr/cius2007/offenses/expanded_information/data/shrtable_02.html (accessed October 20, 2008)

TABLE 2.2

TABLE 2.3

Details on murder circumstances, 2007

Circumstances	2007
Total	14,831
Felony type total	**2,184**
Rape	31
Robbery	924
Burglary	86
Larceny-theft	11
Motor vehicle theft	20
Arson	58
Prostitution and commercialized vice	11
Other sex offenses	9
Narcotic drug laws	583
Gambling	4
Other—not specified	447
Suspected felony type	**67**
Other than felony type total	**7,105**
Romantic triangle	105
Child killed by babysitter	34
Brawl due to influence of alcohol	117
Brawl due to influence of narcotics	61
Argument over money or property	192
Other arguments	3,645
Gangland killings	77
Juvenile gang killings	676
Institutional killings	11
Sniper attack	1
Other—not specified	2,186
Unknown	**5,475**

SOURCE: Adapted from "Expanded Homicide Data Table 9. Murder Circumstances, by Relationship, 2007," in *Crime in the United States, 2007*, U.S. Department of Justice, Federal Bureau of Investigation, September 2008, http://www.fbi.gov/ucr/cius2007/offenses/expanded_information/data/shrtable_09.html (accessed October 3, 2008)

MURDER CIRCUMSTANCES. Table 2.2 describes the circumstances for 14,831 of the total murders reported in 2007. Of the reported murders, 15% (2,184) were associated with known felonies, mostly robberies and narcotic drug law violations. Nearly half (7,105 or 48%) of the reported murders occurred due to other circumstances, mainly arguments and brawls between people. Juvenile gang killings accounted for 676 of the reported murders, and 77 of the murders were attributed to gangland killings, including organized crime syndicates.

The FBI reports in *Crime in the United States, 2007* that the relationship between murder offender and victim was unknown in 6,848 of the 14,831 murders reported to the UCR Program in 2007. Of the 7,983 murders in which the relationship could be ascertained, the vast majority were committed by someone known to the victim. The breakdown was:

• Acquaintances (neighbor, friend, boyfriend, etc.)—4,289 (54%)

• Strangers—1,924 (24%)

• Family members—1,770 (22%)

MURDER WEAPONS. Table 2.3 shows the weapons used in 14,831 of the murders committed during 2007.

Murder victims, by weapon used, 2007

Weapons	2007
Total	14,831
Total firearms:	10,086
Handguns	7,361
Rifles	450
Shotguns	455
Other guns	115
Firearms, type not stated	1,705
Knives or cutting instruments	1,796
Blunt objects (clubs, hammers, etc.)	647
Personal weapons (hands, fists, feet, etc.)*	854
Poison	10
Explosives	1
Fire	130
Narcotics	49
Drowning	12
Strangulation	134
Asphyxiation	108
Other weapons or weapons not stated	1,004

*Pushed is included in personal weapons.

SOURCE: Adapted from "Expanded Homicide Data Table 7. Murder Victims, by Weapon, 2003–2007," in *Crime in the United States, 2007*, U.S. Department of Justice, Federal Bureau of Investigation, September 2008, http://www.fbi.gov/ucr/cius2007/offenses/expanded_information/data/shrtable_07.html (accessed October 20, 2008)

More than two-thirds (10,086 or 68%) of these murders involved firearms, primarily handguns. Knives or other cutting instruments were used in 1,796 murders in 2007. Murderers used their hands, fists, and feet as weapons in 854 murders. Blunt objects, such as clubs and hammers, were used in 647 murders.

Forcible Rape

Rape is a crime of violence in which the victim may suffer serious physical injury and long-term psychological pain. In *Crime in the United States, 2007*, the FBI defines forcible rape as "the carnal knowledge of a female forcibly and against her will." The FBI includes assaults and attempts to commit rape by force or threat of force, but statutory rape and other sex offenses are not included.

Rape is a very intimate crime, and rape victims may be unwilling, afraid, or ashamed to discuss it. As a result, many rapes are not reported to law enforcement authorities. In 2007, 90,427 forcible rapes were reported to law enforcement agencies for a rate of 30 forcible rapes per 100,000 female inhabitants. (See Table 2.1.) Forcible rape rates have declined dramatically since the early 1990s, when rates of more than 40 rapes per 100,000 female inhabitants were recorded. The FBI notes that 92.2% of forcible rapes recorded by law enforcement agencies in 2007 were rapes by force, and 7.8% were attempted rapes.

Robbery

According to the FBI, in *Crime in the United States, 2007*, robbery is defined as "the taking or attempting to

FIGURE 2.2

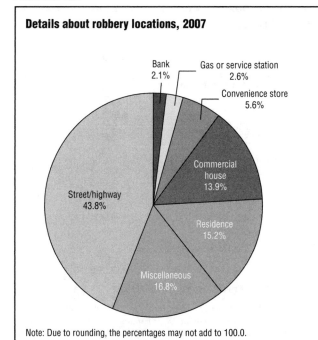

Details about robbery locations, 2007

Bank 2.1%

Gas or service station 2.6%

Convenience store 5.6%

Commercial house 13.9%

Street/highway 43.8%

Residence 15.2%

Miscellaneous 16.8%

Note: Due to rounding, the percentages may not add to 100.0.

SOURCE: "Robbery Location Figure: Percent Distribution, 2007," in *Crime in the United States, 2007*, U.S. Department of Justice, Federal Bureau of Investigation, September 2008, http://www.fbi.gov/ucr/cius 2007/offenses/violent_crime/robbery.html (accessed October 22, 2008)

FIGURE 2.3

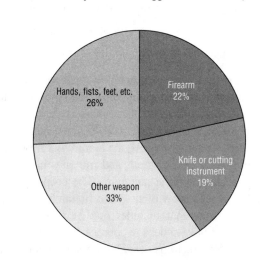

Details about weapons used in aggravated assaults, 2007

Hands, fists, feet, etc. 26%

Firearm 22%

Knife or cutting instrument 19%

Other weapon 33%

SOURCE: Adapted from "Table 15. Crime Trends: Additional Information about Selected Offenses by Population Group, 2006–2007," in *Crime in the United States, 2007*, U.S. Department of Justice, Federal Bureau of Investigation, September 2008, http://www.fbi.gov/ucr/cius2007/data/table_15.html (accessed October 22, 2008)

take anything of value from the care, custody, or control of a person or persons by force or threat of force or violence and/or by putting the victim in fear." The robbery rate peaked in 1991 at 272.7 per 100,000 inhabitants. (See Table 2.1.) Over the following decade it declined dramatically, and between 2000 and 2007 the rate stayed below 150 robberies per 100,000 inhabitants.

Figure 2.2 shows the locations of 345,200 robberies that were reported in 2007. Nearly 44% of these robberies occurred on the street or highway, 16.8% occurred in miscellaneous locations, 15.2% occurred at residences, and 13.9% occurred at commercial houses (i.e., nonresidential structures used for businesses other than gas stations, banks, or convenience stores). Robberies at convenience stores comprised 5.6% of the total, with gas or service station locations accounting for 2.6% and banks 2.1%.

Aggravated Assault

Aggravated assault is defined by the FBI in *Crime in the United States, 2007* as "an unlawful attack by one person upon another for the purpose of inflicting severe or aggravated bodily injury." The agency further notes that aggravated assault typically involves the use of a weapon or other means "likely to produce death or great bodily harm." Attempted aggravated assaults that involve weapons or the threat to use weapons are included in this category. However, an aggravated assault that occurs during a robbery is categorized as a robbery.

In 2007, 855,856 aggravated assaults were reported to law enforcement agencies nationwide for a rate of 283.8 aggravated assaults per 100,000 inhabitants. (See Table 2.1.) During the early to mid-1990s the rate was more than 400 aggravated assaults per 100,000 inhabitants. The rate has declined dramatically since that time period, falling nearly 36% from the peak of 441.9 aggravated assaults reported per 100,000 inhabitants in 1992.

WEAPONS INVOLVED IN AGGRAVATED ASSAULTS. Figure 2.3 shows the weapons involved in 731,864 of the aggravated assaults that occurred in 2007. In 26% of these aggravated assaults the perpetrators used their hands, fists, and feet as weapons. Firearms were involved in 22% of these crimes, and knives or other cutting instruments were involved in 19% of aggravated assaults in 2007. The remaining third (33%) of these crimes involved other weapons.

Violent Crime and Property Crime

As noted earlier, the FBI includes four crimes in the category of violent crime: forcible rape, murder and nonnegligent manslaughter, aggravated assault, and robbery. A crime that includes more than one of these violent acts is counted only once under the most serious offense committed. According to the FBI, in *Crime in the United States, 2007*, the hierarchy is murder and nonnegligent homicide, forcible rape, robbery, and aggravated assault. Thus, a forcible rape in which the victim is also robbed would be counted as a forcible rape, not as a forcible rape and a robbery. In 2007, 1.4 million violent crimes were reported by law enforcement agencies for a rate of 466.9 per 100,000 inhabitants. (See Table 2.1.) The following is a breakdown of reported violent crimes by percentage:

- Murder and nonnegligent homicide—1.2% of reported violent crimes

- Forcible rape—6.4% of reported violent crimes

- Robbery—31.6% of reported violent crimes

- Aggravated assault—60.8% of reported violent crimes

The FBI includes four crimes in the category of property crime: larceny-theft, burglary, arson, and motor vehicle theft. In 2007, 9.8 million of these property crimes were reported for a rate of 3,263.5 per 100,000 inhabitants. (See Table 2.1.) According to the FBI, the hierarchy for property crimes is burglary, larceny-theft, and motor vehicle theft; arson is not included in the hierarchy. The property crime hierarchy lies below the violent crime hierarchy, meaning that a violent crime that includes one or more property crimes is counted only under the appropriate violent crime. The following four sections describe the statistics for individual property crimes.

Burglary

According to the FBI, in *Crime in the United States, 2007*, burglary is defined as "the unlawful entry of a structure to commit a felony or theft." Unlawful entry includes both forcible and nonforcible entry (e.g., entering a home through an unlocked door without the owner's permission). The FBI's definition of structure includes houses, apartments, offices, barns, stables, and so on, but does not include automobiles. Attempted forcible entries are included in the burglary category.

Nearly 2.2 million burglaries were reported in 2007 for a rate of 722.5 per 100,000 inhabitants. (See Table 2.1.) This rate is down dramatically from the late 1980s and early 1990s, when the rate was more than 1,000 burglaries per 100,000 inhabitants. Most (61.1%) of the burglaries in 2007 involved forcible entry. Nearly a third (32.4%) were nonforcible unlawful entries, and 6.5% were attempted forcible entries.

A separate data set by the FBI covering nearly 1.7 million burglaries in 2007 indicates that the vast majority of these burglaries (nearly 1.2 million) occurred at residences. The remainder were at nonresidences, such as stores or offices. The time of day in which the residence burglaries occurred could not be identified in 21.5% of the cases. Nighttime burglaries accounted for 28.5% of the residence total, whereas daytime burglaries accounted for 49.9% of the residence total.

Larceny-Theft

Larceny-theft is defined by the FBI in *Crime in the United States, 2007* as "the unlawful taking, carrying, leading, or riding away of property from the possession or constructive possession of another." Larceny-theft does not involve the use of force, violence, or fraud. Examples of fraud-based crimes are embezzlement, forgery, and passing

TABLE 2.4

Details about larceny-theft crimes, 2007

Classification	Number of offenses 2007	Percent distribution*
Larceny-theft (except motor vehicle theft):		
Larceny-theft by type		
Total	5,268,582	100.0
Pocket-picking	21,984	0.4
Purse-snatching	30,526	0.6
Shoplifting	785,228	14.9
From motor vehicles (except accessories)	1,369,150	26.0
Motor vehicle accessories	480,502	9.1
Bicycles	179,945	3.4
From buildings	632,947	12.0
From coin-operated machines	24,894	0.5
All others	1,743,406	33.1
Larceny-theft by value		
Over $200	2,313,327	43.9
$50 to $200	1,179,936	22.4
Under $50	1,775,319	33.7

*Because of rounding, the percentages may not add to 100.0.

SOURCE: Adapted from "Table 23. Offense Analysis, Number and Percent Change, 2006–2007," in *Crime in the United States,* 2007, U.S. Department of Justice, Federal Bureau of Investigation, September 2008, http://www.fbi.gov/ucr/cius2007/data/table_23.html (accessed October 3, 2008)

bad checks. Larceny-theft does include offenses such as shoplifting, pocket picking, purse snatching, stealing items from motor vehicles, stealing bicycles, and so on. Attempted larceny-thefts are also included.

In 2007 law enforcement agencies reported nearly 6.6 million larceny-thefts for a rate of 2,177.8 per 100,000 inhabitants. (See Table 2.1.) This rate is down from a peak of 3,229.1 larceny-thefts per 100,000 inhabitants in 1991. According to the FBI, the total value of property lost by victims to larceny-theft during 2007 was approximately $5.8 billion.

Table 2.4 provides details about 5.3 million of the larceny-thefts that occurred in 2007. Thefts from motor vehicles (excluding accessories) accounted for nearly 1.4 million of the offenses. This was, by far, the largest category among the specifically identified larceny-theft crimes. It accounted for 26% of the total. Shoplifting crimes and thefts from buildings made up 14.9% and 12%, respectively, of the total.

Motor Vehicle Theft

The FBI defines motor vehicle theft in *Crime in the United States, 2007* as "the theft or attempted theft of a motor vehicle." Included in the definition of motor vehicles are cars, trucks, sport utility vehicles, buses, motorcycles and motor scooters, snowmobiles, and all-terrain vehicles. Other types of motorized vehicles (such as boats, tractors, or construction equipment) are not included.

In 2007 about 1.1 million cases of motor vehicle theft were reported in the United States for a rate of 363.3 per

100,000 inhabitants. (See Table 2.1.) This rate is down considerably from the early 1990s, when the rate was more than 650 motor vehicle thefts per 100,000 inhabitants. According to the FBI, the total value of the stolen motor vehicles in 2007 was $7.4 billion.

Arson

Arson is defined by the FBI in *Crime in the United States, 2007* as "any willful or malicious burning or attempting to burn, with or without intent to defraud, a dwelling house, public building, motor vehicle or aircraft, personal property of another, etc." Arson statistics do not include fires that have been classified as suspicious or of unknown origin.

The FBI states that incomplete statistics are available on arson crimes due to limited reporting by law enforcement agencies. Reports from law enforcement agencies indicate that 64,332 arson offenses occurred in 2007. Approximately 42.9% of these arsons involved buildings, such as residences or other structures. Another 29.2% of the arsons involved miscellaneous types of property, such as crops or fences, and 27.9% involved mobile property, such as cars.

GUNS AND CRIME

The FBI reports that firearms were used in 68% of the murders, 43% of the robberies, and 21% of the aggravated assaults reported in 2007. (See Figure 2.4.) It does not, however, specify the number of total offenses or the number of reporting agencies involved in calculating these percentages.

Figure 2.5 shows the number of violent crimes (murders, robberies, and aggravated assaults) committed with firearms between 1973 and 2006. The number of violent crimes committed with firearms skyrocketed during the early 1990s, reaching nearly 600,000 per year in 1993. Since

FIGURE 2.5

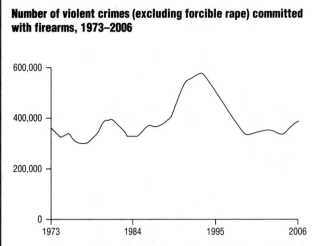

Number of violent crimes (excluding forcible rape) committed with firearms, 1973–2006

SOURCE: "Crimes Committed with Firearms, 1973–2006," in *Additional Crime Facts at a Glance*, U.S. Department of Justice, Office of Justice Programs, Bureau of Justice Statistics, January 25, 2008, http://www.ojp.usdoj.gov/bjs/glance/guncrime.htm (accessed October 24, 2008)

that time the number has dropped dramatically, dipping below 400,000 per year, which is similar to the levels recorded back in the 1970s and 1980s.

Background Checks for Firearms

In 1993 Congress passed the Brady Handgun Violence Prevention Act. The law requires federal firearms licensees to perform a criminal history background check on customers before selling them firearms. The licensing of firearms dealers is handled by the Bureau of Alcohol, Tobacco, Firearms, and Explosives, a division of the U.S. Department of Justice (DOJ). Table 2.5 lists the types of people who are prohibited from buying firearms under the Brady Act and similar state laws. The list includes convicted felons, people under indictment for felony offenses, people who have been convicted of misdemeanor domestic violence, and people subject to a restraining order due to harassment, stalking, or threatening of an intimate partner or child.

The DOJ reports in "Background Checks for Firearm Transfers, 2007—Statistical Tables" (July 16, 2008, http://www.ojp.usdoj.gov/bjs/pub/html/bcft/2007/bcft07st.htm) that 8.7 million applications for firearm transfers or permits were subject to background checks in 2007 under the Brady Act and similar state laws. Only 1.6% of the applications were denied. The most common reason for denial was a felony conviction or indictment of the applicant.

HATE CRIMES

As noted in Chapter 1, hate crimes are crimes motivated by the offender's personal prejudice or bias against the victim. The FBI includes hate crimes in the UCR Program. The UCR Program's first publication on hate crimes was

FIGURE 2.4

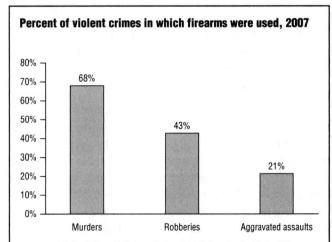

Percent of violent crimes in which firearms were used, 2007

SOURCE: Adapted from "Violent Crime," in *Crime in the United States, 2007*, U.S. Department of Justice, Federal Bureau of Investigation, September 2008, http://www.fbi.gov/ucr/cius2007/offenses/violent_crime/index.html (accessed October 22, 2008)

TABLE 2.5

Types of persons to whom the transfer of a firearm is prohibited under the Brady Act

The Brady Act prohibits transfer of a firearm to a person who—

• is under indictment for, or has been convicted of, a crime punishable by imprisonment for more than 1 year
• is a fugitive from justice
• is an unlawful user of, or addicted to, a controlled substance
• has been adjudicated as a mental defective or committed to a mental institution
• is an illegal alien or has been admitted to the U.S. under a nonimmigrant visa
• was dishonorably discharged from the U.S. Armed Forces
• has renounced U.S. citizenship
• is subject to a court order restraining him or her from harassing, stalking, or threatening an intimate partner or child
• has been convicted of a misdemeanor crime of domestic violence
• is under age 18 for long guns or under age 21 for handguns.

SOURCE: "The Brady Act Prohibits Transfer of a Firearm to a Person Who—," in *Background Checks for Firearm Transfers, 2007—Statistical Tables*, U.S. Department of Justice, Office of Justice Programs, Bureau of Justice Statistics, July 16, 2008, http://www.ojp .usdoj.gov/bjs/pub/html/bcft/2007/bcft07st.htm (accessed October 24, 2008)

Hate Crime Statistics, 1990: A Resource Book, which compiled hate crime data from 11 states that had collected the information under state authority in 1990. The UCR Program continued to work with agencies that were already investigating hate crimes and collecting related information to develop a more uniform method of nationwide data collection. *Hate Crime Statistics, 1992* offered the first data reported by law enforcement agencies across the country that participated in UCR hate crime data collection. In the Violent Crime and Law Enforcement Act of 1994, Congress added hate-motivated crimes against disabled people to the list of bias crimes; the FBI began gathering data on hate crimes against this population on January 1, 1997.

Data on hate crimes are likely incomplete because many incidents may not be reported or cannot be verified as hate crimes. Some victims may not report hate crimes due to fear that the criminal justice system is biased against the group to which the victim belongs and that law enforcement authorities will not be responsive. Attacks against homosexuals may not be reported because the victims do not want to reveal their sexual orientation to others. In addition, proving that an offender acted from bias can be a long, tedious process, requiring much investigation. Until a law enforcement investigator can find enough evidence in a particular case to be sure the offender's actions came, at least in part, from bias, the crime is not counted as a hate crime.

Hate Crime Statistics

The most recent UCR Program–based report on hate crimes is *Hate Crime Statistics, 2007* (October 2008, http://www.fbi.gov/ucr/hc2007/index.html). It covers crimes motivated by offender bias against the race, ethnicity or national origin, sexual orientation, religion, or disability of the vic-

tim. The UCR Program notes that in 2007 law enforcement agencies reported 7,624 hate crime incidents involving 9,006 specific offenses. Almost all the incidents (8,999) were due to a single bias on behalf of the offender:

• Racial bias—52.8%

• Religious bias—16.4%

• Sexual-orientation bias—16.2%

• Ethnicity/national origin bias—13.9%

• Disability bias—0.9%

Concerning the remaining seven hate crime incidents reported in 2007, multiple biases by the offender were recorded.

The following is a breakdown by crime of the 9,006 offenses reported in 2007:

• Destruction/damage/vandalism—32.4%

• Intimidation—28.5%

• Simple assault—18.7%

• Aggravated assault—12.4%

• Other offenses—8.1%

THE DECLINE OF CRIME

The number of crimes reported each year and the crime rate decreased for all the crimes monitored by the DOJ under the UCR Program between 1988 and 2007. (See Table 2.1.) The UCR Program relies on information from law enforcement agencies. The DOJ also conducts an annual victimization survey in which a random group of U.S. inhabitants are quizzed about their experiences with crime during the previous year. Because not all crimes are reported to law enforcement, the victimization surveys provide information about the true extent of crime in the United States.

Violent Crime Decreases

Figure 2.6 includes data from the UCR Program and victimization studies dating back to 1973. It shows four measures of serious violent crime: homicide, rape, robbery, and aggravated assault.

"Total violent crime" is based on the number of homicides committed against people aged 12 years and older as reported by law enforcement agencies plus the number of rapes, robberies, and aggravated assaults tallied in victimization surveys regardless of whether or not these crimes were reported to law enforcement agencies by victims. "Victimizations reported to the police" include homicides committed against people aged 12 years and older as reported by law enforcement agencies plus the number of rapes, robberies, and aggravated assaults tallied in victimization surveys that the victims claim were reported to law enforcement agencies. "Crimes recorded by police" are based on UCR

FIGURE 2.6

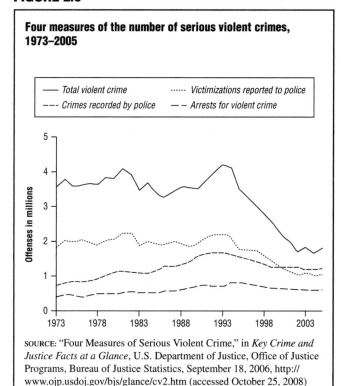

Four measures of the number of serious violent crimes, 1973–2005

SOURCE: "Four Measures of Serious Violent Crime," in *Key Crime and Justice Facts at a Glance*, U.S. Department of Justice, Office of Justice Programs, Bureau of Justice Statistics, September 18, 2006, http://www.ojp.usdoj.gov/bjs/glance/cv2.htm (accessed October 25, 2008)

FIGURE 2.7

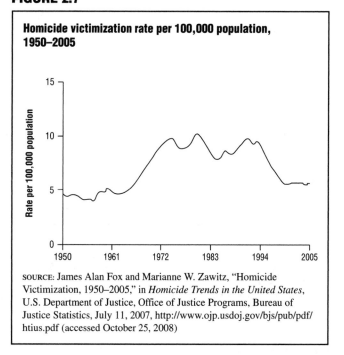

Homicide victimization rate per 100,000 population, 1950–2005

SOURCE: James Alan Fox and Marianne W. Zawitz, "Homicide Victimization, 1950–2005," in *Homicide Trends in the United States*, U.S. Department of Justice, Office of Justice Programs, Bureau of Justice Statistics, July 11, 2007, http://www.ojp.usdoj.gov/bjs/pub/pdf/htius.pdf (accessed October 25, 2008)

FIGURE 2.8

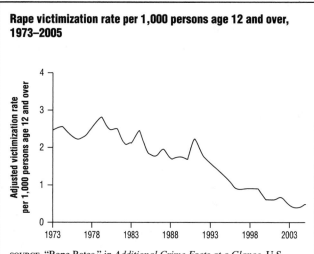

Rape victimization rate per 1,000 persons age 12 and over, 1973–2005

SOURCE: "Rape Rates," in *Additional Crime Facts at a Glance*, U.S. Department of Justice, Office of Justice Programs, Bureau of Justice Statistics, September 10, 2006, http://www.ojp.usdoj.gov/bjs/glance/rape.htm (accessed October 27, 2008)

Program records, but include only crimes committed against people aged 12 years and older. "Arrests for violent crime" are also based on UCR records.

Figure 2.6 indicates that the total number of serious violent crimes hovered between 3 million and just over 4 million offenses per year from the early 1970s through the early 1990s. The number peaked at nearly 4.2 million offenses in 1993 and then began a steady decline that lasted until 2002. From 2002 to 2005 the total number of violent crimes stabilized at just under 2 million per year.

A similar pattern is evident in Figure 2.7, which shows the number of homicides per 100,000 U.S. inhabitants from 1950 to 2005. The homicide rate more than doubled between 1950 and 1980 from 4.6 to 10.2 homicides per 100,000 inhabitants. Then it began to decline. By 1999 the homicide rate was less than 6 offenses per 100,000 inhabitants. It stabilized near that level through 2005.

Figure 2.8 shows the rape rate per 1,000 people aged 12 years and older from 1973 to 2005. The rate peaked in 1979 at 2.8 rapes per 1,000 people, then underwent a general decline over the following two decades. In 1996 the rate dropped below 1 rape per 1,000 people. Between 2003 and 2005 the rate was at or below 0.5 rapes per 1,000 people aged 12 years and older.

Figure 2.9 shows the robbery rate per 1,000 people aged 12 years and older from 1973 to 2005. The rate peaked in 1981 at 7.4 robberies per 1,000 people. It declined temporarily and then slowly rose through the mid-1990s, when it

exceeded 6 robberies per 1,000 people. Over the following decade the robbery rate declined dramatically, dropping below 3 robberies per 1,000 people in 2001. The rate hovered just above 2.5 robberies per 1,000 people through 2005.

A decline among assault cases is less dramatic, but still obvious. Figure 2.10 shows the rates of aggravated and simple assault per 1,000 people aged 12 years and older from 1973 to 2005. In 1973 the aggravated assault rate was 12.5 assaults per 1,000 people. After decreasing slightly through the remainder of the 1970s and the 1980s, the rate surged briefly above 10 in the early 1990s before beginning

FIGURE 2.9

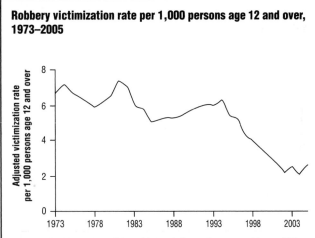

Robbery victimization rate per 1,000 persons age 12 and over, 1973–2005

SOURCE: "Robbery Rates," in *Additional Crime Facts at a Glance*, U.S. Department of Justice, Office of Justice Programs, Bureau of Justice Statistics, September 10, 2006, http://www.ojp.usdoj.gov/bjs/glance/rob.htm (accessed October 27, 2008)

FIGURE 2.10

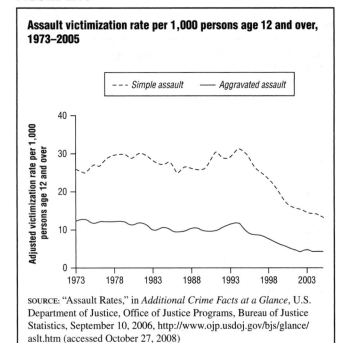

Assault victimization rate per 1,000 persons age 12 and over, 1973–2005

SOURCE: "Assault Rates," in *Additional Crime Facts at a Glance*, U.S. Department of Justice, Office of Justice Programs, Bureau of Justice Statistics, September 10, 2006, http://www.ojp.usdoj.gov/bjs/glance/aslt.htm (accessed October 27, 2008)

a steady decline. By 2005 the aggravated assault rate was 4.3 assaults per 1,000 people aged 12 years and older. The simple assault rate hovered between 25 and just over 30 assaults per 1,000 people for two decades, from 1973 through 1993. In 1994 it peaked at 31.5 assaults per 1,000 people. The rate then underwent a dramatic decline, reaching 13.5 assaults per 1,000 people aged 12 years and older in 2005.

Property Crime Decreases

The number of property crimes (burglary, theft, and motor vehicle theft) per 1,000 households is shown in

FIGURE 2.11

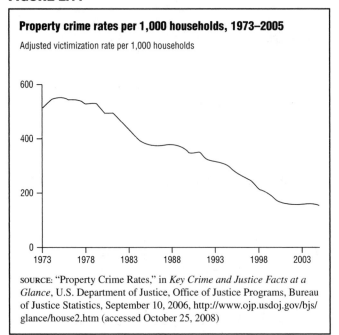

Property crime rates per 1,000 households, 1973–2005

Adjusted victimization rate per 1,000 households

SOURCE: "Property Crime Rates," in *Key Crime and Justice Facts at a Glance*, U.S. Department of Justice, Office of Justice Programs, Bureau of Justice Statistics, September 10, 2006, http://www.ojp.usdoj.gov/bjs/glance/house2.htm (accessed October 25, 2008)

Figure 2.11 from 1973 to 2005. In the mid-1970s the property crime rate was over 500 crimes per 1,000 households. It began a steady decline, dropping below 200 crimes per 1,000 households in 1999 before leveling off.

WHY DID CRIME RISE AND FALL?

According to Arthur J. Lurigio, in "Crime and Communities: Prevalence, Impact, and Programs" (Lawrence B. Joseph, ed., *Crime, Communities, and Public Policy*, 1995), the national crime rate fell from 1900 until the era of Prohibition in the 1920s. Crime spiked during Prohibition and then fell and leveled off until World War II (1939–1945). Crime dropped dramatically during the war because many young men were away. Following the war, a baby boom occurred, meaning that there was a dramatic increase in births. The baby boom lasted from the late 1940s into the 1960s, resulting in a huge surge of teenagers and young adults in the population from the 1960s through the 1980s.

Figure 2.12 shows historical crime rates for violent crimes and property crimes from 1960 to 2006. In both categories a huge increase occurred from 1960 through the 1980s and 1990s. A variety of social, economic, and even environmental reasons have been proposed to explain this increase:

- Huge influx in youth due to the baby boom

- Decrease in high-paying blue-collar manufacturing jobs for low-skilled workers

- Growth of ghettos and low-income housing projects in the inner cities

FIGURE 2.12

Historical rate of violent crimes and property crimes per 100,000 inhabitants, 1960–2006

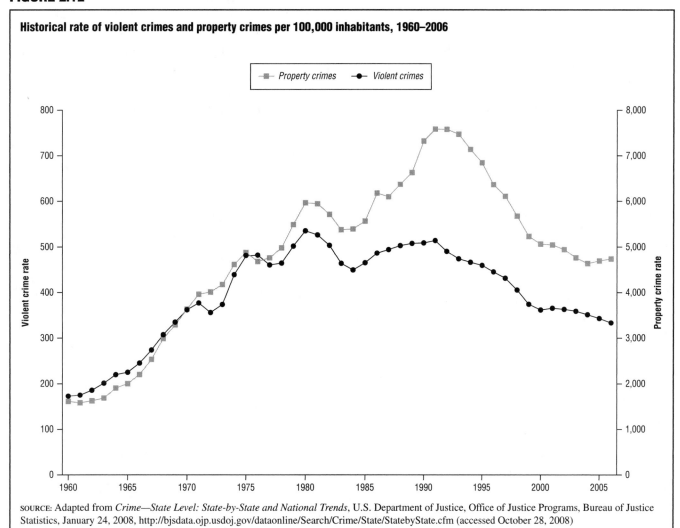

SOURCE: Adapted from *Crime—State Level: State-by-State and National Trends*, U.S. Department of Justice, Office of Justice Programs, Bureau of Justice Statistics, January 24, 2008, http://bjsdata.ojp.usdoj.gov/dataonline/Search/Crime/State/StatebyState.cfm (accessed October 28, 2008)

• Breakdown of the traditional family structure

• New drug culture, particularly heroin and cocaine in the 1970s and crack cocaine in the 1980s

• Growth of youth gangs

• Easy availability of firearms

• Better crime-tracking methods

• Exposure of infants and children to lead in paint and gasoline before the late 1970s. (Lead exposure has been linked to a range of developmental and behavioral issues, including inattention, irritability, aggressiveness, and violent behavior.)

During the early 1990s the crime rate began a dramatic and sustained decline. (See Figure 2.12.) Many of the conditions that had been blamed for the crime surge continued into the 1990s and the first decade of the twenty-first century, even as the crime rate decreased. The breakdown of the traditional family, the growth of youth gangs, and the loss of

high-paying blue-collar jobs continued to occur even as the crime rate plummeted. Likewise, crime-tracking methods continued to improve over time. Sociologists and criminologists have struggled to explain why the crime rate increased and then decreased. Some of the reasons suggested for the decrease are:

• A strong economy in the 1990s provided many job opportunities

• Tougher sentencing rules took hardcore criminals off the streets and kept them behind bars for longer periods of time

• Tougher gun control laws made firearms less accessible to criminals

• The U.S. population aged as baby boomers got older and less prone to criminal behavior

• Some ghettos and low-income housing projects that had been hotbeds for crime in the inner cities were dismantled

- There were more police officers per capita

- Policing methods improved

- People increased their crime prevention efforts, such as the use of security systems and neighborhood watch programs

- The crack cocaine epidemic subsided

- The national legalization of abortion in 1973 prevented unwanted babies from being born and potentially growing up to become criminals

- Lead exposure in infants and children decreased dramatically after the 1970s

It remains to be seen whether these explanations for the crime decline will hold up to future scrutiny.

CHAPTER 3
CRIME VICTIMS

As described in Chapter 2, the Federal Bureau of Investigation (FBI) operates the Uniform Crime Reports (UCR) Program, which compiles national crime data that are submitted by thousands of law enforcement agencies from around the country. The UCR Program provides data on the types of crimes reported to law enforcement agencies. It also includes some data on the victims of these crimes. Another, more detailed examination of crime victims is conducted by the Bureau of Justice Statistics (BJS), an agency within the U.S. Department of Justice (DOJ). This program is called the National Crime Victimization Survey (NCVS).

THE NATIONAL CRIME VICTIMIZATION SURVEY

Since 1972 the BJS has conducted an annual survey measuring the levels of victimization resulting from criminal activity in the United States. The survey was previously known as the National Crime Survey, but was renamed in 1991 to emphasize the measurement of victimization experienced by U.S. residents and households. Each year the NCVS collects data from thousands of households on the frequency, characteristics, and consequences of criminal victimization in the United States. The most recent survey data are reported in *Criminal Victimization in the United States, 2006 Statistical Tables* (August 2008, http://www.ojp.usdoj.gov/bjs/pub/pdf/cvus06.pdf). According to the BJS, in "Crime and Victims Statistics" (August 29, 2008, http://www.ojp.usdoj.gov/bjs/cvict.htm#ncvs), NCVS data cover "a nationally representative sample of 76,000 households comprising nearly 135,300 people."

The NCVS measures the levels of criminal victimization of people and households for the following crimes: rape and sexual assault, robbery, aggravated and simple assault, purse snatching and pocket picking (all of which are called personal crimes), and household burglary, motor vehicle theft, and other thefts (all of which are called household

crimes). Murder and other killing crimes are not counted in the NCVS, because the data are gathered only through interviews with victims. The BJS uses NCVS data to calculate victimization rates as follows:

- Personal crimes—number of victims per 1,000 U.S. residents aged 12 and older

- Household crimes—number of incidents per 1,000 U.S. households

According to the BJS, in *Criminal Victimization in the United States, 2006 Statistical Tables*, neither interviewers nor victims classify events as specific crimes during the interviews. A computer program later performs crime classification based on victim answers to specific detailed questions about the nature of each event. For events that include more than one crime (e.g., rape and burglary), only the most serious crime is counted using the following hierarchy: rape, sexual assault, robbery, assault, burglary, motor vehicle theft, and theft.

Comparing NCVS and UCR Data

The NCVS was created because of a concern that the FBI's UCR Program did not fully portray the true volume of crime in the United States. The UCR provides data on crimes reported to law enforcement authorities, but not all crimes are reported by victims.

Some observers believe the NCVS is a better indicator than the UCR statistics of the volume of crime in the United States. Nonetheless, like all surveys, the NCVS is subject to error. The accuracy of the survey data depends on people's truthful and complete reporting of incidents and events that have happened to them. Also, the NCVS and the UCR sometimes define and track crimes differently. As noted in Chapter 2, the FBI defines rape for UCR purposes as "the carnal knowledge of a female forcibly and against her will." Assaults and attempts to commit rape by force or threat of force are included in this category. By contrast, the

NCVS counts as rape victims both female and male victims who have been subjected to "forced sexual intercourse." The NCVS also counts verbal threats of rape as attempted rapes. In addition, the UCR Program counts crimes committed against babies and children (i.e., people less than 12 years old), whereas the NCVS only counts crimes against people aged 12 and older. Thus, direct comparisons between UCR and NCVS data are difficult.

The NCVS and the UCR are generally considered the primary sources of statistical information on crime in the United States. Like all reporting systems, both have their shortcomings, but each provides valuable insights into crime in the United States.

Comparing Old and New NCVS Data

Beginning in 1979 the NCVS underwent a thorough, decade-long redesign. The new design was intended to improve the survey's ability to measure both victimization and difficult-to-measure crimes, such as rape, sexual assault, and domestic violence. Improvements included the introduction of "short cues" or techniques to jog respondents' memories of events. As anticipated, the redesign resulted in an increased number of crimes counted by the survey. Therefore, pre-1993 raw data cannot be directly compared to the later raw data. The DOJ does, however, provide graphs in which pre-1993 raw data have been adjusted to make them comparable with data collected in later years.

In 2006 the methodology of the NCVS was changed to reflect new population data collected by the U.S. Census Bureau and to increase the use of computers during the interviewing process. These changes are described at length by Michael Rand and Shannan Catalano of the BJS in *Criminal Victimization, 2006* (December 2007, http://www.ojp .usdoj.gov/bjs/pub/pdf/cv06.pdf). According to Rand and Catalano, these changes mean that 2006 NCVS victimization rates are not directly comparable to rates calculated for previous years.

CRIME VICTIMIZATIONS IN 2006

According to the NCVS, nearly 6.3 million U.S. residents aged 12 and older were victims of personal crime during 2006. (See Table 3.1.) More than 18.9 million U.S. households were reportedly victimized by property crimes in 2006.

Victims of Violent Crimes

The NCVS considers rape/sexual assault, robbery, and simple and aggravated assault to be violent crimes. Approximately 6.1 million U.S. residents aged 12 and older were victims of these violent crimes during 2006. (See Table 3.1.) This is a victimization rate of 24.7 violent crimes per 1,000 U.S. residents aged 12 and older. The rate for attempted violent crimes (16.5 per 1,000 population aged 12 and older) was much higher than the rate for completed violent crimes (8.2 per 1,000 population aged 12 and older). Overall, the highest victimization rates per 1,000 population aged 12 and

TABLE 3.1

Number and percent of victimizations, by type of crime, and rate per 1,000 persons or households, 2006

Type of crime	Number of victimizations	Percent of all victimizations	Rate per 1,000 persons or households
All crimes	25,183,350	100.0%	—
Personal crimes	6,267,610	24.9%	25.4
Crimes of violence	6,094,390	24.2	24.7
Completed violence	2,019,260	8.0	8.2
Attempted/threatened violence	4,075,130	16.2	16.5
Rape/sexual assault	260,940	1.0	1.1
Rape/attempted rape	192,320	0.8	0.8
Rape	116,600	0.5	0.5
Attempted rape[a]	75,720	0.3	0.3
Sexual assault[b]	68,620	0.3	0.3
Robbery	712,610	2.8	2.9
Completed/property taken	482,290	1.9	2.0
With injury	208,140	0.8	0.8
Without injury	274,150	1.1	1.1
Attempted to take property	230,320	0.9	0.9
With injury	43,340	0.2	0.2
Without injury	186,980	0.7	0.8
Assault	5,120,840	20.3	20.7
Aggravated	1,344,280	5.3	5.4
With injury	466,610	1.9	1.9
Threatened with weapon	877,670	3.5	3.5
Simple	3,776,550	15.0	15.3
With minor injury	900,850	3.6	3.6
Without injury	2,875,700	11.4	11.6
Purse snatching/pocket picking	173,220	0.7	0.7
Completed purse snatching	34,250*	0.1*	0.1*
Attempted purse snatching	6,870*	0.0*	0.0*
Pocket picking	132,110	0.5	0.5
Total population age 12 and over	247,233,080	—	—
Property crimes	**18,915,740**	**75.1%**	**160.5**
Household burglary	3,560,920	14.1	30.2
Completed	2,848,210	11.3	24.2
Forcible entry	1,024,030	4.1	8.7
Unlawful entry without force	1,824,180	7.2	15.5
Attempted forcible entry	712,710	2.8	6.0
Motor vehicle theft	992,260	3.9	8.4
Completed	791,840	3.1	6.7
Attempted	200,410	0.8	1.7
Theft	14,362,570	57.0	121.9
Completed	13,791,020	54.8	117.0
Less than $50	3,822,200	15.2	32.4
$50–$249	4,940,790	19.6	41.9
$250 or more	3,718,530	14.8	31.6
Amount not available	1,309,500	5.2	11.1
Attempted	571,550	2.3	4.8
Total number of households	117,858,380	—	—

Note: Due to changes in methodology, the 2006 national crime victimization rates are not comparable to previous years and cannot be used for yearly trend comparisons. However, the overall patterns of victimization at the national level can be examined. Detail may not add to total shown because of rounding.
*Estimate is based on 10 or fewer sample cases.
Percent distribution is based on unrounded figures.
—Not applicable.
[a]Includes verbal threats of rape.
[b]Includes threats.

SOURCE: "Table 1. Personal and Property Crimes, 2006: Number, Percent Distribution, and Rate of Victimizations, by Type of Crime," in *Criminal Victimization in the United States, 2006 Statistical Tables*, U.S. Department of Justice, Office of Justice Programs, Bureau of Justice Statistics, August 2008, http://www.ojp.usdoj.gov/bjs/pub/pdf/cvus06.pdf (accessed October 3, 2008)

older were for simple assault without injury (11.6), simple assault with minor injury (3.6), and aggravated assault involving threatening with a weapon (3.5).

Victims of Property Crimes

The NCVS counts household burglaries (forced and unforced), motor vehicle thefts, and other thefts (excluding purse snatching and pocket picking) as property crimes. According to NCVS data, more than 18.9 million U.S. households were victimized by these crimes during 2006. (See Table 3.1.) This is a victimization rate of 160.5 property crimes per 1,000 households in 2006. The most common self-reported property crime was theft (other than motor vehicle theft). Thefts made up nearly 14.4 million of the total victimizations. The vast majority of the thefts (13.8 million) were completed thefts, rather than attempted thefts (572,000).

VICTIM DEMOGRAPHICS

The Department of Justice uses both UCR and NCVS data to characterize the demographic qualities of crime victims. Victims are characterized by sex, age, race, and family income. In addition, some information is provided about victim activities at the time of the crime, victim-offender relationships, and weapons used against the victims. As of early 2009, UCR data were available through 2007, whereas NCVS data were available only through 2006.

Crime Victims by Sex

In 2006 male respondents to the NCVS experienced a victimization rate of 27.4 personal crimes per 1,000 people aged 12 and older. (See Table 3.2.) The rate for females was slightly lower at 23.4 personal crimes per 1,000 people aged 12 and older. Personal crimes include rape/sexual assault, robbery, aggravated and simple assault, and purse snatching/pocket picking. Males experienced higher rates of all personal crimes except rape/sexual assault and simple assault with minor injury. The breakdown for crimes of violence in Table 3.2 indicates that the victimization rates for males and females in 2006 were 26.7 and 22.7, respectively.

According to the BJS, in *Criminal Victimization in the United States, 2006 Statistical Tables*, females who experienced violent personal crimes in 2006 were more often the victims of relatives or people well-known to them than casual acquaintances or strangers. By contrast, male victims of violent personal crimes in 2006 were more likely to

TABLE 3.2

Number of victimizations and victimization rates for persons age 12 and over, by type of crime and gender of victims, 2006

| | Rate per 1,000 persons age 12 and over | | | | | |
| | Both genders | | Male | | Female | |
Type of crime	Number	Rate	Number	Rate	Number	Rate
All personal crimes	6,267,610	25.4	3,301,950	27.4	2,965,670	23.4
Crimes of violence	6,094,390	24.7	3,215,590	26.7	2,878,800	22.7
Completed violence	2,019,260	8.2	989,590	8.2	1,029,660	8.1
Attempted/threatened violence	4,075,130	16.5	2,225,990	18.5	1,849,140	14.6
Rape/sexual assault	260,940	1.1	27,970*	0.2*	232,960	1.8
Rape/attempted rape	192,320	0.8	27,970*	0.2*	164,340	1.3
Rape	116,600	0.5	6,520*	0.1*	110,080	0.9
Attempted rape[a]	75,720	0.3	21,460*	0.2*	54,270	0.4
Sexual assault[b]	68,620	0.3	0*	0.0*	68,620	0.5
Robbery	712,610	2.9	465,130	3.9	247,490	2.0
Completed/property taken	482,290	2.0	316,590	2.6	165,700	1.3
With injury	208,140	0.8	132,390	1.1	75,750	0.6
Without injury	274,150	1.1	184,200	1.5	89,950	0.7
Attempted to take property	230,320	0.9	148,540	1.2	81,780	0.6
With injury	43,340	0.2	23,480*	0.2*	19,860*	0.2*
Without injury	186,980	0.8	125,060	1.0	61,920	0.5
Assault	5,120,840	20.7	2,722,480	22.6	2,398,350	18.9
Aggravated	1,344,280	5.4	757,500	6.3	586,780	4.6
With injury	466,610	1.9	241,700	2.0	224,910	1.8
Threatened with weapon	877,670	3.5	515,800	4.3	361,880	2.9
Simple	3,776,550	15.3	1,964,980	16.3	1,811,570	14.3
With minor injury	900,850	3.6	424,780	3.5	476,070	3.8
Without injury	2,875,700	11.6	1,540,200	12.8	1,335,510	10.5
Purse snatching/pocket picking	173,220	0.7	86,360	0.7	86,870	0.7
Population age 12 and over	247,233,080	—	120,465,800	—	126,767,280	—

Note: Due to changes in methodology, the 2006 national crime victimization rates are not comparable to previous years and cannot be used for yearly trend comparisons. However, the overall patterns of victimization at the national level can be examined.

Detail may not add to total shown because of rounding.

*Estimate is based on 10 or fewer sample cases.

—Not applicable.

[a]Includes verbal threats of rape.

[b]Includes threats.

SOURCE: "Table 2. Personal Crimes, 2006: Number of Victimizations and Victimization Rates for Persons Age 12 and over, by Type of Crime and Gender of Victims," in *Criminal Victimization in the United States, 2006 Statistical Tables*, U.S. Department of Justice, Office of Justice Programs, Bureau of Justice Statistics, August 2008, http://www.ojp.usdoj.gov/bjs/pub/pdf/cvus06.pdf (accessed October 3, 2008)

FIGURE 3.1

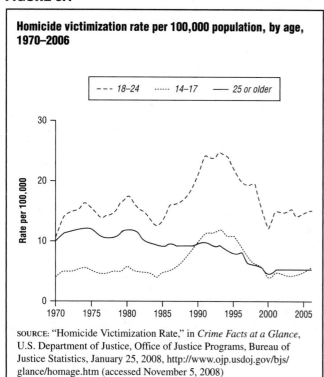

Homicide victimization rate per 100,000 population, by age, 1970–2006

SOURCE: "Homicide Victimization Rate," in *Crime Facts at a Glance*, U.S. Department of Justice, Office of Justice Programs, Bureau of Justice Statistics, January 25, 2008, http://www.ojp.usdoj.gov/bjs/glance/homage.htm (accessed November 5, 2008)

FIGURE 3.2

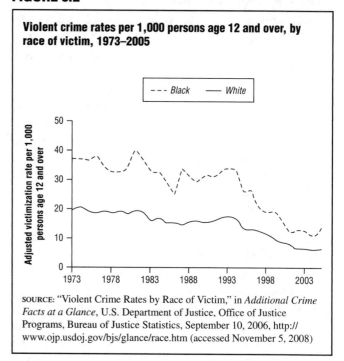

Violent crime rates per 1,000 persons age 12 and over, by race of victim, 1973–2005

SOURCE: "Violent Crime Rates by Race of Victim," in *Additional Crime Facts at a Glance*, U.S. Department of Justice, Office of Justice Programs, Bureau of Justice Statistics, September 10, 2006, http://www.ojp.usdoj.gov/bjs/glance/race.htm (accessed November 5, 2008)

have been victimized by casual acquaintances and strangers than relatives or people well known to them.

Crime Victims by Age

The BJS (September 10, 2006, http://www.ojp.usdoj.gov/bjs/glance/vage.htm) reports that people aged 12 to 24 experience higher violent crime victimization rates than people of older ages. This includes homicides, rapes, robberies, and aggravated assaults. Figure 3.1 shows homicide victimization rates from 1970 through 2006 for three age groups: 14 to 17 years old, 18 to 24 years old, and 25 years and older. The data indicate that older teens and young adults aged 18 to 24 experienced the highest homicide rates, by far, over this time period.

The BJS notes in *Criminal Victimization in the United States, 2006 Statistical Tables* that the victimization rates for personal crimes reported in the 2006 NCVS were:

- People aged 12 to 15—47.8 personal crimes per 1,000 people in this age group

- People aged 16 to 19—52.8 personal crimes per 1,000 people in this age group

- People aged 20 to 24—45.1 personal crimes per 1,000 people in this age group

- People aged 25 to 34—36.6 personal crimes per 1,000 people in this age group

- People aged 35 to 49—20.6 personal crimes per 1,000 people in this age group

- People aged 50 to 64—13.6 personal crimes per 1,000 people in this age group

- People aged 65 and older—3.9 personal crimes per 1,000 people in this age group

Crime Victims by Race

Figure 3.2 shows violent crime rates per 1,000 people aged 12 and older from 1973 through 2005 based on the race of the victim. The violent crimes included in this analysis are homicide, rape, robbery, and aggravated assault. Homicide data were collected from the UCR Program, whereas data for the other crimes were collected from the NCVS. African-Americans suffered higher victimization rates than whites over the entire time period shown. However, the difference between the races has narrowed somewhat since the early 1990s.

In 2006 for people aged 12 and older, African-American males had, by far, the highest victimization rate of 34.5, followed by African-American females at 30.1. (See Figure 3.3.) White males experienced a victimization rate of 25.7, and the rate for white females was 21.

Crime Victims by Annual Family Income

Figure 3.4 provides a breakdown by annual family income in 2006 for victims aged 12 and older of violent personal crimes. NCVS data indicate that individuals from low-income households experienced a much higher victimization rate than did individuals from high-income households. The violent crime victimization rate for people from households making less than $7,500 per year was 63.5 per 1,000 people aged 12 and older. This was more than twice the rate for people from

FIGURE 3.3

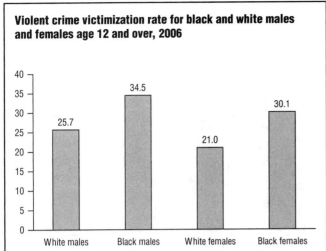

Violent crime victimization rate for black and white males and females age 12 and over, 2006

SOURCE: Adapted from "Table 6. Personal Crimes, 2006: Number of Victimizations and Victimization Rates for Persons Age 12 and over, by Type of Crime and Gender and Race of Victims," in *Criminal Victimization in the United States, 2006 Statistical Tables*, U.S. Department of Justice, Office of Justice Programs, Bureau of Justice Statistics, August 2008, http://www.ojp.usdoj.gov/bjs/pub/pdf/cvus06.pdf (accessed October 3, 2008)

households with annual incomes of $15,000 to $24,999 and four and a half times the rate for people from households with annual incomes of $75,000 or more.

Crime Victim Activities

NCVS data for 2006 indicate the activities that crime victims were reportedly doing when they became victims. More than a quarter (26%) of these incidents occurred while the victims were engaged in activities at home other than sleeping. (See Figure 3.5.) About two-thirds of incidents occurred while victims were away from home, including conducting a leisure activity (23%), while at work or school (21%), or while shopping, running errands, or en route (21%). Only 3% of incidents occurred while victims were sleeping at home. Another 6% of the incidents occurred while victims were engaged in other activities, or their activities at the time of the crime are unknown.

Figure 3.6 provides a similar analysis for victims of property crimes during 2006. These crimes include household burglary, motor vehicle thefts, and other thefts. The largest portion (28%) of the incidents occurred while the victims were sleeping at home. Nearly a fifth (18%) of the incidents

FIGURE 3.4

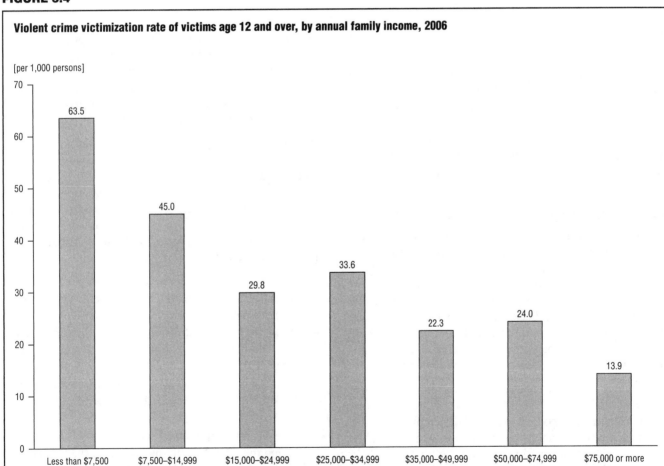

Violent crime victimization rate of victims age 12 and over, by annual family income, 2006

SOURCE: Adapted from "Table 14. Personal Crimes, 2006: Victimization Rates for Persons Age 12 and over, by Type of Crime and Annual Family Income of Victims," in *Criminal Victimization in the United States, 2006 Statistical Tables*, U.S. Department of Justice, Office of Justice Programs Bureau of Justice Statistics, August 2008, http://www.ojp.usdoj.gov/bjs/pub/pdf/cvus06.pdf (accessed October 3, 2008)

FIGURE 3.5

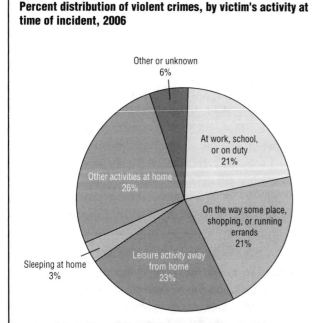

Percent distribution of violent crimes, by victim's activity at time of incident, 2006

SOURCE: Adapted from "Table 64. Personal and Property Crimes, 2006: Percent Distribution of Incidents, by Victim's Activity at Time of Incident and Type of Crime," in *Criminal Victimization in the United States, 2006 Statistical Tables*, U.S. Department of Justice, Office of Justice Programs, Bureau of Justice Statistics, August 2008, http://www.ojp.usdoj.gov/bjs/pub/pdf/cvus06.pdf (accessed October 3, 2008)

FIGURE 3.6

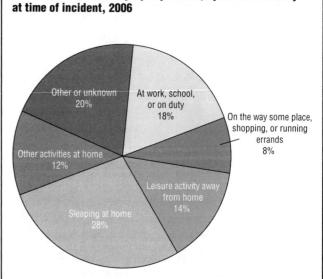

Percent distribution of property crimes, by victim's activity at time of incident, 2006

SOURCE: Adapted from "Table 64. Personal and Property Crimes, 2006: Percent Distribution of Incidents, by Victim's Activity at Time of Incident and Type of Crime," in *Criminal Victimization in the United States, 2006 Statistical Tables*, U.S. Department of Justice, Office of Justice Programs, Bureau of Justice Statistics, August 2008, http://www.ojp.usdoj.gov/bjs/pub/pdf/cvus06.pdf (accessed October 3, 2008)

occurred while victims were at work, school, or on duty, and 14% of the incidents occurred while the victims were engaged in leisure activities away from their homes. Smaller percentages occurred while victims were at home conducting activities other than sleeping (12%) or were on their way some place, shopping, or running errands (8%); 20% of the incidents occurred during other or unknown activities.

REPORTING VICTIMIZATIONS TO POLICE

More than half (58.2%) of all victimizations compiled in the 2006 NCVS were not reported by the victims to the police. (See Table 3.3.) Just over 40% of the victimizations were reported to the police. Personal crime victimizations (49% reported) were more reported than property crime victimizations (37.8%). Personal crimes include rape/sexual assault, robbery, aggravated and simple assault, and purse snatching and pocket picking. Property crimes include household burglary, motor vehicle theft, and other thefts.

Violent crimes are personal crimes excluding purse snatching and pocket picking. In 2006, 48.8% of violent victimizations were reported to police by victims, and 49.4% of these crimes were not reported to police. According to the BJS, in *Criminal Victimization in the United States, 2006 Statistical Tables*, the reporting rate for female victims of violent crime in 2006 was 52.5%, whereas the reporting rate for men victimized by violent crimes was 45.6%. African-American victims reported 54.7% of violent crimes commit-

ted against them, whereas white victims reported 48.1% of their violent victimizations. Older victims reported much higher numbers of victimizations than did younger victims. Victims aged 65 and older reported 63.4% of their victimizations to police, whereas victims aged 12 to 19 only reported 34.3% of their victimizations to police.

The personal crimes most often reported to police by victims in 2006 were completed purse snatching (78.9% reported), aggravated assault with injury (76% reported), and attempted robbery with injury (66.3% reported). (See Table 3.3.) The personal crimes least often reported to police by victims were attempted purse snatching (0% reported), attempted rape (25.7% reported), and simple assault without injury (38.8% reported).

The property crimes most often reported to police by victims in 2006 were completed motor vehicle theft (89% reported), household burglary with forcible entry (71.1%), and completed theft of $250 or more (56.4% reported). (See Table 3.3.) The property crimes least often reported to police by victims were completed theft of less than $50 (17.3% reported), completed theft of $50 to $249 (26% reported), and attempted theft (28.5% reported).

Reasons for Not Reporting Victimizations

During the 2006 NCVS, interviewers asked crime victims who had not reported their victimizations to police why they chose not to do so. The largest single reason given for not reporting a personal crime was that the victim considered the incident a private or personal matter. (See

TABLE 3.3

Number and percent of victimizations, by type of crime and whether or not reported to the police, 2006

Sector and type of crime	Number of victimizations	Percent of victimizations reported to the police			
		Total	Yes[a]	No	Not known and not available
All crimes	**25,183,350**	**100.0%**	**40.6%**	**58.2%**	**1.2%**
Personal crimes	**6,267,610**	**100.0%**	**49.0%**	**49.2%**	**1.8%**
Crimes of violence	6,094,390	100.0	48.8	49.4	1.8
Completed violence	2,019,260	100.0	62.6	35.7	1.7*
Attempted/threatened violence	4,075,130	100.0	42.0	56.2	1.8
Rape/sexual assault	260,940	100.0	43.4	56.6	0.0*
Rape/attempted rape	192,320	100.0	39.9	60.1	0.0*
Rape	116,600	100.0	49.2	50.8	0.0*
Attempted rape[b]	75,720	100.0	25.7*	74.3	0.0*
Sexual assault[c]	68,620	100.0	53.2*	46.8*	0.0*
Robbery	712,610	100.0	56.8	41.9	1.3*
Completed/property taken	482,290	100.0	59.8	39.5	0.7*
With injury	208,140	100.0	60.8	37.5	1.7*
Without injury	274,150	100.0	58.9	41.1	0.0*
Attempted to take property	230,320	100.0	50.8	46.9	2.4*
With injury	43,340	100.0	66.3*	21.0*	12.7*
Without injury	186,980	100.0	47.2	52.8	0.0*
Assault	5,120,840	100.0	48.0	50.1	2.0
Aggravated	1,344,280	100.0	59.6	37.4	3.0
With injury	466,610	100.0	76.0	22.3	1.7*
Threatened with weapon	877,670	100.0	50.9	45.4	3.7*
Simple	3,776,550	100.0	43.9	54.6	1.6
With minor injury	900,850	100.0	59.9	37.6	2.5*
Without injury	2,875,700	100.0	38.8	59.9	1.3
Purse snatching/pocket picking	173,220	100.0	55.9	42.4	1.7*
Completed purse snatching	34,250*	100.0*	78.9*	12.3*	8.7*
Attempted purse snatching	6,870*	100.0*	0.0*	100.0*	0.0*
Pocket picking	132,110	100.0	52.8	47.2	0.0*
Property crimes	**18,915,740**	**100.0%**	**37.8%**	**61.2%**	**1.1%**
Household burglary	3,560,920	100.0	49.5	49.0	1.5
Completed	2,848,210	100.0	50.5	48.0	1.5
Forcible entry	1,024,030	100.0	71.1	28.5	0.4*
Unlawful entry without force	1,824,180	100.0	39.0	58.9	2.1
Attempted forcible entry	712,710	100.0	45.5	53.0	1.5*
Motor vehicle theft	992,260	100.0	80.9	18.8	0.3*
Completed	791,840	100.0	89.0	11.0	0.0*
Attempted	200,410	100.0	48.8	49.7	1.5*
Theft	14,362,570	100.0	31.9	67.1	1.0
Completed	13,791,020	100.0	32.0	67.0	1.0
Less than $50	3,822,200	100.0	17.3	81.5	1.1
$50–$249	4,940,790	100.0	26.0	73.0	0.9
$250 or more	3,718,530	100.0	56.4	43.2	0.5*
Amount not available	1,309,500	100.0	28.6	69.0	2.4*
Attempted	571,550	100.0	28.5	70.2	1.3*

Note: Many incident characteristics were unaffected or minimally affected by changes in methodology in the 2006 National Crime Victimization Survey. However, caution should be used in comparing 2006 rates of individual variables, particularly those with small sample sizes, to previous years.
Detail may not add to total shown because of rounding.
*Estimate is based on 10 or fewer sample cases.
[a]Figures in this column represent the rates at which victimizations were reported to the police, or "police reporting rates."
[b]Includes verbal threats of rape.
[c]Includes threats.

SOURCE: "Table 91. Personal and Property Crimes, 2006: Percent Distribution of Victimizations, by Type of Crime and Whether or Not Reported to the Police," in *Criminal Victimization in the United States, 2006 Statistical Tables*, U.S. Department of Justice, Office of Justice Programs, Bureau of Justice Statistics, August 2008, http://www.ojp.usdoj.gov/bjs/pub/pdf/cvus06.pdf (accessed October 3, 2008).

Figure 3.7.) About one-fifth (21%) of those asked gave this reason. Other oft-cited reasons were that the stolen object was recovered or the offender was unsuccessful in the crime (17%) or the victim reported the crime to an official other than the police (13%).

Figure 3.8 shows the reasons given by victims for not reporting property crimes to police in 2006. The largest single reason given was that the stolen object was recovered or the offender was unsuccessful in the crime (28%). In

10% of the cases the victims stated the police would not want to be bothered about the victimization or there was lack of proof to support the crime.

TRENDS IN VICTIMIZATION, 1973 TO 2005

As stated earlier, the NCVS underwent a major methodology change in 2006 rendering data collected in that year incompatible with data collected in earlier years. However, the BJS has analyzed trends for NCVS data collected from

FIGURE 3.7

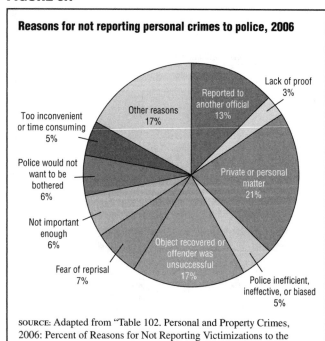

Reasons for not reporting personal crimes to police, 2006

SOURCE: Adapted from "Table 102. Personal and Property Crimes, 2006: Percent of Reasons for Not Reporting Victimizations to the Police, by Type of Crime," in *Criminal Victimization in the United States, 2006 Statistical Tables*, U.S. Department of Justice, Office of Justice Programs, Bureau of Justice Statistics, August 2008, http://www.ojp.usdoj.gov/bjs/pub/pdf/cvus06.pdf (accessed October 3, 2008)

FIGURE 3.8

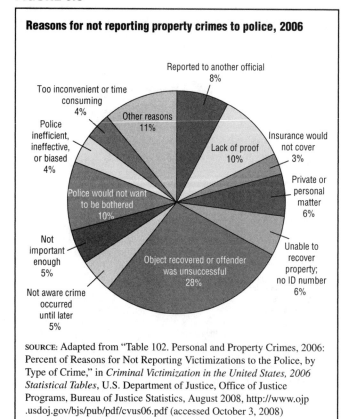

Reasons for not reporting property crimes to police, 2006

SOURCE: Adapted from "Table 102. Personal and Property Crimes, 2006: Percent of Reasons for Not Reporting Victimizations to the Police, by Type of Crime," in *Criminal Victimization in the United States, 2006 Statistical Tables*, U.S. Department of Justice, Office of Justice Programs, Bureau of Justice Statistics, August 2008, http://www.ojp.usdoj.gov/bjs/pub/pdf/cvus06.pdf (accessed October 3, 2008)

1973 to 2005. NCVS data are similar to UCR data in that both indicate overall levels of violent crime and property crime decreased between 1973 and 2005. According to the BJS, in "Key Facts at a Glance: Violent Crime Trends" (September 10, 2006, http://www.ojp.usdoj.gov/bjs/glance/tables/viortrdtab.htm), the violent crime victimization rate increased between 1973 and 1981 and then declined until 1986. From 1986 to 1994 the violent crime victimization rate increased, reaching 51.2 per 1,000 people aged 12 and older in 1994. From 1994 to 2005, however, violent crime victimization rates fell by 59%, to 21 per 1,000 people aged 12 and older. The victimization rates of most violent crimes dropped significantly between 1973 and 2005. The exception is murder, which remained at a steady rate of 0.1 per 1,000 people aged 12 and older every year between 1973 and 2005. In contrast, the rate of robbery reported in the NCVS declined from 6.7 per 1,000 people aged 12 and older in 1973 to 2.6 per 1,000 in 2005, aggravated assault from 12.5 per 1,000 to 4.3 per 1,000, and simple assault from 25.9 per 1,000 to 13.5 per 1,000.

In "Key Facts at a Glance: Property Crime Trends" (September 10, 2006, http://www.ojp.usdoj.gov/bjs/glance/tables/proptrdtab.htm), the BJS states that total property crime victimization rates fell dramatically between 1973 and 1995. After a slight increase from 1973 (519.9 per 1,000 households) to 1975 (553.6 per 1,000 households),

the rates dropped more or less consistently through 2005, when the total property crime rate was 154 per 1,000 households. The rates of all property crime types on which the NCVS collects data fell significantly from 1973 to 2005. The burglary rate fell from 110 per 1,000 households in 1973 to just 29.5 per 1,000 in 2005; the theft rate fell from 390.8 per 1,000 households to 116.2 per 1,000; and the motor vehicle theft rate fell from 19.1 per 1,000 households to 8.4 per 1,000.

COST OF VICTIMIZATION

The costs borne by crime victims include direct costs, such as the value of items that have been stolen, and indirect costs, such as the expenses of the criminal justice system, which must be shared by the entire society. In 2006 victims suffered a total economic loss of $18.4 billion due to crime. (See Table 3.4.) This is the cost of property losses and does not include additional expenses such as medical or insurance costs. Even though material losses are very important, emotional costs can also be significant by affecting victims for the rest of their lives.

Property crimes accounted for more than $16.5 billion in economic losses to victims in 2006. (See Table 3.4.) The highest mean (average) dollar loss was $5,690 due to motor vehicle theft.

TABLE 3.4

Economic losses of crime victims, by type of crime, 2006

Type of crime	All crimes			
	Gross loss (in millions of dollars)	Total crimes	Mean dollar loss	Median dollar loss
All crimes	$18,410	25,183,350	731	100
Personal crimes	1,896	6,267,610	303	100
Crimes of violence	1,860	6,094,390	305	100
Rape/sexual assault	45	260,940	171	350
Rape/attempted rape	45	192,320	233	350
Rape	43	116,600	371	500
Attempted rape[a]	1	75,720	19	50
Sexual assault[b]	0	68,620	0	0
Robbery	904	712,610	1,269	100
Assault	911	5,120,840	178	100
Purse snatching	4	41,110	107	70
Pocket picking	32	132,110	239	87
Property crimes	16,513	18,915,740	873	100
Household burglary	4,427	3,560,920	1,243	280
Motor vehicle theft	5,646	992,260	5,690	2,500
Theft	6,441	14,362,570	448	100

*Estimate is based on 10 or fewer sample cases.
[a]Includes verbal threats of rape.
[b]Includes threats.

SOURCE: Adapted from "Table 82. Personal and Property Crimes, 2006: Total Economic Loss to Victims of Crime," in *Criminal Victimization in the United States, 2006 Statistical Tables*, U.S. Department of Justice, Office of Justice Programs, Bureau of Justice Statistics, August 2008, http://www.ojp.usdoj.gov/bjs/pub/pdf/cvus06.pdf (accessed October 3, 2008)

VICTIMS' RIGHTS

For many years victims received little consideration in justice proceedings; to some it seemed that victims were victimized again by the very system to which they had turned for help. In *Final Report of the President's Task Force on Victims of Crime* (December 1982, http://www.ojp.gov/ovc/publications/presdntstskforcrprt/87299.pdf), Lois Haight Herrington observes that "somewhere along the way, the system began to serve lawyers and judges and defendants, treating the victim with institutionalized disinterest."

Revictimization may take several forms. For example, police questioning might seem to accuse a rape victim of enticing her attacker or participating willingly in the act. An assault victim might find that the hospital is more concerned about whether he or she can pay for treatment than about helping him or her recover from the incident. In their efforts to make sure each defendant receives a fair trial, judges and lawyers might seem to be more concerned about the accused offender than the victim. Crime victims might not be informed of court dates, sentencing hearings, or probation or parole hearings concerning their cases. They might not be informed when their attacker escapes or is released from prison. Victims who do participate in a trial might be kept outside the courtroom without ever being called to the witness stand. Situations such as these led many to advocate for victims' rights, including the right to be protected from harassment and the right to communicate to the court the effect the crime had on their life.

Attempts to improve the situation for victims gained momentum during the 1980s and 1990s. State and federal governments, the judicial system, and private groups all reflected an increased awareness of victims' concerns. Organizations began offering services to victims of crime. These organizations include domestic violence shelters, rape crisis centers, and child abuse programs. Law enforcement agencies, hospitals, and social services agencies also provide victims' services. The types of services provided include:

- Crisis intervention
- Counseling
- Emergency shelter and transportation
- Legal services

FEDERAL ACTIONS TO AID VICTIMS
The Federal Victim and Witness Protection Act of 1982

In 1982 Congress enacted the federal Victim and Witness Protection Act, a bill designed to protect and assist victims and witnesses of federal crimes. The law permits victim-impact statements in sentencing hearings to provide judges with information concerning financial, psychological, or physical harm suffered by victims. The law also provides for restitution (monetary compensation) to victims and prevents victims and/or witnesses from being intimidated by threatening verbal harassment. The law establishes penalties for acts of retaliation by defendants against those who testify against them.

Victims who provide addresses and telephone numbers are to be notified of major events in the criminal proceedings, including the arrest of the accused, the times of any court appearances at which the victim may appear, the release or detention of the accused, and the victim's opportunities to address the sentencing court. The guidelines also recommend that federal officials consult victims and witnesses to obtain their views on procedures such as proposed dismissals and plea negotiations. Officials must not disclose the names and addresses of victims and witnesses.

The Comprehensive Crime Control Act of 1990

In 1990 President George H. W. Bush (1924–) signed the Comprehensive Crime Control Act, which addressed many aspects of crime control, including protection for victims of child abuse, penalties for savings-and-loan fraud, and mandatory death penalties. The law includes the Victims' Rights and Restitution Act of 1990, which provides victims of federal crimes with the right to be treated with fairness and respect, be reasonably protected from the accused, be notified of court proceedings, be afforded an opportunity to meet with a federal prosecutor, and be provided with restitution. The act also bars criminals and convicted drunken drivers from declaring bankruptcy to avoid paying restitution.

Compensation and Assistance to Victims of Terrorism or Mass Violence (1996)

Title II of the Antiterrorism and Effective Death Penalty Act of 1996 included two laws designed to assist victims of terrorism and mass violence. The Mandatory Victims Restitution Act of 1996 provided for mandatory restitution for victims of certain federal crimes. The Justice for Victims of Terrorism Act of 1996 authorized compensation for citizens victimized by terrorist acts, both at home and abroad. It also allows the director of the Victims Crime Fund to make supplemental grants to states to assist residents who are victims of terrorism. Following the September 11, 2001 (9/11), terrorist attacks, the Uniting and Strengthening America by Providing Appropriate Tools Required to Intercept and Obstruct Terrorism (USA Patriot) Act of 2001 authorized the transfer of emergency supplemental appropriation funding into the Emergency Reserve account to assist victims of the attacks.

The Air Transportation Safety and System Stabilization Act

On September 22, 2001, Congress enacted the Air Transportation Safety and System Stabilization Act. Besides requiring the federal government to compensate the air carriers for losses incurred as a result of the 9/11 attacks, the act established the September 11th Victim Compensation Fund of 2001. The fund provided compensation to victims of the attacks who chose not to join in litigation (lawsuits) seeking additional money. The fund compensated any individual who was physically injured and the families and beneficiaries of victims killed as a result of the terrorist-related aircraft crashes on 9/11.

Keeping Children and Families Safe Act of 2003

The U.S. government has passed several laws intended to strengthen the legal rights of victims and make social services more widely accessible to crime victims. The Keeping Children and Families Safe Act of 2003 was signed into law on June 25, 2003. The act supports state efforts toward preventing and treating child abuse and neglect, including a basic grant program for improving state child protective services. The Justice for All Act of 2004, which was signed into law on October 30, 2004, contains four major sections related to crime victims and the criminal justice process. The act also includes provisions intended to protect crime victims' rights, eliminate the substantial backlog of deoxyribonucleic acid (DNA) samples collected from crime scenes and convicted offenders, and improve and expand the DNA testing capacity of federal, state, and local crime laboratories. The Crime Victims' Rights Act is a key component of the Justice for All Act. It guarantees crime victims the following rights:

1. The right to be reasonably protected from the accused

2. The right to reasonable, accurate, and timely notice of any public court proceeding, or any parole proceeding, involving the crime or of any release or escape of the accused

3. The right not to be excluded from any such public court proceeding, unless the court, after receiving clear and convincing evidence, determines that testimony by the victim would be materially altered if the victim heard other testimony at that proceeding

4. The right to be reasonably heard at any public proceeding in the district court involving release, plea, sentencing, or any parole proceeding

5. The reasonable right to confer with the attorney for the government in the case

6. The right to full and timely restitution as provided in law

7. The right to proceedings free from unreasonable delay

8. The right to be treated with fairness and with respect for the victim's dignity and privacy

The National Center for Victims of Crime (2007, http://www.ncvc.org/ncvc/main.aspx?dbID=DB_About189) calls itself "the nation's leading resource and advocacy organization for crime victims and those who serve them." The organization operates the online database VictimLaw (http://www.victimlaw.info/victimlaw/start.do), which is funded by the DOJ's Office for Victims of Crime (OVC) and serves as a clearinghouse of information regarding victim rights at the federal, state, and tribal levels.

VICTIM SERVICES AND ASSISTANCE

Programs that offer assistance to crime victims have received widespread public and legislative support in the United States. Restitution paid to victims is the most fundamental type of victim assistance because it represents an attempt to repay the victim for what was lost during the commission of a crime. Restitution for criminal acts has a long history that dates back to biblical times. The Bible often cites money payments for injuries, and this practice continued well into the Middle Ages. In about 1100, King Henry I (1068–1135) of England began to take a portion of each restitution payment as compensation for holding a trial and for injury inflicted on the state because the criminal act had disturbed the peace within his kingdom. Eventually, assault on an individual began to be considered an assault on society, and the king took the entire payment.

Victims' Participation at Sentencing

According to the National Center for Victims of Crime, every state allows courts to consider or ask for information from victims concerning the effects of the offense on their lives. Most states permit victim input at sentencing and most allow written victim-impact statements (detailing the impact the crime has had on the victim or, in the case of murder, on the victim's family). The Child Protection Restoration and Penalties Enhancement Act of 1990 permits child victims of federal crimes to present statements commensurate with their age, including drawings. Even though most impact statements are used at sentencing and parole hearings, victims often have input at bail hearings, pretrial release hearings, and plea-bargaining hearings.

Several state legislatures have developed strong victims' rights legislation. For example, Section 1191.1 of the California Penal Code (http://www.leginfo.ca.gov/cgi-bin/displaycode?section=pen&group=01001-02000&file=1191-1210.5) states: "The victim...or the next of kin... have the right to appear, personally or by counsel, at the sentencing proceeding and to reasonably express his, her, or their views concerning the crime, the person responsible, and the need for restitution. The court in imposing sentence shall consider the statements of victims, parents or guardians, and next of kin...and shall state on the record its conclusion concerning whether the person would pose a threat to public safety if granted probation."

Victim Compensation

Victim compensation programs pay money from a public fund to help victims with expenses incurred because of a violent crime. The U.S. government maintains the Crime Victims Fund, which is administered by the OVC. The federal Victims of Crime Act (VOCA) of 1984 established the fund, which supports the Victim Compensation and Victim Assistance grant programs. Victim compensation grants cover medical treatment and physical therapy costs, counseling fees, lost wages, funeral and burial expenses, and loss of support to dependents of homicide victims. Victim assistance funds cover the costs of crisis intervention, counseling, emergency shelter, and criminal justice advocacy. Deposits to the fund come from fines, penalty assessments, and bond forfeitures collected from convicted federal criminal offenders. In 2001 legislation was passed allowing the fund to receive gifts, donations, and bequests from private entities.

The OVC explains in *Rebuilding Lives, Restoring, Hope: OVC Report to the Nation 2007* (2007, http://www.ojp.usdoj .gov/ovc/welcovc/reporttonation2007/ReporttoNation07full .pdf) that as of 2007 it had distributed $7 billion in funds to assist millions of crime victims over the previous two decades. In fiscal years 2005 and 2006, $1.5 billion was deposited into the fund. Most of this money came from a handful of extremely large criminal fines levied against corporations.

The primary programs supported by the fund are:

- State crime victim assistance program grants
- State crime victim compensation grants
- Victim-witness coordinators who assist victims of federal crimes
- FBI victim specialists who assist victims of federal crimes

TABLE 3.5

Victims served by Victims of Crime Act (VOCA) assistance programs in fiscal years 2005 and 2006

Total victims	Number of victim categories	Percentage of victims served
Domestic violence	3,608,012	52
Child sexual abuse	691,519	10
Assault	613,301	10
Adult sexual assault	475,515	7
Child physical abuse	285,499	4
Robbery	225,851	3
Survivors of homicide victims	223,070	3
Adults molested as children	156,519	2
DUI/DWI crashes	110,729	2
Elder abuse	94,588	1
Other	432,915	6
Total	**6,917,518**	**100**

Note: DUI = Driving Under the Influence. DWI = Driving While Intoxicated.

SOURCE: "Figure 6. Victims Served by VOCA Assistance Programs in FYs 2005 and 2006 by Type of Victimization," in *OVC Report to the Nation 2007: Rebuilding Lives, Restoring Hope*, U.S. Department of Justice, Office of Justice Programs, Office for Victims of Crime, October 2008, http://www .ojp.usdoj.gov/ovc/welcovc/reporttonation2007/ReporttoNation07full.pdf (accessed November 7, 2008)

- The federal Victim Notification System, which notifies victims of federal crimes about key events, such as offender release dates
- The Children's Justice Act grant program for state and tribal programs handling crimes against children

According to the OVC, in fiscal years 2005 and 2006 VOCA distributed nearly $350 million to thousands of state-based crime victim programs that assisted nearly 7 million victims. Victims of domestic violence constituted just over half (52%) of all victims receiving VOCA assistance during this time period. (See Table 3.5.) Assault victims and child victims of sexual abuse each made up 10% of the total number of victims.

National Crime Victims' Rights Week

In 1981 the OVC initiated a nationwide program encouraging local communities to observe a National Crime Victims' Rights Week (January 16, 2009, http://www.ojp.usdoj .gov/ovc/ncvrw/welcome.html). The event is held annually in April and includes rallies, candlelight vigils, and other activities designed to honor or memorialize crime victims and highlight their rights in the criminal justice system.

Offender Restitution Programs

Restitution programs require those who have harmed an individual to repay the victim. In the past, the criminal justice system focused primarily on punishing the criminal and leaving victims to rely on civil court cases for damage repayment. By the twenty-first century most states permitted criminal courts to allow restitution payments as a condition of probation and/or parole. In addition, courts had the statutory authority to order restitution, and several states had passed constitutional amendments that specifically enumerated a victim's right to restitution.

Most restitution laws provide for restitution to the direct victim(s) of a crime, including the surviving family members of homicide victims. Restitution is usually only provided to victims of crimes for which a defendant was convicted. Many states allow victims to claim medical expenses and property damage or loss, and several permit families of homicide victims to claim costs for loss of support. In assessing damages, the courts must consider the offender's ability to pay.

Restitution can be ordered for several types of crime-related expenses that a victim experiences. The OVC explains that the restitution amount is typically based on:

- Medical care costs

- Lost wages

- Counseling

- Lost or damaged property

- Funeral expenses

- Other direct out-of-pocket expenses

In "Enforcing Restitution Orders" (March 7, 2007, http://www.ovc.gov/publications/bulletins/legalseries/bulletin5/4.html), the OVC notes that an offender may lose parole privileges and be imprisoned for nonpayment of restitution fees. The courts have upheld the constitutionality of incarcerating offenders for nonpayment, but the U.S. Supreme Court, in *Beardon v. Georgia* (461 U.S. 660 [1983]), ruled that an offender could not be sent to prison for nonpayment if he or she had made a good-faith effort to pay and could not do so. In most cases, offenders must prove their inability to make the payments. When offenders prove that they cannot pay, the courts can reduce the amount, change the schedule of payments, or suspend payment.

Besides threatening offenders with imprisonment, some jurisdictions have other methods of collection. These include garnishment of wages (taking the payment amount from wages before the employee receives his or her salary) or attaching the offender's assets (not allowing the offender to use bank accounts, stocks, or bonds) until he or she pays the restitution. Some jurisdictions can even sell the offender's home.

Civil Suits

A victim can sue in civil court for damages even if the offender has not been found guilty of a criminal offense. Victims often pursue this course of action because it is easier to win civil cases than criminal cases. In a criminal case, a jury or judge can find an alleged offender guilty only if the proof is "beyond a reasonable doubt." In a civil case, the burden of proof requires merely a "preponderance of the evidence" against the accused. Proof is still needed that a crime was committed, that there were damages, and that the accused is liable to pay for those damages. In addition, any restitution amounts that remain unpaid at the end of an offender's parole or probation period may be converted into civil judgments. However, even when victims secure a civil judgment, they often have trouble collecting their damage payments. Such has been the case with O. J. Simpson (1947–), a former professional football player, who was acquitted in 1995 of killing his former wife and her friend. In 1997 the victims' families won a multimillion-dollar civil judgment against Simpson. However, quirks of state laws shielded his pension and primary residence from seizure to pay the debts. In 2008 Simpson was sentenced to 33 years in prison for his role in an armed robbery. Media reports on that incident indicated that the winners of the 1997 civil judgment had collected little of the money owed to them by Simpson.

CHAPTER 4
DRUG CRIMES

As noted in Chapter 2, the Federal Bureau of Investigation's (FBI) Uniform Crime Reports (UCR) Program indicates that reported rates of violent crimes and property crimes have decreased dramatically over the past few decades. The UCR Program does not track the number of drug crimes reported by police, but it does track the number of arrests for drug crimes. State and local arrests for drug crimes skyrocketed from 580,900 in 1980 to 1.9 million in 2006, an increase of 225%. (See Figure 4.1.) According to the FBI, in *Crime in the United States, 2007* (September 2008, http://www.fbi.gov/ucr/cius2007/index.html), there were 1.8 million arrests for drug abuse violations in 2007—the highest number for any single crime category.

The Substance Abuse and Mental Health Services Administration (SAMHSA), a part of the U.S. Department of Health and Human Services, conducts an annual survey on the use of illegal drugs by the U.S. population. In *Results from the 2007 National Survey on Drug Use and Health: National Findings* (September 2008, http://www.oas.samhsa.gov/nsduh/2k7nsduh/2k7Results.pdf), SAMHSA states that in 2007, 19.9 million Americans aged 12 and older had used illicit drugs within the previous month. The vast majority (14.4 million) of these illicit drug users had used marijuana during the past month. Much smaller numbers had used psychotherapeutics (6.9 million), cocaine (2.1 million), hallucinogens (1 million), inhalants (600,000), and heroin (200,000). Psychotherapeutics are defined by SAMHSA as prescription drugs, such as pain relievers, tranquilizers, stimulants, and sedatives, that are used for nonmedical purposes.

The numbers are staggering: 19.9 million admitted users of illegal drugs and 1.8 million drug arrests in 2007. In addition, experts estimate that millions of other crimes are connected to illicit drug use.

THE WAR ON DRUGS
Drug Crime through the 1950s

Throughout its history the United States has struggled with how best to tackle the problem of drug abuse and the crimes linked to it. During the 1700s a number of potions containing opium and promising cures for a variety of ailments were available as so-called patent medicines, and physicians routinely prescribed opium medications to their patients. In 1805 the discovery of morphine by the Swiss pharmacist Friedrich Sertürner (1783–1841) introduced another powerful drug to the medicines of the day. By the end of the nineteenth century cocaine, codeine, and dozens of similar drugs were in common use. However, doctors were increasingly concerned about the side effects and addictiveness of these drugs and began issuing stern warnings about them to the public.

At the federal level, Congress passed the Pure Food and Drug Act of 1906, the Opium Exclusion Act of 1909, and the Harrison Narcotic Act of 1914 in attempts to quell the widespread availability of highly addictive drugs. The Progressive movement and religious revival that swept the country during the late 1800s and early 1900s made drug abuse socially unacceptable. By the 1920s drug use had been driven underground into the criminal world along with alcohol, which was banned by the Eighteenth Amendment in 1919. During the 1930s a flurry of laws was passed against marijuana, including the Marihuana Tax Act of 1937, which imposed high taxes and heavy fines while allowing restricted legal uses of marijuana-based products. By the 1950s drug abuse was considered a problem only among distinct and socially outcast populations. These included the African-American inhabitants of inner-city ghettos and certain bohemian elements that rejected the social norms of the time.

Drug Crime in the 1960s

The 1960s ushered in a completely new drug culture to the United States: recreational drug use among middle- and upper-class white youths in suburban and rural areas. Marijuana and a relatively new hallucinogenic drug called D-lysergic acid diethylamide (LSD) surged in popularity. Other drugs of choice during this era were amphetamines

FIGURE 4.1

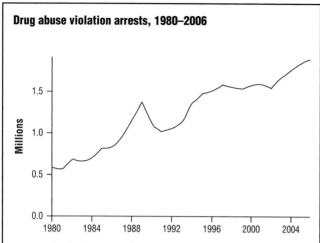

Drug abuse violation arrests, 1980–2006

SOURCE: Tina L. Dorsey, Doris J. James, and Priscilla Middleton, "Drug Abuse Violation Arrests, 1980–2006," in *Drugs and Crime Facts*, U.S. Department of Justice, Office of Justice Programs, Bureau of Justice Statistics, August 14, 2008, http://www.ojp.usdoj.gov/bjs/pub/pdf/dcf.pdf (accessed October 7, 2008)

(also called speed or uppers). Amphetamines stimulate the central nervous system. The drugs were widely dispensed by U.S. military authorities during World War II (1939–1945) to keep soldiers alert during battle. After the war amphetamines remained popular among students and workers who wanted to stay awake for long periods. They also used them to lose weight, because amphetamines suppress the appetite. According to Celinda Franco of the Congressional Research Service (CRS), in *Methamphetamine: Background, Prevalence, and Federal Drug Control Policies* (January 24, 2007, http://assets.opencrs.com/rpts/RL33857_20070124.pdf), amphetamines could be easily purchased over the counter (i.e., without a prescription) until 1951. By the end of the 1960s, new laws had been passed to combat growing problems with LSD and amphetamine abuse.

A National Emergency Is Declared

In 1969 President Richard M. Nixon (1913–1994) asked Congress to pass extensive legislation giving the federal government more control over the problem of drug abuse. The result was the Comprehensive Drug Abuse Prevention and Control Act of 1970. The act gave the U.S. attorney general greater jurisdiction over drug crimes and provided for the rehabilitation of drug addicts. It also placed tight new restrictions on the pharmaceutical industry and medical professionals to better control and monitor the supply and dispensing of prescription drugs. On June 17, 1971, Nixon addressed Congress about the nation's drug problem with this warning: "We must now candidly recognize that the deliberate procedures embodied in present efforts to control drug abuse are not sufficient in themselves. The problem has assumed the dimensions of a national emergency" (http://www.presidency.ucsb.edu/ws/index.php?pid=3048&st=drug+abuse&st1=). In a statement to the public made

that same day, Nixon said, "America's public enemy number one in the United States is drug abuse. In order to fight and defeat this enemy, it is necessary to wage a new, all-out offensive" (http://www.presidency.ucsb.edu/ws/index.php?pid=3047&st=drug+abuse&st1=). Over time, Nixon's statement became known as the declaration of the War on Drugs. In 1973 he created the U.S. Drug Enforcement Administration (DEA) to coordinate drug control efforts for the federal government.

Drug Crime in the 1970s and 1980s

Despite the declaration of war against drugs, illicit drug use continued to thrive. During the 1970s the sedative methaqualone, commonly known by the brand name Quaalude, became a popular street drug. It was heartily embraced by the American medical establishment as a safe and nonaddictive alternative to barbiturates, and easily found its way from medicine cabinets to the streets.

Another drug that gained prominence during this period was 3,4 methylenedioxymethamphetamine (MDMA, also known as ecstasy). In "MDMA (Ecstasy)" (August 2008, http://www.nida.nih.gov/InfoFacts/ecstasy.html), the National Institute on Drug Abuse notes that ecstasy is a synthetic psychoactive drug. It initially became popular among middle-class white teens and young adults at youth-friendly nightclubs and dance parties called raves. Ecstasy is one of several so-called club drugs associated with these types of users.

During the 1970s and 1980s cocaine use soared in the United States with the rise of large well-funded drug cartels in South America, particularly in Colombia. The cartels used their extensive criminal networks to import the drug into the United State and sell it for premium prices. Cocaine became the drug of choice for wealthy celebrities and professionals. It developed a reputation as a trendy, glamorous, and nonaddictive drug that was too expensive for street users. Meanwhile, a cheaper form of cocaine called crack cocaine was introduced to the street users. Unlike powdered cocaine, the crack version was a crystal that could be smoked. It was also more powerful than the same amount of powder cocaine and cost much less. A crack cocaine epidemic developed in U.S. cities, particularly in inner cities with large populations of low-income African-Americans. Gang wars and other crack-related crimes skyrocketed.

Drug Crime in the 1990s and 2000s

By the early 1990s the crack epidemic was over, and the United States enjoyed a brief downturn in the number of drug arrests. (See Figure 4.1.) This decline coincided with a national drop in overall crime that was described in Chapter 2. However, the overall crime rate continued a downward trend through the end of the decade, even as drug crime began to increase again. Drug arrests reached nearly 1.4 million in 1989, but decreased to 1.1 million by 1992. They then began

FIGURE 4.2

Drug arrests, by drug type, 1982–2006

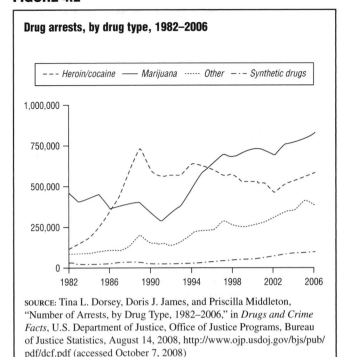

SOURCE: Tina L. Dorsey, Doris J. James, and Priscilla Middleton, "Number of Arrests, by Drug Type, 1982–2006," in *Drugs and Crime Facts*, U.S. Department of Justice, Office of Justice Programs, Bureau of Justice Statistics, August 14, 2008, http://www.ojp.usdoj.gov/bjs/pub/pdf/dcf.pdf (accessed October 7, 2008)

a sustained rise that lasted through 2006. As noted earlier, there were nearly 1.9 million drug arrests in 2006, and approximately 1.8 million drug arrests in 2007. It remains to be seen whether the decrease from 2006 to 2007 is a temporary blip or the beginning of a downturn in drug crime.

The most striking feature of drug crime in the 1990s and the first decade of the twenty-first century, as compared to previous decades, has been the dramatic comeback of marijuana as the drug of choice among users. Since the early 1990s there has been a large increase in the number of marijuana arrests. (See Figure 4.2.) This occurred after a 10-year decline from 1982 to 1991, when marijuana arrests were down to 290,000. Over the following decade they climbed to 735,000 arrests and continued to increase through 2006. SAMHSA indicates in *Results from the 2007 National Survey on Drug Use and Health* that marijuana was the most-used drug in 2007. More than 14 million people aged 12 and older admitted they had used marijuana during the previous month.

ILLICIT DRUG SCHEDULES

Titles II and III of the Comprehensive Drug Abuse Prevention and Control Act of 1970 are called the Controlled Substances Act (CSA). The CSA places all illicit drugs into one of five categories or schedules based on the characteristics of the drugs and their potential for abuse. According to the DEA, in *Drugs of Abuse* (June 2004, http://www.usdoj.gov/dea/pubs/abuse/doa-p.pdf), the five schedules are:

- Schedule I—the drugs have a high potential for abuse, have no accepted use in medical treatment in the United States, and lack acceptable safety for use even under medical supervision.

- Schedule II—the drugs have a high potential for abuse that could cause severe psychological or physical dependence. They have accepted uses in medical treatment in the United States (perhaps with many restrictions).

- Schedule III—the drugs have a lower abuse potential than Schedule I or II drugs, and such abuse "may lead to moderate or low physical dependence or high psychological dependence." They have accepted uses in medical treatment in the United States.

- Schedule IV—the drugs have a lower abuse potential than Schedule III drugs, and such abuse could cause limited physical or psychological dependence. They have accepted uses in medical treatment in the United States.

- Schedule V—the drugs have a lower abuse potential than Schedule IV drugs, and such abuse could cause limited physical or psychological dependence. They have accepted uses in medical treatment in the United States.

Table 4.1 lists common illicit drugs and their medical uses (if any), CSA schedule numbers, and levels of physical and psychological dependence. Heroin, morphine, cocaine, and the cannabis drugs (e.g., marijuana) are derived primarily from organic sources. Heroin, morphine, and cocaine originate from opium poppies. Cannabis is a species of flowering plants. Some illicit drugs are considered synthetic drugs, because their origins are not primarily organic. Examples include amphetamines, methamphetamines, MDMA drugs (e.g., ecstasy), and LSD.

DRUG LAW VIOLATIONS

Drug offenses include the possession, sale, or manufacture of illicit drugs. Many drug offenses are felonies and are punishable by at least one year in prison. Some drug offenses—particularly the possession of small amounts of marijuana—are misdemeanors. People convicted of misdemeanor drug crimes may receive a fine and/or a sentence of less than one year in a local jail. Some jurisdictions treat the possession of very small amounts of marijuana (e.g., less than 1 ounce [28 g]) as an infraction, rather than as a misdemeanor. Infractions are minor offenses, such as traffic violations, that are punishable only with fines, not with incarceration.

Drug laws are complex and can differ between jurisdictions. In general, the seriousness of an offense and the harshness of its penalty are based on the type and amount of drug involved and whether the offender possesses the drug for his or her own use or is a seller, manufacturer, or distributor. Other factors also play a role. For example, first-time offenders may receive less harsh charges and sentences than repeat offenders. New York City treats possession of very

TABLE 4.1

Characteristics of commonly abused drugs

Drugs	CSA, Schedules	Trade or other names	Medical uses	Dependence	
				Physical	Psychological
Narcotics					
Heroin	Substance I	Diamorphine, Horse, Smack, Black tar, *Chiva, Negra (black tar)*	None in U.S., analgesic, antitussive	High	High
Morphine	Substance II	MS-Contin, Roxanol, Oramorph SR, MSIR	Analgesic	High	High
Hydrocodone	Substance II, Product III, V	Hydrocodone w/Acetaminophen, Vicodin, Vicoprofen, Tussionex, Lortab	Analgesic, antitussive	High	High
Hydromorphone	Substance II	Dilaudid	Analgesic	High	High
Oxycodone	Substance II	Roxicet, Oxycodone w/Acetaminophen, OxyContin, Endocet, Percocet, Percodan	Analgesic	High	High
Codeine	Substance II, Products III, V	Acetaminophen, Guaifenesin or Promethazine w/ Codeine, Fiorinal, Fioricet or Tylenol w/Codeine	Analgesic, antitussive	Moderate	Moderate
Other narcotics	Substance II, III, IV	Fentanyl, Demerol, Methadone, Darvon, Stadol, Talwin, Paregoric, Buprenex	Analgesic, antidiarrheal, antitussive	High-Low	High-Low
Depressants					
gamma Hydroxybutyric Acid	Substance I, Product III	GHB, Liquid Ecstasy, Liquid X, Sodium Oxybate, Xyrem®	None in U.S., anesthetic	Moderate	Moderate
Benzodiazepines	Substance IV	Valium, Xanax, Halcion, Ativan, Restoril, Rohypnol (Roofies, R-2), Klonopin	Antianxiety, sedative, Anticonvulsant, Hypnotic, Muscle Relaxant	Moderate	Moderate
Other depressants	Substance I, II, III, IV	Ambien, Sonata, Meprobamate, Chloral Hydrate, Barbiturates, Methaqualone (Quaalude)	Antianxiety, Sedative, Hypnotic	Moderate	Moderate
Stimulants					
Cocaine	Substance II	Coke, Flake, Snow, Crack, *Coca, Blanca, Perico, Nieve, Soda*	Local anesthetic	Possible	High
Amphetamine/ Methamphetamine	Substance II	Crank, Ice, Cristal, Krystal Meth, Speed, Adderall, Dexedrine, Desoxyn	Attention deficit/hyperactivity disorder, narcolepsy, weight control	Possible	High
Methylphenidate	Substance II	Ritalin (Illy's), Concerta, Focalin, Metadate	Attention deficit/hyperactivity disorder	Possible	High
Other stimulants	Substance III, IV	Adipex P, Ionamin, Prelu-2, Didrex, Provigil	Vasoconstriction	Possible	Moderate
Hallucinogens					
MDMA and Analogs	Substance I	(Ecstasy, XTC, Adam), MDA (Love Drug), MDEA (Eve), MBDB	None	None	Moderate
LSD	Substance I	Acid, Microdot, Sunshine, Boomers	None	None	Unknown
Phencyclidine and Analogs	Substance I, II, III	PCP, Angel Dust, Hog, Loveboat, Ketamine (Special K), PCE, PCPy, TCP	Anesthetic (Ketamine)	Possible	High
Other hallucinogens	Substance I	Psilocybe mushrooms, Mescaline, Peyote Cactus Ayahuasca, DMT, Dextromethorphan* (DXM)	None	None	None
Cannabis					
Marijuana	Substance I	Pot, Grass, Sinsemilla, Blunts, *Mota, Yerba, Grifa*	None	Unknown	Moderate
Tetrahydrocannabinol	Substance I, Product III	THC, Marinol	Antinauseant, Appetite stimulant	Yes	Moderate
Hashish and Hashish Oil	Substance I	Hash, Hash oil	None	Unknown	Moderate
Anabolic Steroids					
Testosterone	Substance III	Depo Testosterone, Sustanon, Sten, Cypt	Hypogonadism	Unknown	Unknown
Other Anabolic Steroids	Substance III	Parabolan, Winstrol, Equipose, Anadrol, Dianabol, Primabolin-Depo, D-Ball	Anemia, breast cancer	Unknown	Yes
Inhalants					
Amyl and Butyl Nitrite		Pearls, Poppers, Rush, Locker Room	Angina (Amyl)	Unknown	Unknown
Nitrous Oxide		Laughing gas, balloons, Whippets	Anesthetic	Unknown	Low
Other inhalants		Adhesives, spray paint, hair spray, dry cleaning fluid, spot remover, lighter fluid	None	Unknown	High
Alcohol		Beer, wine, liquor	None	High	High

SOURCE: Adapted from "Drugs of Abuse/Uses and Effects," in *Drugs of Abuse: 2005 Edition*, U.S. Department of Justice, Drug Enforcement Administration, undated, http://www.usdoj.gov/dea/pubs/abuse/doa-p.pdf (accessed October 8, 2008)

small amounts of marijuana as an infraction, unless the drug is "in public view," upon which the offense is a misdemeanor.

Drug Arrests by Type of Drug Law Violation

Figure 4.3 shows the number of drug crime arrests from 1982 to 2006 in two violation categories: possession and sales/manufacture. In 1982 nearly 540,000 of the arrests were for possession, whereas less than 140,000 of the arrests were for sales/manufacture. Overall, 79.6% of drug arrests that year were for possession offenses, and 20.4% were for sales/manufacture offenses. During the next two and a half decades, arrests for drug possession increased dramatically, reaching nearly 1.6 million in 2006. Sales/manufacture arrests totaled almost 330,000 in 2006. Possession arrests made up 82.5% of total drug arrests in 2006, whereas sales/manufacture arrests made up 17.5% of

FIGURE 4.3

Drug arrests, by type of drug law violation, 1982–2006

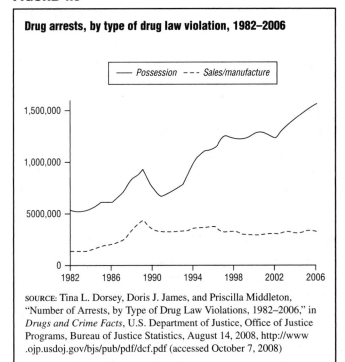

Possession — — — Sales/manufacture

SOURCE: Tina L. Dorsey, Doris J. James, and Priscilla Middleton, "Number of Arrests, by Type of Drug Law Violations, 1982–2006," in *Drugs and Crime Facts*, U.S. Department of Justice, Office of Justice Programs, Bureau of Justice Statistics, August 14, 2008, http://www.ojp.usdoj.gov/bjs/pub/pdf/dcf.pdf (accessed October 7, 2008)

FIGURE 4.4

Arrests for drug violations, by drug type, 2006

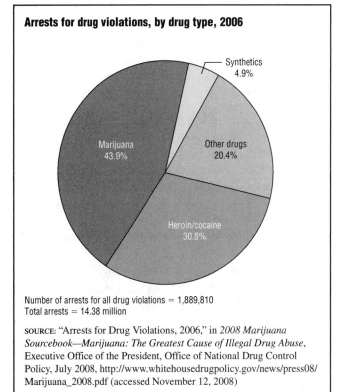

Number of arrests for all drug violations = 1,889,810
Total arrests = 14.38 million

SOURCE: "Arrests for Drug Violations, 2006," in *2008 Marijuana Sourcebook—Marijuana: The Greatest Cause of Illegal Drug Abuse*, Executive Office of the President, Office of National Drug Control Policy, July 2008, http://www.whitehousedrugpolicy.gov/news/press08/Marijuana_2008.pdf (accessed November 12, 2008)

TABLE 4.2

Drug arrests, by violation type and drug type, 2007

[In percent]

Drug abuse violations	United States total
Total*	100
Sale/manufacturing	
Total	17.5
Heroin or cocaine and their derivatives	7.9
Marijuana	5.3
Synthetic or manufactured drugs	1.5
Other dangerous nonnarcotic drugs	2.8
Possession	
Total	82.5
Heroin or cocaine and their derivatives	21.5
Marijuana	42.1
Synthetic or manufactured drugs	3.3
Other dangerous nonnarcotic drugs	15.6

*Because of rounding, the percentages may not add to 100.0.

SOURCE: Adapted from "Arrest Table: Arrests for Drug Abuse Violations, Percent Distribution by Region, 2007," in *Crime in the United States, 2007: Persons Arrested*, U.S. Department of Justice, Federal Bureau of Investigation, September 2008, http://www.fbi.gov/ucr/cius2007/arrests/index.html (accessed November 19, 2008)

Figure 4.2.) In 2006 law enforcement agencies made over 580,000 arrests for heroin/cocaine offenses. Marijuana arrests declined during the 1980s and then climbed significantly through the 1990s and into the first decade of the twenty-first century. In 2006 there were 830,000 marijuana arrests—the highest number of arrests for any drug type. In 1982 synthetic drug arrests totaled less than 30,000; by 2006 they exceeded 90,000. Arrests for other drugs increased from around 80,000 in 1982 to over 380,000 in 2006.

A breakdown of drug arrests by drug type for 2006 is shown in Figure 4.4 and is summarized as follows:

- Marijuana—43.9% of drug arrests
- Heroin/cocaine—30.8% of drug arrests
- Other illicit drugs—20.4% of drug arrests
- Synthetic drugs—4.9% of drug arrests

A breakdown of drug arrests by drug type for 2007 can be calculated from the data in Table 4.2 as follows:

- Marijuana—47.4% of drug arrests
- Heroin/cocaine—29.4% of drug arrests
- Other illicit drugs—18.4% of drug arrests
- Synthetic drugs—4.8% of drug arrests

The Crack Epidemic

Arrests for heroin and cocaine skyrocketed during the 1980s. (See Figure 4.2.) Cocaine, in particular, was popular

the total. The exact same ratio occurred in drug arrests in 2007: 82.5% were for possession, and 17.5% were for possession. (See Table 4.2.)

DRUG ARRESTS BY DRUG TYPE

Arrests for heroin/cocaine peaked in 1989 at 730,000 before beginning a sustained decline until 2002. (See

during the 1980s in two forms: powdered cocaine that was snorted or liquefied and injected into the veins and rock crystal cocaine (or crack) that was smoked in pipes. Both are considered highly addictive. Nonmedical use of cocaine has been illegal since the passage of the Harrison Narcotics Act of 1914. In 1970 cocaine was classified as a CSA Schedule II drug.

During the early 1980s crack cocaine was introduced as a much cheaper alternative to the powdered form of the drug. It also provided a much quicker high than powdered cocaine. Crack soon became the drug of choice among low-income users, particularly in inner cities with large minority populations. The country experienced a so-called crack epidemic. Americans were appalled by media reports about crack-induced street crime and crack-addicted babies born to mothers abusing the drug. The social effects of the crack epidemic are described by the DEA (2008, http://www.usdoj.gov/dea/pubs/history/1985-1990.pdf): "The crack trade had created a violent sub-world, and crack-related murders in many large cities were skyrocketing. For example, a 1988 study by the Bureau of Justice Statistics found that in New York City, crack use was tied to 32% of all homicides and 60% of drug-related homicides. On a daily basis, the evening news reported the violence of drive-by shootings and crack users trying to obtain money for their next hit."

THE CRACK CRACKDOWN. In 1986 Congress passed the Anti-Drug Abuse Act, a comprehensive law that imposed mandatory minimum prison sentences for people convicted of federal drug crimes. The new law made an important distinction between powdered cocaine and crack cocaine. A person convicted of possessing only 5 grams (0.2 ounces) of crack cocaine faced the same mandatory prison sentence as a person convicted of possessing 500 grams (17.6 ounces) of powdered cocaine. In other words, there was a 100 to 1 sentencing disparity between the two forms of the drug. At the time, politicians defended the disparity as a reasonable response to the harm that crack cocaine was doing to American society. However, the law soon became controversial because relatively low-level crack users and suppliers (many of whom were low-income African-Americans) received harsher sentences than users and suppliers of much larger amounts of powdered cocaine. Because most of the latter offenders were white, activists decried the law as racist.

After nearly two decades of controversy, the issue was addressed by the U.S. Supreme Court in *Kimbrough v. United States* (552 U.S. ___ [2007]). The case involved Derrick Kimbrough, an African-American defendant who had pleaded guilty in federal court to offenses involving both powdered and crack cocaine. The original court sentenced Kimbrough in accordance with the federal guidelines for powdered cocaine, rather than with the harsher crack cocaine sentence structure. The court ruled in December 2007 that federal judges can use discretion in such cases and impose shorter sentences for crack cocaine offenses than

called for by federal guidelines to reduce the powder-crack disparity. That same month the U.S. Sentencing Commission (USSC) ruled that crack cocaine sentences imposed by federal courts in the past could be shortened accordingly following petition by the convicted defendants. The USSC also recommended that Congress eliminate the 100 to 1 disparity in crack sentencing compared with sentencing for powdered cocaine offenses. As of early 2009, Congress had not acted on this recommendation.

Kevin Bohn reports in "First of Crack Convicts Freed after Sentencing Reform" (CNN.com, March 3, 2008) that the first inmates to have their sentences reduced as a result of the Supreme Court ruling were released in March 2008 from federal prison. According to Bohn, as many as 20,000 federal inmates are eligible for the sentence reductions.

THE CRACK EPIDEMIC ENDS. Heroin and cocaine arrests plummeted suddenly in 1990 after peaking at 730,000 arrests in 1989. (See Figure 4.2.) By 2002 arrests were down to 460,000. Criminologists and sociologists present a number of possible causes for the sudden end to the crack epidemic. Some tie it to the overall downward trend in crime that occurred during the 1990s. As noted in Chapter 2, the reasons for the crime decline are not known for certain, but could include tougher sentencing laws, higher incarceration rates, better policing, and a robust economy.

Some analysts believe the epidemic's end was precipitated, in part, by changing consumer tastes. During the 1990s crack lost favor as the drug of choice among inner-city youths as they increasingly turned to marijuana. Denise Herd of the University of California, Berkeley, suggests in "Changes in Drug Use Prevalence in Rap Music Songs, 1979–1997" (*Addiction Research and Theory*, vol. 16, no. 2, April 2008) that rap music may have played a role in this social trend. Herd finds that popular rap songs decried the "destructiveness" of crack in the 1980s, but glorified marijuana in the 1990s by tying the drug to "creativity, wealth and status."

Marijuana

As the crack epidemic was ending in the early 1990s, another drug began gaining prominence in arrest records: marijuana. Marijuana arrests fell throughout the 1980s, dropping to about 290,000 arrests in 1991. (See Figure 4.2.) Over the following decade arrests nearly tripled, reaching nearly 730,000 in 2000. By 2006 there were 830,000 marijuana arrests, which made up 44% of all drug arrests.

In *Drugs and Crime Facts* (August 14, 2008, http://www.ojp.usdoj.gov/bjs/pub/pdf/dcf.pdf), Tina L. Dorsey, Doris J. James, and Priscilla Middleton of the Bureau of Justice Statistics (BJS) report that 39.1% of the drug arrests in 2006 were for marijuana possession. This would equate to approximately 739,000 arrests for marijuana possession. Only 4.8% of the total drug arrests in 2006 were for marijuana sale/manufacture. This would equate to approximately 91,000 arrests for marijuana sale/manufacture.

MARIJUANA MISDEMEANORS AND INFRACTIONS. In *Beyond Our Control?: Confronting the Limits of Our Legal System in the Age of Cyberspace* (2003), Stuart Biegel reports that marijuana arrests in the United States doubled from 7,000 to 15,000 between 1964 and 1966. By 1969 the national total for marijuana arrests had increased nearly 700% to 118,903. Court systems became overrun with cases involving marijuana possession, which at that time could elicit a prison sentence as long as five years for possession of only a single marijuana cigarette (or joint). In response, many jurisdictions began lowering the penalties for possession of small amounts of marijuana. In some areas this offense was essentially decriminalized, meaning that it became an infraction, rather than a misdemeanor. Decriminalization began in Oregon in 1973 and then spread to other states: Colorado, Alaska, Ohio, and California in 1975; Mississippi, North Carolina, and New York in 1977; and Nebraska in 1978. However, the decriminalization trend faded in the 1980s as marijuana use declined and other drugs came into prominence. Also, the movement to decriminalize was not embraced at the federal level.

As a result, some jurisdictions categorize the possession of small amounts of marijuana as either a misdemeanor or infraction, depending on the circumstances of the offense. This distinction has been a source of great controversy for some social activists. Harry G. Levine and Deborah Peterson Small suggest in *Marijuana Arrest Crusade: Black Bias and Police Policy in New York City, 1997–2007* (April 2008, http://graphics8.nytimes.com/packages/pdf/nyregion/20080429_MARIJUANA.pdf) that marijuana possession arrests in New York City are racially skewed in that African-American and Hispanic offenders are far more likely than white offenders to be charged with misdemeanor possession as opposed to being issued an infraction. Levine and Small note that misdemeanor marijuana possession arrests in New York City skyrocketed between 1997 and 2006, totaling approximately 353,000 arrests for this period. By contrast, only approximately 30,000 arrests were made for misdemeanor marijuana possession in each of the 10-year periods of 1977–86 and 1987–96. In New York City, simple possession of less than 0.875 of an ounce (24.8 g) of marijuana is an infraction, rather than a misdemeanor. Possession of even small amounts of marijuana is a misdemeanor if the drug is "in public view." Levine and Small claim that New York City cops target African-American and Hispanic youths for "stop and frisk" encounters that are intended to bully the offenders into showing their marijuana so they can be arrested under the misdemeanor clause, rather than charged with an infraction.

SELF-REPORTED MARIJUANA USE. SAMHSA finds in *Results from the 2007 National Survey on Drug Use and Health* that 14.4 million Americans aged 12 and older had used marijuana within the previous month.

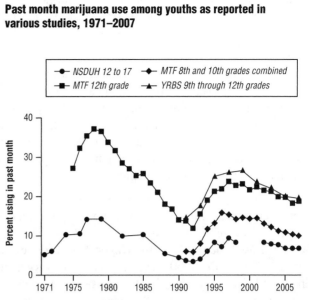

FIGURE 4.5

Past month marijuana use among youths as reported in various studies, 1971–2007

MTF = Monitoring the Future; NSDUH = National Survey on Drug Use and Health; YRBS = Youth Risk Behavior Survey.

SOURCE: "Figure 9.1. Past Month Marijuana Use among Youths in NSDUH, MTF, and YRBS: 1971–2007," in *Results from the 2007 National Survey on Drug Use and Health: National Findings*, Department of Health and Human Services, Substance Abuse and Mental Health Services Administration, Office of Applied Studies, September 2008, http://www.oas.samhsa.gov/nsduh/2k7nsduh/2k7Results.pdf (accessed November 19, 2008)

Figure 4.5 compares past-month marijuana use among juveniles from 1971 to 2007 based on historical National Survey on Drug Use and Health surveys and two other data sources. Monitoring the Future (MTF) is a national survey of middle and high school students. MTF is funded by the National Institute on Drug Abuse. The Youth Risk Behavior Survey (YRBS) also focuses on middle and high school students. The YRBS is conducted by the Centers for Disease Control and Prevention. Past-month marijuana use among youths increased during the 1970s and then decreased dramatically during the 1980s. (See Figure 4.5.) In the early 1990s marijuana usage started to rise again. It reached a plateau in the latter part of the decade and then began a slight decline. During the late 1990s some states began legalizing the use of small amounts of marijuana for medical reasons, for example, to relieve pain or nausea. According to the nonprofit educational organization ProCon.org (April 21, 2009, http://medicalmarijuana.procon.org/viewresource.asp?resourceID=000881), as of April 2009, 13 states had legalized medical marijuana usage. However, marijuana usage has remained a crime under federal law.

A Meth Epidemic?

Methamphetamine (or meth) is a stimulant in the amphetamine group. During the 1990s and the first decade of the twenty-first century methamphetamine abuse became a major problem in some parts of the United States. The rise of this previously obscure drug is described by Franco in *Methamphetamine: Background, Prevalence, and Federal Drug Control Policies.*

Methamphetamine can be synthesized from a naturally occurring chemical called ephedrine. This so-called precursor chemical is commonly synthesized, as are two other methamphetamine precursors: phenylpropanolamine and pseudoephedrine. Both of the latter are widely used in cold and sinus medications, many of which can be purchased over the counter (i.e., without a prescription).

THE EVOLUTION OF ILLICIT METHAMPHETAMINE LABORATORIES. Franco notes that methamphetamine is classified as a Schedule II drug under the CSA. The drug had been used medically in the United States for several decades. During the 1950s methamphetamine was widely prescribed for a variety of ailments; however, growing concern about the abuse of methamphetamine (and amphetamines, in general) led to severe government restrictions on dispensing the drug. In response, underworld methamphetamine laboratories began springing up during the 1960s. These illicit labs were primarily located in the western United States and mostly operated by outlaw motorcycle gangs. They produced a crude form of methamphetamine that was known as crank on the streets. Crank was less potent than pharmaceutical-grade methamphetamine, but it still became popular with certain users. In the 1980s more sophisticated amateur chemists developed a new method for synthesizing a much more potent form of crank using ephedrine-based reactions. This led to a variety of forms that could be ingested, snorted, injected, or smoked. A popular type of smokable methamphetamine is a crystalline powder known as ice.

During the 1990s illicit amateur methamphetamine laboratories became a cause of great concern. Many of the labs were operated in homes, putting the residents at great danger of fires and explosions due to the volatile nature of the chemicals involved. In *Drug Endangered Children* (February 2009, http://www.whitehousedrugpolicy.gov/enforce/dr_endangered_child.html), the Office of National Drug Control Policy states that in 2008 law enforcement agencies found 1,025 children residing or visiting in homes containing clandestine methamphetamine laboratories. Of these, six children were injured in laboratory mishaps at their homes. These numbers were down considerably from 2004, when three children were killed, 13 children were injured, and 3,088 more were endangered by visiting or residing in a home with a clandestine meth lab.

As the so-called meth epidemic attracted national attention, legislators rushed to pass laws making it more difficult for amateur chemists to obtain the ephedrine-type precursors used to synthesize methamphetamine. The Comprehensive Methamphetamine Control Act of 1996 added the precursor

chemicals to Schedule II of the CSA. That act and a subsequent law—the Methamphetamine Trafficking Penalty Enhancement Act of 1998—increased the penalties for manufacturing and selling methamphetamine. After 2000 legislators tackled the easy availability of precursor chemicals in over-the-counter cold and sinus medications. By 2006 many states and the federal government had laws in place restricting purchases by individual consumers of these medications from retail and mail order stores. The clampdown is believed to have reduced the number of amateur methamphetamine laboratories in the United States. The DEA notes in "Maps of Methamphetamine Lab Incidents" (September 2008, http://www.usdoj.gov/dea/concern/map_lab_seizures.html) that the number of these laboratories known to law enforcement decreased from 17,356 in 2003 to only 5,910 in 2007. Figure 4.6 shows the locations of the laboratories (and related facilities) reported during 2007.

Franco notes that by 2007 the clampdown on ephedrine-containing medications had made it much more difficult for the so-called mom-and-pop methamphetamine laboratories to operate. As a result, large-scale methamphetamine production has shifted to more sophisticated super laboratories often under the control of Mexican drug-trafficking organizations. According to Franco, DEA officials estimated in 2007 that more than 80% of illicit methamphetamine in the United States was supplied by these Mexican drug cartels. They reportedly purchase tons of precursor chemicals from companies around the world and synthesize a potent form of methamphetamine in large laboratories in Mexico and in the western United States.

SELF-REPORTED METHAMPHETAMINE ABUSE. In 2002, 12.4 million people reported using meth at some point during their lifetime. (See Table 4.3.) By 2005 this number had dropped to 10.4 million. In 2002 more than 1.5 million people said they had used meth within the previous year. This number was down below 1.3 million in 2005. The number of people claiming that they became new meth users within the previous year also decreased from 299,000 in 2002 to 192,000 in 2005. People reporting illicit use of methamphetamine within the previous month are considered current users by SAMHSA. The number of current meth users rose from 597,000 in 2002 to 607,000 in 2003, but then dropped over the following two years, reaching 512,000 in 2005. In *Results from the 2007 National Survey on Drug Use and Health*, SAMHSA indicates that the number of current users increased to 731,000 in 2006 and then dropped to 529,000 in 2007.

METHAMPHETAMINE HOT SPOTS. Even though meth abuse is often described by the media as a national epidemic, analysts assert that it is actually a regional problem in that certain so-called hot spots exist around the country. Franco notes that methamphetamine abuse is largely associated with states in the Midwest and in some parts of the West and south central United States. In 2007 clandestine

FIGURE 4.6

Number of methamphetamine clandestine laboratory incidents, 2007

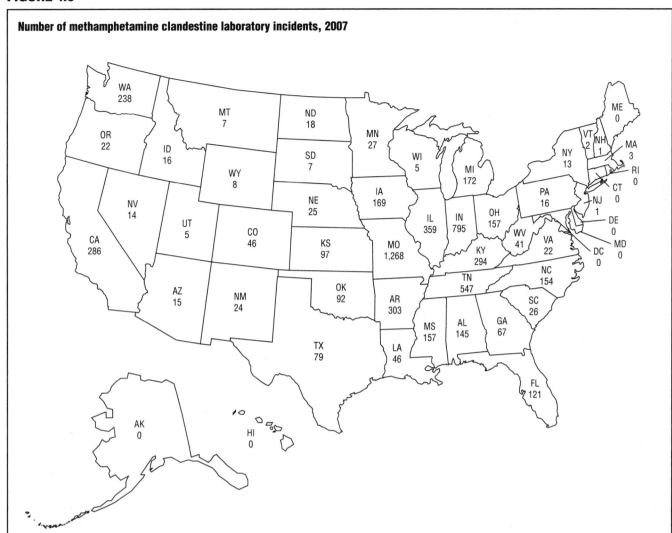

Notes: Incidents includes labs, dumpsites, chemicals, glass and equipment. Map was last updated September 2008.

SOURCE: "Total of All Meth Clandestine Laboratory Incidents, Including Labs, Dumpsites, Chem/Glass/Equipment, Calendar Year 2007," in *Maps of Methamphetamine Lab Incidents*, U.S. Department of Justice, Drug Enforcement Administration September 2008, http://www.usdoj.gov/dea/concern/map_lab_seizures_2007p.html (accessed October 8, 2008)

methamphetamine laboratory incidents occurred mainly in Missouri (1,268 incidents), Indiana (795 incidents), Tennessee (547 incidents), Illinois (359 incidents), and Arkansas (303 incidents). (See Figure 4.6.)

Multnomah County, Oregon, is just one example of a methamphetamine hot spot. To help combat the growing trend of methamphetamine use, local authorities established the project Faces of Meth (http://www.facesofmeth.us/main.htm), which shows the before and after pictures of people suffering from methamphetamine addiction.

DRUG USE REPORTED BY PRISON INMATES

In *Drug Use and Dependence, State and Federal Prisoners, 2004* (October 2006, http://www.ojp.usdoj.gov/bjs/pub/pdf/dudsfp04.pdf), Christopher J. Mumola and Jennifer C. Karberg of the BJS note that in 2004, 56% of all state prisoners reported using drugs in the month before commit-

ting their offense(s). This percentage changed little from 1997, when 57% of state prisoners reported previous drug use. A slightly lower percentage of federal prison inmates, 50%, reported drug use in the month before their offense in 2004, compared with 45% in 1997.

Nearly one-third (32.1%) of state prison inmates in 2004 said they had committed their current offense while under the influence of drugs. The most common drug used by state prisoners was marijuana; 77.6% of state prisoners in 2004 reported they had used marijuana at some time in their life. The percentage of prisoners who said they used cocaine or crack cocaine in the month before their offense declined from 25% in 1997 to 21.4% in 2004. During this period the use of heroin and other opiates in the month preceding the offense dropped slightly from 9.2% in 1997 to 8.2% in 2004, whereas the use of hallucinogens rose from 4% to 5.9%.

TABLE 4.3

Methamphetamine use among persons aged 12 or older, 2002–05

[In thousands]

Use	2002	2003	2004	2005
Lifetime use	12,383	12,303	11,726	10,357
Age 12–17	366	328	299	296
Age 18–25	1,756	1,650	1,688	1,682
26 years of age or older	10,261	10,325	9,739	8,379
Use in last year	1,541	1,315	1,440	1,297
Age 12–17	226	174	163	170
Age 18–25	525	506	516	482
26 years of age or older	790	636	761	645
New users in last year	299	260	318	192
Use in the last month	597	607	583	512
Age 12–17	63	69	57	66
Age 18–25	160	185	186	194
26 years of age or older	375	353	340	252
Dependent use in last month	164	250	346	257
Stimulant is primary drug of abuse	63	92	130	103
Other illicit drug is primary drug of abuse	101	158	216	154

SOURCE: Celinda Franco, "Table 1. Methamphetamine Use among Persons Aged 12 or Older, 2002–2005," in *Methamphetamine: Background, Prevalence, and Federal Drug Control Policies*, Congressional Research Service, January 24, 2007, http://assets.opencrs.com/rpts/RL33857_20070124.pdf (accessed November 13, 2008)

FIGURE 4.7

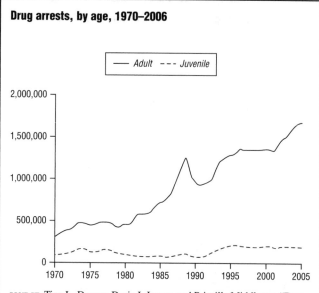

Drug arrests, by age, 1970–2006

SOURCE: Tina L. Dorsey, Doris J. James, and Priscilla Middleton, "Drug Arrests by Age, 1970–2006," in *Drugs and Crime Facts*, U.S. Department of Justice, Office of Justice Programs, Bureau of Justice Statistics, August 14, 2008, http://www.ojp.usdoj.gov/bjs/pub/pdf/dcf.pdf (accessed October 7, 2008)

According to Mumola and Karberg, 26.4% of federal prison inmates reported using drugs at the time of their offense in 2004, an increase from 22.4% in 1997. Between 1997 and 2004 marijuana use increased from 30.4% to 36.2%. However, the percentage of federal prisoners who reported using cocaine or crack cocaine in the month before their offense fell from 20% in 1997 to 18% in 2004, and use at the time of the offense dropped from 9.3% in 1997 to 7.4% in 2004.

IS THE UNITED STATES WINNING ITS WAR ON DRUGS?

In 1971 President Nixon launched the nation's War on Drugs. After nearly four decades of battle, analysts disagree on whether the United States is winning or losing this war. Researchers point hopefully to data indicating that juvenile drug use and arrest rates are not increasing as rapidly as they once did. Juvenile drug arrests generally increased in the early 1970s and then slowly declined through the mid-1980s. (See Figure 4.7.) After a brief surge they decreased again through the early 1990s. In 1991, 80,000 juveniles were arrested for drug crimes. By 1997 that number had climbed to 210,000. The number of juvenile arrests then leveled off just below 200,000 from 2004 to 2006.

SAMHSA notes in *Results from the 2007 National Survey on Drug Use and Health* that self-reported drug abuse by youths aged 12 to 17 declined for many drugs between 2002 and 2007, including marijuana, cocaine, LSD, hallucinogenic drugs, ecstasy, and methamphetamine. The percent of all youths reporting illicit drug use decreased from 11.6% in 2002 to 9.5% in 2007.

For the adult population, drug arrests have climbed sharply since undergoing a brief decline in the late 1980s. (See Figure 4.7.) SAMHSA indicates that the percentage of young adults aged 18 to 25 reporting current illicit use of prescription pain relievers increased from 4.1% to 4.6% between 2002 and 2007. There were slight decreases during this period in current use of hallucinogens, ecstasy, and methamphetamines. People aged 50 to 54 reported increased current use of illicit drugs between 2002 (3.4%) and 2007 (5.7%). A similar increase was seen in people aged 55 to 59. The percentage of current illicit drug users in this survey group increased from 1.9% in 2002 to 4.1% in 2007.

Like all commodities, illicit drugs operate under the economic principles of supply and demand. Federal, state, and local law enforcement officials attack the supply side by arresting and prosecuting sellers and manufacturers of illicit drugs. Because many illicit drugs are imported from foreign countries, the federal government plays an active role in trying to control and stop these international suppliers. This has proved to be extremely difficult. In *Drug Control: International Policy and Approaches* (February 2, 2006, http://fpc.state.gov/documents/organization/61518.pdf), Raphael Perl of the CRS states that "efforts to significantly reduce the flow of illicit drugs from abroad into the United States have so far not succeeded. Moreover, over the past decade, worldwide production of illicit drugs has risen dramatically: opium and marijuana production has roughly doubled and coca production tripled. Street prices of cocaine and heroin have fallen significantly in the past 20 years, reflecting increased availability."

Opium production in war-torn Afghanistan is of particular concern to authorities. In "Opium Trade Finances Taliban War Machine, Says UN Drug Tsar" (November 27, 2008, http://www.un.org/apps/news/story.asp?NewsID=29099&Cr=Afghan&Cr1=UNODC;), the United Nations reports that Afghanistan's opium industry was a major source of funding for the Taliban and other terrorist and criminal groups in the country. The UN Office on Drugs and Crime estimates that these organizations generated $70 million in income in 2008 from opium farming, and another $400 million in production and trafficking. This money helps fund terrorist operations in Afghanistan against a coalition of military forces from the United States and other countries that are trying to restore peace there.

The War on Drugs is an expensive war. According to Perl, the United States spent $8.6 billion between 1981 and 2001 on international narcotics control, primarily in South America. Nevertheless, estimated cocaine production in that region nearly quadrupled during that same period and the average price per gram of cocaine in the United States nearly halved. To make matters worse, the average purity of a gram of cocaine sold on U.S. streets increased by 69%. Similar results occurred for heroin, which decreased in price by 77%, but was 147% higher in purity. Table 4.4 shows the federal government budget for drug control by agency for fiscal years 2007, 2008, and 2009. The federal government spent $13.8 billion in fiscal year 2007 on drug control and was expected to spend $14.1 billion in fiscal year 2009.

TABLE 4.4

Drug control funding, by national agency, fiscal years 2007–09

[Budget authority in millions]

	FY 2007 final	FY 2008 enacted	FY 2009 request
Department of Defense	1,329.8	1,177.4	1,060.5
Department of Education	495.0	431.6	218.1
Department of Health and Human Services			
Centers for Medicare & Medicaid Services	—	45.0	265.0
Indian Health Service	148.2	173.2	162.0
National Institute on Drug Abuse	1,000.0	1,000.7	1,001.7
Substance Abuse and Mental Health Services Administration	2,443.2	2,445.8	2,370.6
Total HHS	**3,591.4**	**3,664.8**	**3,799.3**
Department of Homeland Security			
Office of Counternarcotics Enforcement	2.5	2.7	4.0
Customs and Border Protection	1,968.5	2,130.9	2,191.9
Immigration and Customs Enforcement	422.8	412.3	428.9
U.S. Coast Guard	1,080.9	1,004.3	1,071.0
Total DHS	**3,474.8**	**3,550.1**	**3,695.8**
Department of the Interior			
Bureau of Indian Affairs	2.6	6.3	6.3
Total DOI	**2.6**	**6.3**	**6.3**
Department of Justice			
Bureau of Prisons	65.1	67.2	69.2
Drug Enforcement Administration	1,969.1	2,105.3	2,181.0
Interagency Crime and Drug Enforcement	497.9	497.9	531.6
Office of Justice Programs	245.5	222.8	114.2
Total DOJ	**2,777.7**	**2,893.2**	**2,896.0**
ONDCP			
Counterdrug Technology Assessment Center	20.0	1.0	5.0
High Intensity Drug Trafficking Area Program	224.7	230.0	200.0
Other Federal Drug Control Programs	193.0	164.3	189.7
Drug-Free Communities (non-ad)	79.2	90.0	80.0
National Youth Anti-Drug Media Campaign (non-ad)	99.0	60.0	100.0
Salaries and Expenses	26.8	26.4	26.8
Total ONDCP	**464.4**	**421.7**	**421.5**
Small Business Administration	1.0	1.0	1.0
Department of State			
Bureau of International Narcotics and Law Enforcement Affairs	1,055.7	640.8	1,173.2
United States Agency International Development	239.0	361.4	315.8
Total State	**1,294.7**	**1,002.2**	**1,489.0**
Department of Transportation			
National Highway Traffic Safety Administration	2.9	2.7	2.7
Department of Treasury			
Internal Revenue Service	55.6	57.3	59.2
Department of Veterans Affairs			
Veterans Health Administration	354.1	447.2	465.0
Total	**$13,844.0**	**$13,655.4**	**$14,114.4**

Note: Detail may not add due to rounding.
In addition to the resources displayed in the table above, the administration requests $385.1 million in fiscal year 2008 supplemental funding for counternarcotics support to Mexico and Central America.

SOURCE: "Agency Summary, FY 2007–FY 2009," in *National Drug Control Strategy 2008 Annual Report*, U.S. Department of Justice, Office of National Drug Control Policy, 2008, http://www.ondcp.gov/publications/policy/ndcs08/app_b.html (accessed November 17, 2008)

CHAPTER 5
WHITE-COLLAR CRIME

DEFINING WHITE-COLLAR CRIME

The term *white-collar crime* was first used by the American criminologist Edwin H. Sutherland (1883–1950) to define a violation of the criminal law committed by "a person of respectability and high social status in the course of his occupation" (Cornell University Law School, "White Collar Crime," 2009, http://topics.law.cornell.edu/wex/White-collar_crime). Over time, the definition has become much broader and can include a variety of crimes committed by perpetrators that use deceptive means for financial gain. The Federal Bureau of Investigation (FBI) investigates violations of federal laws. In *Financial Crimes Report to the Public, Fiscal Year 2007 (October 1, 2006–September 30, 2007)* (May 21, 2008, http://www.fbi.gov/publications/financial/fcs_report2007/financial_crime_2007.htm), the FBI notes that white-collar crimes are "characterized by deceit, concealment, or violation of trust and are not dependent upon the application or threat of physical force or violence."

Thus, the term *white-collar crime* is a generic term for a broad set of criminal offenses that include fraud, embezzlement, bribery, swindles, counterfeiting, identity theft, confidence games, money laundering, environmental crimes, copyright violations, computer hacking, and a number of other offenses.

ARRESTS FOR WHITE-COLLAR CRIMES

The FBI's Uniform Crime Reporting (UCR) Program gathers crime data from law enforcement agencies around the country and publishes selected data in an annual report. Arrest data for 2007 are provided in *Crime in the United States, 2007* (September 2008, http://www.fbi.gov/ucr/cius2007/index.html). The UCR Program provides 2007 arrest data for only three crimes widely considered to be white-collar crimes:

- Fraud—252,873 arrests

- Forgery and counterfeiting—103,448 arrests

- Embezzlement—22,381 arrests

The FBI defines these crimes as:

- Fraud—"The intentional perversion of the truth for the purpose of inducing another person or other entity in reliance upon it to part with something of value or to surrender a legal right. Fraudulent conversion and obtaining of money or property by false pretenses. Confidence games and bad checks, except forgeries and counterfeiting, are included."

- Forgery and counterfeiting—"The altering, copying, or imitating of something, without authority or right, with the intent to deceive or defraud by passing the copy or thing altered or imitated as that which is original or genuine; or the selling, buying, or possession of an altered, copied, or imitated thing with the intent to deceive or defraud. Attempts are included."

- Embezzlement—"The unlawful misappropriation or misapplication by an offender to his/her own use or purpose of money, property, or some other thing of value entrusted to his/her care, custody, or control."

The FBI reported more than 14.2 million arrests in 2007; thus, arrests for these three white-collar crimes made up only a very small portion (less than 3%) of the total arrests.

In *Crime in the United States, 2007*, the FBI provides a breakdown of arrests by age; however, the numbers differ from the overall arrest data because the ages of all arrestees may not be included in law enforcement reports to the UCR. The 2007 data included the ages of 78,005 people arrested for forgery and counterfeiting, 185,229 arrested for fraud arrests, and 17,015 for embezzlement. Forgery and counterfeiting crimes for which age information was reported included 24,739 arrestees who were under the age of 25; 36,245 who were between the ages of 25 and 39; 15,312 who were aged 40 to 54; and 1,709 who were aged 55 or older. Of those arrested for fraud in 2007, 47,593 were under age 25; 84,689 were 25 to 39; 45,126 were aged

40 to 54; and 7,821 were age 55 or older. Of those arrested for embezzlement in 2007, 7,871 were under the age of 25; 5,767 were aged 25 to 39; 2,943 were aged 40 to 54; 434 were aged 55 or older.

White arrestees for these three white-collar crimes outnumbered African-American arrestees in 2007 by a margin of approximately two to one. White arrestees made up 63.8% to 69.6% of the total, whereas African-American arrestees made up 28.9% to 34.3% of the total.

The FBI provides 10-year arrest trends for all crimes tracked through the UCR. The data indicate that arrests for fraud between 1998 and 2007 decreased by 28.2% among male offenders and by 33.7% among female offenders. Arrests for embezzlement increased 22.7% among males and by 30.5% among females. Arrests for forgery and counterfeiting decreased by 12.7% for males and by 14.2% for females.

SURVEY RESULTS ON WHITE-COLLAR CRIME VICTIMIZATIONS

The National White Collar Crime Center (NW3C) is a congressionally funded nonprofit corporation whose members are involved in the investigation and enforcement of laws dealing with white-collar crime. In 2005 the NW3C conducted a national survey of 1,605 adults in which the participants were asked about their experiences and those of their households with white-collar crime during the previous 12 months. The results are presented by John Kane and April Wall in *The 2005 National Public Survey on White Collar Crime* (2006, http://www.nw3c.org/research/national_public_survey.cfm).

Almost half (46.5%) of households and 36% of individuals surveyed reported they had been a victim of white-collar crime during the previous year; 62.5% of individuals had experienced at least one type of white-collar crime in their lifetime. The most common white-collar crimes experienced by households included being misled about the price of a product or service (35.9% of reported incidents), having a credit card misused (24.5%), and being directly affected by a national corporate scandal (21.4%). Of households that experienced a white-collar crime, 67% reported the crime to at least one organization (such as a credit card company, business, or personal attorney), and 30.1% reported the crime to a law enforcement or other crime control agency. The most commonly reported crimes by individuals were pricing schemes (33.2%), credit card misuse (21.8%), and the effects of national corporate scandals (20.6%).

Perceptions of White-Collar Crimes

Kane and Wall explain that the NW3C survey included questions about the perceived seriousness of several types of crime, including white-collar crimes. The most serious crime according to respondents was carjacking and murder,

which received a score of 6.9 on a scale of 0 (not serious) to 7 (very serious). Car theft was perceived as the least serious crime, with a score of 4. All the white-collar crimes included in the survey were perceived to be more serious than car theft, including omission of a safety report (6.2), insurance fraud (5.8), hacking into a database (5.6), embezzlement (5.6), overcharging for insurance (5.5), submitting a false earnings report (5.4), and auction fraud (5.1).

IDENTITY THEFT STATISTICS FROM THE BUREAU OF JUSTICE STATISTICS

In recent years more and more transactions of every type are handled remotely using telephones, computers, and the Internet. Identity thieves steal personal information from victims, such as their Social Security, driver's license, credit card, or other identification numbers, and then set up new bank or credit card accounts or otherwise misrepresent themselves as their victims to obtain money, goods, or services fraudulently.

As noted in Chapter 3, the Bureau of Justice Statistics (BJS) performs a detailed examination of U.S. crime victims through its National Crime Victimization Survey (NCVS). This is an annual survey that measures the levels of victimization resulting from specific criminal acts. The data collected are extrapolated to the entire U.S. population to provide estimates of criminal victimization at the national level.

In 2004 the BJS first added questions about identity theft to the NCVS survey. The results for the 2005 survey are reported by Katrina Baum of the BJS in *Identity Theft, 2005* (November 2007, http://www.ojp.usdoj.gov/bjs/pub/pdf/it05.pdf).

According to Baum, the NCVS defines identity theft as any one of the following criminal acts:

- Unauthorized use or attempted unauthorized use of a victim's credit cards

- Unauthorized use or attempted unauthorized use of a victim's accounts, for example, checking or savings accounts

- Misuse of a victim's personal information for the purpose of opening new accounts, obtaining loans, or committing other crimes

Baum estimates that 6.4 million U.S. households experienced identity theft in 2005. About 46% of the victimized households experienced unauthorized use of credit cards, 25% had unauthorized use of other existing accounts (such as a bank account), and 17% reported misuse of their personal information. Another 12% of victimized households experienced multiple types of identity theft.

According to Baum, demographic data reveal that non-Hispanic whites suffered the most identity theft victimizations in 2005. White victims numbered more than 5.4

million, accounting for 84% of all victims. High-income households (i.e., those with annual incomes of $75,000 or more) were more highly victimized than lower-income households. Households in the West experienced slightly more identity thefts than households in other parts of the country.

Baum states that seven out of 10 identity theft victims participating in the NCVS were aware of their personal monetary losses from the crimes. Overall, the average loss per household from all types of identity theft was $1,620. Households that experienced misuse of personal information lost approximately three times the average amount. The most common ways in which victimized households became aware of the crime were noticing missing money or unfamiliar charges on an existing account (30.8%), being contacted about late or unpaid bills (20.6%), or experiencing banking problems (13.1%).

IDENTITY THEFT AND CONSUMER FRAUD REPORTED BY THE FEDERAL TRADE COMMISSION

The Federal Trade Commission (FTC) operates a complaint database known as Consumer Sentinel that compiles complaints from a variety of organizations. The agency also maintains a database known as the Identity Theft Data Clearinghouse. These databases are made available to law enforcement agencies to assist in their investigations of white-collar crimes. The FTC publishes an annual report that summarizes data collected within the previous year from Consumer Sentinel and the Identity Theft Data Clearinghouse. Data for calendar year 2007 are presented in *Consumer Fraud and Identity Theft Complaint Data, January–December 2007* (February 2008, http://www.ftc.gov/senti nel/reports/sentinel-annual-reports/sentinel-cy2007.pdf).

Consumer Sentinel was launched in 1997 and includes more than 4.3 million complaints received through 2007. Figure 5.1 provides a breakdown by complaint type (identity theft or consumer fraud) for calendar years 2005 to 2007. In 2007 the FTC recorded 813,899 complaints. More than two-thirds (555,472 or 68% of the total) of the complaints were for fraud, and the remaining complaints (258,427 or 32%) were for identity theft. Overall, the number of complaints was up from 2006, when 674,283 complaints were received and up from 2005, when 693,526 complaints were received. The number of identity theft complaints increased only slightly between 2005 and 2007 from 255,627 to 258,427. Much larger gains were recorded in fraud complaints; they grew from 437,899 in 2005 to 555,472 in 2007.

Table 5.1 lists the top 20 complaint categories for 2007. Identity theft (32%) was the most prevalent single complaint. The most common consumer fraud complaints involved shop-at-home and catalog sales (8%), Internet services (5%), foreign money offers (4%), and prizes, sweepstakes, and lotteries (4%).

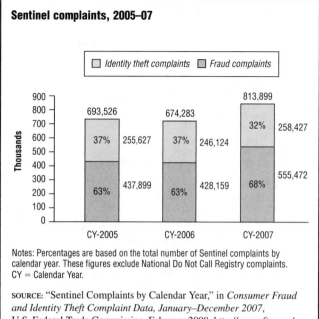

FIGURE 5.1

Sentinel complaints, 2005–07

Notes: Percentages are based on the total number of Sentinel complaints by calendar year. These figures exclude National Do Not Call Registry complaints. CY = Calendar Year.

SOURCE: "Sentinel Complaints by Calendar Year," in *Consumer Fraud and Identity Theft Complaint Data, January–December 2007*, U.S. Federal Trade Commission, February 2008, http://www.ftc.gov/ sentinel/reports/sentinel-annual-reports/sentinel-cy2007.pdf (accessed October 3, 2008)

FTC Identity Theft Complaints

According to the FTC, in *Consumer Fraud and Identity Theft Complaint Data*, fraudulent use of a credit card was reported by 23% of identity theft complainants during 2007. This entails thieves using stolen identities to open new credit card accounts or tapping into victims' existing credit card accounts. Another significant type of identity theft was phone or utilities fraud, which accounted for 18% of the total complaints. Stolen identities were used by thieves to open new telephone, wireless, or utilities accounts or to fraudulently make charges to victims' existing accounts. Another 14% of complaints involved employment-related fraud, for example, obtaining employment by pretending to be someone else. Bank fraud made up 13% of the complaints. In these cases thieves used stolen identities to open new bank accounts, access victims' existing bank accounts, or electronically transfer money from victims' bank accounts to their own bank accounts. Government documents/benefits fraud accounted for 11% of the total. Thieves used stolen identities to file fraudulent tax returns or to apply for or obtain government benefits or documents, such as driver's licenses or Social Security cards.

The FTC reports that the U.S. metropolitan areas associated with the highest rates of identity theft complaints in 2007 were Napa, California (302.6 complaints per 100,000 population), Madera, California (280.2), and Greeley, Colorado (228). Nearly two-thirds (65%) of identity theft victims in 2007 indicated they did not notify the police about the theft.

TABLE 5.1

Sentinel top twenty complaint categories, 2007

Rank	Top categories	Complaints	Percentage[a]
1	Identity theft	258,427	32%
2	Shop-at-home/catalog sales	62,811	8%
3	Internet services[b]	42,266	5%
4	Foreign money offers	32,868	4%
5	Prizes/sweepstakes and lotteries	32,162	4%
6	Computer equipment and software[b]	27,036	3%
7	Internet auctions	24,376	3%
8	Health care	16,097	2%
9	Travel, vacations and timeshare	14,903	2%
10	Advance-fee loans and credit protection/repair	14,342	2%
11	Investments	13,705	2%
12	Magazines and buyers clubs	12,970	2%
13	Business opps and work-at-home plans	11,362	1%
14	Real estate (not timeshares)	9,475	1%
15	Office supplies and services	9,211	1%
16	Telephone services	8,155	1%
17	Employ agencies/job counsel/overseas work	5,932	1%
18	Debt management/credit counseling	3,442	1%
19	Multi-level mktg/pyramids/chain letters	3,092	1%
20	Charitable solicitations	1,843	1%

[a]Percentages are based on the total number of Sentinel complaints (813,899) received by the Federal Trade Commission (FTC) between January 1 and December 31, 2007. Twenty-five percent (200,136) of the Sentinel complaints received by the FTC did not contain specific product service codes.

[b]In previous reports, complaints for "Internet services" and "computer equipment and software" were reported under a combined category.

SOURCE: "Sentinel Top Complaint Categories, January 1–December 31, 2007," in *Consumer Fraud and Identity Theft Complaint Data, January–December 2007*, U.S. Federal Trade Commission, February 2008, http://www.ftc.gov/sentinel/reports/sentinel-annual-reports/sentinel-cy2007.pdf (accessed October 3, 2008)

FIGURE 5.2

Company's method of contacting consumers who reported fraud complaints to Sentinel, 2007

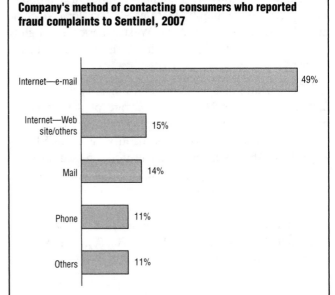

Notes: Percentages are based on the total number of fraud complaints for each calendar year where company's method of initial contact was reported by consumers: CY (calendar year)-2005 = 323,690; CY-2006 = 306,335; and CY-2007 = 291,780. 53% of consumers reported this information during CY-2007, 74% and 72% for CY-2005 and CY-2006, respectively.

SOURCE: "Company's Method of Contacting Consumers, January 1–December 31, 2007," in *Consumer Fraud and Identity Theft Complaint Data, January–December 2007*, U.S. Federal Trade Commission, February 2008, http://www.ftc.gov/sentinel/reports/sentinel-annual-reports/sentinel-cy2007.pdf (accessed October 3, 2008)

FTC Consumer Fraud Complaints

Figure 5.2 provides a breakdown of the methods used by companies to initially contact consumers who ultimately complained about fraud to the FTC. In 49% of the cases initial contact was by e-mail. Another 15% of complaining consumers reported they had contact with the business through an Internet Web site or similar means. Some 14% of complaint contacts involved contact by mail, and 11% involved phone contact. An additional 11% of the complaints involved contact by other means.

In 2007, 89% of fraud complainants specified their monetary losses to the FTC. Over $1.2 billion in total losses were reported, with a median loss of $349. This means that half of the complainants lost more than this amount and the other half lost less than this amount.

DATA BREACHES AND IDENTITY THEFT

In recent years well-organized rings of identity thieves have emerged that engage in large-scale thefts known as data breaches. These are crimes in which the computer records of businesses, government agencies, universities, or other organizations are breached for the purpose of obtaining the personal and/or financial data of large numbers of people. The phenomenon is described by Kimberly Kiefer Peretti of the U.S. Department of Justice (DOJ) in *Data*

Breaches: What the Underground World of "Carding" Reveals (May 2008, http://www.cybercrime.gov/DataBreachesArticle.pdf).

Peretti defines *carding* as the large-scale theft of credit and/or debit card account numbers and other financial information. (See Table 5.2.) She notes that carding is an especially worrisome crime, because carders have created fast and effective methods for disseminating the stolen information to other criminals. This is achieved through Web sites known as carding forums, where fraudsters buy and sell stolen personal and financial information. Large-scale data breaches first gained public attention in 2005, when carders stole the financial records of 163,000 consumers from the computer systems of Choicepoint, Inc. The company notified California consumers about the breaches in accordance with a 2003 law requiring companies to alert individuals whose data records have been stolen. Since that time other large data breaches have prompted many states to pass similar legislation.

Peretti recommends a four-pronged approach to combating carding and large-scale data breaches:

- Mandatory reporting by organizations that experience data breaching to alert individuals that their information has been stolen and to notify law enforcement about the breaches

TABLE 5.2

Definitions of various white–collar crimes

Account takeover	A type of identity theft involving fraud on existing financial accounts, for example, when a criminal uses a stolen credit card number to make fraudulent purchases on an existing credit line.
Carders	Individuals engaged in criminal carding activities.
Carding	Large scale theft of credit and/or debit card account numbers and other financial information.
Carding forums	Criminal Web sites dedicated to the sale of stolen personal and financial information to fraudsters worldwide.
Carding online	Using stolen credit card information to make purchases of goods and services online from merchants.
Cashing	Obtaining money, rather than retail goods and services, with the unauthorized use of stolen financial information, for example, withdrawing cash at ATMs.
Data breach	An organization's unauthorized or unintentional exposure, disclosure, or loss of sensitive personal information, such as Social Security numbers or credit card numbers.
Dumps	Information electronically copied from the magnetic stripe on the back of credit and debit cards. This information includes customer name, account number, etc.
Dumpster diving	Rummaging through garbage cans or trash bins to obtain copies of checks, credit card or bank statements, etc., and using this information to assume a person's identity.
Full info (or fulls)	A package of data about a victim, including address, phone number, Social Security number, credit or debit account numbers and PINs, credit history report, mother's maiden name, and other identifying information.
Gift card vending	Purchasing gift cards from retail merchants at their physical stores using counterfeit credit cards and reselling the gift cards for a percentage of their actual value.
In-store carding	Presenting a counterfeit credit card that had been encoded with stolen account information to a cashier at a physical retail store location.
Malicious code	For hacking purposes, this is a computer program placed unknowingly on a victim's computer that allows for the capture of personal and financial data.
New account creation	A type of identity theft involving fraudulent creation of new accounts, for example, when a criminal uses stolen data to open a bank or credit card account in someone else's name.
Phishing	Using 'spoofed' emails to "lead consumers to counterfeit Web sites designed to trick them into divulging financial data such as credit card numbers. Phishing can also involve placing malicious code onto an individual's computer without the individual's awareness to steal personal information directly.
Skimming	Criminal use of an electronic storage device to read and record the encoded data on the magnetic stripe on the back of a credit or debit card. Typical examples involve rogue employees at restaurants that swipe a patron's card in the skimming device prior to swiping it through the restaurant's own card reader or attaching the skimming device to an ATM.
Wardriving	Driving around in a vehicle with a laptop and a high-powered antenna to locate, and potentially exploit, wireless computer systems of vulnerable targets. Once inside the system, a criminal can intercept wireless communications and capture credit card numbers and other personal identification information.

SOURCE: Adapted from Kimberly Kiefer Peretti, *Data Breaches: What the Underground World of "Carding" Reveals*, U.S. Department of Justice, Computer Crime and Intellectual Property Section, May 2008, http://www.cybercrime.gov/DataBreachesArticle.pdf (accessed November 20, 2008)

- Additional legislation to criminalize carding and related activities

- Stricter sentences to reflect the seriousness of carding

- Greater cooperation with foreign law enforcement agencies to combat carding activities that originate in foreign nations

FINANCIAL CRIMES REPORTED BY THE FBI

The FBI's Financial Crime Section investigates certain offenses relating to fraud, theft, and embezzlement. According to the FBI, in *Financial Crimes Report to the Public*, these white-collar crimes include corruption by public officials, corporate fraud, mortgage fraud, securities and commodities fraud, health care fraud, financial institution fraud, insurance fraud, and money laundering. Data on all these offenses, excluding corruption by public officials, are addressed in the FBI report.

Corporate Fraud Reported by the FBI

According to the FBI, most of the corporate fraud cases it investigates involve accounting schemes that businesses use to deceive their investors, analysts, or auditors about the financial soundness of their companies. Corporations may overstate their financial worth to artificially inflate the value of their stock on the stock markets. Executives participating in these schemes often sell their stock for a high profit before the deception is discovered, bringing them signifi-

cant personal financial gain. Other investors lose large sums of money after the truth comes out and the company's stock plummets in value.

Figure 5.3 shows the number of corporate fraud cases pending in federal courts from fiscal years (FYs) 2003 to 2007. The number grew from 279 cases in FY 2003 to 529 cases in FY 2007, a 90% increase. The FBI's investigations into corporate fraud resulted in 183 indictments and 173 convictions during this period. During FY 2007, $12.6 billion in restitutions (an amount of money set by a court to be paid to the victim of a crime for property losses or injuries caused by the crime) and $38.6 million in fines were secured by the federal government from convicted corporate criminals.

Mortgage Fraud Reported by the FBI

The FBI indicates that mortgage fraud typically involves "material misstatement, misrepresentation, or omission relating to the property or potential mortgage relied on by an underwriter or lender to fund, purchase or insure a loan." These cases fall into two broad categories: fraud for profit and fraud for housing. Fraud for profit is conducted by industry insiders, for example, loan officers or appraisers. Fraud for housing is perpetrated by individuals who seek housing through false pretenses, for example, by lying about their assets or income on a mortgage loan application. The FBI notes that 80% of the mortgage fraud cases it investigates involve fraud for profit.

FIGURE 5.3

Pending federal court cases of corporate fraud, mortgage fraud, securities and commodities fraud, and health care fraud, 2003–07

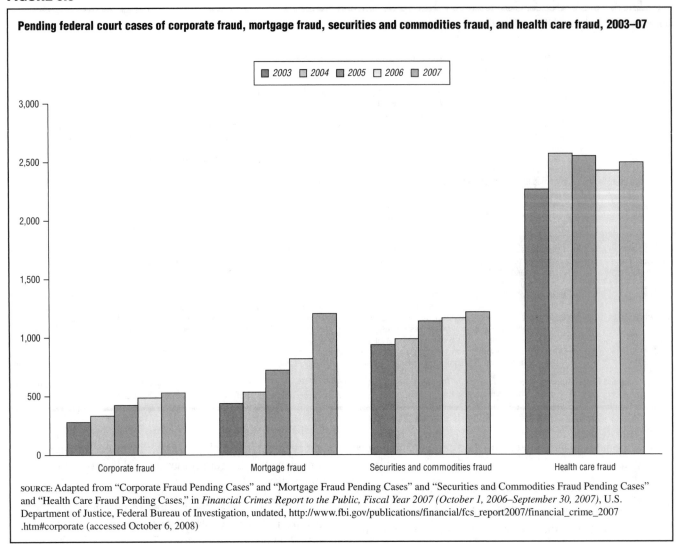

SOURCE: Adapted from "Corporate Fraud Pending Cases" and "Mortgage Fraud Pending Cases" and "Securities and Commodities Fraud Pending Cases" and "Health Care Fraud Pending Cases," in *Financial Crimes Report to the Public, Fiscal Year 2007 (October 1, 2006–September 30, 2007)*, U.S. Department of Justice, Federal Bureau of Investigation, undated, http://www.fbi.gov/publications/financial/fcs_report2007/financial_crime_2007.htm#corporate (accessed October 6, 2008)

Figure 5.3 shows the number of mortgage fraud cases pending in federal courts from FYs 2003 to 2007. The number grew from 436 cases in FY 2003 to 1,204 cases in FY 2007, an increase of 176%. The FBI achieved 321 indictments and 260 convictions for mortgage fraud through FY 2007. Approximately $595.9 million in restitutions, $21.8 million in recoveries, and $1.7 million in fines were collected.

Mortgage fraud is often brought to the FBI's attention through the filing of a Suspicious Activity Report (SAR) by a financial institution or the U.S. Department of Housing and Urban Development. SARs are filed with the U.S. Department of the Treasury and shared with law enforcement agencies. They can be triggered by any financial transaction that arouses the suspicion of a participating business. The number of mortgage-related SARs skyrocketed 574%, from 6,936 in FY 2003 to 46,717 in FY 2007. (See Figure 5.4.) This huge increase is believed to be related to the significant downturn in the real estate and housing market that hit the United States after 2003. The

FBI notes that many mortgage industry insiders are paid by commission and faced a tremendous loss of personal income when the industry crashed. This likely encouraged fraudulent activity in the mortgage markets.

Securities and Commodities Fraud Reported by the FBI

Securities are financial instruments, such as stocks, bonds, and mutual funds. Commodities are raw materials, foreign currencies, or other objects of investment. Securities and commodities fraud offenses are complicated crimes in which investment companies or managers use sophisticated schemes to trick investors out of their money. According to the FBI, the most common schemes involve manipulating the price of securities or commodities or selling them under false pretenses.

Figure 5.3 shows the number of securities and commodities fraud cases pending in federal courts from FYs 2003 to 2007. The number grew from 937 cases in FY 2003 to 1,217 cases in FY 2007, a 30% increase. The FBI reports

FIGURE 5.4

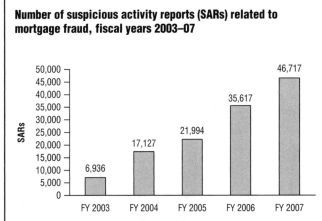

Number of suspicious activity reports (SARs) related to mortgage fraud, fiscal years 2003–07

SOURCE: "Figure 1. Mortgage Fraud Related SARs, FYs 2003 to 2007," in *2007 Mortgage Fraud Report*, U.S. Department of Justice, Federal Bureau of Investigation, April 2008, http://www.fbi.gov/publications/fraud/mortgage_fraud07.htm (accessed October 3, 2008)

achieving 320 indictments and 289 convictions by yearend 2007 for these types of fraud cases. During FY 2007, $1.7 billion in restitutions, $24 million in recoveries, and $202.7 million in fines were collected.

Health Care Fraud Reported by the FBI

Health care fraud occurs when individuals or businesses cheat public or private health care systems out of money. Many of these crimes are perpetrated by insiders, for example, by doctors or other practitioners who overbill insurance companies or perform unnecessary services. Many other offenses are included in this category, such as selling medical equipment or prescription drugs under false pretenses. The latter can occur through Internet pharmacies or businesses that illegally sell prescription-only drugs or appliances or sell counterfeit or stolen pharmaceuticals.

Figure 5.3 shows the number of health care fraud cases pending in federal courts from FYs 2003 to 2007. The number rose from 2,262 cases in FY 2003 to 2,493 cases in FY 2007, a 9% increase. FBI investigations produced 839 indictments and 635 convictions through FY 2007. In addition, the agency secured $1.1 billion in restitutions, $4.4 million in recoveries, $34 million in fines, and 308 seizures valued at $61.2 million in FY 2007.

Insurance Fraud Reported by the FBI

Insurance fraud involves a number of crimes that may be perpetrated by industry insiders against policyholders or vice versa. Note that fraud involving health care insurance is not included in this category, but is tracked separately. The FBI reports that the most common types of insider insurance fraud involve misuse of policyholder premiums. This can occur when insurance agents or brokers keep premiums for their own financial gain. Fraud by policyholders most often takes the form of willful destruction of

property (e.g., arson to collect insurance proceeds) or making other false claims.

Figure 5.5 shows the number of insurance fraud cases pending in federal courts from FYs 2003 to 2007. The number decreased from 326 cases in FY 2003 to 209 cases in FY 2007, a 36% decline. The FBI expects the number of cases to increase significantly in coming years due to many ongoing investigations along the Gulf Coast that are related to Hurricane Katrina. The hurricane and subsequent flooding caused enormous damage there in August 2005. The agency reports "a marked increase" in insurance fraud claims in the region and estimates that these claims total as much as $4 billion to $6 billion.

During FY 2007 the FBI achieved 39 indictments and 47 convictions for insurance fraud. In addition, more than $27.2 million in restitutions and $427,000 in fines were secured.

Mass Marketing Fraud Reported by the FBI

Mass marketing fraud is a general term for fraud perpetrated by a form of mass communications, such as the telephone or Internet. Typically, the victim of the scam is asked to pay some fee to secure a prize from a lottery or sweepstakes or to facilitate the transfer of a larger sum of money to the victim's possession. One of the best-known schemes in this category is the so-called Nigerian e-mail fraud wherein victims are asked to pay fees to help transfer a large sum of money out of Nigeria. For their help, the victims are promised a substantial payment from the transferred funds. Victims pay the up-front fee, but never receive the promised payment.

Figure 5.5 shows the number of mass marketing fraud cases pending in federal courts from FYs 2003 to 2007. The number decreased from 236 cases in FY 2003 to 127 cases in FY 2007, a decrease of 46%. The FBI acknowledges that many of these crimes are perpetrated by criminals in foreign nations, making them difficult to prosecute. The agency believes the best solution for combating mass marketing fraud lies in better consumer education.

Money Laundering Reported by the FBI

The FBI defines money laundering as "the process by which criminals conceal or disguise the proceeds of their crimes or convert those proceeds into goods and services. It allows criminals to infuse their illegal money into the stream of commerce, thus corrupting financial institutions and the money supply, thereby giving criminals unwarranted economic power." In other words, money laundering is the process of making criminally obtained money look legitimate. The FBI's Financial Crimes Section focuses only on money laundering cases in which the money is derived from other white-collar crimes, for example, securities fraud.

Figure 5.5 shows the number of money laundering fraud cases pending in federal courts from FYs 2003 to

FIGURE 5.5

Pending federal court cases of insurance fraud, mass marketing fraud, and money laundering, 2003–07

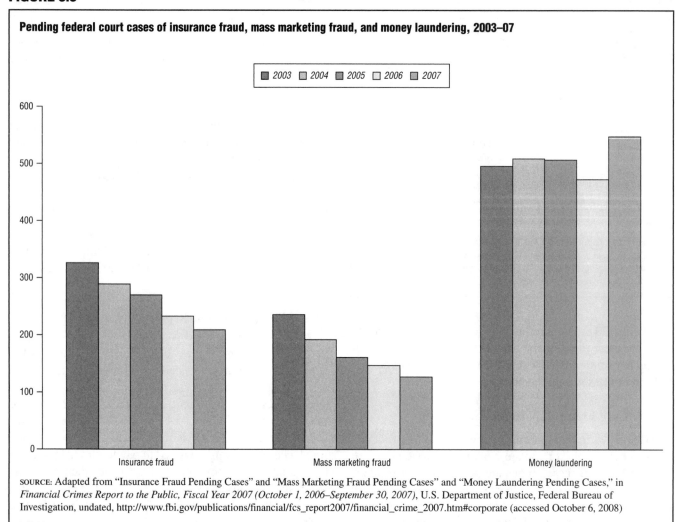

SOURCE: Adapted from "Insurance Fraud Pending Cases" and "Mass Marketing Fraud Pending Cases" and "Money Laundering Pending Cases," in *Financial Crimes Report to the Public, Fiscal Year 2007 (October 1, 2006–September 30, 2007)*, U.S. Department of Justice, Federal Bureau of Investigation, undated, http://www.fbi.gov/publications/financial/fcs_report2007/financial_crime_2007.htm#corporate (accessed October 6, 2008)

2007. The number increased from 496 cases in FY 2003 to 548 cases in FY 2007, an increase of 10%. During FY 2007 the FBI secured $66.9 million in restitutions, $2.6 million in recoveries, and $11.4 million in fines associated with these types of cases.

FAMOUS CORPORATE CRIMES: ENRON

The collapse of Enron Corporation is one of the most glaring examples of corporate crime and falsification of corporate data in recent history. Enron, based in Houston, Texas, was an energy broker trading in electricity and other energy commodities. In the late 1990s, however, instead of simply brokering energy deals, Enron devised increasingly complex contracts with buyers and sellers that allowed Enron to profit from the difference in the selling price and the buying price of commodities such as electricity. Enron executives created a number of partnerships—in effect, companies that existed only on paper whose sole function was to hide debt and make Enron appear to be much more profitable than it actually was.

On December 2, 2001, Enron filed for bankruptcy protection, listing some $13.1 billion in liabilities and $24.7 billion in assets—$38 billion less than the assets listed only two months earlier. As a result, thousands of Enron employees lost their jobs. In addition, many Enron staff—who had been encouraged by company executives to invest monies from their 401k retirement plans in Enron stock—had their retirement savings reduced to almost nothing as a result of the precipitous decline in value of Enron stock.

In the wake of Enron's collapse, several committees in the U.S. Senate and House of Representatives began to investigate whether Enron defrauded investors by deliberately concealing financial information. Many lawsuits were filed against Enron, its accounting firm Arthur Andersen, and former Enron executives including the former chairman Kenneth L. Lay (1942–2006) and the former chief executive officer Jeffrey Skilling (1953–).

The Enron treasurer Ben Glisan Jr. (1966–) was convicted of conspiracy charges to commit wire and securities fraud. He was sentenced to five years in prison and was released in January 2007. Lay and Skilling went on trial in January 2006. Kristen Hays reports in "Prosecutor: Lay, Skilling Committed Crimes" (Associated Press, May 16, 2006) that the federal prosecutor Kathryn H. Ruemmler

(1935–) accused the men of using "accounting tricks, fiction, hocus-pocus, trickery, misleading statements, half-truths, omissions and outright lies" in committing their crimes. On May 25 a jury found Lay guilty of all six counts against him in the corporate trial; he was also convicted of four counts of fraud in a separate trial relating to his personal finances. He faced 20 to 30 years in prison but died of a heart attack on July 5, 2006, before the judge set his sentence. The jury found Skilling guilty of 19 of the 28 counts against him, and he was sentenced to 24 years and four months in federal prison. Skilling began serving his sentence at a low-security federal facility in Waseca, Minnesota, and is projected to be released in 2028. Dozens of other people were charged in the Enron scandal. In February 2008 three British bankers prosecuted for their roles were given 37-month prison terms.

On June 15, 2002, a New York jury found the accounting firm Arthur Andersen guilty of obstructing justice in connection with the Enron collapse. Arthur Andersen was convicted of destroying Enron documents during an ongoing federal investigation of the company's accounting practices. As a result of the verdict, Andersen faced a fine of $500,000 and a probation term of up to five years. In 2005 the U.S. Supreme Court overturned the conviction due to flaws in the instructions that had been given to the jury. However, the firm was effectively out of the accounting business with its few remaining U.S. employees responsible for administrating the many legal cases generated by the scandal.

The Enron scandal helped lead to the passage of the Sarbanes-Oxley Act (SOX), which was signed into law on July 30, 2002. The law was designed to rebuild public trust in the U.S. corporate sector by imposing new criminal and civil penalties for security violations and establishing a new certification system for internal audits. SOX also grants independent auditors more access to company data and requires increased disclosure of compensation methods and systems, especially for upper management.

FAMOUS INVESTMENT CRIMES: BERNARD MADOFF

In perhaps the most notable white-collar crime since the Enron collapse earlier in the decade, the financial world was rocked in December 2008 by the disclosure of a far-reaching Ponzi scheme managed by Bernard Madoff (1938–), an influential Wall Street executive who had served as chairman of NASDAQ during the 1990s. Named after Charles Ponzi (1882–1949), an Italian immigrant who defrauded investors in Boston in the early twentieth century, a Ponzi scheme is also known as a pyramid scheme. Its victims are lured with promises of large, quick returns on their investments. Rather than providing legitimate investment services, however, the swindler uses the investment monies of those lower on the pyramid (new investors)

to provide payouts to those higher up in the scheme. Larger and larger numbers of investors are always needed to keep sending money up the levels of the pyramid, a situation that cannot be sustained forever, and the scheme is eventually exposed. At the time of Madoff's arrest, the Securities and Exchange Commission (SEC; December 11, 2008, http://www.sec.gov/news/press/2008/2008-293.htm) reported that he estimated the fraud losses to his victims to total "at least $50 billion."

Madoff was the founder and chairman of Bernard L. Madoff Investment Securities LLC, a leading Wall Street firm established in 1960. At the time of his arrest, the firm had approximately 8,000 clients, claimed $700 million in capital, and prided itself, according to its Web site, on the "unblemished record of value, fair-dealing, and high ethical standards that has always been the firm's hallmark." However, in addition to the investment firm, Madoff also conducted a side business as an investment adviser, kept multiple sets of books, maintained secrecy about his investments, and provided false reports of his activities to federal regulators and to his clients. The extent of his influence among U.S. financial experts included an advisory role to the SEC, a relationship Madoff used to his advantage and one that led SEC staff to dismiss accusations against him that first came to their attention in the late 1990s (December 16, 2008, http://www.sec.gov/news/press/2008/2008-297.htm).

When the list of Madoff's clients was made public in early February 2009, it included thousands of institutions and individuals worldwide, including investment funds, pension funds, charitable organizations, financiers, Hollywood celebrities, and many private investors who expressed alarm at the sudden, unsought media exposure of their personal finances (February 6, 2009, http://online.wsj.com/article/SB1233845 33479552435.html?mod=googlenews_wsj). On March 12, 2009, Madoff pleaded guilty to 11 felony counts against him in federal court, including securities fraud, investment adviser fraud, mail fraud, wire fraud, money laundering, making false statements, perjury, making false filings with the SEC, and theft from an employee benefit plan. His sentencing was set for June 2009.

COMPUTER CRIME
Federal Computer Crime Legislation

In 1986 Congress passed the Computer Fraud and Abuse Act (CFAA), which makes it illegal to perpetrate fraud on a computer. Table 5.3 lists the major offenses covered by CFAA provisions and the federal prison sentences prescribed for people who are convicted of these crimes.

The Computer Abuse Amendments Act of 1994 makes it a federal crime "through means of a computer used in interstate commerce or communications . . . [to] damage, or cause damage to, a computer, computer system, network,

Crime, Prisons, and Jails

White-Collar Crime 59

TABLE 5.3

Summary of provisions under the Computer Fraud and Abuse Act

Offense	Section	Sentence*
Obtaining national security information	(a)(1)	10 (20) years
Compromising the confidentiality of a computer	(a)(2)	1 or 5
Trespassing in a government computer	(a)(3)	1 (10)
Accessing a computer to defraud & obtain value	(a)(4)	5 (10)
Knowing transmission and intentional damage	(a)(5)(A)(i)	10 (20 or life)
Intentional access and reckless damage	(a)(5)(A)(ii)	5 (20)
Intentional access and damage	(a)(5)(A)(iii)	1 (10)
Trafficking in passwords	(a)(6)	1 (10)
Extortion involving threats to damage computer	(a)(7)	5 (10)

*The maximum prison sentences for second convictions are noted in parentheses.

SOURCE: "Table 1. Summary of CFAA Provisions," in *Prosecuting Computer Crimes*, U.S. Department of Justice, Computer Crime and Intellectual Property Section, Criminal Division, February 2007, http://www.cybercrime.gov/ccmanual/ccmanual.pdf (accessed November 20, 2008)

information, data, or program ... with reckless disregard" for the consequences of these actions to the computer owner. This law pertains to maliciously destroying or changing computer records or knowingly distributing malware (i.e., malicious software or programs, such as viruses, Trojans, or worms designed to interfere in the working of a computer system and/or allow a perpetrator access to someone else's computer system). Malware can be transmitted by sharing disks and programs or through e-mail.

The 2001 Uniting and Strengthening America by Providing Appropriate Tools Required to Intercept and Obstruct Terrorism (USA PATRIOT) Act, which gave increased powers to U.S. government law enforcement and intelligence agencies to help prevent terrorist attacks, amended the CFAA. The act was expanded to include the types of electronic records that law enforcement authorities may obtain without a subpoena, including records of Internet session times and durations, as well as temporarily assigned network addresses. The PATRIOT Act was reauthorized on March 9, 2006, in the USA PATRIOT Improvement and Reauthorization Act of 2005.

Internet Fraud

In *IC3 2008 Internet Crime Report* (2009, http://www.ic3.gov/media/annualreport/2008_IC3Report.pdf), the Internet Crime Complaint Center (IC3) notes that it received 275,284 complaints of Internet crime in 2008. This represents a 33.1% increase from 2007, when the center received 206,884 complaints. The total dollar cost of all cases of Internet fraud referred to law enforcement agencies was $265 million, with a median loss of $931 per complaint. This shows a significant upward trend from $68 million in 2004, to $198.4 million in losses reported in 2006, and $239 million in losses in 2007. According to IC3, the top three complaint categories in 2008 were nondelivered merchandise and/or payment (32.9% of complaints), Internet auction fraud

(25.5% of complaints), and credit card/debit card fraud (9% of complaints).

SPAM. The IC3 defines the term *spam* as unsolicited bulk e-mail. According to IC3, spam is widely used to commit traditional white-collar crimes, including financial institution fraud, credit card fraud, and identity theft. Spam messages are usually considered unsolicited because the recipients have not chosen to receive the messages. Generally, spam involves multiple identical messages sent simultaneously. Spam can also be used to access computers and servers without authorization and transmit viruses or forward spam. Spam senders often sell open proxy information, credit card information, and e-mail lists illegally.

The Controlling the Assault of Non-Solicited Pornography and Marketing (CAN-SPAM) Act of 2003 established requirements for those who send commercial e-mail. CAN-SPAM requires that all spam contain a legitimate return address as well as instructions on how to opt out of receiving additional spam from the sender. Spam must also state in the subject line if the e-mail is pornographic in nature. Violators of these rules are subject to heavy fines.

The law's main provisions include:

• Banning false or misleading header information—the "from," "to," and routing information (including the originating name and e-mail address) must be accurate and identify the person who initiated the e-mail

• Prohibiting deceptive subject lines—the subject line must not mislead the recipient about the message's contents or subject matter

• Requiring an opt-out method—senders must provide a return e-mail address or another Internet-based way that allows the recipient to ask the sender not to send any more e-mail messages to him or her

The first person convicted by a jury in a CAN-SPAM case was Jeffrey Brett Goodin (1961–) of California. He was found guilty in January 2007 of operating an Internet-based scheme to obtain personal and credit card information. Goodin sent e-mails to AOL users that appeared to be from AOL's billing department. The messages, which instructed recipients to update their AOL billing information or lose service, referred users to Web pages that were actually scam pages set up by Goodin to collect the users' personal and credit card information.

SPYWARE. The Anti-Spyware Coalition (October 1, 2007, http://www.antispywarecoalition.org/about/FAQ.html), a group composed of software manufacturers, academics, and consumer advocates, defines spyware as:

Technologies deployed without appropriate user consent and/or implemented in ways that impair user control over:

• Material changes that affect their user experience, privacy, or system security

- Use of their system resources, including what programs are installed on their computers, and/or

- Collection, use and distribution of their personal or other sensitive information

Some states have enacted antispyware legislation. California's Consumer Protection against Computer Spyware Act makes it illegal for anyone to install software on someone else's computer deceptively and use it to modify settings, including the user's home page, default search page, or bookmarks. The act also outlaws collecting, through intentionally deceptive means, personally identifiable information by logging keystrokes, tracking Web site visits, or extracting personal information from a user's hard drive.

Computer Hacking

Computer hacking takes place when an outsider gains unauthorized access to a secure computer by identifying and exploiting system vulnerabilities. Criminal hackers use their software expertise to crack security codes to access stored information or hijack a computer (i.e., take it over and instruct it to generate spam or perform other malicious actions). The Web Application Security Consortium tracks hacking incidents that have been reported in the media and that result from vulnerabilities in Web application security. The consortium (February 17, 2008, http://www.webappsec.org/projects/whid/statistics.shtml) reports that the number of Web hacking incidents has increased significantly in recent years, from just five in 2000 to 82 in 2007.

INTELLECTUAL PROPERTY

According to the World Intellectual Property Organization (July 25, 2008, http://www.wipo.int/about-ip/en/), intellectual property consists of "creations of the mind: inventions, literary and artistic works, and symbols, names, images, and designs used in commerce." These include industrial property such as trademarks, chemical formulas, patents, and designs, and copyrighted material such as literary works, films, musical compositions and recordings, graphic and architectural designs, works of art in any medium, and domain names.

In the United States intellectual property is protected by the joint efforts of the U.S. Patent and Trademark Office, the U.S. Copyright Office, the DOJ, the U.S. Department of Commerce, and two agencies that focus on international aspects of intellectual property: the U.S. Customs Service, which monitors incoming goods arriving from other nations, and the Office of the U.S. Trade Representative, which negotiates on behalf of U.S. interests and develops and implements trade agreements and policies.

To coordinate the wide-ranging efforts of these organizations, the administration of President Bill Clinton established the National Intellectual Property Law Enforcement Coordination Council (NIPLECC) in 2000. In its 2008

annual report (January 2008, http://www.usdoj.gov/criminal/pr/press_releases/2008/02/012008-nipleccrprt.pdf), the NIPLECC reported an increase in federal investigations and prosecutions of intellectual property cases during FY 2007 over the previous two fiscal years. In FY 2007 the Department of Justice filed 217 intellectual property cases, an increase of 7% over FY 2006 (204 cases) and an increase of 33% over FY 2005 (169 cases). In addition, the Department of Homeland Security reported border seizure of pirated and counterfeit goods valued at nearly $200 million. Most of the seized items came from Asia, with 80% ($158 million) originating in China, 6% ($12.7 million) in Hong Kong, 2% ($3.4 million) in Taiwan, and the remaining 12% ($22.6 million) from all other countries.

TAX FRAUD

For most Americans, failure to pay the correct amount of taxes to the Internal Revenue Service (IRS) results in an agreement to pay off the taxes in some manner. However, when the IRS believes it has found a pattern of deception designed to avoid paying taxes, criminal charges can be brought against someone. The Criminal Investigations Division (October 9, 2008, http://www.irs.gov/compliance/enforcement/article/0,,id=106791,00.html) of the IRS notes that in FY 2008 it initiated 1,603 cases, slightly lower than 1,780 cases initiated in FY 2007 and 1,863 in FY 2006. Of the cases investigated in FY 2008, the IRS recommended prosecution in 1,129 cases, and in 1,038 cases criminal charges were filed or brought by indictment. The IRS reported 734 convictions for tax fraud, with an average sentence of 28 months.

FORGERY AND COUNTERFEITING

As technology advances, forgers can use sophisticated computers, scanners, and laser printers to make copies of more and more documents, including counterfeit checks, identification badges, driver's licenses, and money.

Making counterfeit U.S. currency or altering genuine currency to increase its value is punishable by a fine, imprisonment of up to 15 years, or both. Possession of counterfeit U.S. currency is also a crime, punishable by a fine, imprisonment of up to 15 years, or both. Counterfeiting is not limited to paper money. Manufacturing counterfeit U.S. coins in any denomination above five cents is subject to the same penalties as all other counterfeit activities. Anyone who alters a real coin to increase its value to collectors can be punished by a fine, imprisonment for up to five years, or both.

In response to the growing use of computer-generated counterfeit money, the Department of the Treasury redesigned the $50 and $100 bills in the 1990s and introduced new $5, $10, and $20 bills between 1998 and 2000. These bills contain a watermark making them harder to copy accurately. According to the Bureau of Engraving and Printing, in "Currency Redesign Timeline" (2009, http://

www.moneyfactory.gov/newmoney/main.cfm/media/rede sign), another change in currency design was introduced in October 2003: a new $20 bill with shades of green, peach, and blue in the background. A blue eagle and metallic green eagle and shield have also been added to the bill's design. A new $50 note was issued in 2004, a new $10 note in 2006, and new $5 notes in 2007 and 2008.

The U.S. Secret Service (2008, http://www.secretservi ce.gov/counterfeit.shtml) explains that many counterfeiters have abandoned the traditional method of offset printing, which requires specialized skills and machinery. Instead, counterfeiters produce fake currency with basic computer training and typical office equipment. The number of coun- terfeit bills in circulation is likely to increase because more people have access to the machines and methods required to produce them, but the security features added to the design and manufacture of U.S. currency have also made it easier to detect bogus bills.

PUBLIC CORRUPTION

The abuse of public trust may be found wherever the interest of individuals or businesses overlaps with govern- ment interest. It ranges from the health inspector who accepts a bribe from a restaurant owner or the police officer who "shakes down" a drug dealer, to the council member or legislator who accepts money to vote a certain way. These crimes are often difficult to uncover as typically few willing witnesses are available.

The DOJ states in *Report to Congress on the Activities and Operations of the Public Integrity Section for 2007* (2008, http://www.usdoj.gov/criminal/pin/docs/arpt-2007 .pdf) that the number of people indicted for offenses involving the abuse of public office has remained relatively stable since 1998. In 2007, 1,141 people were indicted and 1,014 were convicted in public corruption cases. Of those indicted, 426 were elected or appointed federal officials, 128 were state officials, 284 were local officials, and the remaining 303 were private citizens not employed by the government.

Jack Abramoff

In one of the most notable cases involving bribery and kickbacks, Jack Abramoff (1958–), a prominent lobbyist in Washington, D.C., pleaded guilty to fraud, tax evasion, and conspiracy to bribe public officials in January 2006. He was originally sentenced to 70 months in prison. However, because of the assistance he provided federal prosecutors, his sentence was reduced to 48 months in September 2008. The court also ordered him to pay more than $23 million in restitution to his victims.

Abramoff received kickbacks from his former business partner, Michael Scanlon (1970–), in a conspiracy to defraud Native American tribes who sought government approval to operate casinos. The tribes hired Abramoff to represent their

interests, and he then recommended Scanlon's public rela- tions firm to the tribes. Abramoff received a kickback from Scanlon for the referral. Abramoff and Scanlon supplied financial incentives, trips, and entertainment expenses to public officials whose support was needed for the projects they represented.

Abramoff was also listed as a coconspirator in the charges against Representative Robert W. Ney (1954–; R-OH), who was sentenced in January 2007 to 30 months in prison and two years of supervised release. In addition, Ney was ordered to serve 100 hours of community service for each year of supervised release and to pay a $6,000 fine. Ney pleaded guilty on October 13, 2006, to honest services fraud, lobbying violations, and making false statements to the House of Representatives. Ney represented the 18th District of Ohio from 1995 to 2006. He admitted that he accepted domestic and international trips, meals, sports and concert tickets, and other incentives from Abramoff and others in exchange for his support on matters before the House of Representatives. Besides Abramoff and Scanlon, a foreign businessman also provided financial incentives to Ney in return for his support in obtaining a travel visa and an exemption from legal restrictions against foreign nation- als selling U.S. aircraft abroad.

Public Corruption Cases

Because public officials have sworn to uphold the law and to act in the interest of the communities they represent, their failure to do so is considered particularly reprehensible, and cases of public corruption often receive much media attention. Common public corruption charges include per- jury, obstruction of justice, and bribery. "Pay-to-play" is a form of bribery in which a public official demands benefits— often in the form of campaign contributions—in exchange for government appointments or contracts. Some notable recent corruption cases involving public officials include:

KWAME KILPATRICK. Mayor Kwame Kilpatrick (1970–) of Detroit, Michigan, pleaded guilty to two felony counts of obstruction of justice and resigned from office as part of a September 2008 plea agreement. The charges arose from the settlement of a 2007 court case, for which the city of Detroit paid a premium to hide evidence that the mayor and his chief of staff had an affair and lied about it under oath. In the case, two whistleblowers—a deputy chief of police and one of Kilpatrick's former bodyguards— claimed to have been dismissed in retaliation for their parts in an investigation of the mayor and his security detail on accusations that included throwing wild parties at the may- or's residence, improper use of city vehicles, and inflated overtime claims. During the trial Kilpatrick and his former chief of staff, Christine Beatty (1970–), had testified that they had not had an affair; however, after the whistle- blowers won a $6.5 million judgment, they discovered thousands of text messages sent by the couple to each other that revealed an intimate relationship. Faced with evidence that he and Beatty had perjured themselves, Kilpatrick pushed through a city-funded $8.4 million settlement of the case in order to keep the text messages from becoming public.

TED STEVENS. In October 2008, Alaska Senator Ted Stevens (1923–)—the longest-serving Republican in Senate history—was convicted on bribery charges related to gifts allegedly given to him by an oil company executive. Less than a week after his conviction, Stevens was narrowly defeated in his reelection bid by Democratic challenger Mark Begich (1962–). On April 1, 2009, the Justice Department (http://www.usdoj.gov/opa/pr/2009/April/09-ag-288.html) moved to have Stevens's conviction dismissed on procedural grounds. Attorney General Eric Holder (1954–) said of the Stevens case, "After careful review, I have concluded that certain information should have been provided to the defense for use at trial. In light of this conclusion, and in consideration of the totality of the circumstances of this particular case, I have determined that it is in the interest of justice to dismiss the indictment and not proceed with a new trial."

LARRY P. LANGFORD. In what the U.S. Attorney's office called a "classic pay-to-play scheme," Larry P. Langford (1948–), the mayor of Birmingham, Alabama, and former president of the Jefferson County commission, was indicted December 1, 2008, along with two associates—investment banker William B. Blount and lobbyist Albert W. LaPierre—on charges of conspiracy, bribery, fraud, money laundering, and filing false tax returns. According to the Department of Justice (http://birmingham.fbi.gov/dojpressrel/pressrel08/bh120108.htm), while acting on behalf of the county commission, Langford negotiated financial transactions that benefited Blount and LaPierre. In return Blount and LaPierre allegedly paid bribes to Langford that included at least $235,000 in cash, loan pay offs, expensive clothing, and jewelry.

COOK COUNTY SHERIFF'S OFFICE. Charges were brought against 15 law enforcement officers in suburban Chicago, Illinois, in December 2008 for allegedly providing security for purported drug transactions. According to the Department of Justice (http://chicago.fbi.gov/dojpressrel/pressrel08/dec02_08.pdf), the accused were paid between $400 and $4,000 each by an undercover FBI agent who hired the officers to accompany him on staged transactions involving what the defendants understood to be large amounts of heroin and cocaine. Armed with their service weapons, the officers (10 corrections officers from the Cook County Sheriff's department, four Village of Harvey police officers, and one Chicago police officer) served as lookouts and were reportedly prepared to intervene on behalf of the "dealer" should on-duty police interfere in the drug transactions. At the time the charges were announced, Patrick J. Fitzgerald, the U.S. Attorney for the Northern District of Illinois, said: "Ideally, it should be hard to find one corrupt police officer, and it should never be easy to find 15 who allegedly used their guns and badges to protect people they believed were dealing drugs instead of arresting them."

ROD BLAGOJEVICH. The Illinois governor Rod Blagojevich (1956–) was impeached and removed from office in January 2009 following his arrest the previous month on federal charges of solicitation of bribery, mail fraud, and abuse of power. The accusations against Blagojevich included charges that he attempted to sell to the highest bidder the Senate seat vacated by Barack Obama (1961–) at the time of his election to the presidency; that Blagojevich demanded editorial favor with the *Chicago Tribune* in exchange for state funds for a large financial transaction being negotiated by the newspaper's parent company; and that he solicited bribes in the form of campaign contributions from various sources in exchange for favorable treatment in state business. On April 2, 2009, the federal charges against Blagojevich were expanded in a 19-count indictment that included wire fraud, attempted extortion, and racketeering conspiracy, among other charges. According to the Department of Justice (http://www.usdoj.gov/usao/iln/pr/chicago/2009/pr0402_01.pdf), Blagojevich conspired with his brother, Robert Blagojevich, his chief of staff, John Harris, and others in various influence-peddling and pay-to-play activities that comprised "a wide-ranging scheme to deprive the people of Illinois of honest government."

CHAPTER 6
CONTROLLING CRIME

Criminologists state that every criminal act involves three elements: motivation, resources, and opportunity. A person who is motivated to commit a crime and has the resources to do so (e.g., a weapon or the physical or mental prowess needed to carry out a crime) seeks criminal opportunities, such as victims or targets. Societies try to control crime by controlling these three primary elements of criminality.

Controlling crime in the United States is a multipronged effort that includes interrelated acts of prevention, deterrence, and punishment. Private citizens may take actions designed to prevent and deter crimes on their person and property. Examples include alarm systems, self-defense classes, and neighborhood watch programs. Taxpayer funds are used by governments to establish crime-controlling entities at the local, state, and federal levels for the overall good of society. There are four major governmental components that work together to control crime:

- Law enforcement agencies
- The legal system
- The judicial system
- The corrections system

LAW ENFORCEMENT AGENCIES

The primary role of law enforcement agencies is to investigate crimes, gather evidence, and arrest suspected perpetrators. Agencies differ by geographic jurisdictions (e.g., federal, state, or local) and by enforcement responsibilities (e.g., the types of laws they enforce or the types of crimes they investigate).

Agencies and Employees

The vast majority of law enforcement in the United States is carried out by local agencies. The Federal Bureau of Investigation (FBI) tracks local law enforcement employment as part of its Uniform Crime Reporting (UCR) Pro-

gram. In 2007 the UCR Program reported the employee count of 14,676 city and county police agencies around the country. (See Table 6.1.) These agencies had just over 1 million full-time employees. Of these employees, 699,850 were law enforcement officers, such as police officers or sheriff deputies, and the remainder were civilian employees (e.g., receptionists or clerks). More than half of all local law enforcement employees worked for city governments, most for cities with populations of 250,000 or more.

As of February 2009, every state except Hawaii had a state police agency or highway patrol force. These officers patrol state highways and often provide law enforcement assistance to local agencies within their state, particularly those in rural areas or small towns.

The federal government has several law enforcement agencies with specific responsibilities. The largest agencies are:

- FBI
- U.S. Drug Enforcement Administration
- Bureau of Alcohol, Tobacco, Firearms, and Explosives
- U.S. Customs and Border Protection
- U.S. Immigration and Customs Enforcement
- U.S. Secret Service

The latter three agencies operate under the U.S. Department of Homeland Security.

OFFICERS KILLED IN THE LINE OF DUTY. Between 1998 and 2007 felons killed 549 federal, state, and local law enforcement officers. (See Table 6.2.) This excludes officers who were killed in the terrorist attacks of September 11, 2001. The largest number of officers (127) were feloniously killed during arrest situations. Another 110 of the officers were killed during ambushes, and 103 were killed during traffic pursuits or stops.

TABLE 6.1

Number of full-time law enforcement employees (officers and civilians) and number of law enforcement agencies, total and by jurisdiction size, 2007

Population group	Total law enforcement employees	Total officers	Total civilians	Number of agencies	2007 estimated population
Total agencies	1,017,954	699,850	318,104	14,676	285,866,466
Total cities	581,888	446,669	135,219	11,112	192,561,315
Group I (250,000 and over)	203,771	152,594	51,177	71	53,815,350
1,000,000 and over (Group I subset)	113,693	83,852	29,841	10	25,220,230
500,000 to 999,999 (Group I subset)	51,812	40,163	11,649	23	15,276,719
250,000 to 499,999 (Group I subset)	38,266	28,579	9,687	38	13,318,401
Group II (100,000 to 249,999)	69,425	52,329	17,096	181	27,270,252
Group III (50,000 to 99,999)	68,944	53,271	15,673	441	30,331,106
Group IV (25,000 to 49,999)	64,503	50,728	13,775	806	27,684,136
Group V (10,000 to 24,999)	70,372	56,134	14,238	1,826	28,984,708
Group VI (under 10,000)	104,873	81,613	23,260	7,787	24,475,763
Metropolitan counties	301,088	173,546	127,542	1,333	65,514,896
Nonmetropolitan counties	134,978	79,635	55,343	2,231	27,790,255
Suburban area*	471,974	302,867	169,107	7,594	121,917,604

*Suburban area includes law enforcement agencies in cities with less than 50,000 inhabitants and county law enforcement agencies that are within a Metropolitan Statistical Area. Suburban area excludes all metropolitan agencies associated with a principal city. The agencies associated with suburban areas also appear in other groups within this table.

SOURCE: Adapted from "Table 74. Full-Time Law Enforcement Employees, by Population Group, Percent Male and Female, 2007," in *Crime in the United States, 2007*, U.S. Department of Justice, Federal Bureau of Investigation, September 2008, http://www.fbi.gov/ucr/cius2007/data/table_74.html (accessed November 24, 2008)

Key Law Enforcement Agency Components

Even though law enforcement agencies differ in their geographic and criminal jurisdictions, there are some components that are considered key to modern crime control, particularly at the local level. These components are neighborhood patrols, detectives, and forensic science.

Local law enforcement agencies may assign uniformed officers to regularly patrol specific neighborhoods for the purpose of developing relationships with the residents and business owners in the area. These officers are known informally as "beat cops," because each officer patrols a particular "beat" within the community. The use of beat cops is an example of community policing, whereby law enforcement agencies seek to forge a cooperative bond with people in the community to better fight crime.

Community policing was commonly practiced in the United States in the early part of the twentieth century. However, beginning in the 1950s and 1960s police departments shifted beat cops from their foot patrols to patrol cars so that larger areas could be covered. Eventually law enforcement agencies became almost completely reactive—that is, they reacted after a crime was committed with officers dispatched in response to 911 calls. During the high-crime decades of the 1970s and 1980s, some criminologists began advocating a return to community policing. Joseph F. Ryan describes this evolution in "Community Policing and the Impact of the COPS Federal Grants: A Potential Tool in the Local War on Terrorism" (Joseph F. Ryan, ed., *Critical Issues in Crime and Justice*, 2003). Ryan notes that community policing was a key component of the Violent Crime Control and Law Enforce-

ment Act of 1994, which allocated billions of federal dollars for the hiring of more police officers and the development of community policing programs.

Community policing is an example of proactive policing. Proactive means taking action before a situation or event becomes a problem. Proactive policies are designed to prevent crimes from occurring in the first place. Activities designed to deter criminals include visible police patrols, such as beat cops regularly walking or driving around neighborhoods. Some jurisdictions install video cameras in public places, such as parks or street corners, to deter criminal activity. Local law enforcement agencies also work with private citizens and business owners to encourage the reporting of suspicious-acting people or situations that present opportunities to criminals.

Many law enforcement agencies also employ detectives. These are plainclothes officers specially trained to investigate particular crimes (such as homicides). Detectives interview witnesses and suspects, gather facts, examine records, and collect evidence. They may also participate in the apprehension of perpetrators.

Forensic science is the application of scientific knowledge and methods to solve crime. Forensic investigators (or criminalists) are employed by some law enforcement agencies. These specialists commonly investigate crime scenes where they collect and analyze physical evidence. They may perform deoxyribonucleic acid (DNA) or firearms analyses or conduct laboratory tests on blood, semen, hair, tissue, fibers, and other evidentiary materials associated with criminal acts.

TABLE 6.2

Number of law enforcement officers feloniously killed, 1998–2007

Circumstance	Total	1998	1999	2000	2001*	2002	2003	2004	2005	2006	2007
Number of victim officers											
Total	549	61	42	51	70	56	52	57	55	48	57
Disturbance call											
Total	91	16	5	8	13	9	10	10	7	8	5
Disturbance (bar fight, person with firearm, etc.)	41	7	4	4	5	4	5	1	2	6	3
Domestic disturbance (family quarrel, etc.)	50	9	1	4	8	5	5	9	5	2	2
Arrest situation											
Total	127	15	9	12	24	10	8	13	8	12	16
Burglary in progress/pursuing burglary suspect	11	0	0	3	3	0	1	2	1	0	1
Robbery in progress/pursuing robbery suspect	39	3	3	1	4	4	1	7	4	6	6
Drug-related matter	27	7	2	3	8	3	1	0	0	2	1
Attempting other arrest	50	5	4	5	9	3	5	4	3	4	8
Civil disorder (mass disobedience, riot, etc.)											
Total	0	0	0	0	0	0	0	0	0	0	0
Handling, transporting, custody of prisoner											
Total	16	4	2	2	2	0	2	1	1	1	1
Investigating suspicious person/circumstance											
Total	60	5	7	6	8	6	4	7	7	6	4
Ambush situation											
Total	110	10	6	10	9	17	9	15	8	10	16
Entrapment/premeditation	43	4	4	2	3	4	6	6	4	1	9
Unprovoked attack	67	6	2	8	6	13	3	9	4	9	7
Investigative activity (surveillance, search, interview, etc.)											
Total	7	0	0	0	0	0	2	0	4	0	1
Handling person with mental illness											
Total	12	0	0	0	3	4	0	2	2	1	0
Traffic pursuit/stop											
Total	103	10	8	13	8	10	14	6	15	8	11
Felony vehicle stop	38	5	4	4	5	6	4	0	5	0	5
Traffic violation stop	65	5	4	9	3	4	10	6	10	8	6
Tactical situation (barricaded offender, hostage taking, high-risk entry, etc.)											
Total	23	1	5	0	3	0	3	3	3	2	3

*The 72 deaths that resulted from the events of September 11, 2001, are not included in this table.

SOURCE: "Table 19. Law Enforcement Officers Feloniously Killed, Circumstance at Scene of Incident, 1998–2007," in *Law Enforcement Officers Killed and Assaulted, 2007,* U.S. Department of Justice, Federal Bureau of Investigation, October 2008, http://www.fbi.gov/ucr/killed/2007/data/table_19.html (accessed November 24, 2008)

Arrests

One of the most important aspects of crime control practiced by law enforcement agencies is the apprehension and arrest of suspected perpetrators. The FBI reports that in 2007 law enforcement agencies made 14.2 million arrests for all criminal infractions, excluding traffic violations. (See Table 6.3.)

The FBI notes that there were 597,447 arrests for violent crimes (murder, forcible rape, robbery and aggravated assault) and 1.6 million arrests for property crimes (burglary, larceny-theft, motor vehicle theft, and arson) in 2007. (See Table 6.3.) Of the arrests for specific offenses on which

the FBI collects statistics, the five crimes with the most arrests were:

- Drug abuse violations—1.8 million arrests
- Driving under the influence—1.4 million arrests
- Assaults, other than aggravated assaults—1.3 million arrests
- Larceny-theft—1.2 million arrests
- Disorderly conduct—709,105 arrests

AGE OF ARRESTEES. Age data were reported to the FBI in 2007 for nearly 10.7 million arrestees. Of this number,

TABLE 6.3

Estimated number of arrests, 2007

Total[a]	14,209,365
Murder and nonnegligent manslaughter	13,480
Forcible rape	23,307
Robbery	126,715
Aggravated assault	433,945
Burglary	303,853
Larceny-theft	1,172,762
Motor vehicle theft	118,231
Arson	15,242
Violent crime[b]	597,447
Property crime[b]	1,610,088
Other assaults	1,305,693
Forgery and counterfeiting	103,448
Fraud	252,873
Embezzlement	22,381
Stolen property; buying, receiving, possessing	122,061
Vandalism	291,575
Weapons; carrying, possessing, etc.	188,891
Prostitution and commercialized vice	77,607
Sex offenses (except forcible rape and prostitution)	83,979
Drug abuse violations	1,841,182
Gambling	12,161
Offenses against the family and children	122,812
Driving under the influence	1,427,494
Liquor laws	633,654
Drunkenness	589,402
Disorderly conduct	709,105
Vagrancy	33,666
All other offenses	3,931,965
Suspicion	2,176
Curfew and loitering law violations	143,002
Runaways	108,879

[a]Does not include suspicion.
[b]Violent crimes are offenses of murder and nonnegligent manslaughter, forcible rape, robbery, and aggravated assault. Property crimes are offenses of burglary, larceny-theft, motor vehicle theft, and arson.

SOURCE: "Table 29. Estimated Number of Arrests, United States, 2007," in *Crime in the United States, 2007*, U.S. Department of Justice, Federal Bureau of Investigation, September 2008, http://www.fbi.gov/ucr/cius2007/data/table_29.html (accessed October 3, 2008)

TABLE 6.4

Arrests of persons under 25 years of age, 2007

[11,936 agencies; 2007 estimated population 225,518,634]

Offense charged	Number of persons arrested		Percent of total all ages
	Total all ages	Under 25	Under 25
Total	**10,698,310**	**4,753,345**	**44.4**
Murder and nonnegligent manslaughter	10,082	5,084	50.4
Forcible rape	17,132	7,433	43.4
Robbery	96,720	62,542	64.7
Aggravated assault	327,137	129,264	39.5
Burglary	228,846	134,198	58.6
Larceny-theft	897,626	478,160	53.3
Motor vehicle theft	89,022	50,174	56.4
Arson	11,451	7,614	66.5
Violent crime[a]	451,071	204,323	45.3
Property crime[a]	1,226,945	670,146	54.6
Other assaults	983,964	413,165	42.0
Forgery and counterfeiting	78,005	24,739	31.7
Fraud	185,229	47,593	25.7
Embezzlement	17,015	7,871	46.3
Stolen property; buying, receiving, possessing	92,215	46,285	50.2
Vandalism	221,040	148,140	67.0
Weapons; carrying, possessing, etc.	142,745	83,152	58.3
Prostitution and commercialized vice	59,390	16,180	27.2
Sex offenses (except forcible rape and prostitution)	62,756	25,403	40.5
Drug abuse violations	1,386,394	636,465	45.9
Gambling	9,152	5,013	54.8
Offenses against the family and children	88,887	20,422	23.0
Driving under the influence	1,055,981	311,920	29.5
Liquor laws	478,671	373,174	78.0
Drunkenness	451,055	128,759	28.5
Disorderly conduct	540,270	300,984	55.7
Vagrancy	25,631	8,296	32.4
All other offenses (except traffic)	2,948,031	1,088,202	36.9
Suspicion	1,589	839	52.8
Curfew and loitering law violations	109,815	109,815	100.0
Runaways	82,459	82,459	100.0

[a]Violent crimes are offenses of murder and nonnegligent manslaughter, forcible rape, robbery, and aggravated assault. Property crimes are offenses of burglary, larceny-theft, motor vehicle theft, and arson.

SOURCE: Adapted from "Table 41. Arrests, of Persons under 15, 18, 21, and 25 Years of Age, 2007," in *Crime in the United States, 2007*, U.S. Department of Justice, Federal Bureau of Investigation, September 2008, http://www.fbi.gov/ucr/cius2007/data/table_41.html (accessed October 3, 2008)

4.8 million people arrested nationwide (44.4%) were under the age of 25. (See Table 6.4.) Among those arrestees for whom age is known, people under 25 years old accounted for more than three-quarters (78%) of those arrested for liquor law infractions and nearly two-thirds (67%) of those arrested for vandalism, robbery, or arson. People in this age group made up much lower percentages of those arrested for offenses against the family and children (23%), fraud (25.7%), drunkenness (28.5%), and driving under the influence (29.5%). Arrestees for these crimes were more often people older than 25 years of age.

Overall, people under 25 years old made up 45% of those arrested for violent crimes and 55% of those arrested for property crimes. Figure 6.1 provides a breakdown by age of arrestee in 2007. People aged 25 and older accounted for 56% of arrests for all crimes, 55% of arrests for violent crimes, and 45% of arrests for property crimes. People between the ages of 21 and 24 made up 15% of those arrested for all crimes, 15% of those arrested for violent crimes, and 12% of those arrested for property crimes.

People aged 18 to 20 made up 14% of all arrestees, 14% of arrestees for violent crimes, and 16% of arrestees for property crimes. Juveniles (people under the age of 18) accounted for 15% of those arrested for all crimes, 16% of those arrested for violent crimes, and 26% of those arrested for property crimes. Juvenile crime is discussed in more detail in Chapter 10.

GENDER OF ARRESTEES. A gender breakdown for all the arrests shown in Table 6.3 is not provided by the FBI. However, the FBI estimates that in 2007 male arrestees outnumbered female arrestees by a margin of more than three to one. Out of a total of 8.1 million arrests in 2007 for which sex information was reported, 6.1 million of those arrested were male and 1.9 million were female. (See Table 6.5.)

FIGURE 6.1

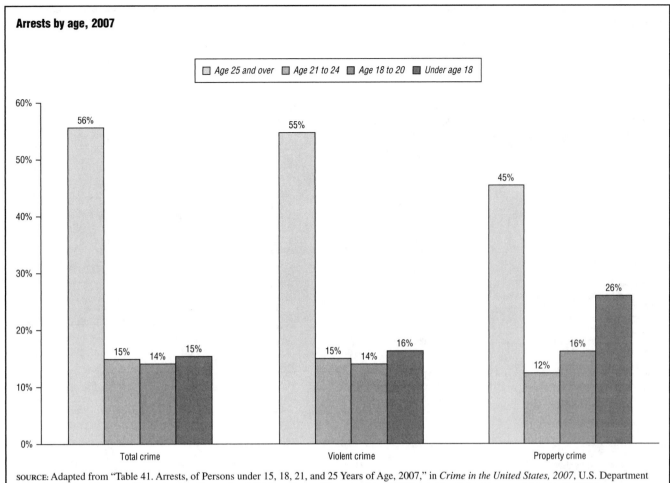

Arrests by age, 2007

SOURCE: Adapted from "Table 41. Arrests, of Persons under 15, 18, 21, and 25 Years of Age, 2007," in *Crime in the United States, 2007*, U.S. Department of Justice, Federal Bureau of Investigation, September 2008, http://www.fbi.gov/ucr/cius2007/data/table_41.html (accessed October 3, 2008)

From 1998 to 2007 the number of males arrested for all offenses declined by 6.1%, whereas female arrests for all offenses increased by 6.6%. (See Table 6.5.) Male arrests during this period increased for only three specifically named crimes: robbery (up 4.2%), drug abuse violations (up 15.3%), and embezzlement (up 22.7%). By contrast, female arrests between 1998 and 2007 increased for most crimes, particularly embezzlement (up 30.5%), driving under the influence (up 28.8%), and drug abuse violations (up 28.6%). Overall, the FBI notes in *Crime in the United States, 2007* (September 2008, http://www.fbi.gov/ucr/cius2007/index.html) that male arrests were down 10.5% for violent crimes and down 17.8% for property crimes between 1998 and 2007. Female arrests decreased by 1.1% for violent crimes and increased by 0.3% for property crimes during this same period.

RACE AND ETHNICITY OF ARRESTEES. Of the nearly 10.7 million arrests reported to the UCR that included race information in 2007, 69.7% of the arrestees were white and 28.2% were African-American. (See Table 6.6.) The remaining arrestees were Native American or Alaskan native (1.3%) and Asian-American or Pacific Islander (0.8%). Whites accounted for large percentages of those arrested for driving

under the influence (88.5%), liquor law violations (85.6%), and drunkenness (83.6%). African-American arrestees accounted for nearly three-fourths (74.4%) of all arrests for illegal gambling. In *Crime in the United States, 2007*, the FBI notes that whites made up 58.9% of arrests for violent crimes, whereas African-Americans accounted for 39%. Whites made up a larger percentage of those arrested for property crimes (67.9%) than did African-Americans (29.8%).

OFFENSES CLEARED BY ARREST OR EXCEPTIONAL MEANS. Table 6.7 shows the number and percentage of known offenses that were cleared by arrest or exceptional means during 2007. Offenses cleared by exceptional means are those for which there can be no arrest, such as in a murder-suicide, when the perpetrator is known to be deceased.

Because murder is considered the most serious crime, it receives the most police attention and, therefore, has the highest arrest rate of all felonies. In 2007, 61.2% of murders were cleared by arrest. (See Table 6.7.)

Making an arrest does not mean the alleged offender is guilty or will be convicted of the crime. Law enforcement agencies do not determine the guilt or innocence of

TABLE 6.5

Ten-year arrest trends, by sex, 1998–2007

[7,946 agencies; 2007 estimated population 171,876,948; 1998 estimated population 154,013,711]

Offense charged	Male Total			Female Total		
	1998	2007	Percent change	1998	2007	Percent change
Total[a]	6,550,864	6,150,145	−6.1	1,846,201	1,968,052	+6.6
Murder and nonnegligent manslaughter	7,342	6,519	−11.2	890	782	−12.1
Forcible rape	16,942	13,079	−22.8	206	133	−35.4
Robbery	61,410	64,004	+4.2	6,943	8,351	+20.3
Aggravated assault	234,040	202,588	−13.4	56,811	54,876	−3.4
Burglary	170,504	154,607	−9.3	25,192	27,945	+10.9
Larceny-thef	514,574	413,125	−19.7	276,511	275,912	−0.2
Motor vehicle theft	68,494	51,382	−25.0	12,431	11,384	−8.4
Arson	8,606	7,685	−10.7	1,449	1,409	−2.8
Violent crime[b]	319,734	286,190	−10.5	64,850	64,142	−1.1
Property crime[b]	762,178	626,799	−17.8	315,583	316,650	+0.3
Other assaults	593,042	560,655	−5.5	174,996	193,625	+10.6
Forgery and counterfeiting	41,508	36,217	−12.7	26,362	22,615	−14.2
Fraud	114,751	82,340	−28.2	99,049	65,645	−33.7
Embezzlement	5,584	6,849	+22.7	5,531	7,216	+30.5
Stolen property; buying, receiving, possessing	66,132	57,865	−12.5	12,239	15,039	+22.9
Vandalism	147,331	139,748	−5.1	26,286	29,067	+10.6
Weapons; carrying, possessing, etc.	100,973	97,822	−3.1	8,560	8,258	−3.5
Prostitution and commercialized vice	20,745	11,485	−44.6	29,337	27,596	−5.9
Sex offenses (except forcible rape and prostitution)	48,658	42,369	−12.9	3,869	3,502	−9.5
Drug abuse violations	723,435	833,941	+15.3	154,920	199,262	+28.6
Gambling	4,568	2,769	−39.4	499	520	+4.2
Offenses against the family and children	67,843	53,754	−20.8	17,980	17,551	−2.4
Driving under the influence	676,911	626,371	−7.5	126,119	162,493	+28.8
Liquor laws	294,553	242,820	−17.6	80,456	89,411	+11.1
Drunkenness	409,100	345,502	−15.5	59,696	65,081	+9.0
Disorderly conduct	293,691	261,327	−11.0	93,843	97,101	+3.5
Vagrancy	14,281	12,761	−10.6	3,713	3,627	−2.3
All other offenses (except traffic)	1,732,271	1,744,417	+0.7	453,592	522,728	+15.2
Suspicion	2,766	1,031	−62.7	697	268	−61.5
Curfew and loitering law violations	73,163	51,116	−30.1	31,813	22,101	−30.5
Runaways	40,412	27,028	−33.1	56,908	34,822	−38.8

[a]Does not include suspicion.

[b]Violent crimes are offenses of murder and nonnegligent manslaughter, forcible rape, robbery, and aggravated assault. Property crimes are offenses of burglary, larceny-theft, motor vehicle theft, and arson.

SOURCE: Adapted from "Table 33. Ten-Year Arrest Trends, by Sex, 1998–2007," in *Crime in the United States, 2007*, U.S. Department of Justice, Federal Bureau of Investigation, September 2008, http://www.fbi.gov/ucr/cius2007/data/table_33.html (accessed October 3, 2008)

suspected perpetrators. That task is left up to the judicial system. Figure 6.2 shows the percent of arrested adults that were convicted in state courts on felony charges in 2004. More than two-thirds of adults arrested for murder and nonnegligent homicide (68%) and drug trafficking (71%) were convicted in state courts on felony charges. Roughly half of adults arrested on state charges for rape (56%), robbery (46%), and burglary (44%) received convictions in 2004. Much smaller percentages were reported for adults arrested for aggravated assault (25%) and motor vehicle theft (16%).

THE LEGAL SYSTEM

Even though *mala in se* (morally wrong or inherently wrong) behaviors are universally condemned as wrong, punishments for these crimes can vary significantly between societies. Many of the legal decisions concerning *mala in se* crimes have evolved over time through what is known as common law. Common law refers to the legal precedents set though court decisions over time, as opposed to laws passed by legislative bodies. The U.S. legal system relies heavily on common-law decisions dating back to the legal system that was used in England before the establishment of the United States.

People enter the U.S. criminal justice system through a variety of means. They may be issued a citation for a traffic violation witnessed by a law enforcement officer. They may be arrested for a more serious crime by a law enforcement officer who has probable cause to believe they committed a crime. They may be arrested due to issuance of a warrant for their arrest by a court. An arrest warrant is a legal document signed by a judge or a magistrate who believes there is compelling evidence that the person named in the warrant has committed a particular crime.

A person charged with a crime falls under the legal and judicial system of the government body with appropriate jurisdiction, for example, the city, county, state, or federal government. These systems may differ in structure and mode

TABLE 6.6

Arrests by race, 2007

[11,929 agencies; 2007 estimated population 225,477,173]

	Total arrests					Percent distribution[a]				
Offense charged	Total	White	Black	American Indian or Alaskan Native	Asian or Pacific Islander	Total	White	Black	American Indian or Alaskan Native	Asian or Pacific Islander
Total	10,656,710	7,426,278	3,003,060	142,969	84,403	100.0	69.7	28.2	1.3	0.8
Murder and nonnegligent manslaughter	10,067	4,789	5,078	99	101	100.0	47.6	50.4	1.0	1.0
Forcible rape	17,058	10,984	5,708	213	153	100.0	64.4	33.5	1.2	0.9
Robbery	96,584	40,573	54,774	602	635	100.0	42.0	56.7	0.6	0.7
Aggravated assault	326,277	208,762	109,985	4,374	3,156	100.0	64.0	33.7	1.3	1.0
Burglary	228,346	156,442	68,052	2,191	1,661	100.0	68.5	29.8	1.0	0.7
Larceny-theft	894,215	610,607	261,730	11,885	9,993	100.0	68.3	29.3	1.3	1.1
Motor vehicle theft	88,843	55,229	31,765	1,041	808	100.0	62.2	35.8	1.2	0.9
Arson	11,400	8,510	2,666	119	105	100.0	74.6	23.4	1.0	0.9
Violent crime[b]	449,986	265,108	175,545	5,288	4,045	100.0	58.9	39.0	1.2	0.9
Property crime[b]	1,222,804	830,788	364,213	15,236	12,567	100.0	67.9	29.8	1.2	1.0
Other assaults	980,512	641,991	316,217	14,028	8,276	100.0	65.5	32.3	1.4	0.8
Forgery and counterfeiting	77,757	54,136	22,460	414	747	100.0	69.6	28.9	0.5	1.0
Fraud	184,446	127,377	54,575	1,369	1,125	100.0	69.1	29.6	0.7	0.6
Embezzlement	16,954	10,813	5,818	95	228	100.0	63.8	34.3	0.6	1.3
Stolen property; buying, receiving, possessing	91,937	57,870	32,570	735	762	100.0	62.9	35.4	0.8	0.8
Vandalism	220,055	166,201	48,642	3,340	1,872	100.0	75.5	22.1	1.5	0.9
Weapons; carrying, possessing, etc.	142,369	82,311	57,745	1,061	1,252	100.0	57.8	40.6	0.7	0.9
Prostitution and commercialized vice	59,307	34,190	23,251	550	1,316	100.0	57.6	39.2	0.9	2.2
Sex offenses (except forcible rape and prostitution)	62,586	45,961	15,372	633	620	100.0	73.4	24.6	1.0	1.0
Drug abuse violations	1,382,783	880,742	485,054	8,872	8,115	100.0	63.7	35.1	0.6	0.6
Gambling	9,141	2,199	6,805	20	117	100.0	24.1	74.4	0.2	1.3
Offenses against the family and children	88,437	60,124	26,090	1,686	537	100.0	68.0	29.5	1.9	0.6
Driving under the influence	1,050,803	929,453	97,472	14,251	9,627	100.0	88.5	9.3	1.4	0.9
Liquor laws	474,726	406,221	49,434	14,422	4,649	100.0	85.6	10.4	3.0	1.0
Drunkenness	449,117	375,440	62,278	8,891	2,508	100.0	83.6	13.9	2.0	0.6
Disorderly conduct	537,809	342,169	183,810	8,376	3,454	100.0	63.6	34.2	1.6	0.6
Vagrancy	25,584	15,493	9,474	501	116	100.0	60.6	37.0	2.0	0.5
All other offenses (except traffic)	2,936,233	1,969,862	905,656	40,546	20,169	100.0	67.1	30.8	1.4	0.7
Suspicion	1,571	904	649	4	14	100.0	57.5	41.3	0.3	0.9
Curfew and loitering law violations	109,575	69,950	37,532	964	1,129	100.0	63.8	34.3	0.9	1.0
Runaways	82,218	56,975	22,398	1,687	1,158	100.0	69.3	27.2	2.1	1.4

[a]Because of rounding, the percentages may not add to 100.0.
[b]Violent crimes are offenses of murder and nonnegligent manslaughter, forcible rape, robbery, and aggravated assault. Property crimes are offenses of burglary, larceny-theft, motor vehicle theft, and arson.

SOURCE: "Table 43A. Arrests, by Race, 2007," in *Crime in the United States, 2007*, U.S. Department of Justice, Federal Bureau of Investigation, September 2008, http://www.fbi.gov/ucr/cius2007/data/table_43.html (accessed October 3, 2008)

of operation, but under U.S. law they all must provide certain legal rights to arrested people.

The Rights of the Arrested

People placed under arrest (with or without a warrant) must be told their Miranda rights before being questioned about their alleged crime by law enforcement. Miranda rights stem from the 1966 U.S. Supreme Court decision *Miranda v. Arizona* (384 U.S. 436). The court ruled that arrested individuals must be told about their constitutional right to an attorney and against self-incrimination before they are subjected to any questioning about the crime. Even though the so-called Miranda warning takes several forms, it must cover the following basic concepts:

- The arrestee has the right to remain silent during police questioning

- Anything the arrestee says to police can be used against him or her at trial

- The arrestee has the right to an attorney

- If the arrestee cannot afford an attorney, one will be appointed for him or her at the government's expense

In addition, arrested individuals have the right to know the charges against them and to see any arrest warrants used to make the arrest. According to the American Bar Association, in "Arrest Procedures" (2008, http://www.abanet.org/publiced/courts/arrestprocedure.html), a person arrested without a warrant can only be held by the police for a limited time period (typically 48 hours) before making his or her first court appearance, or arraignment, before a judge or magistrate. The granting of bail is not specifically a right, but most arrestees are given a bail hearing during which a court sets the

TABLE 6.7

Percent of offenses cleared by arrest or exceptional means, 2007

Population group		Violent crime	Murder and nonnegligent manslaughter	Forcible rape	Robbery	Aggravated assault	Property crime	Burglary	Larceny-theft	Motor vehicle theft	Arson*	Number of agencies	2007 estimated population
Total all agencies:	Offenses known	1,227,330	14,811	78,740	383,749	750,030	8,716,315	1,946,803	5,774,598	994,914	62,248	14,108	262,114,256
	Percent cleared by arrest	44.5	61.2	40.0	25.9	54.1	16.5	12.4	18.6	12.6	18.3		

*Not all agencies submit reports for arson to the FBI. As a result, the number of reports the FBI uses to compute the percent of offenses cleared for arson is less than the number it uses to compute the percent of offenses cleared for all other offenses.

SOURCE: Adapted from "Table 25. Percent of Offenses Cleared by Arrest or Exceptional Means, by Population Group, 2007," in *Crime in the United States, 2007,* U.S. Department of Justice, Federal Bureau of Investigation, September 2008, http://www.fbi.gov/ucr/cius2007/data/table_25.html (accessed October 3, 2008)

FIGURE 6.2

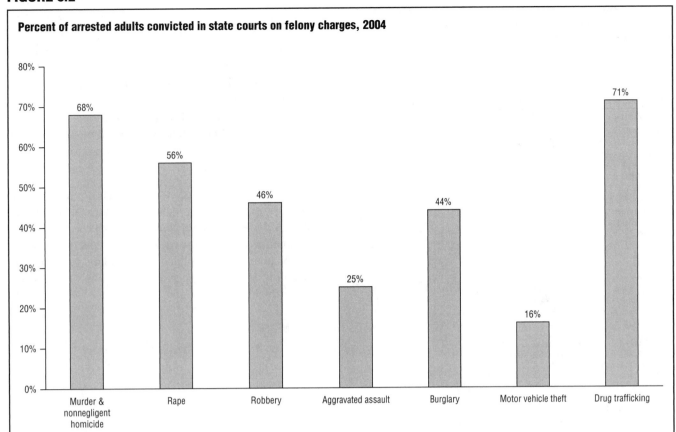

Percent of arrested adults convicted in state courts on felony charges, 2004

SOURCE: Adapted from Matthew R. Durose, "Table 1.8. Felony Convictions and Sentences in State Courts Relative to the Number of Arrests, 2004," in *State Court Sentencing of Convicted Felons, 2004—Statistical Tables*, U.S. Department of Justice, Office of Justice Programs, Bureau of Justice Statistics, July 25, 2007, http://www.ojp.usdoj.gov/bjs/pub/html/scscf04/tables/scs04108tab.htm (accessed December 2, 2008)

monetary amount for bail. The U.S. Constitution prohibits excessive bail. It also guarantees the defendant the right to a speedy trial and prohibits the imposition of cruel and unusual punishment.

The Role of Prosecutors

Government jurisdictions have their own unique legal systems. Each system is typically headed by a public official. At the state level, this official may be called the state attorney. At the lower levels of government, such as counties or cities, officials may be called district attorneys, county or city attorneys, or simply prosecutors. A prosecutor represents the legal authority of his or her geographical area and supervises the legal prosecution of suspected criminals. These cases are often referred to prosecutors' offices by law enforcement agencies. Some states also use grand juries to file criminal charges against suspected criminals. Grand juries consist of local citizens summoned by a court to serve for a specified period of time. They do not determine the guilt or innocence of the accused, rather they determine if there is enough evidence to bind over the accused to stand trial. If so, the grand jury issues a formal charge called an indictment.

Some district attorneys are elected into office, whereas others are appointed by higher public officials. A prosecu-

tor acts on behalf of the people within a jurisdiction to ensure that its criminal laws are enforced and that criminals are prosecuted. Prosecution for criminal activity sometimes proceeds to court, where the guilt or innocence of the defendant is determined during a trial. The judicial system tries perpetrators in a court of law and, if they are found guilty, sentences them to a period of incarceration or some other form of punishment, restitution (an amount of money that is set by a court to be paid to the victim of a crime for property losses or injuries caused by the crime), and/or treatment.

Not all criminal cases proceed to trial. In fact, many are settled through alternative means, such as plea bargains.

PLEA BARGAINS. In a plea bargain a prosecutor (acting on behalf of the people of the jurisdiction) and the defendant's attorney reach an agreement about how a case should be settled before it goes to trial. A typical example involves an offer from a prosecutor for the alleged criminal to plead guilty to a lesser charge than the one originally filed against him or her. Another common plea bargain occurs when a defendant agrees to plead guilty to a charge in exchange for a recommendation by the prosecutor for a lighter sentence than would be expected to result from a guilty verdict if the

TABLE 6.8

Distribution of means by which felons were convicted in state courts, by offense, 2004

Most serious conviction offense	Total	Percent of felons convicted by —			
		Trial			Guilty plea
		Total	Jury	Bench	
All offenses	100%	5	2	3	95
Violent offenses	100%	9	6	3	91
Murder[a]	100%	31	27	4	69
Sexual assault[b]	100%	11	8	3	89
Rape	100%	17	13	3	83
Other sexual assault	100%	8	5	4	92
Robbery	100%	8	6	2	92
Aggravated assault	100%	7	4	4	93
Other violent[c]	100%	6	4	2	94
Property offenses	100%	4	1	3	96
Burglary	100%	5	2	3	95
Larceny[d]	100%	4	1	3	96
Motor vehicle theft	100%	3	2	1	97
Fraud[e]	100%	4	1	4	96
Drug offenses	100%	4	2	2	96
Possession	100%	4	1	3	96
Trafficking	100%	4	2	2	96
Weapon offenses	100%	7	3	4	93
Other offenses[f]	100%	4	1	3	96

Note: Detail may not add to the total because of rounding.
This table is based on an estimated 582,480 cases.
[a]Includes nonnegligent manslaughter.
[b]Includes rape.
[c]Includes offenses such as negligent manslaughter and kidnapping.
[d]Includes motor vehicle theft.
[e]Includes forgery and embezzlement.
[f]Composed of nonviolent offenses such as receiving stolen property and vandalism.

SOURCE: Matthew R. Durose, "Table 4.1. Distribution of Types of Felony Convictions in State Courts, by Offense, 2004," in *State Court Sentencing of Convicted Felons, 2004—Statistical Tables*, U.S. Department of Justice, Office of Justice Programs, Bureau of Justice Statistics, July 25, 2007, http://www.ojp.usdoj.gov/bjs/pub/html/scscf04/tables/scs04401tab.htm (accessed December 2, 2008)

case went to trial. Prosecutors are motivated to negotiate plea bargains, because criminal trials can be long and costly, and their outcomes are not certain. Defendants may choose to plea bargain to avoid the publicity and legal expense of a trial and the likely harsher sentence that will result from a guilty verdict. The American Bar Association states in "Plea Bargaining" (2008, http://www.abanet.org/publiced/courts/plea bargaining.html) that plea bargains resolve most of the criminal cases in most jurisdictions in the United States.

Table 6.8 shows that 95% of all felons convicted in state courts in 2004 pleaded guilty, presumably as a result of plea bargains. Only 5% of state felony cases went to trial in 2004. Of these, 3% were tried by the bench (i.e., by a judge) and 2% were tried by juries. The percentage of felons convicted in 2004 by a guilty plea exceeded 90% for all felonies except murder (69% convicted by a guilty plea) and rape (83% convicted by a guilty plea).

THE JUDICIARY SYSTEM

The judiciary system includes all criminal courts and the judges and juries that operate within them. There are two main levels of the judiciary system in the United States:

federal courts and state/local courts. In "United States District Courts" (December 30, 2008, http://www.uscourts.gov/districtcourts.html), U.S. Courts states that the federal judiciary system includes 94 U.S. judicial districts organized into 12 regional circuits. (See Figure 6.3; note that the 12th circuit is the District of Columbia.) The district courts serve as trial courts in the federal system. Each circuit has a U.S. court of appeals. The U.S. Supreme Court is the highest court in the United States. It hears a limited number of cases each year that primarily address issues related to federal law or the U.S. Constitution.

Every state has its own court system. These systems differ by state, but in general they include local or municipal courts, county-level courts, district courts, state appeals courts, and state supreme courts. Figure 6.4 shows the court structure for Texas. Note that municipal and county courts have jurisdiction over misdemeanors, whereas district courts have jurisdiction over felony criminal cases.

Sentences

One of the roles of the judiciary system is to impose sentences on convicted criminals. Most convicted felons are sentenced to incarceration. Nonincarceration sentences include probation (a period of intense supervision) and other alternatives, such as a fine or community service.

Every two years the U.S. Department of Justice (DOJ) publishes statistics on the sentencing of convicted felons in state and federal courts. The most recent report, *State Court Sentencing of Convicted Felons, 2004—Statistical Tables* (July 2007, http://www.ojp.usdoj.gov/bjs/abstract/scscf04st.htm) by Matthew R. Durose of the Bureau of Justice Statistics (BJS), includes data through 2004. There were over 1.1 million felony convictions in state and federal courts in 2004. (See Table 6.9.) Only 5.8% of the convictions were in federal court. The vast majority (94.2%) were in state courts. At the state and federal levels, 70% and 85%, respectively, of convicted felons were sentenced to prison or jail. The mean (average) maximum sentence length for felons sentenced to incarceration was 37 months at the state level and 61 months at the federal level. Average maximum incarceration lengths were much higher for the most serious violent crimes, such as murder, rape, and robbery.

Table 6.10 shows the percent of felons sentenced in 2004 by state courts to prison, jail, probation, or other nonincarceration options. Note that only the most severe penalty is counted for felons who received a combination of sentences. Overall, 70% of state-convicted felons (40% in prisons and 30% in jails) were sentenced to incarceration. Another 28% of state-convicted felons were sentenced to probation. Only 2% received another type of sentence, such as a fine or community service. The incarceration rate was much higher for felons convicted of the most violent offenses, such as murder and nonnegligent manslaughter. Of these felons, 92% (89% in prisons and 3% in jails) received a sentence

FIGURE 6.3

Map of the geographical boundaries of the U.S. Courts of Appeal and U.S. District Courts

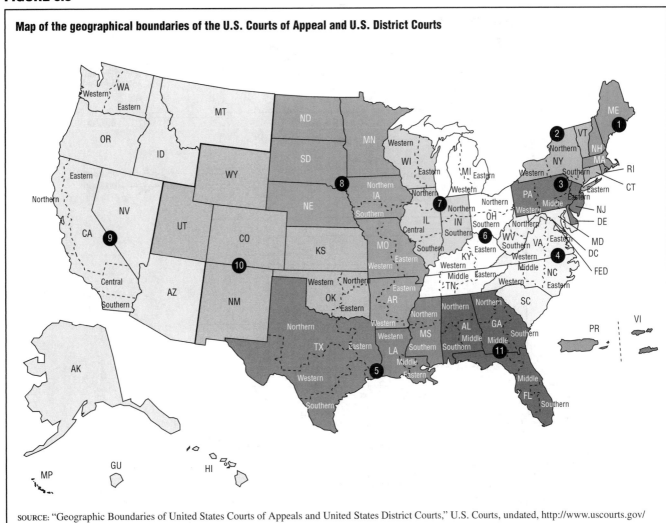

SOURCE: "Geographic Boundaries of United States Courts of Appeals and United States District Courts," U.S. Courts, undated, http://www.uscourts.gov/images/CircuitMap.pdf (accessed December 1, 2008)

of incarceration, whereas only 7% received probation and 1% were given another nonincarceration sentence.

Truth-in-Sentencing

During the 1970s and early 1980s the United States experienced a historically high crime rate. Politicians responded to public pressure with policies aiming to "get tough on crime," including new sentencing guidelines that imposed mandatory minimum sentences and other reforms that imposed stiffer penalties for certain offenses. Sentence reforms enacted by states came to be known as "truth-in-sentencing" statutes. The first such statute was enacted by Washington State in 1984. Also that year, Congress established the U.S. Sentencing Commission (USSC) in the Sentencing Reform Act. Congress charged this new federal agency with developing sentencing guidelines for federal courts. The Sentencing Reform Act was the federal enactment of truth-in-sentencing.

Truth-in-sentencing is intended to tell the public that a sentence announced by the court will actually be served—rather than the criminal serving only some small fraction of

the sentence, the prisoner being released on parole, or the individual having the sentence commuted to probation and serving no time at all. Under truth-in-sentencing statutes, offenders are required to spend substantial portions of their sentences in prison.

With truth-in-sentencing came the distinction between determinate and indeterminate sentencing. Determinate sentencing takes decision-making power away from parole boards, fixes the term to be served, and provides or denies the means to shorten the sentence by good behavior or other "earned" time. Indeterminate sentencing gives parole boards the authority to release offenders at their option after a process of review. Part of the truth-in-sentencing statutes is mandatory minimum sentences for specific offenses and circumstances. Guidelines define the range of sentences the judge may apply, which are governed by the offense and the prior history of the offender (e.g., first-time or repeat-offender, severity of the offense, etc.).

Setting uniform sentences for offenses and requiring that fixed proportions of them be served by those convicted

FIGURE 6.4

Court structure of Texas, September 15, 2008

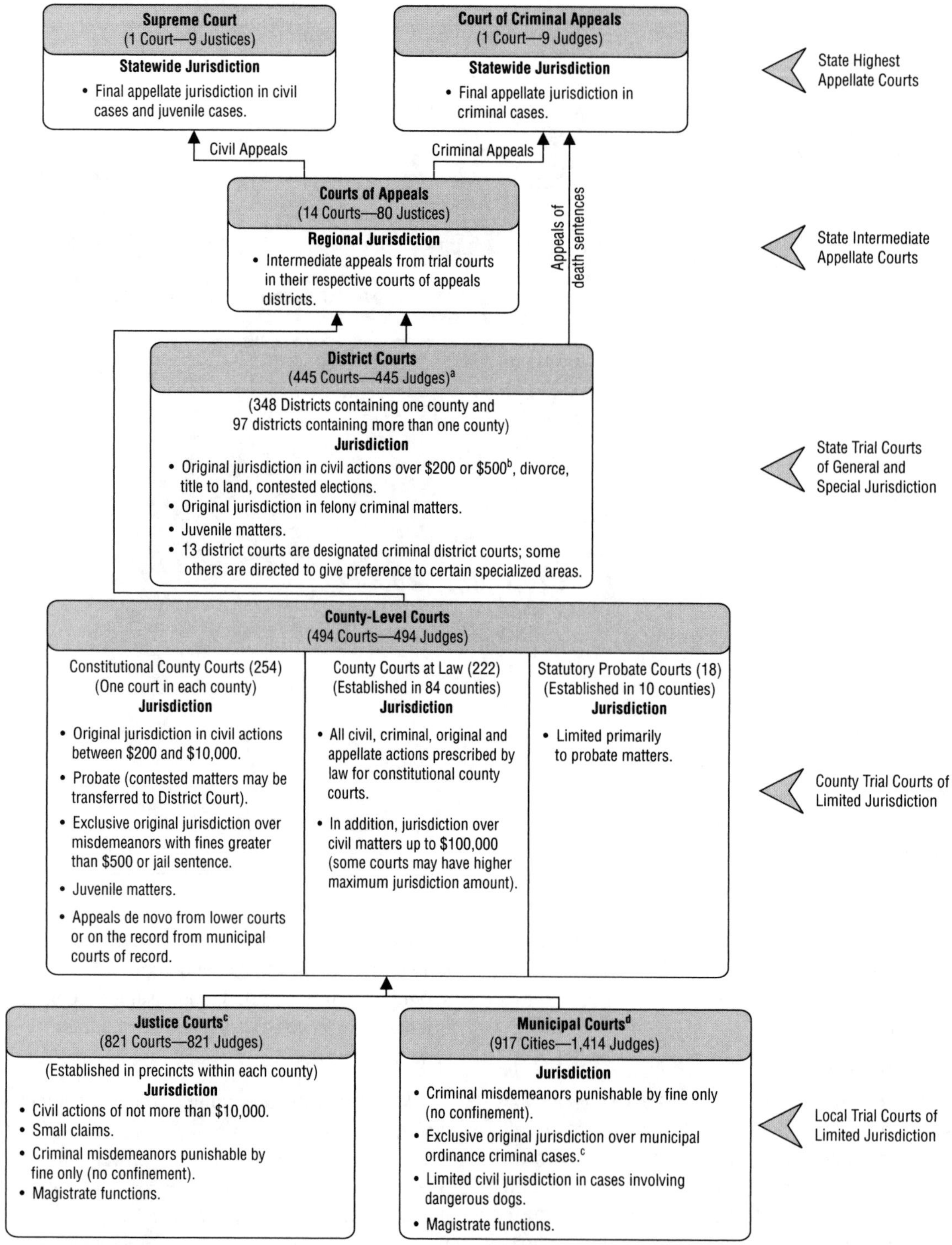

Supreme Court
(1 Court—9 Justices)
Statewide Jurisdiction
• Final appellate jurisdiction in civil cases and juvenile cases.

Court of Criminal Appeals
(1 Court—9 Judges)
Statewide Jurisdiction
• Final appellate jurisdiction in criminal cases.

State Highest Appellate Courts

Civil Appeals

Criminal Appeals

Appeals of death sentences

Courts of Appeals
(14 Courts—80 Justices)
Regional Jurisdiction
• Intermediate appeals from trial courts in their respective courts of appeals districts.

State Intermediate Appellate Courts

District Courts
(445 Courts—445 Judges)[a]

(348 Districts containing one county and 97 districts containing more than one county)
Jurisdiction
• Original jurisdiction in civil actions over $200 or $500[b], divorce, title to land, contested elections.
• Original jurisdiction in felony criminal matters.
• Juvenile matters.
• 13 district courts are designated criminal district courts; some others are directed to give preference to certain specialized areas.

State Trial Courts of General and Special Jurisdiction

County-Level Courts
(494 Courts—494 Judges)

Constitutional County Courts (254) (One court in each county) **Jurisdiction**	County Courts at Law (222) (Established in 84 counties) **Jurisdiction**	Statutory Probate Courts (18) (Established in 10 counties) **Jurisdiction**
• Original jurisdiction in civil actions between $200 and $10,000. • Probate (contested matters may be transferred to District Court). • Exclusive original jurisdiction over misdemeanors with fines greater than $500 or jail sentence. • Juvenile matters. • Appeals de novo from lower courts or on the record from municipal courts of record.	• All civil, criminal, original and appellate actions prescribed by law for constitutional county courts. • In addition, jurisdiction over civil matters up to $100,000 (some courts may have higher maximum jurisdiction amount).	• Limited primarily to probate matters.

County Trial Courts of Limited Jurisdiction

Justice Courts[e]
(821 Courts—821 Judges)

(Established in precincts within each county)
Jurisdiction
• Civil actions of not more than $10,000.
• Small claims.
• Criminal misdemeanors punishable by fine only (no confinement).
• Magistrate functions.

Municipal Courts[d]
(917 Cities—1,414 Judges)

Jurisdiction
• Criminal misdemeanors punishable by fine only (no confinement).
• Exclusive original jurisdiction over municipal ordinance criminal cases.[c]
• Limited civil jurisdiction in cases involving dangerous dogs.
• Magistrate functions.

Local Trial Courts of Limited Jurisdiction

[a]As of September 15, 2008 there were 445 district courts. The 80th Legislature authorized the creation of 3 additional new courts as of September 1, 2007. However, these courts had yet to be implemented.
[b]The dollar amount is currently unclear.
[c]All justice courts and most municipal courts are not courts of record. Appeals from these courts are by trial de novo in the county-level courts, and in some instances in the district courts.
[d]Some municipal courts are courts of record—appeals from those courts are taken on the record to the county-level courts.
[e]An offense that arises under a municipal ordinance is punishable by a fine not to exceed: (1) $2,000 for ordinances that govern fire safety, zoning, and public health or (2) $500 for all others.

SOURCE: "Court Structure of Texas," Texas Office of Court Administration, September 15, 2008, http://www.courts.state.tx.us/oca/pdf/Court_Structure_Chart.pdf (accessed December 1, 2008).

TABLE 6.9

Comparison of felony convictions in state and federal courts, 2004

Most serious conviction offense	Felony convictions			Federal felony convictions as percent of total	Percent of felons sentenced to prison or jail—		Mean maximum sentence length (in months) for felons sentenced to prison or jail—	
	Total	State	Federal		State	Federal	State	Federal
All offenses	**1,145,438**	**1,078,920**	**66,518**	**5.8%**	**70%**	**85%**	**37mo**	**61 mo**
Violent offenses	197,138	194,570	2,568	1.3	78	94	68	96
Murder[a]	8,590	8,400	190	2.2	92	92	232	111
Sexual assault[b]	33,605	33,190	415	1.2	81	94	93	112
Rape	12,409	12,310	99	0.8	89	88	123	141
Other sexual assault	21,196	20,880	316	1.5	76	96	72	105
Robbery	40,230	38,850	1,380	3.4	87	98	86	105
Aggravated assault	94,845	94,380	465	0.5	73	83	41	45
Other violent[c]	19,868	19,750	118	0.6	73	82	38	88
Property offenses	322,501	310,680	11,821	3.7	68	60	29	26
Burglary	93,923	93,870	53	0.1	75	83	40	28
Larceny[d]	120,705	119,340	1,365	1.1	69	54	21	31
Motor vehicle theft	16,968	16,910	58	0.3	86	67	17	27
Other theft	103,737	102,430	1,307	1.3	67	53	22	31
Fraud	107,873	97,470	10,403	9.6	60	60	26	26
Fraud[e]	57,883	48,560	9,323	16.1	56	60	24	26
Forgery	49,990	48,910	1,080	2.2	63	64	28	24
Drug offenses	387,322	362,850	24,472	6.3	67	93	31	84
Possession	163,112	161,090	2,022	1.2	64	90	23	82
Trafficking	224,210	201,760	22,450	10	69	93	37	84
Weapon offenses	41,092	33,010	8,082	19.7	72	93	32	84
Other offenses[f]	197,385	177,810	19,575	9.9	69	86	24	30

[a]Includes nonnegligent manslaughter.
[b]Includes rape.
[c]Includes offenses such as negligent manslaughter and kidnapping.
[d]Includes motor vehicle theft.
[e]Includes embezzlement.
[f]Composed of nonviolent offenses such as receiving stolen property and vandalism.

SOURCE: Matthew R. Durose, "Table 1.10. Comparison of Felony Convictions in State and Federal Courts, 2004," in *State Court Sentencing of Convicted Felons, 2004—Statistical Tables*, U.S. Department of Justice, Office of Justice Programs, Bureau of Justice Statistics, July 25, 2007, http://www.ojp.usdoj.gov/bjs/pub/html/scscf04/tables/scs04110tab.htm (accessed December 2, 2008)

put pressure on prison and jail capacities. In response, Congress passed the Violent Crime Control and Law Enforcement Act of 1994. The act gave the federal government the authority to offer grants to states to expand their prison capacity if they imposed truth-in-sentencing requirements on violent offenders. To qualify for the grants, the states had to pass laws requiring that serious violent offenders serve at least 85% of their imposed sentences in prison.

Federal Sentencing Guidelines

The Sentencing Reform Act of 1984 is the federal approach to truth-in-sentencing, or determinate sentencing. The USSC lists in *Fifteen Years of Guidelines Sentencing* (November 2004, http://www.ussc.gov/15_year/15year.htm) the goals of the act:

1. Elimination of unwarranted disparity

2. Transparency, certainty, and fairness

3. Proportionate punishment

4. Crime control through deterrence, incapacitation, and the rehabilitation of offenders

The act was designed to eliminate the unregulated power of federal judges to impose sentences of indeterminate length. Because of this unregulated power, some people were convicted of the same crime but sentenced by different judges to receive entirely different terms of incarceration. The USSC developed federal guidelines to give a range of sentencing options to federal judges while guaranteeing minimum and maximum sentencing lengths.

The USSC continues to update the guidelines as laws administered by the federal courts are changed or new laws are passed. The USSC also issues supplemental volumes. As of April 2009, the most recent edition of the guidelines is *Guidelines Manual* (November 1, 2008, http://www.ussc.gov/2008guid/GL2008.pdf).

At the core of the guidelines are offenses as defined by federal statutes. The USSC assigns an offense level to each offense, known as the base offense level, which ranges from 1 to 43. The lowest actual offense for which the USSC has a level is trespass. Trespass is level 4. First-degree murder has a base offense level of 43. Based on the circumstances associated with an offense, additional levels can be

TABLE 6.10

Distribution of types of felony sentences imposed in state courts, by offense, 2004

| | | Percent of felons sentenced to — | | | |
| | | Incarceration | | Nonincarceration | |
Most serious conviction offense	Total	Prison	Jail	Probation	Other
All offenses	**100%**	**40**	**30**	**28**	**2**
Violent offenses	100%	54	24	20	2
Murder[a]	100%	89	3	7	1
Sexual assault[b]	100%	61	20	17	2
Rape	100%	69	20	9	2
Other sexual assault	100%	57	19	22	2
Robbery	100%	72	15	12	1
Aggravated assault	100%	43	30	26	2
Other violent[c]	100%	41	32	25	2
Property offenses	100%	37	31	30	2
Burglary	100%	49	26	24	1
Larceny[d]	100%	34	35	28	2
Motor vehicle theft	100%	41	45	11	3
Fraud[e]	100%	30	29	37	3
Drug offenses	100%	37	30	30	3
Possession	100%	35	29	31	4
Trafficking	100%	39	30	28	2
Weapon offenses	100%	44	28	27	1
Other offenses[f]	100%	34	35	29	2

Note: For persons receiving a combination of sentences, the sentence designation came from the most severe penalty imposed—prison being the most severe, followed by jail, probation, and then other sentences, such as a fine or community service. Prison includes death sentences. In this table "probation" is defined as straight probation. Detail may not sum to total because of rounding. This table is based on an estimated 1,062,629 cases.
[a]Includes nonnegligent manslaughter.
[b]Includes rape.
[c]Includes offenses such as negligent manslaughter and kidnapping.
[d]Includes motor vehicle theft.
[e]Includes forgery and embezzlement.
[f]Composed of nonviolent offenses such as receiving stolen property and vandalism.

SOURCE: Matthew R. Durose,"Table 1.2. Distribution of Types of Felony Sentences Imposed in State Courts, by Offense, 2004," in *State Court Sentencing of Convicted Felons, 2004—Statistical Tables*, U.S. Department of Justice, Office of Justice Programs, Bureau of Justice Statistics, July 25, 2007, http://www .ojp.usdoj.gov/bjs/pub/html/scscf04/tables/scs04102tab.htm (accessed December 2, 2008)

added or taken away until a particular offense has been assigned to the appropriate level. Judges and prosecutors use the levels to find the relevant sentence in the federal sentencing table, which determines the number of months of imprisonment.

An illustration is provided for kidnapping, abduction, and unlawful restraint in Table 6.11. The table displays the USSC's guideline for this offense. The offense has a base offense level of 32, but additional levels can be added. For example, if the victim sustained serious bodily injury, the level is increased by four, to 36. If the victim was sexually exploited, the level is increased by six levels, to 38. If the victim was not released before seven days had passed, the level is increased by one, to 33.

According to the USSC's 2008 sentencing table, level 28, for example, points to six columns of sentence ranges indicating a minimum and a maximum sentence in each column. (See Table 6.12.) The first column, where the sentence range is 78 to 97 months, applies to offenders with no prior convictions or one prior conviction. The sixth column, where the sentence is 140 to 175 months, provides sentencing guidelines for offenders with 13 or more prior convictions. A single level thus provides six different levels of confinement, and, within each level, a minimum and maximum number of

months of imprisonment. This leaves judges with some discretion to determine sentencing.

Level 28 falls into the sentencing table's Zone D. (See Table 6.12.) Individuals in this zone are not permitted to receive any probation and must serve at least the minimum sentence shown in the applicable column. A three-time offender would be sentenced to a minimum of 87 months in prison and, under the USSC guidelines, could receive at most 54 days off per year for good behavior. Thus, this offender would serve at least 85% of the minimum sentence. If a case of kidnapping involved sexual exploitation, the offender would also be charged with criminal sexual abuse (a base offense level of 24) or sexual abuse of a minor (level 18 to 24 depending on whether the abuse was attempted or committed). Parole is not available in any of the guideline cases.

Property crimes are handled in the USSC guidelines in a similar manner. The base level is increased with the amount of property involved. For example, for larceny, embezzlement, and other forms of theft, the base offense level is 6 in cases where the loss to the victim is $5,000 or less. If the loss is greater than $5,000 but less than $10,000, the level rises to 8 and continues to rise as the amount of the loss increases. If the loss is more than $200,000 but less

TABLE 6.11

Federal sentencing guidelines on kidnapping, 2008

(a) Base offense level: 32

(b) Specific offense characteristics

    (1) If a ransom demand or a demand upon government was made, increase by 6 levels.

    (2) (A) If the victim sustained permanent or life-threatening bodily injury, increase by 4 levels; (B) if the victim sustained serious bodily injury, increase by 2 levels; or (C) if the degree of injury is between that specified in subdivisions (A) and (B), increase by 3 levels.

    (3) If a dangerous weapon was used, increase by 2 levels.

    (4) (A) If the victim was not released before thirty days had elapsed, increase by 2 levels.

        (B) If the victim was not released before seven days had elapsed, increase by 1 level.

    (5) If the victim was sexually exploited, increase by 6 levels.

    (6) If the victim is a minor and, in exchange for money or other consideration, was placed in the care or custody of another person who had no legal right to such care or custody of the victim, increase by 3 levels.

    (7) If the victim was kidnapped, abducted, or unlawfully restrained during the commission of, or in connection with, another offense or escape therefrom; or if another offense was committed during the kidnapping, abduction, or unlawful restraint, increase to—

        (A) the offense level from the chapter two offense guideline applicable to that other offense if such offense guideline includes an adjustment for kidnapping, abduction, or unlawful restraint, or otherwise takes such conduct into account; or

        (B) 4 plus the offense level from the offense guideline applicable to that other offense, but in no event greater than level 43, in any other case, if the resulting offense level is greater than that determined above.

SOURCE: "§2A4.1. Kidnapping, Abduction, Unlawful Restraint," in *Guidelines Manual*, U.S. Sentencing Commission, November 2008, http://www.ussc .gov/2008guid/GL2008.pdf (accessed December 2, 2008)

than $400,000, the level is 18. If the loss is greater than $100 million, the level is 32—which will result in a mandatory sentence of at least 121 months in prison for a first-time offender. A person who earned the maximum days for good behavior could expect to be out of incarceration in 103 months if he or she received the minimum sentence. Fines and restitution of stolen money or property would also be required.

DEPARTURES FROM THE GUIDELINES. U.S. Supreme Court decisions in 2004 and 2005 modified sentencing guidelines. In 2004 the court ruled in *Blakely v. Washington* (542 U.S. 296) that a state judge cannot impose a longer sentence when the basis for the enhanced sentence was not admitted by the subject or found by a jury. In the *Blakely* case, the subject admitted to kidnapping his estranged wife. The maximum sentence for the crime was 53 months in prison, but the judge imposed a sentence of 90 months after determining that Ralph Howard Blakely had acted with deliberate cruelty, a factor that allowed a longer sentence under existing statutes. However, the charge of deliberate cruelty had not been part of Blakely's plea, and it had not been determined by a jury. The court found that the Sixth Amendment right to a trial by jury had thus been violated. The *Blakely* ruling means that only facts proved to a jury can justify an enhanced sentence.

In 2005 the Supreme Court made a related ruling in *United States v. Booker* (543 U.S. 220). In this case the subject had been charged with possession with intent to distribute 50 grams (1.8 ounces) of crack cocaine, a crime for which the federal sentencing guidelines set a 262-month sentence. However, the judge later determined that Booker had possessed 92 grams (3.2 ounces) of crack cocaine and had obstructed justice as well. Because of these additional offenses, the judge sentenced Booker to 360 months in prison. In language similar to the *Blakely* ruling, the court ruled that federal judges cannot determine facts that are used to increase a defendant's punishment beyond what is authorized by a jury verdict or the defendant's own admissions. In its ruling, the court struck down the mandatory application of sentencing guidelines and instructed courts to apply reasonableness in determining sentences. Guidelines should be considered, but judges are not required to follow them. The legal impact of these two decisions continues to be worked out in the courts.

In *Final Report on the Impact of* United States v. Booker *on Federal Sentencing* (March 2006, http://www.ussc.gov/ booker_report/Booker_Report.pdf), the USSC finds that most federal cases are sentenced according to the sentencing guidelines. The USSC concludes, "When within-range sentences and government-sponsored, below-range sentences are combined, the rate of sentencing in conformance with the sentencing guidelines is 85.9 percent." It also determines that the average sentence length since *Booker* has increased.

The rate of government-sponsored, below-range sentences experienced a minor increase after the *Booker* decision. Below-range sentences are permissible because of stipulations in the guidelines for so-called departures from the guidelines' provisions. Upward departures are used for cases where special circumstances merit longer incarceration than the maximum sentence in the guidelines, whereas downward departures authorize shorter sentences than the minimum for extenuating circumstances or because the defendant provided substantial assistance to federal authorities, typically by helping with a broader investigation or providing testimony against other suspects.

According to the USSC, in an analysis of cases decided in fiscal year 2007, 60.8% of offenders were sentenced within the guideline range. (See Table 6.13.) Another 1.5% of offenders received departures above the guideline range, and 37.6% received departures below the guideline range. Of the latter, 25.6% received government-sponsored below-range sentences, and 12% received nongovernment-sponsored below-range sentences.

"Three Strikes, You're Out"

Nine years after passing the first truth-in-sentencing law, Washington State passed the first of the so-called three-strikes laws in December 1993. The measure took effect in the wake of a voter initiative, which passed by a

TABLE 6.12

Federal sentencing table, November 1, 2008

[In months of imprisonment]

Zone	Offense level	Criminal history category (criminal history points)					
		I (0 or 1)	II (2 or 3)	III (4, 5, 6)	IV (7, 8, 9)	V (10, 11, 12)	VI (13 or more)
Zone A	1	0–6	0–6	0–6	0–6	0–6	0–6
	2	0–6	0–6	0–6	0–6	0–6	1–7
	3	0–6	0–6	0–6	0–6	2–8	3–9
	4	0–6	0–6	0–6	2–8	4–10	6–12
	5	0–6	0–6	1–7	4–10	6–12	9–15
	6	0–6	1–7	2–8	6–12	9–15	12–18
	7	0–6	2–8	4–10	8–14	12–18	15–21
	8	0–6	4–10	6–12	10–16	15–21	18–24
Zone B	9	4–10	6–12	8–14	12–18	18–24	21–27
	10	6–12	8–14	10–16	15–21	21–27	24–30
Zone C	11	8–14	10–16	12–18	18–24	24–30	27–33
	12	10–16	12–18	15–21	21–27	27–33	30–37
Zone D	13	12–18	15–21	18–24	24–30	30–37	33–41
	14	15–21	18–24	21–27	27–33	33–41	37–46
	15	18–24	21–27	24–30	30–37	37–46	41–51
	16	21–27	24–30	27–33	33–41	41–51	46–57
	17	24–30	27–33	30–37	37–46	46–57	51–63
	18	27–33	30–37	33–41	41–51	51–63	57–71
	19	30–37	33–41	37–46	46–57	57–71	63–78
	20	33–41	37–46	41–51	51–63	63–78	70–87
	21	37–46	41–51	46–57	57–71	70–87	77–96
	22	41–51	46–57	51–63	63–78	77–96	84–105
	23	46–57	51–63	57–71	70–87	84–105	92–115
	24	51–63	57–71	63–78	77–96	92–115	100–125
	25	57–71	63–78	70–87	84–105	100–125	110–137
	26	63–78	70–87	78–97	92–115	110–137	120–150
	27	70–87	78–97	87–108	100–125	120–150	130–162
	28	78–97	87–108	97–121	110–137	130–162	140–175
	29	87–108	97–121	108–135	121–151	140–175	151–188
	30	97–121	108–135	121–151	135–168	151–188	168–210
	31	108–135	121–151	135–168	151–188	168–210	188–235
	32	121–151	135–168	151–188	168–210	188–235	210–262
	33	135–168	151–188	168–210	188–235	210–262	235–293
	34	151–188	168–210	188–235	210–262	235–293	262–327
	35	168–210	188–235	210–262	235–293	262–327	292–365
	36	188–235	210–262	235–293	262–327	292–365	324–405
	37	210–262	235–293	262–327	292–365	324–405	360–life
	38	235–293	262–327	292–365	324–405	360–life	360–life
	39	262–327	292–365	324–405	360–life	360–life	360–life
	40	292–365	324–405	360–life	360–life	360–life	360–life
	41	324–405	360–life	360–life	360–life	360–life	360–life
	42	360–life	360–life	360–life	360–life	360–life	360–life
	43	Life	Life	Life	Life	Life	Life

SOURCE: "Sentencing Table," in *Guidelines Manual*, U.S. Sentencing Commission, November 2008, http://www.ussc.gov/2008guid/Chap5.pdf (accessed November 24, 2008)

three-to-one margin. Three-strikes laws are the functional equivalent of sentencing guidelines in that they mandate a fixed sentence length for repeat offenders for specified crimes or a mix of crimes—but their formulation in public debate, using the baseball analogy, is much easier to understand than the complexities of thick books of codes and sentencing tables. Under three-strikes laws, the offender receives a mandatory sentence upon conviction for the third offense—life imprisonment without parole (as in Washington State), 25 years without parole (as in California), or some variant of a long sentence. These laws are designed to remove the criminal from society for a long period of time or, in some instances, for life. Even though three strikes laws are best known for their imposition of long sentences on a third offense, they typically feature longer-than-average sentences for second offenses, as well.

The Washington law identifies specific offenses that are "strikable." California, which passed its own (and more famous) three-strikes law just months after Washington passed its measure, specifies the categories of offenses that must precede the third felony conviction.

OPPOSITION AND CHALLENGES TO THREE-STRIKES LAWS. Opponents of three-strikes laws charge that the laws unfairly target African-Americans, who are disproportionately represented among felony convicts. They argue that three-strikes laws remove proportion and reasonableness from sentencing by making all third strikes punishable by the same prison sentence, whether it be stealing a small item or killing someone. Opponents also note that incarcerating more people for longer periods requires more prisons and increases corrections costs for maintaining prisoners.

TABLE 6.13

National comparison of federal sentences imposed relative to federal sentencing guideline ranges[a], fiscal year 2007

	N	%
Total cases	69,893	100.0
Cases sentenced within guideline range	42,504	60.8
Cases sentenced above guideline range	1,060	1.5
Departure above guideline range	467	0.7
Upward departure from guideline range[b]	324	0.5
Upward departure with *Booker*/18 U.S.C. § 3553[c]	143	0.2
Otherwise above guideline range	593	0.8
Above guideline range with *Booker*/18 U.S.C. § 3553[d]	491	0.7
All remaining cases above guideline range[e]	102	0.1
Government sponsored below range[f]	17,896	25.6
§5K1.1 Substantial assistance departure	10,049	14.4
§5K3.1 Early disposition program departure	5,233	7.5
Other government sponsored below range	2,614	3.7
Non-government sponsored below range	8,433	12.0
Departure below guideline range	2,770	3.9
Downward departure from guideline range[b]	1,757	2.5
Downward departure with *Booker*/18 U.S.C. § 3553[c]	1,013	1.4
Otherwise below guideline range	5,663	8.1
Below guideline range with *Booker*/18 U.S.C. § 3553[d]	4,957	7.1
All remaining cases below guideline range[e]	706	1.0

[a]This table reflects the 72,865 cases sentenced in fiscal year 2007. Of these, 2,972 cases were excluded because information was missing from the submitted documents that prevented the comparison of the sentence and the guideline range.
[b]All cases with departures in which the court did not indicate as a reason either *U.S. v. Booker*, 18 U.S.C. § 3553, or a factor or reason specifically prohibited in the provisions, policy statements, or commentary of the *Guidelines Manual*.
[c]All cases sentenced outside of the guideline range in which the court indicated both a departure (see footnote b) and a reference to either *U.S. v. Booker*, 18 U.S.C. § 3553, or related factors as a reason for sentencing outside of the guideline system.
[d]All cases sentenced outside of the guideline range in which no departure was indicated and in which the court cited *U.S. v. Booker*, 18 U.S.C. § 3553, or related factors as one of the reasons for sentencing outside of the guideline system.
[e]All cases sentenced outside of the guideline range that could not be classified into any of the three previous outside of the range categories. This category includes cases in which no reason was provided for a sentence outside of the guideline range.
[g]Cases in which a reason for the sentence indicated that the prosecution initiated, proposed, or stipulated to a sentence outside of the guideline range, either pursuant to a plea agreement or as part of a non-plea negotiation with the defendant.

SOURCE: "Table N. National Comparison of Sentence Imposed and Position Relative to the Guideline Range, Fiscal Year 2007," in *Sourcebook of Federal Sentencing Statistics*, U.S. Sentencing Commission, 2008, http://www.ussc.gov/ANNRPT/2007/TableN.pdf (accessed November 27, 2008)

Reducing the possibility of parole results in an increasing number of elderly prisoners, who are statistically much less likely to commit crimes than younger prisoners and who have increasing health care needs. Finally, some critics suggest the finality of three-strikes laws may make active criminals more desperate and, thus, more violent. According to this view, if criminals know they will be sentenced to life in prison, then they have nothing to lose and might be more likely to kill witnesses or to resist arrest through violent means.

On April 1, 2002, the U.S. Supreme Court agreed to consider whether California's three-strikes law, considered to be one of the toughest in the country, violates the Eighth Amendment's ban against cruel and unusual punishment. More than half of California prisoners sentenced under the three-strikes law were convicted of nonviolent third-strike felonies, including drug possession and petty theft, and are serving mandatory sentences of 25 years to life without the possibility of parole. In *Lockyer v. Andrade* (538 U.S. 63 [2003]), the court considered the case of Leandro Andrade, an inmate serving two consecutive 25-year sentences in California for stealing videotapes valued at $150 from two different video stores. Because each theft counted as an offense and Andrade had two prior convictions, the new crimes counted as his third and fourth strikes for purposes of sentencing. In a 5–4 decision, the court upheld the sentence imposed on Andrade and thereby upheld the right of states to impose long sentences on repeat felony offenders, regardless of the relative seriousness of the third-strike felony.

In 2003 the Supreme Court again ruled on the constitutionality of the California three-strikes law. The case involved the defendant Gary Albert Ewing, who had been sentenced to 25 years to life for a third offense, the theft of three golf clubs, with each valued at $399. His previous offenses included (among others) a burglary and a robbery while threatening his victim with a knife. *Ewing v. California* (538 U.S. 11 [2003]) was a good test of the California statute because neither of Ewing's first two offenses were seriously violent and the third, the triggering offense, was what is known under California law as a "wobbler," namely an offense that can be tried, at the prosecutor's option, as either a felony or a misdemeanor.

The petition in *Ewing* argued that the punishment was cruel, unusual, and disproportionate to the offense committed. In effect, Ewing had the profile of a habitual but petty criminal whose theft of golf clubs should have been tried as a misdemeanor. In this case the court dismissed the proportionality argument and, instead, affirmed the state's right to set policy for the protection of the public. Quoting from another case, the court said, "The Eighth Amendment does not require strict proportionality between crime and sentence [but] forbids only extreme sentences that are 'grossly disproportionate' to the crime." California had the right to incapacitate repeat offenders by incarcerating them. According to the court, the Constitution did not mandate that the states apply any one penological theory.

IMPACT AND EFFECTIVENESS OF THREE-STRIKES LAWS. Vincent Schiraldi, Jason Colburn, and Eric Lotke note in *An Examination of the Impact of 3-Strike Laws, 10 Years after Their Enactment* (September 2004, http://www.soros.org/initiatives/usprograms/focus/justice/articles_publications/publications/threestrikes_20040923/three_strikes.pdf) that during the previous decade 23 states had passed three-strikes laws.

According to Schiraldi, Colburn, and Lotke, the three-strikes laws had little impact on state prison populations after they were enacted, except for California, Florida, and Georgia. Of the 21 three-strikes states on which data on the number of people incarcerated were available, 14 had incarcerated fewer than 100 people under three strikes. Only three states had more than 400 people imprisoned under three strikes: California (42,322 inmates), Georgia (7,631), and Florida (1,628). The researchers also report that between 1993 and 2002 states with three-strikes laws experienced a decline in serious crime rates only slightly greater (26.8%) than states without three-strikes laws (22.3%).

Further scientific analyses of three-strikes laws have been conducted by Brian Brown and Greg Jolivette of the Legislative Analyst's Office in *A Primer: Three Strikes—The Impact after More Than a Decade* (October 2005, http://www.lao.ca.gov/2005/3_strikes/3_strikes_102005.htm), by Eric Helland and Alexander Tabarrok in *Does Three Strikes Deter? A Non-parametric Estimation* (2007, http://mason.gmu.edu/~atabarro/ThreeStrikes.pdf), and by Radha Iyengar in *I'd Rather Be Hanged for a Sheep Than a Lamb: The Unintended Consequences of "Three-Strikes" Laws* (February 2008, http://www.nber.org/papers/w13784).

Brown and Jolivette report that as of yearend 2004 there were nearly 43,000 inmates in California prisons who had been sentenced under the three-strikes law. They made up just over one-fourth (26%) of the state's total prison population. Most of the "strikers" (more than 35,000) were serving time for their second strike. Approximately 7,500 of the strikers were so-called third strikers. From 1994 to 2001 the percent of second and third strikers grew quickly from less than 5% to approximately 25% of California's total prison population. Through 2004 the percentage remained about 25%. Most of the strikers were convicted of serious crimes, such as assault, robbery, and burglary. Nearly one-fourth (23%) of the strikers were serving time for drug charges. More than half (56%) of the strikers had been most recently convicted of a nonviolent nonserious crime. However, Brown and Jolivette find that the criminal histories of the strikers were "more serious," on average, than the criminal histories of nonstrikers.

Brown and Jolivette list the racial makeup of California's second and third strikers as 37% African-American, 33% Hispanic, and 26% white. This breakdown is described as "similar" to the overall prison population in the state. African-Americans make up 45% of the third-striker population, but only 30% of the overall prison population. The researchers examine the effects of California's three-strikes law on public safety. The state's crime rate had already begun to decline at the time the law was implemented in 1994 and continued to decline over the following decade. However, a variety of factors are believed to have played a role in the decline. They conclude that it is "difficult to conclusively evaluate the law's impact on crime and safety."

Helland and Tabarrok examine the arrest and conviction records of a large subset of criminals who were released from California prisons in 1994. They determine that the state's three-strikes law reduced felony arrest rates by 17% to 20% among second strikers and kept them from committing further serious crimes.

Iyengar finds a similar result in her study. She estimates that California's three-strikes law "reduced participation in criminal activity" by 28% for second strikers and by 20% for first strikers (i.e., criminals facing second-strike sentences on their next offense). However, Iyengar concludes that second strikers who did choose to commit further crimes were more likely to commit more violent crimes than they otherwise would have committed because the consequences were the same regardless of the violent nature of the third strike. For example, second strikers were more willing to commit robbery than burglary and more willing to commit a rape or assault during the commission of a burglary. In addition, Iyengar claims the state's three-strikes law encouraged some strikers to commit their next serious crime outside of the state. According to Iyengar, "Three strikes appears to have imposed 50,000 crimes on other states due to the migration of criminals out of California."

Alternative Sentencing

Forms of sentencing other than probation, prison, or a combination of the two (split sentences) are widely used in virtually every state. State departments of correction, the District of Columbia, and the Federal Bureau of Prisons offer a range of alternative sentencing options for criminal offenders. Even though programs can vary among regions, those options include work release and weekend sentencing, shock incarceration (sometimes called boot camp), community service programs, day fines, day reporting centers, house arrest and electronic monitoring, residential community corrections, and diversionary treatment programs. Other types of alternative sentencing options, such as mediation and restitution, are sometimes available.

MEDIATION AND RESTITUTION. In mediation the victim and the offender meet under the auspices of a community representative and work out a "reconciliation," usually involving some type of restitution and requiring offenders to take responsibility for their actions. This technique is used mainly for minor crimes and often involves private organizations; therefore, the judiciary does not always accept its resolution. Most often, restitution is not considered the complete punishment but part of a broader punishment, such as probation or working off the restitution dollar amount while in prison.

WORK RELEASE AND WEEKEND SENTENCING. Work-release programs permit selected prisoners nearing the end of their terms to work in the community and return to prison facilities or community residential facilities during non-working hours. Such programs are designed to prepare inmates to return to the community in a relatively controlled environment while they are learning how to work productively. Work release also allows inmates to earn an income, reimburse the state for part of their confinement costs, build up savings for their eventual full release, and acquire more positive living habits. Those on weekend sentencing programs spend certain days in prison, usually weekends, but are free the remainder of the time. Both of these types of sentences are known as intermittent incarceration. Violent offenders and those convicted of drug offenses are usually excluded from such programs by the courts.

SHOCK INCARCERATION. Shock incarceration is another name for reformatories or boot camps that use military discipline for juveniles and adults. The name comes from the British home secretary William Whitelaw (1918–1999), who called for a "short, sharp shock" that would end teenagers' criminal careers. Boot camps established in Great Britain attracted youths who liked the challenge. In "Crime Record Shows Boot Camps Works" (*Sunday Times*, June 12, 2005), Robert Winnett reports that the British government believes boot camps are effective. Statistics show that the reconviction rate of offenders who attended the Thorn Cross boot camp in Cheshire, England, a particularly regimented institution, was considerably lower than average for similar institutions.

The DOJ explains in *Correctional Boot Camps: Lessons from a Decade of Research* (June 2003, http://www.ncjrs.gov/pdffiles1/nij/197018.pdf) that boot camps became popular in the United States in the 1980s and early 1990s. By 1995 more than 120 of them were in operation. Most boot camp sentences were short, for example, three to four months.

Typically, boot camp programs include physical training and regular drill-type exercise, housekeeping and maintenance of the facility, and often hard labor. Programs closely regulate dress, talking, movement, eating, hygiene, and other behaviors. Obedience to rules reinforces submission to authority and forces the prisoners to handle a challenge that is both tedious and demanding. Boot camps are intended to be both punitive in their rigid discipline and rehabilitative by enhancing self-esteem upon successful completion of the program. Shock incarceration is intended to motivate prisoners, teach respect for themselves and others, and break destructive cycles of behavior. Virtually all these programs are based on the assumption that a military regimen is beneficial.

Despite great public expectations, by 2009 many boot camps had closed for failing to meet their primary objectives: reduce recidivism (relapse into criminal activity) and reduce prison populations. According to the DOJ, research indicates that boot camps are effective only at achieving short-term changes in inmate attitudes and behavior.

COMMUNITY SERVICE PROGRAMS. Community service is most often a supplement to other penalties and mainly given to white-collar criminals, juvenile delinquents, and those who commit nonserious crimes. Offenders are usually required to work for government or private nonprofit agencies cleaning parks, collecting roadside trash, setting up chairs for community events, painting community projects, and helping out at nursing homes.

DAY FINES. Under the day fines type of alternative sentence, the offender pays a monetary sum rather than spending time in jail or prison. Most judges assess fixed, flat-fee fines sparingly. The fees are tied to the seriousness of the crimes and the criminal records of the offenders, and they bear no relationship to the offender's wealth. As a result, judges often think the fixed fines are too lenient for wealthy offenders and too harsh for poor ones.

When setting a day fine, the judge first determines how much punishment an offender deserves. For example, a judge may decide that the gravity of the offense is worth 15, 60, or 120 punishment units, without regard to income. The value of each unit is set at a percentage of the offender's daily income, and the total fine amount is determined by simple multiplication. The fine is paid into the jurisdiction's treasury.

DAY REPORTING CENTERS. Day reporting centers (DRCs) allow offenders to reside in the community. DRCs are often populated by people with drug and alcohol problems and require offenders to appear on a frequent and regular basis to participate in services or activities provided by the center or other community agencies. Random drug screening and breathalyzer tests may be administered. The centers may provide employment and educational training and conduct classes on topics such as anger management, substance abuse, life skills, and cognitive skills. Failure to adhere to program requirements or to report at stated intervals can lead to commitment to prison or jail. DRC participation can also be terminated if the offender is charged with a new crime.

INTENSIVE PROBATION SUPERVISION. Intensive Probation Supervision (IPS) is another method of closely supervising offenders while they reside in the community. Routine probation is not designed or structured to handle high-risk probationers. Therefore, IPS was developed as an alternative that is stricter than routine probation.

The caseloads of officers assigned to IPS offenders are kept low. In typical programs, the offender must contact a supervising officer frequently, pay restitution to victims, participate in community service, have and keep a job, and, if appropriate, undergo random and unannounced drug testing. Offenders are often required to pay a probation fee.

HOUSE ARREST AND ELECTRONIC MONITORING PROGRAM. Some nonviolent offenders are sentenced to house arrest (or home confinement), which means that they are legally required to remain confined in their own home. They are allowed to leave only for medical purposes or to go to work, although some curfew programs permit offenders to work during the day and have a specified number of hours of free time before returning home. The idea began as a way to keep drunk drivers off the street, but it quickly expanded to include other nonviolent offenders.

The most severe type of house arrest is home incarceration, where the offender's home actually becomes a prison that he or she cannot leave except for very special reasons, such as medical emergencies. Home-detention programs require the offender to be at home when he or she is not working. Some offenders are required to perform a certain number of hours of community service and, if they are employed, to repay the cost of probation and/or restitution.

An electronic monitoring program (EMP) that is used in tandem with house arrest involves attaching a small radio transmitter to the offender in a nonremovable bracelet or anklet. Some systems send a signal to a small monitoring box, which is programmed to call a department of corrections computer if the signal is broken; other systems randomly call probationers and the computer verifies the prisoner's identity through voice recognition software. In some cases, a special device in the electronic monitor sends a confirmation to the computer. Some systems have global positioning system technologies to help corrections officers ensure that offenders are not violating any territorial restrictions.

EMPs are often used to monitor the whereabouts of those under house arrest and permitted to be only at home or at work. Electronic monitoring is sometimes used to ensure that child molesters stay a specified distance from schools. EMPs cost much less than building new prison cells or housing more inmates. However, close supervision by officers is crucial to the success of any home confinement or electronic monitoring. Officers must ensure that the participants are indeed working when they leave the house and that they are not using illegal drugs. Electronic monitoring equipment must also be checked periodically to determine whether the offender has attempted to disable the equipment.

RESIDENTIAL COMMUNITY CORRECTIONS. Residential community corrections facilities are known less formally as halfway houses, because they are designed to help prisoners reintegrate into community life. Some offenders are sentenced to halfway houses directly in lieu of incarceration if their offenses and general profile indicate they will benefit from the structure and counseling available in such facilities. Many states frequently use halfway houses to relieve prison overcrowding.

Residential programs house offenders in a structured environment. Offenders work full time, maintain the residence center, perform community service, and sometimes attend educational or counseling programs. They may leave the centers only for work or approved programs such as substance-abuse treatment. One type of residential program, called the restitution center, allows offenders to work to pay restitution and child support. The centers regularly test the residents for drugs.

DIVERSIONARY TREATMENT PROGRAMS. Probation combined with mandatory treatment programs is used as an alternative sentence for nonviolent offenders convicted of drug offenses, alcohol abuse, or sex offenses. Sentenced individuals are free on probation but typically are required to attend group therapy and supervised professional treatment sessions.

Death Penalty

The ultimate penalty that can be imposed by the U.S. judiciary system is the death penalty, also known as capital punishment. The Eighth Amendment of the U.S. Constitution guarantees that "cruel and unusual punishments [not be] inflicted." In recent decades debates have raged about the morality and deterrent effect of the death penalty and whether or not capital punishment is cruel and unusual punishment under the Constitution. According to the BJS (December 2008, http://www.ojp.usdoj.gov/bjs/glance/tables/drtab.htm), 3,220 prisoners were under a sentence of death at yearend 2007.

KEY SUPREME COURT CASES. Three Supreme Court cases, all decided in the 1970s, have produced the current interpretation of the Eighth Amendment relative to the death penalty. In *Furman v. Georgia* (408 U.S. 238 [1972]), the court held that the death penalty in three cases under review was cruel and unusual because under the then-prevailing statutes juries had "untrammeled discretion . . . to pronounce life or death in capital cases." Due process required procedural fairness, including consideration of the severity of the crime and the circumstances. In the three cases decided in *Furman*, three individuals were condemned to die, two for rape and one for murder. All three of the offenders were African-American.

In response to *Furman*, states modified their statutes. North Carolina imposed a mandatory death sentence for first-degree murder. This law was tested by the Supreme Court in *Woodson v. North Carolina* (428 U.S. 280 [1976]). The court held that even though the death penalty was not cruel and unusual punishment in every circumstance, a mandatory death sentence did not satisfy the requirements laid down in *Furman*. The court stated, "North Carolina's mandatory death penalty statute for first-degree murder departs markedly from contemporary standards respecting the imposition of the punishment of death and thus cannot be applied consistently with the Eighth and Fourteenth Amendments' requirement that the State's power to punish 'be exercised within the limits of civilized standards.'" The court overturned the North Carolina law.

Woodson was decided on July 2, 1976. On that same day the court rendered its judgment in *Gregg v. Georgia* (428 U.S. 153), the case of a man sentenced to death for murder and robbery under new legislation that passed in Georgia following *Furman*. In this case, the court upheld the death penalty saying, in part:

The Georgia statutory system under which petitioner was sentenced to death is constitutional. The new procedures on their face satisfy the concerns of *Furman*, since before the death penalty can be imposed there must be specific jury findings as to the circumstances of the crime or the character of the defendant, and the State Supreme Court thereafter reviews the comparability of each death sentence with the sentences imposed on similarly situated defendants to ensure that the sentence of death in a particular case is not disproportionate. Petitioner's contentions that the changes in Georgia's sentencing procedures have not removed the elements of arbitrariness and capriciousness condemned by *Furman* are without merit.

Death Penalty for Juveniles

In *Roper v. Simmons* (543 U.S. 551 [2005]), the Supreme Court ruled that the death penalty for minors is cruel and unusual punishment. In a 5–4 ruling, the court found it unconstitutional to sentence someone to death for a crime he or she committed when he or she was younger than age 18. As a result of the ruling, dozens of prisoners were removed from death row.

As part of its argument for outlawing the death penalty for minors, the court cited scientific opinion that teenagers are too immature to be held accountable in the same way as adults for the crimes they commit. Justice Anthony M. Kennedy (1936–), speaking for the majority, explained that "from a moral standpoint it would be misguided to equate the failings of a minor with those of an adult, for a greater possibility exists that a minor's character deficiencies will be reformed."

THE CORRECTIONS SYSTEM

Correction agencies house convicted criminals in prisons, jails, treatment centers, or other places of confinement. The corrections system operates prisons, oversees parole, and administers probation. Parole and probation are systems for monitoring and controlling criminals without removing them from the general population.

FIGURE 6.5

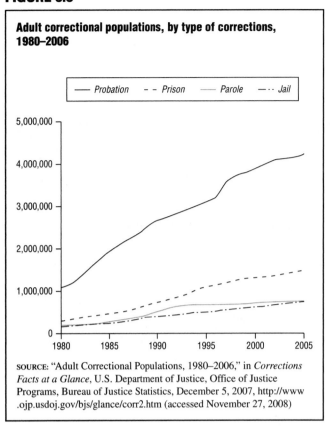

Adult correctional populations, by type of corrections, 1980–2006

SOURCE: "Adult Correctional Populations, 1980–2006," in *Corrections Facts at a Glance*, U.S. Department of Justice, Office of Justice Programs, Bureau of Justice Statistics, December 5, 2007, http://www.ojp.usdoj.gov/bjs/glance/corr2.htm (accessed November 27, 2008)

Figure 6.5 shows the adult correctional population in the United States from 1980 to 2006. According to Lauren E. Glaze and Thomas P. Bonczar of the BJS, in *Probation and Parole in the United States, 2007 Statistical Tables* (December 2008, http://www.ojp.usdoj.gov/bjs/pub/pdf/ppus07st.pdf), 3.2% of the U.S. adult population was incarcerated or on probation or parole at yearend 2007. Detailed information about correctional facilities, inmates, and people on probation or parole is provided in Chapters 7, 8, and 9, respectively.

CHAPTER 7
CORRECTIONAL FACILITIES: PRISONS AND JAILS

Public views of crime and punishment have changed over the centuries. In general, most societies have moved from the extraction of personal or family justice—vengeful acts such as blood feuds or the practice of taking "an eye for an eye"—toward formal systems based on written codes and orderly processes. Prisons and jails have changed from being holding places where prisoners awaited deportation, maiming, whipping, or execution to places of extended—even lifelong—incarceration. Confinement itself has become the punishment.

THE HISTORY OF CORRECTIONS IN THE UNITED STATES

During the colonial period in U.S. history physical punishment was more common than incarceration. Stocks, pillories, branding, flogging, and maiming—such as cutting off an ear or slitting the nostrils—were typical punishments meted out to offenders. The death penalty was also used frequently. The Puritans of Massachusetts believed that humans were naturally depraved, which made it easier for some of the colonies and the first states to enforce harsh punishments. In addition, because Puritans maintained the view that individuals had no control over their fate (predestination), few early Americans supported the idea that criminals could be rehabilitated.

The Quakers, led by William Penn (1644–1718), made colonial Pennsylvania an exception to the harsh practices often found in the other colonies. The early criminal code of colonial Pennsylvania abolished executions for all crimes except homicide, replaced physical punishments with imprisonment and hard labor, and did not charge the prisoners for their food and housing.

The Reform Movement

The idea of individual freedom and the concept that people could change society for the better by using reason permeated American society during the 1800s. Reformers worked to abolish slavery, secure women's rights, and prohibit liquor, as well as to change the corrections system. Rehabilitation of prisoners became the goal of criminal justice, and inmates were given work to keep them busy and to defray the cost of their confinement. Prison administrators began constructing factories within prison walls or hiring inmates out as laborers in chain gangs. In rural areas inmates worked on prison-owned farms. In the South prisoners were often leased out to local farmers. Prison superintendents justified the hard labor by arguing that it taught the offenders the value of work and self-discipline. With the rise of labor unions in the North, the 1930s saw an end to the large-scale prison industry. Unions complained about competing with the inmates' free labor, especially amid the rising unemployment of the Great Depression (1929–1939). As such, states began limiting what inmates could produce.

As crime increased during the 1970s and 1980s, criminal justice practices such as indeterminate sentencing, probation, parole, and treatment programs came under attack. Support decreased for rehabilitative programs and increased for keeping offenders incarcerated; many people subscribed to the idea that keeping criminals off the streets is the surest way to keep them from committing more crimes. As a result, the federal government and a growing number of states introduced mandatory sentencing and life terms for habitual criminals. They also limited the use of probation, parole, and time off for good behavior.

PRISONS AND JAILS COMPARED

Corrections institutions are organized into tiers by level of government, and at each level (federal, state, and local) specific types of institutions provide corrections functions based on the relative severity of the offenses committed. The most restrictive form of corrections is incarceration in a prison. Both the federal and the state governments operate their own prison systems; within the federal government, the military maintains its own prisons. Prison inmates serve time for serious offenses that carry a sentence of at least one year of incarceration.

Most people sentenced to jail serve less than a year for misdemeanors and offenses against the public order. Jails are operated at the local level by cities and counties. The federal government operates some jails as well, and within the federal government the U.S. Immigration and Customs Enforcement has its own detention facilities. In some states, jails and prisons are operated under a single state authority but still maintain the distinction—prisons for long terms and serious offenses, jails for lesser terms and less serious offenses.

PUBLIC VERSUS PRIVATE CORRECTIONAL FACILITIES

During the 1980s the rapidly rising prison and jail populations led a few jurisdictions to privatize some of their correctional facilities. The basic assumption behind this idea is that the private sector is inherently more efficient and flexible than the government sector because it is less constrained by bureaucracy and is more cost effective. It is also argued that private facilities save the public the initial costs of prison construction, because those costs are assumed by private contractors. This saves the government from taking on long-term debt to build housing for more prisoners. In this view, a privatized or even a partially privatized corrections system would cost taxpayers less money. Corrections functions, however, are ultimately vested in governmental hands, and private prisons must operate under established rules and regulations.

According to William J. Sabol and Heather Couture of the Bureau of Justice Statistics (BJS), in *Prison Inmates at Midyear 2007* (June 2008, http://www.ojp.usdoj.gov/bjs/pub/pdf/pim07.pdf), 7.4% of state and federal prisoners were held in private correctional facilities in 2007. That percentage was up from 6.5% in 2003.

FEDERAL CORRECTIONS

The Federal Bureau of Prisons (BOP) was established in 1930 as an agency of the U.S. Department of Justice (DOJ) to oversee the corrections system for federal inmates and to administer federal prisons. The BOP notes in "Weekly Population Report" (http://www.bop.gov/locations/weekly_report.jsp) that as of April 2, 2009, it oversaw 204,092 federal inmates. Most of the inmates (167,308 or 82% of the total) were in BOP facilities. An additional 22,622 (11%) inmates were in privately managed facilities, and 14,162 (7%) inmates were held in other contract facilities, such as jails and community corrections centers, or were under home confinement.

The BOP directly operated 180 facilities around the country at that time. The five states with the greatest num-

ber of BOP facilities were Texas (22), California (16), Pennsylvania (14), Florida (12), and Kentucky (10). The 10 BOP facilities housing the largest number of inmates were:

- Fort Dix Federal Correctional Institute, New Jersey—3,885 inmates

- Brooklyn Metropolitan Detention Center, New York—2,843 inmates

- Atlanta U.S. Penitentiary, Georgia—2,076 inmates

- Coleman Low-Security Federal Correctional Institute, Florida—1,993 inmates

- Forrest City Federal Correctional Institute, Arkansas—1,990 inmates

- Elkton Federal Correctional Institute, Ohio—1,899 inmates

- Petersburg Medium-Security Federal Correctional Institute, Virginia—1,876 inmates

- Leavenworth U.S. Penitentiary, Kansas—1,870 inmates

- Beaumont Low-Security Federal Correctional Institute, Texas—1,821 inmates

- Beckley Federal Correctional Institute, West Virgina—1,817 inmates

Security Levels of Federal Prisons

The BOP maintains institutions at five different security levels, and each prisoner is assigned to a particular level based on that individual's offenses and behavioral history:

- Minimum security—at the lowest security level are federal prison camps. These facilities have dormitory housing, a relatively low staff-to-inmate ratio, and limited or no perimeter fencing. They are located on or near larger institutions or military bases, where the inmates participate in work programs.

- Low-security federal correctional institutions (FCIs)—FCIs have fenced perimeters and a dormitory that consists of cubicle housing. Inmates are typically involved in work programs.

- Medium-security FCIs—these facilities feature reinforced perimeter fencing, usually a double fence with an electronic detection system. In addition, inmates are housed in cells and have access to work and treatment programs.

- High-security U.S. penitentiaries (USPs)—the most secure environment in the federal prison system includes highly secured perimeters with walls and reinforced fences. Inmates are held in multiple- or single-occupant cells, are closely watched, and do not have freedom to move around within the facility without supervision.

- Administrative facilities—these facilities hold offenders awaiting trial or treat inmates with serious medical needs. Special facilities may also be used to house the most dangerous, violent, or escape-prone inmates. These include metropolitan correctional centers, metropolitan detention centers, federal detention centers, federal medical centers, the Federal Transfer Center in Oklahoma City, Oklahoma, and the Administrative-Maximum USP in Florence, Colorado.

CENSUS OF STATE AND FEDERAL CORRECTIONAL FACILITIES

In 2005 the DOJ performed a census of state and federal correctional facilities. The results were published by James J. Stephan of the BJS in *Census of State and Federal Correctional Facilities, 2005* (October 2008, http://www.ojp.usdoj .gov/bjs/pub/pdf/csfcf05.pdf). In 2005 there were 1,821 facilities—1,719 state facilities and 102 federal facilities. (See Table 7.1.) The vast majority of the facilities were publicly operated (1,406 facilities) rather than privately operated (415 facilities). Between 2000 and 2005 the total number of state prisons increased by 9%, whereas the total number of federal prisons increased by 21%. The number of inmates housed in state and federal prisons increased by 9.6% during this same period.

In 2005 state prisons housed nearly 1.3 million inmates, whereas federal prisons held less than 146,000 inmates. (See Table 7.1.) The number of state inmates increased by 7.5% between 2000 and 2005. A much larger increase (31.4%) occurred in federal prisons. The number of combined state and federal inmates per 100,000 U.S. residents increased from 464 in 2000 to 480 in 2005.

Figure 7.1 and Figure 7.2 provide details about the sizes and security levels, respectively, of state and federal prisons based on the 2000 and 2005 censuses. In 2005 the largest number of prisons (946) housed fewer than 500 inmates each. Likewise, the largest number of prisons (969) were minimum-security facilities. The number of prisons holding 2,500 inmates or more rose from 65 in 2000 to 76 in 2005, an increase of 17%, which was the largest increase for any size range. The number of minimum-security prisons increased by 19% during this same period, from 814 in 2000 to 969 in 2005.

Correctional Facility Employees

State and federal correctional facilities employed more than 445,000 people as of December 30, 2005. (See Table 7.2.) Nearly two-thirds (67%) of the employees were male. Correctional officers, who work in direct contact with inmates, numbered 295,261 (or 66% of the total). Clerical and maintenance workers include secretaries, clerks, janitors, cooks, and groundskeepers. They accounted for 12% of state and federal prison employees. Professional and technical staff members are doctors, nurses, dentists, counselors, and other medical and social workers. They made up 10% of total employees. Academic and technical educators made up 3% of the workforce, and prison administrators (such as wardens) accounted for 2% of the workforce. Another 7% of state and federal prison workers were not specifically classified in the 2005 census.

State Prisons and Inmates

Table 7.3 lists the number of state prisons and inmates by region and state according to the 2000 and 2005 censuses. As of 2005, the southern states had the most prisons (779) and inmates (561,927). The 10 states with the largest numbers of state prisons in 2005 were:

- Texas—132
- Florida—109
- California—100

TABLE 7.1

Number of state and federal prisons and inmates, population change, and number of inmates per 100,000 U.S. residents, 2000 and 2005

Region and authority	Number of facilities		Number of inmates held		Population change,	Inmates per 100,000 U.S. residents	
	2000	2005	2000	2005	2000–2005	2000	2005
U.S. total	1,668	1,821	1,305,253	1,430,208	9.6%	464	480
Public[a]	1,404	1,406	1,212,176	1,321,685	9	431	444
Private	264	415	93,077	108,523	16.6	33	36
Federal	84	102	110,974	145,780	31.4	39	49
State[b]	1,584	1,719	1,194,279	1,284,428	7.5	424	431

Note: Unless stated otherwise, numbers for 2000 are as of June 30, and numbers for 2005 are as of December 30.
[a]Includes facilities operated by both federal and state authorities.
[b]Includes private facilities.
Some inmates were housed in private facilities under contract to the District of Columbia on December 30, 2005.

SOURCE: Adapted from James J. Stephan, "Appendix Table 1. Number of Correctional Facilities and Inmates under State or Federal Authority, Population Change, and Number of Inmates per 100,000 U.S. Residents, June 30, 2000, and December 30, 2005," in *Census of State and Federal Correctional Facilities, 2005*, U.S. Department of Justice, Office of Justice Programs, Bureau of Justice Statistics, October 2008, http://www.ojp.usdoj.gov/bjs/pub/pdf/csfcf05.pdf (accessed November 27, 2008)

FIGURE 7.1

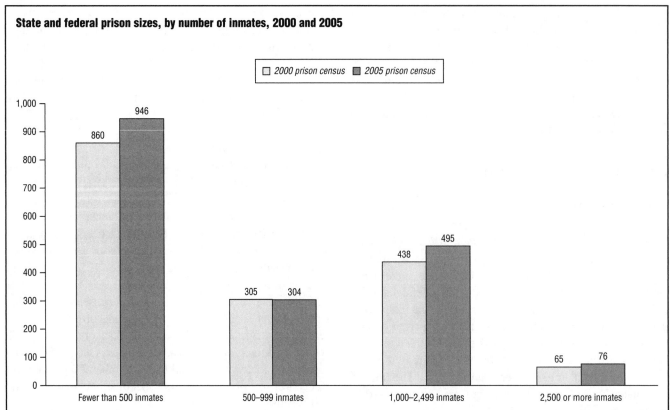

State and federal prison sizes, by number of inmates, 2000 and 2005

☐ *2000 prison census* ■ *2005 prison census*

SOURCE: Adapted from James J. Stephan, "Table 1. Total Number of Correctional Facilities by Characteristic, June 30, 2000, and December 30, 2005," in *Census of State and Federal Correctional Facilities, 2005*, U.S. Department of Justice, Office of Justice Programs, Bureau of Justice Statistics, October 2008, http://www.ojp.usdoj.gov/bjs/pub/pdf/csfcf05.pdf (accessed November 27, 2008)

FIGURE 7.2

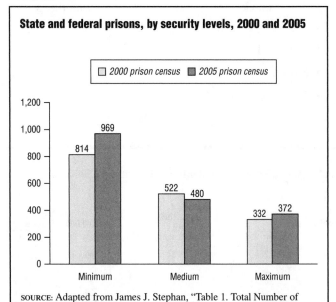

State and federal prisons, by security levels, 2000 and 2005

☐ *2000 prison census* ■ *2005 prison census*

SOURCE: Adapted from James J. Stephan, "Table 1. Total Number of Correctional Facilities by Characteristic, June 30, 2000, and December 30, 2005," in *Census of State and Federal Correctional Facilities, 2005*, U.S. Department of Justice, Office of Justice Programs, Bureau of Justice Statistics, October 2008, http://www.ojp.usdoj.gov/bjs/pub/pdf/csfcf05.pdf (accessed November 27, 2008)

- North Carolina—88
- Georgia—87
- New York—77
- Michigan—62
- Ohio—59
- Virginia—59
- Colorado—58

Between 2000 and 2005 the Midwestern states added 41 state prisons, from 301 to 342. The number of state prisons in the southern region increased by 36, from 743 to 779; the northeastern region increased by 32, from 236 to 268; and the western region increased by 26, from 304 to 330.

In 2005 the states housing the most state inmates were California (169,988), Texas (163,556), Florida (86,705), New York (63,855), and Georgia (51,822). Between the 2000 and 2005 censuses, the western region had the largest rate of inmate population increase of 9%; at 50.8% Idaho had the greatest inmate increase rate of any state.

Work, Educational, and Counseling Programs for Inmates

As of December 30, 2005, a large majority of state and federal prisons offered inmate work, educational, or

TABLE 7.2

Number of employees in state or federal correctional facilities, by gender and occupational category, December 30, 2005

	Number	Percent
Gender		
Male	296,852	67
Female	148,203	33
Occupational category		
Administrators	10,769	2
Correctional officers	295,261	66
Clerical/maintenance	51,993	12
Educational	11,526	3
Professional/technical	46,016	10
Other/not available	29,489	7

SOURCE: James J. Stephan, "Table 4. Number of Employees in Correctional Facilities under State or Federal Authority, by Gender and Occupational Category," in *Census of State and Federal Correctional Facilities, 2005*, U.S. Department of Justice, Office of Justice Programs, Bureau of Justice Statistics, October 2008, http://www.ojp.usdoj.gov/bjs/pub/pdf/csfcf05.pdf (accessed November 27, 2008)

counseling programs. Most facilities (88%) offered inmate work programs, typically in facility support services. (See Table 7.4.) Similarly, 85% of state and federal prisons offered educational programs to the inmates, mostly for secondary education and general education diploma testing. Even more facilities (92%) offered counseling programs, mainly in life skills and community adjustment.

PRISON INMATES AT MIDYEAR 2007

Every year the DOJ collects data on the nation's state and federal inmate population. Surveys are conducted at midyear and at the end of the year. Survey results from midyear 2007 were reported by Sabol and Couture in 2008 in *Prison Inmates at Midyear 2007*. Nearly 1.6 million inmates were under state or federal jurisdiction at midyear 2007. (See Table 7.5.) The vast majority (87.5%) of the inmates were in state prisons, and 12.5% were in federal prisons. Most of the inmates (92.8%) were male, and 95.8% of the inmates were serving a sentence length of more than one year. The imprisonment rate was 509 inmates per 100,000 U.S. residents.

Table 7.6 lists the number of inmates in state and federal prisons by region and state based on yearend surveys from 2000 and 2006 and the midyear 2007 survey. The table also shows the average annual percent change in inmate populations between 2000 and 2006. Overall, state and federal inmate populations increased by 0.3% in the Northeast, by 1.6% in the Midwest, by 1.8% in the South, and by 2.4% in the West.

The states with the highest annual rates of inmate increases from yearend 2000 to yearend 2006 were:

- West Virginia—up 6.8%
- Minnesota—up 6.5%

- Arizona—up 5.2%
- Kentucky—up 5%
- Colorado—up 4.9%
- Florida—up 4.5%
- Vermont—up 4.5%
- Indiana—up 4.4%
- Oregon—up 4.4%
- Idaho—up 4.3%
- South Dakota—up 4.3%

Some states saw declines in their state and federal inmate populations from yearend 2000 to yearend 2006. These states were New York (down 1.7%), New Jersey (down 1.4%), Maryland (down 0.4%), and Illinois (down 0.1%).

Partial Data from Midyear 2008

Initial results from the midyear 2008 survey were released in *Prison Inmates at Midyear 2008—Statistical Tables* (March 31, 2009, http://www.ojp.usdoj.gov/bjs/pub/pdf/pim08st.pdf) by Heather C. West and William J. Sabol. A total of 1,610,584 inmates were under state or federal jurisdiction at midyear 2008, including 1,494,805 males and 115,779 females. The 10 states with the largest state and federal inmate populations at that time were:

- California—173,320 inmates
- Texas—173,232 inmates
- Florida—100,494 inmates
- New York—62,211 inmates
- Georgia—54,016 inmates
- Ohio—51,160 inmates
- Michigan—50,482 inmates
- Illinois—45,675 inmates
- Pennsylvania—46,313 inmates
- Virginia—39,224 inmates

JAILS

Besides confining offenders for short terms (usually a sentence of less than one year), jails administer community justice programs that offer alternatives to incarceration. Jails also hold suspects awaiting arraignment, trial, or sentencing, and such detainees as juveniles and mental patients who are being transferred to other facilities.

Jail Inmates at Midyear 2007

Data from the DOJ survey of the nation's jail population conducted June 30, 2007, were reported by William J. Sabol and Todd D. Minton in *Jail Inmates at Midyear 2007* (June 2008, http://www.ojp.usdoj.gov/bjs/pub/pdf/jim07.pdf). At

TABLE 7.3

State and federal prisons and inmates, by region and state, 2000 and 2005 and population change from 2000 to 2005

Region and authority	Number of facilities		Number of inmates held		Population change, 2000–2005
	2000	2005	2000	2005	
Region (excluding federal)					
Northeast	236	268	171,999	171,465	−0.3%
Connecticut	20	49	16,984	19,019	12
Maine	8	7	1,629	1,968	20.8
Massachusetts	25	17	10,500	10,262	−2.3
New Hampshire	8	8	2,277	2,373	4.2
New Jersey	43	42	27,118	25,724	-5.1
New York	72	77	71,938	63,855	−11.2
Pennsylvania	44	52	36,895	43,254	17.2
Rhode Island	7	7	3,347	3,414	2
Vermont	9	9	1,311	1,596	21.7
Midwest	301	342	233,993	255,134	9%
Illinois[a]	48	44	44,150	44,669	1.2
Indiana	25	23	18,195	23,205	27.5
Iowa	30	31	9,086	10,145	11.7
Kansas	11	13	8,992	9,47t4	5.4
Michigan	70	62	47,639	50,082	5.1
Minnesota	9	18	7,451	9,680	29.9
Missouri	28	28	27,963	31,748	13.5
Nebraska	9	9	3,508	4,371	24.6
North Dakota	3	8	992	1,411	42.2
Ohio	34	59	47,915	44,717	−6.7
South Dakota	4	6	2,591	3,451	33.2
Wisconsin	30	41	15,511	22,181	43
South	743	779	518,912	561,927	8.3%
Alabama	36	33	22,422	23,174	3.4
Arkansas	15	26	10,465	13,921	33
Delaware	9	12	6,023	6,781	12.6
District of Columbia[b]	8	5	3,767	300	−92
Florida	106	109	71,616	86,705	21.1
Georgia	84	87	44,299	51,822	17
Kentucky	25	25	12,378	14,932	20.6
Louisiana	17	23	19,167	20,344	6.1
Maryland	26	29	22,821	22,613	−0.9
Mississippi	28	31	14,823	16,967	14.5
North Carolina	80	88	30,708	38,233	24.5
Oklahoma	52	53	23,858	25,149	5.4
South Carolina	34	33	21,277	22,537	5.9
Tennessee	15	19	18,368	19,484	6.1
Texas	136	132	162,440	163,556	0.7
Virginia	61	59	31,412	31,478	0.2
West Virginia	11	15	3,068	3,931	28.1
West	304	330	269,375	295,902	9.8%
Alaska	24	21	3,248	4,146	27.6
Arizona	18	21	30,832	32,855	6.6
California	92	100	163,383	169,988	4
Colorado	48	58	15,695	20,842	32.8
Hawaii	10	10	3,761	3,951	5.1
Idaho	13	15	3,961	5,975	50.8
Montana	8	11	2,368	3,160	33.4
Nevada	20	22	9,296	11,726	26.1
New Mexico	10	11	5,158	7183	39.3
Oregon	13	15	9,933	13049	31.4
Utah	9	7	4,872	5461	12.1
Washington	30	32	14,682	16146	10
Wyoming	9	7	2,186	1420	−35

Note: Unless stated otherwise, numbers for 2000 are as of June 30, and numbers for 2005 are as of December 30.
[a]2005 data are as of June 30.
[b]As of December 30, 2001, sentenced felons from the District of Columbia were the responsiblity of the Federal Bureau of Prisons. Some inmates were housed in private facilities under contract to the District of Columbia on December 30, 2005.

SOURCE: Adapted from James J. Stephan, "Appendix Table 1. Number of Correctional Facilities and Inmates under State or Federal Authority, Population Change, and Number of Inmates per 100,000 U.S. Residents, June 30, 2000, and December 30, 2005," in *Census of State and Federal Correctional Facilities, 2005*, U.S. Department of Justice, Office of Justice Programs, Bureau of Justice Statistics, October 2008, http://www.ojp.usdoj.gov/bjs/pub/pdf/csfcf05.pdf (accessed November 27, 2008)

TABLE 7.4

TABLE 7.5

Number of state or federal correctional facilities providing work, educational, and counseling programs to inmates, December 30, 2005

	Number of facilities	Percent of all facilities
Inmate work programs	1,594	88%
Facility support services	1,347	74
Public works	798	44
Prison industries	562	31
Work release	502	28
Educational programs	1,550	85%
Secondary education or GED	1,399	77
Literacy or 1st–4th grade	1,229	67
5th–8th grade	1,203	66
Vocational training	956	52
Special education	667	37
College courses	642	35
English as a second language	632	35
Counseling programs	1,676	92%
Life skills and community adjustment	1,421	78
Drug/alcohol dependency	1,344	74
Employment	1,332	73
Psychological or psychiatric	1,054	58
HIV/AIDS	996	55
Parenting	873	48
Sex offender	662	36

SOURCE: James J. Stephan,"Table 6. Number of Correctional Facilities under State or Federal Authority That Provided Work, Educational, and Counseling Programs to Inmates, December 30, 2005," in *Census of State and Federal Correctional Facilities, 2005*, U.S. Department of Justice, Office of Justice Programs, Bureau of Justice Statistics, October 2008, http://www.ojp.usdoj .gov/bjs/pub/pdf/csfcf05.pdf (accessed November 27, 2008)

Characteristics of state and federal inmates, December 31, 2000, December 31, 2006, and June 30, 2007

	Number of prisoners			Percent
	12/31/2000	12/31/2006	06/30/2007	06/30/2007
Total[3]	1,391,261	1,570,115	1,595,034	100%
Federal	145,416	193,046	199,118	12.5
State	1,245,845	1,377,069	1,395,916	87.5
Gender				
Male	1,298,027	1,457,641	1,479,726	92.8%
Female	93,234	112,474	115,308	7.2
Sentence length				
More than 1 year	1,331,278	1,502,179	1,528,041	95.8%
1 year or less[b]	59,983	67,936	66,993	4.2
Sentenced imprisonment rate[c]				
Total	478	501	509	
Male	915	943	957	
Female	59	68	69	

[a]Includes prisoners under the authority of state or federal correctional officials regardless of the facility in which they were held.
[b]Includes unsentenced prisoners.
[c]Imprisonment rates are based on U.S. Census Bureau population estimates per 100,000 U.S. residents. Resident population estimates are as of January 1 for yearend and July 1 for midyear.

SOURCE: William J. Sabol and Heather Couture, "Table 1. Prisoners under State or Federal Jurisdiction by Selected Characteristics, December 31, 2000 and 2006, and June 30, 2007," in *Prison Inmates at Midyear 2007*, U.S. Department of Justice, Office of Justice Programs, Bureau of Justice Statistics, June 2008, http://www.ojp.usdoj.gov/bjs/pub/pdf/pim07.pdf (accessed November 27, 2008)

midyear 2007, 780,581 inmates were being held in local jails. The number of local jail inmates was 621,148 in 2000. (See Figure 7.3.) The population grew at an average annual rate of 3.3% between 2000 and 2007. The annual rate increase varied from a low of 1.5% in 2001 to a high of 5.5% in 2002. Between 2005 and 2007 the annual growth rate decreased each year, reaching 1.9% in 2007.

Local Jail Sizes

Table 7.7 breaks down the nation's local jail jurisdictions by size of facility from 1999 to 2007. The midyear 2007 DOJ survey included 2,860 local jurisdictions. Nearly 1,097 (38%) of the jurisdictions had jail facilities that held fewer than 50 inmates each. A much smaller number of jurisdictions (173 or 6%) had facilities that held 1,000 or more inmates each. Figure 7.4 provides a breakdown of the number of jail inmates by jail size at midyear 2007. Sabol and Minton note that of the 780,581 inmates in local jails at that time, 402,300 (51.5%) were in jails that each held 1,000 or more inmates. Even though jails holding fewer than 50 inmates each were much more prevalent, they held only 22,460 (2.9%) inmates.

Local Jail Programs Besides Incarceration

Table 7.8 lists the number of people that were held in local jails or under local correctional supervision as of mid-

year 2000, 2006, and 2007. Of the 848,826 people under confinement status as of midyear 2007, the vast majority (780,581 or 92% of the total) were incarcerated full time. The remaining 8% (68,245) were in various types of supervised programs outside of jail facilities. At midyear 2007, 15,327 people were involved in community service programs under the supervision of local jurisdictions. Nearly 10,500 people were in weekender programs. These programs allow sentenced individuals (typically those convicted of nonserious, nonviolent misdemeanors) to serve jail time on the weekends only.

Partial Data from Midyear 2008

On March 31, 2009, the BJS reported initial results from the midyear 2008 survey in *Jail Inmates at Midyear 2008—Statistical Tables* (http://www.ojp.usdoj.gov/bjs/pub/pdf/ jim08st.pdf) by Todd D. Minton and William J. Sabol. A total of 785,556 inmates were held in local jails as of June 30, 2008, including 685,882 males and 99,673 females. A preliminary breakdown of jail inmates by race and ethnicity in 2008 included 333,300 non-Hispanic white inmates (42.4% of the total), 308,000 African-Americans (39.2%), 128,500 Hispanics (16.4%), 15,300 of other or mixed races (1.9%).

Minton and Sabol state that the 10 largest local jail jurisdictions (based on the number of inmates held) at midyear 2008 were:

TABLE 7.6

Inmates in state or federal prison, by region and state, December 31, 2000, December 31, 2006, and June 30, 2007, and average annual change between December 31, 2000 and December 31, 2006

Region and jurisdiction	Number of prisoners			Average annual change 12/31/00– 12/31/06
	12/31/00	12/31/06	6/30/07	
U.S. total	1,391,261	1,570,115	1,595,034	2.0%
Northeast	174,826	177,817	180,980	0.3%
Connecticut[a]	18,355	20,566	20,780	1.9
Maine	1,679	2,120	2,185	4.0
Massachusetts	10,722	11,032	11,440	0.5
New Hampshire	2,257	2,805	2,814	3.7
New Jersey	29,784	27,371	28,378	−1.4
New York	70,199	63,315	63,536	−1.7
Pennsylvania	36,847	44,397	45,563	3.2
Rhode Island[a]	3,286	3,996	4,119	3.3
Vermont[a]	1,697	2,215	2,165	4.5
Midwest	237,378	261,466	264,066	1.6%
Illinois	45,281	45,106	45,565	−0.1
Indiana	20,125	26,091	26,833	4.4
Iowa[b]	7,955	8,875	8,837	1.8
Kansas	8,344	8,816	8,850	0.9
Michigan	47,718	51,577	50,648	1.3
Minnesota	6,238	9,108	9,891	6.5
Missouri	27,543	30,167	29,942	1.5
Nebraska	3,895	4,407	4,435	2.1
North Dakota	1,076	1,363	1,435	4.0
Ohio	45,833	49,166	50,418	1.2
South Dakota	2,616	3,359	3,446	4.3
Wisconsin	20,754	23,431	23,766	2.0
South	561,214	622,817	633,236	1.8%
Alabama	26,332	28,241	29,244	1.2
Arkansas	11,915	13,729	13,914	2.4
Delaware[a]	6,921	7,206	7,521	0.7
District of Columbia[c]	7,456	~	~	~
Florida	71,319	92,969	95,078	4.5
Georgia[b]	44,232	52,792	53,226	3.0
Kentucky	14,919	20,000	21,644	5.0
Louisiana	35,207	37,012	36,981	0.8
Maryland	23,538	22,945	23,123	−0.4
Mississippi	20,241	21,068	21,758	0.7
North Carolina	31,266	37,460	38,179	3.1
Oklahoma	23,181	25,497	25,686	1.6
South Carolina	21,778	23,616	24,093	1.4
Tennessee	22,166	25,745	26,453	2.5
Texas	166,719	172,116	172,626	0.5
Virginia	30,168	36,688	37,824	3.3
West Virginia	3,856	5,733	5,886	6.8

- Los Angeles County, California—19,533 inmates
- New York City, New York—13,804 inmates
- Harris County, Texas—10,063 inmates
- Cook County, Illinois—9,984 inmates
- Maricopa County, Arizona—9,536 inmates
- Philadelphia City, Pennsylvania—8,824 inmates
- Miami-Dade County, Florida—7,082 inmates
- Dallas County, Texas—6,252 inmates
- Orange County, California—6,216 inmates
- Shelby County, Tennessee—5,925 inmates

TABLE 7.6

Inmates in state or federal prison, by region and state, December 31, 2000, December 31, 2006, and June 30, 2007, and average annual change between December 31, 2000 and December 31, 2006 [CONTINUED]

Region and jurisdiction	Number of prisoners			Average annual change 12/31/00– 12/31/06
	12/31/00	12/31/06	6/30/07	
West	272,427	314,969	317,634	2.4%
Alaska[a]	4,173	5,069	5,312	3.3
Arizona[b]	26,510	35,892	37,088	5.2
California	163,001	175,512	176,059	1.2
Colorado	16,833	22,481	22,662	4.9
Hawaii[a]	5,053	5,967	6,039	2.8
Idaho	5,535	7,124	7,357	4.3
Montana	3,105	3,572	3,469	2.4
Nevada	10,063	12,901	13,034	4.2
New Mexico	5,342	6,639	6,526	3.7
Oregon	10,580	13,707	14,012	4.4
Utah	5,637	6,430	6,524	2.2
Washington	14,915	17,561	17,438	2.8
Wyoming	1,680	2,114	2,114	3.9

~ Not applicable. See footnote c.
[a]Prisons and jails form one integrated system. Data include total jail and prison populations.
[b]Population based on custody counts.
[c]As of December 30, 2001, sentenced felons from the District of Columbia were the responsibility of the Federal Bureau of Prisons.

SOURCE: Adapted from William J. Sabol and Heather Couture, "Table 2. Prisoners under the Jurisdiction of State or Federal Correctional Authorities, by Region and Jurisdiction, December 31, 2000 and 2006, and June 30, 2007" in *Prison Inmates at Midyear 2007*, U.S. Department of Justice, Office of Justice Programs, Bureau of Justice Statistics, June 2008, http://www.ojp .usdoj.gov/bjs/pub/pdf/pim07.pdf (accessed November 27, 2008)

OVERALL INCARCERATION NUMBERS AND RATES

The BJS keeps track of the total number of inmates in state and federal prisons and local jails (http://www.ojp.us doj.gov/bjs/glance/corr2.htm; and http://www.albany.edu/ sourcebook/pdf/t6132007.pdf). The total number of inmates in the United States has risen steadily for more than two decades. Between 1980 and 1990 the prison population more than doubled, from 503,000 inmates to 1,150,000 inmates, and then continued to grow. By 2007 it had doubled from the 1990 number; there were nearly 2.3 million inmates in U.S. prisons and jails.

According to the BJS, in "Key Facts at a Glance: Correctional Populations" (December 11, 2008, http://www.ojp.us doj.gov/bjs/glance/tables/corr2tab.htm), the greatest annual growth in the number of inmates occurred during the 1980s. The average annual increase for this decade was 8.9%. The largest annual increase occurred between 1988 and 1989, when the inmate population grew from 951,335 to 1,078,920—a rise of 13.4%. The U.S. inmate population topped 1 million in 1989. During the 1990s the average annual increase in the number of inmates was 6.4%. Between 2000 and 2007 the inmate population grew at an average rate of 2.4% per year. Thus, the inmate population grew at a much lower annual rate during the first decade of the twenty-first century than it had in the previous two decades.

Table 7.9 provides a breakdown of the number of inmates in federal, state, and local facilities from 2000 to 2007. The federal and state prison populations are based on annual yearend surveys, whereas the local jail populations are based on midyear surveys. Overall, the inmate population increased by 2.6% between yearend 2000 and yearend 2006. The rate of increase was highest for federal prisoners at 5.3%, compared with 3.6% for jail inmates and 1.7% for state inmates. In other words, the federal inmate population grew at a faster annual rate from 2000 to 2006 than did the state or local jail inmate populations.

FIGURE 7.3

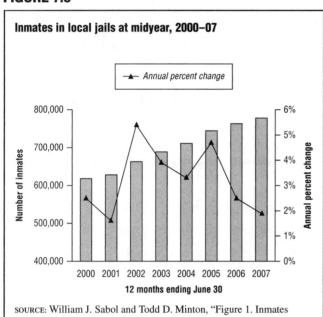

Inmates in local jails at midyear, 2000–07

SOURCE: William J. Sabol and Todd D. Minton, "Figure 1. Inmates Confined in Local Jails at Midyear, 2000–2007," in *Jail Inmates at Midyear 2007*, U.S. Department of Justice, Office of Justice Programs, Bureau of Justice Statistics, June 2008, http://www.ojp.usdoj.gov/bjs/pub/pdf/jim07.pdf (accessed November 27, 2008)

The incarceration rate is the number of people sent by the courts to prisons and jails per 100,000 people in the general population. The incarceration rate for people in state and federal prisons and local jails was 313 in 1985. (See Table 7.10.) By 1996 the rate had more than doubled to 618 inmates per 100,000 U.S. residents. In 2002 the rate surpassed 700 and continued to climb. In 2007 the incarceration rate was 762 inmates per 100,000 U.S. residents.

Crime rates, as calculated by the FBI, have decreased since the 1990s while the incarceration rate has increased. It should be noted, however, FBI crime rate statistics do not include drug offenses—or related money laundering offenses and illegal weapons violations—which have been growing at high rates. Some additional reasons for the rising incarceration rate include:

• More people are serving time in prison; that is, fewer convicts are receiving probation or parole.

• Mandatory sentencing rules require that some criminals be held for longer periods.

• Some courts are requiring stiffer sentences.

• There is a rising incidence of rearrest of those who have been paroled.

OVERCROWDING IN PRISONS AND JAILS

The booming inmate populations in state and federal prisons and local jails have led, in some facilities, to overcrowding. When overcrowding occurs, two inmates are often assigned to a cell designed for one person, or temporary housing units are set up to take prison overflow. Overcrowding makes it more likely that disagreements will rise between inmates, leading to violence and injuries. In addition, diseases are more likely to spread among the inmate population.

TABLE 7.7

Number of local jail jurisdictions, midyear 1999–2007

Jurisdiction size*	Number of jail jurisdictions, midyear								
	1999	2000	2001	2002	2003	2004	2005	2006	2007
Total	2,999	3,001	3,002	3,001	3,003	3,003	2,876	2,861	2,860
Fewer than 50 inmates	1,518	1,512	1,479	1,387	1,369	1,331	1,147	1,130	1,097
50 to 99	547	499	509	535	546	526	559	548	583
100 to 249	471	512	523	554	547	566	564	561	558
250 to 499	212	224	231	255	259	294	286	281	272
500 to 999	128	131	137	141	144	135	161	180	177
1,000 or more	123	123	123	129	138	151	159	161	173

*Based on the average daily population.

SOURCE: William J. Sabol and Todd D. Minton, "Appendix Table 1. Number of Jail Jurisdictions, Midyear 1999–2007," in *Jail Inmates at Midyear 2007*, U.S. Department of Justice, Office of Justice Programs, Bureau of Justice Statistics, June 2008, http://www.ojp.usdoj.gov/bjs/pub/pdf/jim07.pdf (accessed November 27, 2008)

FIGURE 7.4

Local jail inmates, by size of jail, June 30, 2007

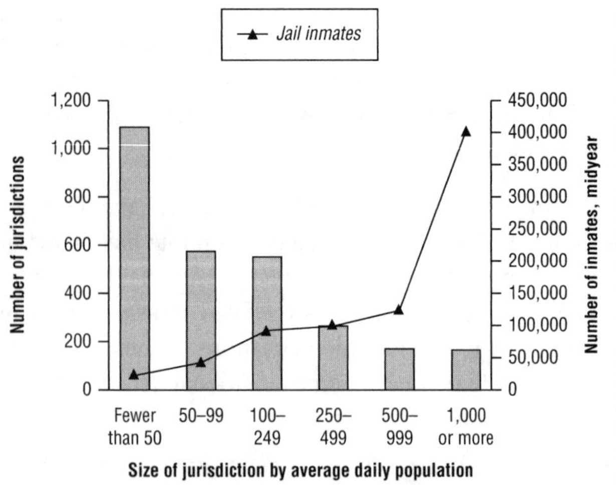

SOURCE: William J. Sabol and Todd D. Minton, "Figure 4. Number of Jail Inmates and Jurisdictions, by Size of Jail Jurisdiction, Midyear 2007," in *Jail Inmates at Midyear 2007*, U.S. Department of Justice, Office of Justice Programs, Bureau of Justice Statistics, June 2008, http://www.ojp.usdoj.gov/bjs/pub/pdf/jim07.pdf (accessed November 27, 2008)

TABLE 7.8

Persons under the supervision of local jail jurisdictions, by confinement status and type of program, 2000, 2006, and 2007

Confinement status and type of program	Number of persons under jail supervision		
	2000	2006	2007
Total	687,033	826,232	848,826
Held in jail	621,149	766,010	780,581
Supervised outside of a jail facility[a]	65,884	60,222	68,245
Weekender programs	14,523	11,421	10,473
Electronic monitoring	10,782	10,999	13,121
Home detention[b]	332	807	512
Day reporting	3,969	4,841	6,163
Community service	13,592	14,667	15,327
Other pretrial supervision	6,279	6,409	11,148
Other work programs[c]	8,011	8,319	7,369
Treatment programs[d]	5,714	1,486	2,276
Other	2,682	1,273	1,857

[a]Excludes persons supervised by a probation or parole agency.
[b]Includes only those without electronic monitoring.
[c]Includes persons in work release programs, work gangs, and other work alternative programs.
[d]Includes persons under drug, alcohol, mental health, and other medical treatment.

SOURCE: William J. Sabol and Todd D. Minton, "Appendix Table 5. Persons under Jail Supervision, by Confinement Status and Type of Program, Midyear 2000, 2006, and 2007," in *Jail Inmates at Midyear 2007*, U.S. Department of Justice, Office of Justice Programs, Bureau of Justice Statistics, June 2008, http://www.ojp.usdoj.gov/bjs/pub/pdf/jim07.pdf (accessed November 27, 2008)

State and Federal Prison Capacity

Table 7.11, from the 2008 BJS publication *Census of State and Federal Correctional Facilities, 2005*, lists the percent of rated capacity occupied by inmates in state and federal prisons as of December 30, 2005. (Rated capacity is the maximum number of beds or inmates that may be housed in a correctional facility.) Overall, U.S. prisons were at 111% of capacity on that date. Publicly operated prisons were at 112% of capacity, whereas privately operated prisons were at 95% of capacity. Federal prisons were much more troubled by overcrowding than state prisons. Federal prisons reported being at 137% of capacity, whereas state prisons were at 108% of capacity. On a regional basis, state prisons in the western United States reported the most overcrowding (120% of capacity), followed by the Midwest (110% of capacity), the South (104% of capacity), and the Northeast (102% of capacity).

The 10 most overcrowded state prison systems were:

- California—141% of capacity
- Illinois—136% of capacity
- Washington—131% of capacity
- Florida—128% of capacity
- Ohio—122% of capacity
- Iowa—116% of capacity
- Hawaii—110% of capacity

- New Hampshire—109% of capacity
- Wisconsin—109% of capacity
- Pennsylvania—108% of capacity

Jail Capacity

Overall, the nation's jails do not suffer as much overcrowding as the state and federal prisons. Figure 7.5 shows the rated capacity of local jails and the percent of capacity occupied from 2000 to 2007. Note that data were compiled based on midyear surveys. According to Sabol and Minton in *Jail Inmates at Midyear 2007*, local jails had a rated capacity of 677,787 in 2000. This is the number of beds that were available. By 2007 local jail capacity had reached 813,502 beds, an average annual increase of 2.6%. In 2000 local jails were at approximately 90% of rated capacity. In 2007 they were at 96% of rated capacity.

The capacities and percents of capacity occupied of local jails differ greatly by jurisdiction. Sabol and Minton note that 16 of the country's 50 largest local jail jurisdictions were over 100% capacity as of midyear 2007:

- Denver County, Colorado—139% of capacity
- Polk County, Florida—136% of capacity
- Maricopa County, Arizona—130% of capacity
- Bernalillo County, New Mexico—118% of capacity
- Jacksonville City, Florida—114% of capacity

TABLE 7.9

Details on inmates in state or federal prison or local jails, 2000–07

				December 31						Average annual change, 2000–2006	Percent change, 12/31/2006–06/30/2007
	2000	2001	2002	2003	2004	2005	2006	June 30, 2007		
Total inmates in custody	1,937,482	1,961,247	2,033,022	2,081,580	2,135,335	2,195,873	2,258,983	2,299,116	2.6%	1.8%
Federal prisons[a]										
Total	140,064	149,852	158,216	168,144	177,600	186,364	190,844	196,804	5.3%	3.1%
Prisons	133,921	143,337	151,618	161,673	170,535	179,220	183,381	188,779	5.4	2.9
Federal facilities	124,540	130,601	137,942	146,279	152,832	159,318	163,118	166,425	4.6	2.0
Privately operated facilities	9,381	12,736	13,676	15,394	17,703	19,902	20,263	22,354	13.7	10.3
Community Corrections Centers[b]	6,143	6,515	6,598	6,471	7,065	7,144	7,463	8,025	3.3	7.5
State prisoners	1,176,269	1,180,155	1,209,331	1,222,135	1,243,745	1,261,980	1,302,129	1,321,731	1.7%	1.5%
Inmates held in local jails[c]	621,149	631,240	665,475	691,301	713,990	747,529	766,010	780,581	3.6	1.9
Incarceration rate[d]	684	685	701	712	723	737	751	762		

Note: Counts include all inmates held in public and private adult correctional facilities and in local jails.

[a]As of December 30, 2001, sentenced felons from the District of Columbia were the responsibility of the Federal Bureau of Prisons.

[b]Non-secure, privately operated community corrections centers.

[c]Counts for inmates held in local jails are for the last working day of June in each year. Counts were estimated from the Annual Survey of Jails in every year except 2005 when a Census of Jail Inmates was conducted.

[d]The total number in custody per 100,000 U.S. residents. Resident population estimates were as of January 1 of the following year for December 31 estimates. Resident population estimates are as of July 1, 2007 for June 30, 2007 estimates.

SOURCE: William J. Sabol and Heather Couture, "Table 8. Prisoners and Inmates Held in Custody in State or Federal Prisons or in Local Jails, December 31, 2000–2006 and June 30, 2007," in *Prison Inmates at Midyear 2007*, U.S. Department of Justice, Office of Justice Programs, Bureau of Justice Statistics, June 2008, http://www.ojp.usdoj.gov/bjs/pub/pdf/pim07.pdf (accessed November 27, 2008)

TABLE 7.10

Adult incarceration rate, 1985 and 1990–2007

	Incarceration rate[a]
1985	313
1990	458
1991	481
1992	505
1993	528
1994	564
1995	601
1996	618
1997	648
1998	669
1999[b]	691
2000	684
2001	685
2002	701
2003	712
2004	723
2005	737
2006	751
2007[c]	762

Note: Jail counts are for the last business day in June; beginning in 1994 counts exclude persons who were supervised outside of a jail facility. State and federal prisoner counts are for December 31 except where indicated otherwise.

[a]Number of prison and jail inmates per 100,000 U.S. residents at yearend.

[b]In 1999, 15 states expanded their reporting criteria to include prisoners held in privately operated correctional facilities. For comparisons with previous years, the state count 1,137,544 and the total 1,869,169 should be used for 1999.

[c]Counts are as of midyear and subject to revision.

SOURCE: Adapted from Ann L. Pastore and Kathleen Maguire, editors, "Table 6.13.2007. Number and Rate (per 100,000 U.S. Residents) of Persons in State and Federal Prisons and Local Jails," in *Sourcebook of Criminal Justice Statistics Online*, U.S. Department of Justice, Office of Justice Programs, Bureau of Justice Statistics, undated, http://www.albany.edu/sourcebook/pdf/t6132007.pdf (accessed December 4, 2008)

- Santa Clara County, California—114% of capacity
- Clark County, Nevada—113% of capacity
- Riverside County, California—112% of capacity
- San Diego County, California—107% of capacity
- Harris County, Texas—105% of capacity
- Milwaukee County, Wisconsin—105% of capacity
- Pinellas County, Florida—105% of capacity
- Marion County, Indiana—104% of capacity
- Mecklenburg County, North Carolina—104% of capacity
- Wayne County, Michigan—104% of capacity
- Cobb County, Georgia—101% of capacity

Together, these local jails held more than 64,000 inmates as of midyear 2007.

COSTS OF CORRECTIONS

In its Justice Expenditures and Employments Extracts series (December 18, 2008, http://www.ojp.usdoj.gov/bjs/glance/expgov.htm), the BJS reports that total spending for all federal, state, and local justice functions in fiscal year 2006 reached $214.5 billion, or $597 per U.S. resident. This represented a 5.1% increase over the previous year, and a 498% increase since 1982, when total direct spending for all federal, state, and local justice functions was $36 billion.

TABLE 7.11

Percent of rated prison capacity occupied by inmates in state or federal prisons, December 30, 2005

Region and authority	Percent of rated capacity occupied	
	2000	2005
U.S. total	102%	111%
Public[a]	103	112
Private	89	95
Federal	134	137
State[b]	100	108
Region (excluding federal)		
Northeast	107%	102%
Connecticut	97	102
Maine	105	107
Massachusetts[c]	87	93
New Hampshire	114	109
New Jersey	101	99
New York	104	101
Pennsylvania	140	108
Rhode Island	90	88
Vermont	97	96
Midwest	109%	110%
Illinois[d]	131	136
Indiana	120	92
Iowa	107	116
Kansas	99	98
Michigan	99	99
Minnesota	91	97
Missouri	94	98
Nebraska	103	n/a
North Dakota	109	97
Ohio	118	122
South Dakota	98	94
Wisconsin	108	109
South	95%	104%
Alabama	101	n/a
Arkansas	104	95
Delaware	105	99
District of Columbia[e]	91	60
Florida	95	128
Georgia	97	97
Kentucky	95	97
Louisiana	97	105
Maryland	93	93
Mississippi	86	93
North Carolina	91	95
Oklahoma	95	96
South Carolina	91	97
Tennessee	96	97
Texas	95	95
Virginia	96	97
West Virginia	99	97

The total amount spent on corrections facilities and functions at the federal, state, and local levels rose by roughly 660% during this period, from $9 billion in 1982 to $68.7 billion in 2006. Corrections costs in 1982 equaled $40 for each U.S. resident, or about $84 in 2006 dollars as computed by the Bureau of Labor Statistics (2009, http://data.bls.gov/cgi-bin/cpicalc.pl). By 2006 corrections costs had risen to $210 per person. By comparison, the per capita cost of police protection rose from $84 ($175 in 2006 dollars) to $264, and judicial and legal costs rose from $34 ($71 in 2006 dollars) to $123.

TABLE 7.11

Percent of rated prison capacity occupied by inmates in state or federal prisons, December 30, 2005 [CONTINUED]

Region and authority	Percent of rated capacity occupied	
	2000	2005
West	98%	120%
Alaska	90	100
Arizona	105	97
California	98	141
Colorado	88	93
Hawaii	109	110
Idaho	76	100
Montana	97	101
Nevada	96	96
New Mexico	85	98
Oregon	87	96
Utah	92	99
Washington	148	131
Wyoming	75	80

[a]Includes facilities operated by both federal and state authorities.
[b]Includes private facilities.
[c]The total number of facilities in 2005 are as of June 30.
[d]2005 population reported by the Illinois Department of Corrections as of June 30. Rated capacity is estimated based on data reported by facilities in 2000 that were in operation in 2005.
[e]As of December 30, 2001, sentenced felons from the District of Columbia were the reponsibility of the Federal Bureau of Prisons. Some inmates were housed in private facilities under contract to the District of Columbia on December 30, 2005.

SOURCE: Adapted from James J. Stephan, "Appendix Table 4. Design and Rated Capacities of Correctional Facilities under State or Federal Authority, June 30, 2000, and December 30, 2005," in *Census of State and Federal Correctional Facilities, 2005*, U.S. Department of Justice, Office of Justice Programs, Bureau of Justice Statistics, October 2008, http://www.ojp.usdoj.gov/bjs/pub/pdf/csfcf05.pdf (accessed November 27, 2008)

Prisoner Work Programs

State and local governments prevent prisoners from working at some jobs because they would be in competition with private enterprise or workers. In 1936 Congress barred convicts from working on federal contracts worth more than $10,000. In 1940 Congress made it illegal to transport convict-made goods through interstate commerce. These rules were changed in 1979, when Congress established the Prison Industry Enhancement Certification Program (PIECP). The PIECP allows state correctional industries that meet certain requirements to sell inmate-produced goods to the federal government and in interstate commerce. The National Correctional Industries Association (NCIA), the professional organization for prison industry employees, provides training and technical assistance to the PIECP.

According to the latest PIECP statistics from the NCIA (2008, http://www.nationalcia.org/wp-content/uploads/2008/10/qtr0208cumulative.pdf), the program paid gross wages of $466.3 million from 1979 through the second quarter of 2008. From this total the following deductions were made: victims programs ($45.3 million), room and board ($134.6 million), family support ($29.8 million), and taxes ($61.7 million). In addition, more than $23.4 million went to mandatory savings accounts. Overall, the program paid nearly $194.9 million in net wages.

FIGURE 7.5

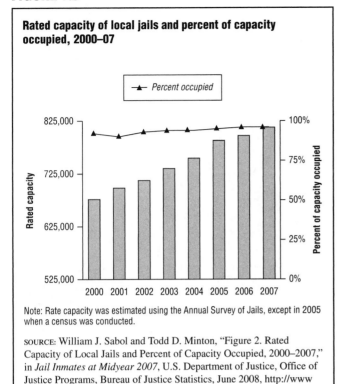

Rated capacity of local jails and percent of capacity occupied, 2000–07

Note: Rate capacity was estimated using the Annual Survey of Jails, except in 2005 when a census was conducted.

SOURCE: William J. Sabol and Todd D. Minton, "Figure 2. Rated Capacity of Local Jails and Percent of Capacity Occupied, 2000–2007," in *Jail Inmates at Midyear 2007*, U.S. Department of Justice, Office of Justice Programs, Bureau of Justice Statistics, June 2008, http://www.ojp.usdoj.gov/bjs/pub/pdf/jim07.pdf (accessed November 27, 2008)

Many prison administrators generally favor work programs. Some believe work keeps prisoners productive and occupied, thus leading to a safer prison environment. Another cited benefit is that work programs prepare prisoners for reentry into the noninstitutionalized world by helping them develop job skills and solid work habits that will be needed for postincarceration employment. Some prisons report that inmates who work in industry are less likely to cause problems in prison or be rearrested after release than convicts who do not participate in work programs.

In addition, many inmates report they like the opportunity to work. They assert that it provides relief from boredom and gives them some extra money. Inmates find that the money they earn helps them to meet financial obligations for their families even while they are in prison.

Work Programs for Federal Inmates

According to the BOP, in "Work Programs" (2008, http://www.bop.gov/inmate_programs/work_prgms.jsp), federal prison inmates are required to work if they are medically able to do so. Their work assignments typically contribute to the facility operations and maintenance in areas such as food service, plumbing, painting, or landscaping. Inmates earn $0.12 to $0.40 per hour for these in-house work assignments. The BOP also reports that 18% of federal prison

inmates work in Federal Prison Industries factories. This program provides slightly higher wages to inmates, from $0.23 to $1.15 per hour as of fiscal year 2008. Work includes manufacturing jobs in areas such as furniture, electronics, textiles, and graphic arts. With a high school diploma or its equivalent inmates can be promoted to a managerial role.

UNICOR. UNICOR is the trade name for Federal Prison Industries, Inc. (FPI), the government corporation that employs inmates in federal prisons. UNICOR should not be confused with state prison industry programs administered by the states. Under UNICOR, which was established in 1934, federal inmates get job training by producing goods and services for federal agencies. In 2009 items produced by inmates included clothing and textiles (military items and apparel, protective clothing for law enforcement, mattresses, and medical textiles), electronics (circuit boards, electrical cables, and outdoor lighting systems/flood lights), industrial products (prescription and nonprescription safety eyewear, traffic and safety signage, license plates, air filters, and perimeter fencing), and office furniture (systems furniture, seating, and filing and storage products). Inmates also provided fleet management and vehicular components (fleet vehicle and vehicular component remanufacturing, fleet vehicle uplifting, and fleet management services), recycling (computers and electronic equipment), and other services (data services, printing and binding, and contact center/help desk support).

UNICOR products and services must be purchased by federal agencies and are not for sale in interstate commerce or to nonfederal entities. UNICOR is not permitted to compete with private industry. If UNICOR cannot make the needed product or provide the required service, federal agencies may buy the product from the private sector through a waiver issued by UNICOR.

According to the FPI, in *2008 Annual Report* (2008, http://www.unicor.gov/information/publications/pdfs/corporate/CATAR2008.pdf), UNICOR employed 21,836 inmates in 109 factories at 76 prison locations at the end of September 2008. Of all eligible inmates in BOP facilities, 17% worked for UNICOR that year. The agency's goal is to employ 25% of all work-eligible prisoners who have no existing job skills.

UNICOR is a self-supporting government corporation that may borrow funds from the U.S. Department of the Treasury and use the proceeds to purchase equipment, pay wages to inmates and staff, and invest in expansion of facilities. However, no funds are appropriated for UNICOR operations. During fiscal year 2008 its net sales were $854.3 million.

CHAPTER 8
CHARACTERISTICS AND RIGHTS OF INMATES

CHARACTERISTICS OF INMATES

Federal and State Prisoners

William J. Sabol and Heather Couture of the Bureau of Justice Statistics (BJS) report in *Prison Inmates at Midyear 2007* (June 2008, http://www.ojp.usdoj.gov/bjs/pub/pdf/pim07.pdf) that as of June 30, 2007, there were nearly 1.6 million federal and state inmates. The vast majority (nearly 1.4 million or 87.5%) were in state prisons. The remaining 199,000 (12.5%) were in federal prisons. State and federal prisoners were overwhelmingly male (92.8%). Between December 31, 2000, and June 30, 2007, the number of male inmates increased 14%, from 1,298,027 to 1,479,726. By contrast, the number of female inmates rose from 93,234 to 115,308 during this same period, an increase of 25%.

The sentenced imprisonment rate (i.e., the number of sentenced prisoners per 100,000 U.S. residents) for state and federal inmates was 509 as of June 30, 2007. (See Table 7.5 in Chapter 7.) The rate for males was 957, and for females was 69. These rates were up from yearend 2000, when the overall rate was 478 and the rates for males and females were 915 and 59, respectively.

At midyear 2007, 95.8% of state and federal inmates were serving sentence lengths greater than one year. The remainder were serving sentences of a year or less.

Federal Inmates Only

The Federal Bureau of Prisons (BOP) is an agency of the U.S. Department of Justice (DOJ). The BOP oversees the corrections system for federal inmates and administers federal prisons. In *Quick Facts about the Bureau of Prisons* (October 25, 2008, http://www.bop.gov/about/facts.jsp), the BOP provides a snapshot in time of the federal inmate population. As of October 25, 2008, the BOP held 201,280 federal inmates. The vast majority (188,007 or 93.4%) of the prisoners were male, and only 13,273 (6.6%) were female. (See Table 8.1.) More than half (57%) of the inmates were white, whereas 39.6% were African-American, 1.7% were

Native American, and 1.7% were Asian-American. Nearly one-third (31.8%) of its prisoners were of Hispanic ethnicity.

Nearly three-fourths (73.5%) of federal inmates were U.S. citizens. (See Table 8.1.) The next largest group of inmates by citizenship was Mexican citizens, which made up 17.3% of the total. Much smaller proportions were citizens of Colombia and the Dominican Republic (1.5% each) and of Cuba (0.9%). The remaining 5.4% of inmates were of other or unknown citizenship. The average inmate age was 38 years old.

Table 8.2 provides a breakdown of federal inmate offenses as of October 25, 2008. More than half (52.5%) of the prisoners were in prison for drug crimes—the largest single category. Another 15.1% of inmates were in prison for charges involving weapons, explosives, and/or arson, and 10.6% of the total had been sentenced for immigration offenses. Together, these three crime categories accounted for 78.2% of the offenses of federal inmates. Each of the other crime categories listed in Table 8.2 accounted for less than 5% of total offenses.

Table 8.3 lists the sentences imposed on federal inmates as of October 25, 2008. The largest single contingent of prisoners (30.1%) were serving a sentence of 5 to 10 years. Approximately 19.9% of the inmates had received a sentence of 10 to 15 years, and nearly 14.8% were serving 3- to 5-year sentences. Smaller contingents were serving sentences of 1 to 3 years (12%), more than 20 years (9.7%), 15 to 20 years (8.8%), and less than 1 year (1.6%). Just over 3% of federal inmates had received life sentences, and 49 inmates had been given death sentences.

State Inmates Only

At yearend 2005 (the most recent year for which complete demographic data were available as of April 2009), there were nearly 1.3 million state inmates, according to Heather C. West and William J. Sabol in *Prisoners in 2007* (December 2008, http://www.ojp.usdoj.gov/bjs/pub/pdf/p07.pdf). The vast majority (1.2 million or 93%) were male. The

TABLE 8.1

Federal inmates, by security level, gender, race, ethnicity, age, and citizenship, October 25, 2008

Inmates by security level

Minimum	16.7 %
Low	38.3 %
Medium	29.1 %
High	11.3 %
Unclassified*	4.4 %

Inmates by gender

Male	188,007	(93.4 %)
Female	13,273	(6.6 %)

Inmates by race

White	114,708	(57.0 %)
Black	79,724	(39.6 %)
Native American	3,494	(1.7 %)
Asian	3,354	(1.7 %)

Ethnicity

Hispanic	63,967	(31.8 %)

Inmate age

Average inmate age	38

Citizenship

United States	147,875	(73.5 %)
Mexico	34,861	(17.3 %)
Colombia	2,948	(1.5 %)
Cuba	1,799	(0.9 %)
Dominican Republic	2,951	(1.5 %)
Other/Unknown	10,846	(5.4 %)

*These inmates have not yet been assigned a security level.

SOURCE: "Inmate Breakdown," in *Quick Facts about the Bureau of Prisons*, U.S. Department of Justice, Federal Bureau of Prisons, October 25, 2008, http://www.bop.gov/about/facts.jsp (accessed December 3, 2008)

TABLE 8.2

Federal inmates, by type of offense, October 25, 2008

Drug offenses	98,168	(52.5%)
Weapons, explosives, arson	28,186	(15.1%)
Immigration	19,860	(10.6%)
Robbery	8,918	(4.8%)
Burglary, larceny, property offenses	6,705	(3.6%)
Extortion, fraud, bribery	9,011	(4.8%)
Homicide, aggravated assault, and kidnapping offenses	5,563	(3.0%)
Miscellaneous	2,039	(1.1%)
Sex offenses	6,297	(3.4%)
Banking and insurance, counterfeit, embezzlement	893	(0.5%)
Courts or corrections	685	(0.4%)
Continuing criminal enterprise	556	(0.3%)
National Security	94	(0.1%)

SOURCE: "Types of Offenses," in *Quick Facts about the Bureau of Prisons*, U.S. Department of Justice, Federal Bureau of Prisons, October 25, 2008, http://www.bop.gov/about/facts.jsp (accessed December 3, 2008)

female inmate population was 88,000, making up 7% of the total. At yearend 2005 African-American state inmates numbered 504,700, accounting for 39% of the total. The 470,700 white inmates accounted for 36% of the total. About 18.5% (240,100) of state prisoners were of Hispanic ethnicity.

West and Sabol report that at yearend 2005, 53% of state inmates were incarcerated for violent offenses, pri-

TABLE 8.3

Federal inmates, by sentence imposed, October 25, 2008

Less than 1 year	2,993	(1.6%)
1–3 years	22,431	(12.0%)
3–5 years	27,605	(14.8%)
5–10 years	56,255	(30.1%)
10–15 years	37,231	(19.9%)
15–20 years	16,391	(8.8%)
More than 20 years	18,225	(9.7%)
Life	5,903	(3.2%)
Death	49	

*Data is only calculated for cases where sentencing information is available.

SOURCE: "Sentence Imposed," in *Quick Facts about the Bureau of Prisons*, U.S. Department of Justice, Federal Bureau of Prisons, October 25, 2008, http://www.bop.gov/about/facts.jsp (accessed December 3, 2008)

marily robbery (13.7%), murder or negligent manslaughter (12.9%), and assault (10%). Another 19.2% of all state prisoners had been sentenced for property offenses, including 9.6% for burglary, 3.5% for larceny, and 2.5% for fraud. Those incarcerated for drug offenses comprised 19.5% of the state inmate population. Another 7.6% were in prison for public-order offenses, such as crimes involving weapons, drunk driving, and so on. An estimated 0.6% of state inmates had been convicted for other or unspecified offenses.

Among male state inmates at yearend 2005, the largest contingents had been convicted of drug offenses (18.9%), robbery (14.1%), murder or negligent manslaughter (13%), assault (10%), and burglary (9.8%). Among female inmates, the five largest crime categories were drug offenses (28.7%), murder or negligent manslaughter (11.2%), fraud (10.4%), assault (8.8%), and robbery (8.6%). A higher percentage of male inmates (54.3%) than female inmates (35.4%) were incarcerated for violent crimes; 18.5% of male inmates and 28.6% of female inmates had been sentenced for property offenses. Similarly, 18.9% of male inmates and 28.7% of female inmates had been convicted of drug offenses.

There were some differences at yearend 2005 between white and African-American prisoners regarding the percentage breakdown by offense. West and Sabol report that half (50.1%) of white inmates were incarcerated for violent crimes, compared with 54.6% of African-American inmates. Nearly a quarter (24.4%) of white inmates were incarcerated for property crimes, compared with 16.1% of African-American inmates. Among white inmates at yearend 2005, the five largest crime categories were drug offenses (15.4%), sexual assault other than rape (12.3%), burglary (11.6%), murder or negligent manslaughter (10.5%), and public order offenses (9.4%). The largest contingents of African-American inmates, according to West and Sabol, had been convicted of drug offenses (22.5%), robbery (18.9%), murder or negligent manslaughter (14.3%), assault (9.5%), and burglary (8.5%). The five largest crime categories for state inmates of Hispanic origin were drug offenses (21.3%), mur-

TABLE 8.4

Characteristics of local jail inmates, midyear 2000 and 2005–07

Characteristic	Number of inmates			
	2000	2005	2006	2007
Average daily population[a]	618,319	733,442	755,896	773,800
Number of inmates at midyear	621,149	747,529	766,010	780,581
Jail incarceration rate[b]	226	252	256	259
Gender				
Male	550,162	652,958	666,985	680,009
Female	70,987	94,571	99,025	100,572
Age				
Adults	613,534	740,770	759,906	773,744
Males	543,120	646,807	661,329	673,697
Female	70,414	93,963	98,577	100,047
Juveniles[c]	7,615	6,759	6,104	6,837
Held as adults[d]	6,126	5,750	4,836	5,652
Held as juveniles	1,489	1,009	1,268	1,185
Race/Hispanic origin[e]				
White[f]	260,500	331,000	336,600	338,400
Black/African American[f]	256,300	290,500	296,000	301,900
Hispanic/Latino	94,100	111,900	119,200	125,600
Other[f, g]	10,200	13,000	13,500	13,900
Two or more races[f]	—	1,000	700	800
Conviction status[e]				
Convicted	270,000	284,400	290,100	296,900
Male	234,200	248,100	251,600	256,500
Female	41,300	36,300	38,500	40,400
Unconvicted	343,600	463,100	475,900	483,700
Male	300,300	405,300	415,900	423,800
Female	49,600	57,900	60,000	59,900

—Not collected.

[a]Average daily population is the sum of the number of inmates in jail each on each day for a year divided by the total number of days in a year.

[b]Number of inmates per 100,000 U.S. resident population.

[c]Juveniles are persons under the age of 18 at midyear.

[d]Includes juveniles who were tried or awaiting trial as adults.

[e]Estimates based on reported data adjusted for nonresponse.

[f]Excludes persons of Hispanic or Latino origin.

[g]Includes American Indians, Alaska Natives, Asians, Native Hawaiians, and other Pacific Islanders

SOURCE: William J. Sabol, "Appendix Table 4. Characteristics of Inmates in Local Jails, Midyear 2000 and 2005–2007," in *Jail Inmates at Midyear 2007*, U.S. Department of Justice, Office of Justice Programs, Bureau of Justice Statistics, June 2008, http://www.ojp.usdoj.gov/bjs/glance/jailrace.htm (accessed November 27, 2008)

FIGURE 8.1

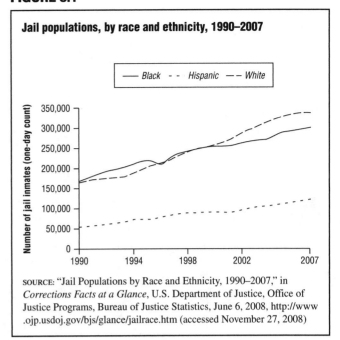

Jail populations, by race and ethnicity, 1990–2007

SOURCE: "Jail Populations by Race and Ethnicity, 1990–2007," in *Corrections Facts at a Glance*, U.S. Department of Justice, Office of Justice Programs, Bureau of Justice Statistics, June 6, 2008, http://www.ojp.usdoj.gov/bjs/glance/jailrace.htm (accessed November 27, 2008)

der or negligent manslaughter (13.4%), assault (13.3%), robbery (12.8%), and sexual assault other than rape (9%).

Local Jail Inmates Only

Table 8.4 provides demographic details about local jail inmates as of midyears 2000, 2005, 2006, and 2007. At midyear 2007 there were 780,581 inmates in local jails for an incarceration rate of 259 jail inmates per 100,000 U.S. resident population. The jail incarceration rate was up from 226 in midyear 2000. At midyear 2007, 680,009 (87%) of jail inmates were male and 100,572 (13%) were female. The racial breakdown was non-Hispanic white (338,400 inmates or 43.4% of the total), non-Hispanic African-American (301,900 inmates or 38.7%), non-Hispanic inmates of other races (13,900 inmates or 1.8%), and non-Hispanic inmates of two or more races (800 inmates or 0.1%). Hispanic

inmates (125,600) made up about 16% of the jail population in 2007.

At midyear 2007 nearly all inmates in local jails were adults. Approximately 6,800 of the inmates were juveniles, making up 0.9% of the total inmate population.

Convicted inmates include those awaiting sentencing, serving a sentence, or returned to jail for a violation of probation or parole. Jails also hold people who have not been convicted of a crime but who are awaiting arraignment and those who are being detained pending transfer to a juvenile or mental health facility. More local jail inmates were classified as unconvicted (483,700 inmates or 62%) than convicted (296,900 inmates or 38%) at midyear 2007. (See Table 8.4.)

Figure 8.1 shows how the racial and ethnic makeup of local jail populations changed over the period from 1990 to 2007. From 1990 to 1997 the African-American inmate population slightly outnumbered the white inmate population. The two were roughly equal near the end of the 1990s. From 2001 through 2007 the white population was higher than the African-American population. Between 1990 and 2007 the white jail population nearly doubled, from 170,000 to 340,000 inmates. By contrast, the African-American jail population increased by approximately 75%, from 170,000 to 300,000 inmates. The Hispanic jail population more than doubled from 58,000 inmates in 1990 to 125,000 inmates in 2007.

Figure 8.2 compares the incarceration rates for non-Hispanic African-Americans, non-Hispanic whites, and Hispanics. The incarceration rate for non-Hispanic whites rose from 89 per 100,000 U.S. residents in 1990 to 170 in 2007,

FIGURE 8.2

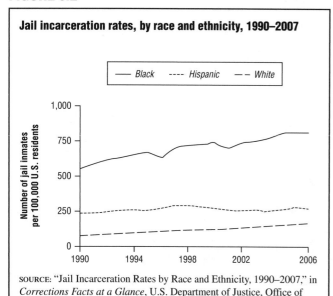

Jail incarceration rates, by race and ethnicity, 1990–2007

— Black   ---- Hispanic   – – White

SOURCE: "Jail Incarceration Rates by Race and Ethnicity, 1990–2007," in *Corrections Facts at a Glance*, U.S. Department of Justice, Office of Justice Programs, Bureau of Justice Statistics, June 6, 2008, http://www.ojp.usdoj.gov/bjs/glance/jailrair.htm (accessed November 27, 2008)

an increase of 91%. The non-Hispanic African-American incarceration rate grew from 560 per 100,000 U.S. residents in 1990 to 815 in 2007, an increase of 46%. The incarceration rate for Hispanics rose from 245 per 100,000 U.S. residents in 1990 to 276 in 2007, an increase of 13%. Overall, in 2007 non-Hispanic African-Americans were almost three times more likely than Hispanics and almost five times more likely than non-Hispanic whites to be in jail.

Comprehensive statistics on jail inmate offenses are provided in *Sourcebook of Criminal Justice Statistics 2003* (2007, http://www.albany.edu/sourcebook/) by Ann L. Pastore and Kathleen Maguire of the Utilization of Criminal Justice Statistics Project. The researchers note that in 1983 the largest proportion of jail inmates had been convicted of property offenses (38.6%), followed by violent offenses (30.7%), public-order offenses (20.6%), and drug offenses (9.3%). (See Table 8.5.) The distribution of offenses had changed drastically by 2002, when approximately equal proportions of prisoners had been convicted of violent offenses (25.4%), public-order offenses (24.9%), drug offenses (24.7%), and property offenses (24.4%).

Federal, State, and Local Inmates

Table 8.6 provides a breakdown of federal, state, and local inmates by age, gender, race, and Hispanic origin as of June 30, 2007. At that time there were 2.3 million inmates—nearly 2.1 million males and 208,000 females. Concerning the male population, there were 814,700 (39% of the total) non-Hispanic African-American, 755,500 (36%) non-Hispanic whites, and 410,900 (20%) Hispanics. Among the female population, there were 96,600 (46%) non-Hispanic

whites, 67,600 (32%) non-Hispanic African-Americans, and 32,100 (15%) Hispanics.

Details on the age distribution of inmates by race and Hispanic origin are shown in Table 8.7. As of June 30, 2007, more than half of male inmates were under age 35, with 4.1% being between the ages of 18 and 19, 16.9% aged 20 to 24, 16.9% aged 25 to 29, and 15.7% aged 30 to 34. Almost half (49.9%) of all female inmates were younger than 35, though the largest numbers were within the age ranges of 35 to 39 (18.7%), 30 to 34 (17%), or 40 to 44 (15.7%). Overall, non-Hispanic African-American male inmates and Hispanic male inmates were younger than non-Hispanic white male inmates. Nearly 70% of non-Hispanic African-American male inmates were less than 40 years old, compared with approximately 62% of non-Hispanic white male inmates. Just over three-fourths of Hispanic male inmates were less than 40 years old. Among female inmates, there was little difference between non-Hispanic African-Americans and non-Hispanic whites regarding the percentage younger than 40. Approximately two-thirds of each group were below this age. By contrast, nearly 75% of female Hispanic inmates were younger than 40.

Table 8.8 shows the incarceration rate for federal, state, and local inmates by age, gender, race, and Hispanic origin as of June 30, 2007. The incarceration rate is the number of inmates per 100,000 U.S. residents. The total rates for males and females were 1,406 and 136, respectively. The rate for non-Hispanic African-American males was 4,618 per 100,000 U.S. residents, whereas for non-Hispanic white males it was 773. The incarceration rate for Hispanics was 1,747. Among females, the rates in descending order were 348 for non-Hispanic African-Americans, 146 for Hispanics, and 95 for non-Hispanic whites. Overall, non-Hispanic African-American males were nearly six times as likely as non-Hispanic white males and nearly three times as likely as Hispanics to be incarcerated. Within every age range non-Hispanic African-American males were incarcerated at higher rates than either non-Hispanic whites or Hispanics. The highest incarceration rates reported in Table 8.8 were for non-Hispanic African-American males aged 30 to 34 (10,688 per 100,000 U.S. residents), 25 to 29 (10,384), and 20 to 24 (9,692).

PRISONERS WITH MINOR CHILDREN

Lauren E. Glaze and Laura M. Maruschak of the BJS estimate in *Parents in Prison and Their Minor Children* (August 2008, http://www.ojp.usdoj.gov/bjs/pub/pdf/pptmc.pdf) that 809,800 state and federal prisoners were parents of minor children (i.e., children under the age of 18) as of midyear 2007. These parents accounted for 52% of state inmates and 63% of federal inmates. Together, the parents had more than 1.7 million minor children, or 2.3% of the total U.S. population of minor children. The breakdown by race and Hispanic origin for the minor children of inmates

TABLE 8.5

Jail inmates by type of offense, 1983, 1989, 1996, 2002

				Percent of jail inmates			
				2002			
Most serious offense	1983	1989	1996	Total	Convicted	Unconvicted	Both[a]
Number of jail inmates	219,573	380,160	496,752	623,492	342,372	178,035	100,348
Violent offenses	30.7%	22.5%	26.3%	25.4%	21.6%	34.4%	22.3%
Murder, nonnegligent manslaughter	4.1	2.8	2.8	2.0	0.9	5.3	NA
Negligent manslaughter	0.6	0.5	0.4	0.5	0.7	0.4	0.3
Kidnapping	1.3	0.8	0.5	0.7	0.4	1.4	0.6
Rape	1.5	0.8	0.5	0.6	0.6	0.8	0.4
Other sexual assault	2.0	2.6	2.7	2.8	2.7	3.6	1.5
Robbery	11.2	6.7	6.5	5.6	3.9	8.7	5.5
Assault	8.6	7.2	11.6	11.7	10.9	12.5	12.7
Other violent[b]	1.3	1.1	1.3	1.4	1.4	1.6	1.1
Property offenses	38.6	30.0	26.9	24.4	24.9	21.5	27.4
Burglary	14.3	10.7	7.6	6.7	6.4	6.8	8.0
Larceny/theft	11.7	7.9	8.0	7.0	7.6	5.3	7.6
Motor vehicle theft	2.3	2.8	2.6	2.0	2.0	1.6	2.6
Arson	0.8	0.7	0.4	0.3	0.3	0.5	0.1
Fraud	5.0	4.0	4.6	4.9	5.3	4.2	4.7
Stolen property	2.5	2.4	2.1	1.7	1.6	1.4	2.5
Other property[c]	1.9	1.6	1.6	1.8	1.8	1.7	1.9
Drug offenses	9.3	23.0	22.0	24.7	24.0	23.4	30.2
Possession	4.7	9.7	11.5	10.8	10.0	10.4	14.6
Trafficking	4.0	12.0	9.2	12.1	12.6	10.6	13.5
Other drug	0.6	1.3	1.3	1.8	1.5	2.3	2.1
Public-order offenses	20.6	22.8	24.4	24.9	29.1	20.2	19.2
Weapons	2.3	1.9	2.3	2.0	2.1	1.9	2.2
Obstruction of justice	2.0	2.8	4.9	3.9	3.5	5.4	2.7
Traffic violations	2.2	2.7	3.2	3.7	4.7	2.3	2.5
Driving while intoxicated[d]	7.0	8.8	7.4	6.4	8.9	2.3	5.1
Drunkenness, morals[e]	3.4	1.7	2.0	1.7	1.8	1.5	1.8
Violation of parole, probation[f]	2.3	3.0	2.6	2.9	3.5	1.5	3.3
Immigration violations	NA	NA	0.2	1.8	1.8	2.5	0.3
Other public-order[g]	1.6	1.8	1.8	2.5	2.8	2.8	1.2
Other offenses[h]	0.8	1.6	0.5	0.5	0.4	0.6	0.9

[a]Includes inmates with a prior conviction, but no new conviction for the current charge.
[b]Includes blackmail, extortion, hit-and-run driving with bodily injury, child abuse, and criminal endangerment.
[c]Includes destruction of property, vandalism, hit-and-run driving without bodily injury, trespassing, and possession of burglary tools.
[d]Includes driving while intoxicated and driving under the influence of drugs or alcohol.
[e]Includes drunkenness, vagrancy, disorderly conduct, unlawful assembly, morals, and commercialized vice.
[f]Includes parole or probation violations, escape, absence without leave (AWOL), and flight to avoid prosecution.
[g]Includes rioting, abandonment, nonsupport, invasion of privacy, liquor law violations, and tax evasion.
[h]Includes juvenile offenses and other unspecified offenses.

SOURCE: Ann L. Pastore and Kathleen Maguire, editors, "Table 6.19. Most Serious Current Offense of Jail Inmates, by Conviction Status, United States, 1983, 1989, 1996, and 2002," in *Sourcebook of Criminal Justice Statistics 2003*, 31st ed., U.S. Department of Justice, Office of Justice Programs, Bureau of Justice Statistics, 2005, http://www.albany.edu/sourcebook/pdf/t619.pdf (accessed December 8, 2008)

was African-American children (6.7%), Hispanic children (2.4%), and white children (0.9%). In other words, African-American children were about seven times more likely than white children and over two and half times more likely than Hispanic children to have an incarcerated parent.

The vast majority of the parents (744,200) were fathers, whereas 65,600 were mothers. Inmate fathers reported having nearly 1.6 million minor children, whereas inmate mothers reported having 147,400 minor children. According to Glaze and Maruschak, the number of minor children with a mother in prison grew by 131% between 1991 and 2006, whereas those with a father in prison grew by 77%.

MEDICAL PROBLEMS IN INMATES

The latest data on the medical problems of state and federal prisoners are addressed by Laura M. Maruschak

of the BJS in *Medical Problems of Prisoners* (April 2008, http://www.ojp.usdoj.gov/bjs/pub/pdf/mpp.pdf). Maruschak presents findings from the 2004 Survey of Inmates in State and Federal Correctional Facilities. According to Maruschak, 44% of state inmates and 39% of federal inmates reported a current medical problem other than a cold or virus. A breakdown of the medical problems by gender and age is presented in Table 8.9. The most common medical problems reported by inmates were arthritis (15.3% of state inmates and 12.4% of federal inmates), hypertension (13.8% of state inmates and 13.2% of federal inmates), and asthma (9.1% of state inmates and 7.2% of federal inmates). Female inmates and inmates older than 45 years of age were much more likely to report having a current medical problem than male inmates and those younger than 45 years of age, respectively.

TABLE 8.6

Inmates held in state or federal prisons or local jails, by gender, race, Hispanic origin, and age, June 30, 2007

Age	Male				Female			
	Total[a]	White[b]	Black[b]	Hispanic	Total[a]	White[b]	Black[b]	Hispanic
Total	2,090,800	755,500	814,700	410,900	208,300	96,600	67,600	32,100
18–19	86,600	27,100	36,500	17,700	5,500	2,300	1,500	1,300
20–24	353,300	108,200	145,600	80,100	31,000	14,200	9,000	6,100
25–29	354,100	106,200	143,400	83,900	32,000	14,500	10,000	5,700
30–34	328,600	109,500	125,600	73,800	35,500	16,400	11,600	5,700
35–39	303,100	113,700	118,200	55,000	39,000	18,300	13,200	5,200
40–44	273,600	114,200	103,300	41,900	32,700	15,000	11,600	3,900
45–49	184,200	77,500	71,200	27,800	18,200	8,400	6,500	2,200
50–54	96,800	43,300	35,500	13,900	8,000	4,200	2,300	1,000
55–59	50,500	26,600	15,000	7,600	3,300	1,800	700	600
60–64	21,700	13,200	5,200	3,300	1,200	700	400	100
65 or older	17,700	10,900	4,500	2,100	800	600	100	100

Note: Detailed categories exclude persons who reported two or more races.
[a]Includes American Indians, Alaska Natives, Asians, Native Hawaiians, other Pacific Islanders, and persons identifying two or more races.
[b]Excludes persons of Hispanic or Latino origin.

SOURCE: William J. Sabol and Heather Couture, "Table 9. Estimated Number of Persons Held in State or Federal Prisons or Local Jails, by Gender, Race, Hispanic Origin, and Age, June 30, 2007," in *Prison Inmates at Midyear 2007*, U.S. Department of Justice, Office of Justice Programs, Bureau of Justice Statistics, June 2008, http://www.ojp.usdoj.gov/bjs/pub/pdf/pim07.pdf (accessed November 27, 2008)

TABLE 8.7

Inmates in state or federal prisons or local jails, by gender, race, ethnicity, and age, June 30, 2007

Age	Male				Female			
	Total[a]	White[b]	Black[b]	Hispanic	Total[a]	White[b]	Black[b]	Hispanic
18–19	4.1%	3.6%	4.5%	4.3%	2.6%	2.4%	2.2%	4.0%
20–24	16.9	14.3	17.9	19.5	14.9	14.7	13.3	19.0
25–29	16.9	14.1	17.6	20.4	15.4	15.0	14.8	17.8
30–34	15.7	14.5	15.4	18.0	17.0	17.0	17.2	17.8
35–39	14.5	15.0	14.5	13.4	18.7	18.9	19.5	16.2
40–44	13.1	15.1	12.7	10.2	15.7	15.5	17.2	12.1
45–49	8.8	10.3	8.7	6.8	8.7	8.7	9.6	6.9
50–54	4.6	5.7	4.4	3.4	3.8	4.3	3.4	3.1
55–59	2.4	3.5	1.8	1.8	1.6	1.9	1.0	1.9
60–64	1.0	1.7	0.6	0.8	0.6	0.7	0.6	0.3
65 or older	0.8	1.4	0.6	0.5	0.4	0.6	0.1	0.3

Note: Detailed categories exclude persons who reported two or more races. Totals do not sum to 100%. Percentage of inmates under 18 years is not shown.
[a]Includes American Indians, Alaska Natives, Asians, Native Hawaiians, and other Pacific Islanders.
[b]Excludes persons of Hispanic or Latino origin.

SOURCE: William J. Sabol and Heather Couture, "Appendix Table 10. Estimated Percentage of Persons Held in State or Federal Prisons or Local Jails, by Gender, Race, Hispanic Origin, and Age, June 30, 2007," in *Prison Inmates at Midyear 2007*, U.S. Department of Justice, Office of Justice Programs, Bureau of Justice Statistics, June 2008, http://www.ojp.usdoj.gov/bjs/pub/pdf/pim07.pdf (accessed November 27, 2008)

HIV/AIDS

Maruschak reports in *HIV in Prisons, 2006* (April 2008, http://www.ojp.usdoj.gov/bjs/pub/html/hivp/2006/hivp06 .htm) that the number of inmates with the human immunodeficiency virus (HIV) in state and federal prisons as of yearend 2006 was 21,980. This number was down 3.1% from 2005 even though the prison population increased by 2.2% during this period. The percentage of inmates with HIV or acquired immunodeficiency syndrome (AIDS) at yearend 2006 was 2.4% for female inmates and 1.6% for male inmates. The three states with the largest contingents of state prisoners known to be infected with HIV or AIDS were New York (4,000 inmates), Florida (3,412 inmates), and Texas (2,693

inmates). Together, these three states accounted for 49% of all HIV/AIDS cases among state inmates.

Concerning prison inmates who were diagnosed with AIDS, the rate was 0.5%, compared with a rate of 0.2% for the general U.S. population. In 2006 there were 167 prisoner deaths related to AIDS. This number was down from 203 deaths reported in 2005.

Mental Health Problems of Inmates

A movement began in the 1970s to deinstitutionalize the mentally ill and reintegrate them into society. This widespread trend resulted in the closing of many large mental hospitals and treatment centers. With fewer options open to

TABLE 8.8

Inmates held in state or federal prisons or local jails per 100,000 residents, by gender, race, Hispanic origin, and age, June 30, 2007

	Male				Female			
Age	Total[a]	White[b]	Black[b]	Hispanic	Total[a]	White[b]	Black[b]	Hispanic
Total	**1,406**	**773**	**4,618**	**1,747**	**136**	**95**	**348**	**146**
18–19	1,995	1,016	5,710	2,383	133	90	245	187
20–24	3,256	1,631	9,692	4,043	304	226	612	357
25–29	3,286	1,686	10,384	3,607	311	233	697	310
30–34	3,317	1,904	10,688	3,388	369	288	893	313
35–39	2,844	1,704	9,577	2,824	371	278	957	309
40–44	2,496	1,566	8,148	2,489	297	205	808	256
45–49	1,630	968	5,665	2,025	157	103	449	167
50–54	940	569	3,300	1,342	74	54	183	94
55–59	571	394	1,751	995	35	26	64	76
60–64	313	242	890	628	16	12	51	22
65 or older	111	84	373	195	4	4	7	4

Note: Based on the U.S. resident population estimates for July 1, 2007, by gender, race, Hispanic origin, and age. Detailed categories exclude persons who reported two or more races.
[a]Includes American Indians, Alaska Natives, Asians, Native Hawaiians, other Pacific Islanders, and persons identifying two or more races.
[b]Excludes persons of Hispanic or Latino origin.

SOURCE: William J. Sabol and Heather Couture, "Table 10. Estimated Number of Inmates Held in State or Federal Prison or in Local Jails per 100,000 Residents, by Gender, Race, Hispanic Origin, and Age, June 30, 2007," in *Prison Inmates at Midyear 2007*, U.S. Department of Justice, Office of Justice Programs, Bureau of Justice Statistics, June 2008, http://www.ojp.usdoj.gov/bjs/pub/pdf/pim07.pdf (accessed November 27, 2008)

TABLE 8.9

Medical problems reported by state and federal inmates, by gender, and age, 2004

		Gender		Age			
Current medical problem	All inmates	Male	Female	24 or younger	25–34	35–44	45 or older
State inmates							
Arthritis	15.3%	14.6%	24.5%	5.4%	8.6%	17.4%	32.6%
Asthma	9.1	8.4	19.2	10.1	9.1	8.3	9.6
Cancer	0.9	0.8	2.4	0.1	0.3	0.6	2.8
Diabetes	4.0	3.9	5.5	0.4	1.5	4.1	11.3
Heart problems	6.1	5.9	9.0	2.7	4.1	5.7	13.3
Hypertension	13.8	13.6	16.8	3.4	8.0	15.4	30.6
Kidney problems	3.2	2.9	6.9	1.5	2.2	3.6	5.7
Liver problems	1.1	1.1	1.3	0.1	0.4	1.4	2.9
Paralysis	1.4	1.4	1.4	0.5	1.0	1.8	2.4
Stroke	2.6	2.5	3.7	1.3	1.7	3.1	4.6
Hepatitis	5.3	5.0	9.5	0.9	2.4	6.8	11.7
HIV	1.6	1.6	1.9	0.3	0.8	2.5	2.6
Sexually transmitted disease	0.8	0.7	2.0	0.6	0.7	1.1	0.7
Tuberculosis*	9.4	9.6	6.1	4.0	6.5	11.5	15.8
Federal inmates							
Arthritis	12.4%	11.5%	23.8%	3.8%	5.7%	10.8%	28.3%
Asthma	7.2	6.7	13.7	10.5	5.5	7.9	7.8
Cancer	0.6	0.6	1.0	0.0	0.1	0.4	2.0
Diabetes	5.1	5.0	6.9	0.7	2.0	4.2	12.9
Heart problems	6.0	5.7	10.0	2.2	3.9	4.4	12.8
Hypertension	13.2	12.6	20.7	2.1	7.5	11.5	28.4
Kidney problems	3.1	2.8	6.9	1.8	2.1	2.7	5.5
Liver problems	1.1	1.1	1.1	0.0	0.3	1.2	2.9
Paralysis	1.6	1.6	1.5	0.2	1.6	1.3	2.6
Stroke	1.7	1.6	2.9	0.1	1.1	1.5	3.7
Hepatitis	4.2	4.2	4.5	0.0	1.9	5.6	7.9
HIV	.0	1.0	1.4	0.7	0.4	1.9	1.1
Sexually transmitted disease	0.4	0.4	0.4	0.5	0.5	0.5	0.2
Tuberculosis*	7.1	7.2	6.2	2.7	5.7	8.0	10.1

*Includes all inmates who reported ever having tuberculosis (TB).

SOURCE: Laura M. Maruschak, "Table 2. Medical Problems Reported by Prison Inmates by Gender and Age, 2004," in *Medical Problems of Prisoners*, U.S. Department of Justice, Office of Justice Programs, Bureau of Justice Statistics, April 2008, http://www.ojp.usdoj.gov/bjs/pub/pdf/mpp.pdf (accessed December 5, 2008)

them, the mentally ill came into contact with law enforcement authorities more often. Holly Hills, Christine Siegfried, and Alan Ickowitz state in *Effective Prison Mental Health Services: Guidelines to Expand and Improve Treatment* (May 2004, http://www.nicic.org/pubs/2004/018604.pdf) that "since the early 1990s, an increasing number of adults with mental illness have become involved with the criminal justice system. State and federal prisons, in particular, have undergone a dramatic transformation, housing a growing number of inmates with serious mental disorders. Complicating this situation is the high proportion of mentally ill inmates who have co-occurring substance use disorders."

In *Mental Health Problems of Prison and Jail Inmates* (September 2006, http://www.ojp.usdoj.gov/bjs/pub/pdf/mhppji.pdf), Doris J. James and Lauren E. Glaze of the BJS report that more than half of all prison and jail inmates had a mental health problem at midyear 2005. Specifically, 705,600 inmates in state prisons (56% of all state prison inmates), 78,800 in federal prisons (45% of all federal prison inmates), and 479,900 in local jails (64% of all local jail inmates) reported symptoms of a mental health problem. For example, 35.1% of federal prisoners, 43.2% of state prisoners, and 54.5% of jail inmates reported symptoms of mania; 16% of federal prisons, 23.5% of state prisoners, and 29.7% of jail inmates reported symptoms of major depression; and 10.2% of federal prisoners, 15.4% of state prisoners, and 23.9% of jail inmates reported symptoms of a psychotic disorder.

DIFFERENCES BY GENDER. James and Glaze indicate that female inmates have much higher rates of mental health problems than male inmates. In midyear 2005, 73% of female state prison inmates had a mental health problem, compared with 55% of male inmates. Similarly, 61% of female federal inmates reported a mental health problem, compared with 44% of males, and 75% of female jail inmates had a mental health problem, compared with 63% of male inmates.

HISTORY OF HOMELESSNESS AND FOSTER CARE. State prison and local jail inmates who reported a mental health problem were more likely than other inmates to have been homeless in the year before they entered prison or jail. Specifically, 13.2% of state prisoners and 17.2% of jail inmates had both a mental health problem and a recent experience of homelessness, compared with 6.3% of state prisoners and 8.8% of jail inmates who did not have a mental health problem but said they had been homeless in the year before they were incarcerated. Some 18.5% of state prisoners who had a mental health problem had lived in a foster home, agency, or institution while growing up, compared with 9.5% of state prisoners who did not report a mental health problem. Similarly, 14.5% of jail inmates who had a mental health problem had lived in a foster home, agency, or institution, compared with 6% of inmates who did not have a mental health problem.

SEXUAL VIOLENCE IN PRISONS AND JAILS

In response to concerns about sexual misconduct in prisons, President George W. Bush (1946–) signed into law the Prison Rape Elimination Act in September 2003. As part of this legislation, the BJS is charged with developing a national data collection on the incidence and prevalence of sexual assault within correctional facilities. The most recent reports on this subject are by Allen J. Beck and Paige M. Harrison of the BJS in *Sexual Victimization in State and Federal Prisons Reported by Inmates, 2007* (December 2007, http://www.ojp.usdoj.gov/bjs/pub/pdf/svsfpri07.pdf) and by Beck and Harrison in *Sexual Victimization in Local Jails Reported by Inmates* (June 2008, http://www.ojp.usdoj.gov/bjs/pub/pdf/svljri07.pdf). Both reports are based on data from the 2007 National Inmate Survey, in which inmates in 146 state and federal prisons and 282 local jails were questioned about acts of nonconsensual sex between inmates or perpetrated by staff against inmates. The results were extrapolated to provide estimates of sexual misconduct in the nation's entire inmate population.

These estimates indicate that 60,500 state and federal inmates have been sexually victimized—2.9% by prison staff and 2.1% by other inmates. There were large differences between prisons in the reported prevalence of sexual misconduct. Inmates in six of the surveyed prisons indicated no sexual misconduct had occurred, whereas those in 10 other prisons reported a sexual victimization rate of at least 9.3%. Inmates in three of the latter prisons reported high rates (greater than 10%) of sexual misconduct by staff against inmates. It is estimated that 24,700 local jail inmates have been sexually victimized—2% by jail staff and 1.6% by other inmates. The rate of sexual victimization is believed to be more than twice as high among female jail inmates (5.1%) than male jail inmates (2.9%).

INMATE DEATHS

The BJS initiated the Deaths in Custody Reporting Program in response to the Deaths in Custody Reporting Act of 2000. The program requires state prisons and local jails to report annually the cause of death and certain demographic data for all inmates who die in their custody. The data are summarized in Table 8.10 for state prisoners from 2001 to 2006 and in Table 8.11 for local jail inmates from 2000 to 2006. In total, 3,242 state inmates died while incarcerated in 2006. The vast majority (2,705) died of illnesses other than AIDS. Other primary causes of death were suicide (220 inmates) and AIDS (131 inmates). Concerning the state inmate deaths in 2006, 1,304 were among prisoners aged 55 and older. The age group with the second largest number of deaths (1,063) was inmates aged 45 to 54 years old. In 2006, 1,097 local jail inmates perished while in custody. The three largest causes of death were illnesses other than AIDS (557), suicide (277), and drug/alcohol intoxication (87). The age bracket with the highest number

TABLE 8.10

Deaths of inmates in state prisons, by cause of death, sex, race and Hispanic origin, and age, 2001–06

[By cause of death and selected prisoner characteristics, 2001–2006][a]

		State prisoner deaths					
	Total	2001	2002	2003	2004	2005	2006
Total[b]	18,550	2,878	2,946	3,167	3,138	3,179	3,242
Cause of death							
Illness	15,335	2,303	2,379	2,633	2,645	2,670	2,705
AIDS	1,154	270	245	210	145	153	131
Suicide	1,172	169	168	200	200	215	220
Homicide	299	39	48	50	51	56	55
Drug/alcohol intoxication	213	36	37	23	23	37	57
Accident	180	23	31	26	37	30	33
Other/unknown	197	38	38	25	37	18	41
Sex							
Male	17,772	2,773	2,811	3,039	3,001	3,036	3,112
Female	751	100	115	126	137	143	130
Race, Hispanic origin							
White, non-Hispanic	9,135	1,343	1,393	1,597	1,552	1,622	1,628
Black, non-Hispanic	7,017	1,159	1,151	1,205	1,187	1,162	1,153
Hispanic	2,026	314	330	311	330	335	406
Other/multiple races	298	52	46	45	68	51	36
Age							
Under 18 years	9	2	1	3	1	1	1
18 to 24 years	431	86	62	58	85	80	60
25 to 34 years	1,529	256	243	278	256	245	251
35 to 44 years	3,776	656	663	669	624	601	563
45 to 54 years	5,829	896	909	983	966	1,012	1,063
55 years and older	6,936	972	1,047	1,171	1,204	1,238	1,304

Note: These data are from the Deaths in Custody Reporting Program, which was launched by the U.S. Department of Justice, Bureau of Justice Statistics (BJS) in 2000 to implement the Death in Custody Reporting Act of 2000 (Public Law 106–297). Data collection on deaths in local jail facilities began in 2000, followed by collection from state prison authorities in 2001. In 2002, collection of records of deaths from state juvenile correctional systems began. The U.S. Census Bureau has collected state data for BJS since 2003.
State prisons were instructed to report the death of any prisoner in their custody, even if the prisoner was held for other jurisdictions, such as county jail, another state, or the federal Government. State prisoner death counts include deaths of any prisoners held in private facilities under contract to the state's department of correction. Deaths of prisoners in private facilities were counted in the state that had jurisdiction over the prisoner, not the state where the private facility was located. State prisons also were instructed to include the death of any prisoner sent outside the prison facility for medical, mental health or substance abuse treatment services, or for work-release programs. Deaths of prisoners who were released on temporary furloughs or who had escaped the prison facility were excluded.
[a]Detail may not add to total because of missing data.
[b]These data do not include deaths by execution.

SOURCE: Ann L. Pastore and Kathleen Maguire, editors, "Table 6.0010.2006. Deaths of Prisoners in State Correctional Facilities," in *Sourcebook of Criminal Justice Statistics Online*, U.S. Department of Justice, Office of Justice Programs, Bureau of Justice Statistics, undated, http://www.albany.edu/sourcebook/pdf/t600102006.pdf (accessed December 4, 2008)

of deaths (313) consisted of inmates aged 35 to 44. For both state and local inmates, deaths were far more common among male jail inmates than female jail inmates and slightly more common among white inmates than African-American inmates.

Figure 8.3 shows the suicide and homicide rates for state and local inmates from 1980 to 2003. The suicide rate (number of suicides per 100,000 inmates) among state prisoners declined slightly from 34 in 1980 to 16 in 2003. The rate among jail inmates decreased dramatically from 129 in 1983 to 43 in 2003. The homicide rate (number of homicides per 100,000 inmates) for state inmates declined from 54 in 1980 to 4 in 2003. The rate for jail inmates showed a slight decrease from 5 in 1983 to 2 in 2003.

PRISONERS' RIGHTS UNDER THE LAW

In 1871 a Virginia court, in *Ruffin v. Commonwealth* (62 Va. 790), commented that a prisoner "has, as a conse-

quence of his crime, not only forfeited his liberty, but all his personal rights except those which the law in its humanity accords to him. He is for the time being the slave of the state." Eight decades later, in *Stroud v. Swope* (187 F. 2d. 850 [1951]), the Ninth Circuit Court asserted that "it is well settled that it is not the function of the courts to superintend the treatment and discipline of prisoners in penitentiaries, but only to deliver from imprisonment those who are illegally confined." The American Correctional Association, in *Legal Responsibility and Authority of Correctional Officers* (1987), explains that correctional administrators believed that prisoners lost all their constitutional rights after conviction. Prisoners had privileges, not rights, and privileges could be taken away arbitrarily.

A significant change in this legal view came during the 1960s. In *Cooper v. Pate* (378 U.S. 546 [1964]), the U.S. Supreme Court held that the Civil Rights Act of 1871 granted protection to prisoners. The code states that "every person who, under color of any statute, ordinance, regulation,

Characteristics and Rights of Inmates

TABLE 8.11

Deaths of inmates in local jails, by cause of death, sex, race and Hispanic origin, and age, 2000–06

[By cause of death and selected inmate characteristics, 2000–2006*]

	Jail inmate deaths							
	Total	2000	2001	2002	2003	2004	2005	2006
Total	7,008	905	947	974	1,003	1,030	1,052	1,097
Cause of death								
Illness	3,311	459	428	459	458	485	465	557
AIDS	368	58	59	50	54	52	40	55
Suicide	2,076	289	314	314	296	300	286	277
Drug/alcohol intoxication	489	37	58	55	90	77	85	87
Accident	210	25	35	35	27	32	25	31
Homicide	147	17	21	17	14	23	21	34
Other/unknown	407	20	32	44	64	61	130	56
Sex								
Male	6,201	814	852	867	868	899	933	968
Female	801	91	91	107	133	131	119	129
Race, Hispanic origin								
White, non-Hispanic	3,641	453	518	537	538	504	561	530
Black, non-Hispanic	2,327	306	283	305	324	363	336	410
Hispanic	847	118	116	114	120	135	118	126
Other/multiple races	153	17	24	18	16	25	23	30
Age								
Under 18 years	43	8	8	7	4	7	5	4
18 to 24 years	717	89	107	101	104	105	108	103
25 to 34 years	1,377	184	193	186	213	212	193	196
35 to 44 years	2,070	266	283	338	283	300	287	313
45 to 54 years	1,835	239	242	238	266	267	277	306
55 years and older	930	115	111	102	127	136	171	168

Note: These data are from the Deaths in Custody Reporting Program, which was launched by the U.S. Department of Justice, Bureau of Justice Statistics (BJS) in 2000 to implement the Death in Custody Reporting Act of 2000 (Public Law 106–297). The U.S. Census Bureau collects the jail deaths data for BJS. Jails were instructed to report the death of any inmate in their custody, even if the inmate was held for other jurisdictions such as the state department of corrections, another state or county, or the federal government. Jails also were instructed to include the death of any inmate sent outside the jail facility for medical, mental health or substance abuse treatment services, or for work-release programs. Deaths that occurred while an inmate was in transit to or from the jail facility were included. Deaths of jail inmates who were released on temporary furloughs or who had escaped the jail facility were excluded.
*Detail may not add to total because of missing data.

SOURCE: Ann L. Pastore and Kathleen Maguire, editors, "Table 6.0012.2006. Deaths of Inmates in Local Jails," in *Sourcebook of Criminal Justice Statistics Online*, U.S. Department of Justice, Office of Justice Programs, Bureau of Justice Statistics, undated, http://www.albany.edu/sourcebook/pdf/t600122006.pdf (accessed December 4, 2008)

custom, or usage, of any State or Territory or the District of Columbia, subjects, or causes to be subjected, any citizen of the United States or other person within the jurisdiction thereof to the deprivation of any rights, privileges, or immunities secured by the Constitution and laws, shall be liable to the party injured in an action at law, suit in equity, or other proper proceeding for redress."

With the *Cooper* decision, the court announced that prisoners had rights guaranteed by the U.S. Constitution and could ask the judicial system for help in challenging the conditions of their imprisonment.

HABEAS CORPUS REVIEW

In *Cooper v. Pate*, the U.S. Supreme Court relied on civil rights. Another source of prisoners' rights arose from the court's reliance on habeas corpus. This Latin phrase means "have the body" with the rest of the phrase "brought before me" implied. A writ of habeas corpus is therefore the command issued by one court to another court (or to a lesser authority) to produce a person and to explain why that

person is being detained. Habeas corpus dates back to an act of the British Parliament passed in 1679. The U.S. Congress enacted the Judiciary Act of 1789 and gave federal prisoners the right to habeas corpus review. The Habeas Corpus Act of 1867 later protected the rights of newly freed slaves and extended habeas corpus protection to state prisoners. The effective meaning of habeas corpus for prisoners is that it enables them to petition federal courts to review any aspect of their cases.

FIRST AMENDMENT CASES

The First Amendment of the U.S. Constitution guarantees that "Congress shall make no law respecting an establishment of religion, or prohibiting the free exercise thereof; or abridging the freedom of speech, or of the press; or the right of the people peaceably to assemble, and to petition the government for a redress of grievances."

Censorship

In *Procunier v. Martinez* (416 U.S. 396 [1974]), the Supreme Court ruled that prison officials cannot censor

FIGURE 8.3

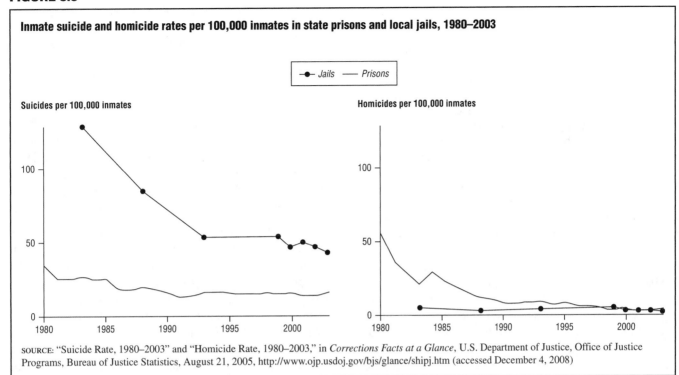

Inmate suicide and homicide rates per 100,000 inmates in state prisons and local jails, 1980–2003

SOURCE: "Suicide Rate, 1980–2003" and "Homicide Rate, 1980–2003," in *Corrections Facts at a Glance*, U.S. Department of Justice, Office of Justice Programs, Bureau of Justice Statistics, August 21, 2005, http://www.ojp.usdoj.gov/bjs/glance/shipj.htm (accessed December 4, 2008)

inmate correspondence unless they "show that a regulation authorizing mail censorship furthers one or more of the substantial governmental interests of security, order, and rehabilitation. Second, the limitation of First Amendment freedoms must be no greater than is necessary or essential to the protection of the particular governmental interest involved."

Prison officials may refuse to send letters that detail escape plans or encoded messages but may not censor inmate correspondence simply to "eliminate unflattering or unwelcome opinions or factually inaccurate statements." Because prisoners retain rights "when a prison regulation or practice offends a fundamental constitutional guarantee, federal courts will discharge their duty to protect constitutional rights."

However, the court recognized that it was "ill equipped to deal with the increasingly urgent problems of prison administration and reform." Running a prison takes expertise and planning, all of which, the court explained, is part of the responsibility of the legislative and executive branches. The task of the judiciary branch is to establish a standard of review for prisoners' constitutional claims that is responsive to both the need to protect inmates' rights and the policy of judicial restraint.

In *Pell v. Procunier* (417 U.S. 817 [1974]), the court ruled that federal prison officials could prohibit inmates from having face-to-face media interviews. The court reasoned that judgments regarding prison security "are peculiarly within the province and professional expertise of corrections officials, and, in the absence of substantial evi-dence in the record to indicate that the officials have exaggerated their response to these considerations, courts should ordinarily defer to their expert judgment in such matters."

The First Circuit Court ruled in *Nolan v. Fitzpatrick* (451 F. 2d 545 [1985]) that inmates had the right to correspond with newspapers. The prisoners were limited only in that they could not write about escape plans or include contraband material in their letters.

The Missouri Division of Corrections permitted correspondence between immediate family members who were inmates at different institutions and between inmates writing about legal matters, and allowed other inmate correspondence only if each prisoner's "classification/treatment team" thought it was in the best interests of the parties. Another Missouri regulation permitted an inmate to marry only with the superintendent's permission, which can be given only when there were "compelling reasons" to do so, such as a pregnancy. In *Turner v. Safley* (482 U.S. 78 [1987]), the Supreme Court found the first regulation constitutional and the second one unconstitutional.

The court held that the "constitutional right of prisoners to marry is impermissibly burdened by the Missouri marriage regulation." The court had ruled earlier in *Zablocki v. Redhail* (434 U.S. 374 [1978]) that prisoners had a constitutionally protected right to marry, subject to restrictions because of incarceration such as time and place and prior approval of a warden. However, the Missouri regulation practically banned all marriages.

The findings in *Turner v. Safley* have become a guide for prison regulations in the United States. In its decision, the court observed that:

> When a prison regulation impinges on inmates' constitutional rights, the regulation is valid if it is reasonably related to legitimate penological interests.... First, there must be a "valid, rational connection" between the prison regulation and the legitimate governmental interest put forward to justify it.... Moreover, the governmental objective must be a legitimate and neutral one.... A second factor relevant in determining the reasonableness of a prison restriction ... is whether there are alternative means of exercising the right that remain open to prison inmates.... A third consideration is the impact accommodation of the asserted constitutional right will have on guards and other inmates, and on the allocation of prison resources generally.

Religious Beliefs

Even though inmates retain their First Amendment right to practice their religion, the courts have upheld restrictions on religious freedom when corrections departments need to maintain security, when economic considerations are involved, and when the regulation is reasonable.

In September 2000 the Religious Land Use and Institutionalized Persons Act was signed into law by President Bill Clinton (1946–). Section 3 of the law requires that prison officials accommodate inmates' religious needs in certain cases, even if this means exempting the inmates from general prison rules. The state of Ohio challenged the act's constitutionality by arguing that it violates the First Amendment's prohibition on the establishment of religion. Because the law does not require prison officials to accommodate inmates' secular needs or desires in similar ways, Ohio claimed the statute impermissibly advances religion. The state also argued that the law creates incentives for prisoners to feign religious belief to gain privileges. The Supreme Court upheld the constitutionality of the act in *Cutter v. Wilkinson* (544 U.S. 709 [2005]), reversing a ruling by the Sixth Circuit Court of Appeals, which had agreed with Ohio's argument.

FOURTH AMENDMENT

The Fourth Amendment guarantees the "right of the people to be secure ... against unreasonable searches and seizures ... and no warrants shall issue, but upon probable cause." The courts have not been as active in protecting prisoners under the Fourth Amendment as under the First and Eighth amendments. In *Bell v. Wolfish* (441 U.S. 520 [1979]), the Supreme Court asserted that:

> simply because prison inmates retain certain constitutional rights does not mean that these rights are not subject to restrictions and limitations.... Maintaining institutional security and preserving internal order and discipline are essential goals that may require limitation or retraction of the retained constitutional rights of both

convicted prisoners and pretrial detainees. Since problems that arise in the day-to-day operation of a corrections facility are not susceptible of easy solutions, prison administrators should be accorded wide-ranging deference in the adoption and execution of policies and practices that in their judgment are needed to preserve internal order and discipline and to maintain institutional security.

Based on this reasoning, the court ruled that body searches did not violate the Fourth Amendment: "Balancing the significant and legitimate security interests of the institution against the inmates' privacy interests, such searches can be conducted on less than probable cause and are not unreasonable."

In another Fourth Amendment case, *Hudson v. Palmer* (468 U.S. 517 [1984]), the court upheld the right of prison officials to search a prisoner's cell and seize property, "The recognition of privacy rights for prisoners in their individual cells simply cannot be reconciled with the concept of incarceration and the needs and objectives of penal institutions.... [However, the fact that a prisoner does not have a reasonable expectation of privacy] does not mean that he is without a remedy for calculated harassment unrelated to prison needs. Nor does it mean that prison attendants can ride roughshod over inmates' property rights with impunity. The Eighth Amendment always stands as a protection against 'cruel and unusual punishments.'"

EIGHTH AMENDMENT

The Eighth Amendment guarantees that "cruel and unusual punishments [not be] inflicted." The Eighth Amendment has been used to challenge the death penalty, three-strikes laws, crowded prisons, lack of health or safety in prisons, and excessive violence by the guards. The Supreme Court has established several tests to determine whether conditions or actions violate the Eighth Amendment:

- Did the actions or conditions offend concepts of "decency and human dignity and precepts of civilization which [Americans] profess to possess"?

- Was it "disproportionate to the offense"?

- Did it violate "fundamental standards of good conscience and fairness"?

- Was the punishment unnecessarily cruel?

- Did the punishment go beyond legitimate penal purposes?

Prison Conditions and Medical Care

In *Rhodes v. Chapman* (452 U.S. 337 [1981]), the Supreme Court ruled that housing prisoners in double cells was not cruel and unusual punishment. The justices maintained that "conditions of confinement, as constituting the punishment at issue, must not involve the wanton and unnecessary infliction of pain, nor may they be grossly disproportionate to the severity of the crime warranting imprisonment. But conditions that cannot be said to be cruel and unusual under contemporary standards are not unconstitutional. To the extent such conditions are restrictive and even harsh, they are part of the penalty that criminals pay for their offenses against society."

The court concluded that the Constitution "does not mandate comfortable prisons" and that only those deprivations denying the "minimal civilized measure of life's necessities" violate the Eighth Amendment.

However, Judge Richard A. Enslen (1931–) of the U.S. District Court ruled in *Hadix v. Caruso* (No. 4:92-CV-110 [2006]) that officials at the Southern Michigan Correctional Facility had to stop using nonmedical restraints on prisoners because the "practice constitutes torture and violates the Eighth Amendment." On November 13, 2006, Judge Enslen issued the opinion in the case of Timothy Souders, a mentally ill detainee who died after spending four days nude and shackled in an isolated cell. Judge Enslen ordered the prison to "immediately cease and desist from the practice of using any form of punitive mechanical restraints [and] shall timely develop practices, protocols and policies to enforce this limitation."

Guards Using Force

The Supreme Court ruled in *Whitney v. Albers* (475 U.S. 312 [1986]) that guards, during prison disturbances or riots, must balance the need "to maintain or restore discipline" through force against the risk of injury to inmates. These situations require prison officials to act quickly and decisively and allow guards and administrators leeway in their actions. In *Whitney*, a prisoner was shot in the knee during an attempt to rescue a hostage. The court found that the injury suffered by the prisoner was not cruel and unusual punishment under the circumstances.

In 1983 Keith Hudson, an inmate at the state penitentiary in Angola, Louisiana, argued with Jack McMillian, a guard. McMillian placed the inmate in handcuffs and shackles to take him to the administrative lockdown area. On the way, according to Hudson, McMillian punched him in the mouth, eyes, chest, and stomach; another guard held him while the supervisor on duty watched. Hudson sued, accusing the guards of cruel and unusual punishment.

A magistrate found that the guards used "force when there was no need to do so," and the supervisor allowed their conduct, thus violating the Eighth Amendment. However, the court of Appeals for the Fifth Circuit reversed the decision, ruling in *Hudson v. McMillian* (929 F. 2d 1014 [1990]) that "inmates alleging use of excessive force in violation of the Eighth Amendment must prove: (1) significant injury; (2) resulting 'directly and only from the use of force that was clearly excessive to the need'; (3) the excessiveness of which was objectively unreasonable; and (4) that the action constituted an unnecessary and wanton infliction of pain."

The court agreed that the use of force was unreasonable and was a clearly excessive and unnecessary infliction of pain. However, the court found against Hudson because his injuries were "minor" and "required no medical attention."

DUE PROCESS COMPLAINTS

The Fifth Amendment provides that no person should "be deprived of life, liberty, or property" by the federal government "without due process of law." The Fourteenth Amendment reaffirms this right and explicitly applies it to the states. Due process complaints brought by prisoners under the Fifth and Fourteenth Amendments are generally centered on questions of procedural fairness. Most of the time disciplinary action in prison is taken on the word of the guard or the administrator, and the inmate has little opportunity to challenge the charges.

The Supreme Court, however, has affirmed that procedural fairness should be used in some institutional decisions. In *Wolff v. McDonnell* (418 U.S. 539 [1974]), the court declared that a Nebraska law providing for sentences to be shortened for good behavior created a "liberty interest." Thus, if an inmate met the requirements, prison officials could not deprive him of the shortened sentence without due process, according to the Fourteenth Amendment.

At the Metropolitan Correctional Center, a federally operated short-term custodial facility in New York City designed mainly for pretrial detainees, inmates challenged the constitutionality of the facility's conditions. As this was a pretrial detention center, the challenge was brought under the due process clause of the Fifth Amendment. The district court and the court of appeals found for the inmates, but the Supreme Court disagreed in *Bell v. Wolfish*.

EARLY RELEASE

Beginning in 1983 the Florida legislature enacted a series of laws authorizing the awarding of early release credits to prison inmates when the state prison population exceeded predetermined levels. In 1986 Kenneth Lynce received a 22-year prison sentence on a charge of attempted murder. He was released in 1992, based on the determination that he had accumulated five different types of early release credits totaling 5,668 days, including 1,860 days of provisional credits awarded as a result of prison overcrowding.

Shortly thereafter, the state attorney general issued an opinion interpreting a 1992 statute as having retroactively canceled all provisional credits awarded to inmates convicted of murder and attempted murder. Lynce was rearrested and returned to custody. He filed a habeas corpus petition alleging that the retroactive cancellation of provisional credits violated the ex post facto (from a thing done afterward) clause of the Constitution.

The Supreme Court agreed with Lynce. In *Lynce v. Mathis* (519 U.S. 443 [1997]), the court ruled that to fall within the ex post facto prohibition a law must be "retrospective" and "disadvantage the offender affected by it." The 1992 statute was clearly retrospective and disadvantaged Lynce by increasing his punishment.

LIMITING FRIVOLOUS PRISONER LAW SUITS

In 1995 the Supreme Court made it harder for prisoners to bring constitutional suits to challenge due process rights. In *Sandin v. Conner* (515 U.S. 472), the majority asserted that it was frustrated with the number of due process cases, some of which, it believed, clogged the judiciary with unwarranted complaints, such as claiming a "liberty interest" in not being transferred to a cell with an electrical outlet for a television set.

Sandin concerned an inmate in Hawaii who was not allowed to call witnesses at a disciplinary hearing for misconduct that had placed him in solitary for 30 days. The Court of Appeals of the Ninth Circuit had held in 1993 that the inmate, Demont Conner, had a liberty interest, allowing him a range of procedural protections in remaining free from solitary confinement. The Supreme Court overruled the court of appeals, stating that the inmate had no liberty interest. Due process protections play a role only if the state's action has infringed on some separate, substantive right that the inmate possesses. For example, in *Wolff v. McDonnell* the petitioner's loss of good-time credit was a substantive right that he possessed. The punishment Conner had received "was within the range of confinement to be normally expected" because he was serving 30 years to life for a number of crimes, including murder.

The court stated, "States may under certain circumstances create liberty interests which are protected by the Due Process Clause," but these should be limited to actions that impose "atypical and significant hardship on the inmate in relation to the ordinary incidents of prison life." According to the court, being put in solitary confinement in a prison where most inmates are limited to their cells most of the day anyway is not a liberty-interest issue. Because there was no liberty interest involved, how the hearing was handled was irrelevant.

Based on this ruling, the court held that a federal court should consider a complaint to be a potential violation of a prisoner's due process rights only when prison staff imposed "atypical and significant hardship on the inmate." Mismanaged disciplinary hearings or temporary placement in solitary were just "ordinary incidents of prison life" and should not be considered violations of the Constitution.

Chief Justice William H. Rehnquist (1924–2005) asserted that past Supreme Court decisions have "led to the involvement of federal courts in the day-to-day management of prisons, often squandering judicial resources with little offsetting benefit to anyone." Judges should allow prison administrators the flexibility to fine-tune the ordinary incidents of prison life.

In 1996 Congress passed the Prison Litigation Reform Act (PLRA) in an effort to limit so-called frivolous lawsuits by prisoners. The PLRA requires inmates to exhaust all possible internal prison grievance processes before filing civil right lawsuits in federal courts. The law states that "no action shall be brought with respect to prison conditions under section 1983 of this title, or any other Federal law, by a prisoner confined in any jail, prison, or other correctional facility until such administrative remedies as are available are exhausted." After a few lower courts handed down controversial rulings on specific procedures that inmates must follow to exhaust administrative grievances, a case was brought before the U.S. Supreme Court. In the consolidated case of *Jones v. Bock* (No. 05-7058 [2007]) and *Williams v. Overton* (No. 05-7142 [2007]), the court overturned strict legal requirements that had been imposed by the Sixth Circuit Court on Michigan inmates with grievances against their prison. Lorenzo Jones claimed that prison officials forced him to do "arduous" work even though he had been seriously injured in a car accident. Williams suffered a debilitating medical condition and claimed that his medical needs were not being properly met in prison. Instead of examining the merits of these claims, the Supreme Court chose to focus on specific legal issues associated with lawsuits that the prisoners had filed under the PLRA.

The court clarified that prisoners alleging federal civil rights violations under the PLRA do not have to prove they have exhausted all administrative remedies before filing lawsuits. The burden is on the defense to prove that administrative remedies were not exhausted. In addition, lower courts cannot dismiss lawsuits including multiple claims, even if some of the claims have not been exhausted. Finally, prisoners filing such lawsuits need not have named specific defendants in the administrative grievances to retain their rights to sue those defendants in court.

INNOCENCE PROTECTION ACT

Deoxyribonucleic acid (DNA) testing has emerged as a powerful tool capable of establishing the innocence of a person in cases where organic matter from the perpetrator of a crime (e.g., blood, skin, and semen) has been obtained by law enforcement officials. This organic matter can be tested against DNA samples taken from an accused or convicted person. If the two samples do not match, then they came from different people and the person being tested is innocent.

The Innocence Protection Act became law in 2004 as part of the Justice for All Act. The act enables people who are "convicted and imprisoned for federal offenses" and who claim to be innocent to have DNA testing on the biological evidence that was originally collected during the investigations of the crimes for which they were convicted. It mandates that the government has to preserve collected biological evidence so that it can be tested after the defendant is convicted. Finally, it provides funds to allow certain agencies to test evidence to identify perpetrators of unsolved crimes.

According to the Innocence Project, in "Facts on Post-conviction DNA Exonerations" (http://www.innocence project.org/Content/351.php), as of March 2009, 235 people had been exonerated by DNA testing, including 17 on death row. In "Access to Post-conviction DNA Testing" (March 2009, http://www.innocenceproject.org/Content/304 .php), the Innocence Project also reports that even though 46 states have postconviction DNA testing access statutes, many of these testing laws are limited. (As of March 2009, Alabama, Alaska, Massachusetts, and Oklahoma did not have any DNA access statutes incorporated into their state laws.) For example, some state legislation does not require adequate safeguards for the preservation of DNA evidence; other states fail to require "full, fair and prompt proceedings" once a DNA testing petition has been filed, which can result in an innocent victim spending long periods being wrongfully imprisoned. Furthermore, despite its ability to prove innocence, some courts still refuse to consider newly discovered DNA evidence after trial.

CHAPTER 9
PROBATION AND PAROLE

Most of the correctional population of the United States—those under the supervision of correctional authorities—are walking about freely. They are people on probation or parole. A probationer is someone who has been convicted of a crime and sentenced—but the person's sentence has been suspended on condition that he or she behaves in a manner ordered by the court. Probation sometimes follows a brief period of incarceration; more often it is granted by the court immediately. A parolee is an individual who has served a part of his or her sentence in jail and prison but, because of good behavior or legislative mandate, has been granted freedom before the sentence is fully served. The sentence remains in effect, however, and the parolee continues to be under the jurisdiction of a parole board. If the person fails to live up to the conditions of the release, the parolee may be confined again.

According to Lauren E. Glaze and Thomas P. Bonczar of the Bureau of Justice Statistics (BJS), in *Probation and Parole in the United States, 2007 Statistical Tables* (December 2008, http://www.ojp.gov/bjs/pub/pdf/ppus07st.pdf), more than 7.3 million people made up the total correctional population in 2007. (See Table 9.1.) More than 5.1 million of these individuals (4.3 million on probation and 824,365 on parole) were under community supervision. Probationers and parolees are still under official supervision and have to satisfy requirements placed on them as a condition of freedom or of early release from correctional facilities.

Glaze and Bonczar indicate that between 2000 and 2007 the number of people on probation and parole grew by 12.5%, from 4.6 million to 5.1 million, with an average annual increase of 1.7%. The increase from 2006 to 2007 was 2.1%, slightly higher than the average annual growth rate. As of 2007 people on probation and parole comprised 69.8% of the total correctional population in the United States and 2.2% of the U.S. adult resident population.

PROBATION
Probation Population

At yearend 1995, according to the BJS, there were nearly 3.1 million probationers. By yearend 2007 the number had reached more than 4.3 million. In each year the number of people entering the system exceeded the number exiting the system. The number of entries grew from approximately 1.6 million in 1995 to 2.2 million in 2007. The number of exits rose from 1.5 million in 1995 to 2.1 million in 2007. The 4.3 million people on probation at the end of 2007 represented 84% of the entire population under community supervision (i.e., total probationers and parolees). Glaze and Bonczar report in *Probation and Parole in the United States, 2007 Statistical Tables* that of the 2.2 million adults entering probation in 2007, 620,840 did so without any incarceration. Another 207,392 of the new probationers received probation with incarceration.

An estimated 2.1 million people exited probation in 2007, down slightly from the 2.2 million people who exited probation in 2006. Nearly half (46.3%; 982,072) of probation exiters in 2007 left the system because they had completed their probation terms successfully. About 12% of the total left the probation system to be incarcerated, including 2.7% (56,335) who received a new sentence for committing a new offense, 5.8% (124,032) who were incarcerated under their original sentence (i.e., they violated the rules of their probation and probation was revoked), and 3.6% (75,462) who were incarcerated under other or unknown circumstances. Overall, 2.5% (52,030) of exiting probationers during 2007 absconded (disappeared). The remaining exiters left the system for a variety of reasons, including 8.4% (177,441) who left for what are called "unsatisfactory" reasons. Unsatisfactory conclusions include those who did not successfully complete all the terms of their supervision, for example, those whose sentences expired before completion and those who failed to fulfill a financial requirement such as restitution. This breakdown of exit

TABLE 9.1

Adults under correctional supervision, 2000–07

Year	Total estimated correctional population[a]	Community supervision[b]	Incarcerated in prison or jail supervision	Percent of U.S. adult resident population on correctional supervision	Percent of total correctional population on community supervision	Percent of U.S. adult resident population on community supervision
2000	6,445,100	4,550,100	1,937,500	3.1%	70.6%	2.2%
2001	6,581,700	4,664,100	1,961,200	3.1	70.9	2.2
2002	6,758,800	4,775,000	2,033,000	3.1	70.6	2.2
2003[c]	6,924,500	4,889,900	2,081,600	3.2	70.6	2.3
2004	6,995,000	4,915,600	2,135,300	3.2	70.3	2.2
2005	7,051,900	4,947,900	2,195,900	3.1	70.2	2.2
2006[d]	7,181,500	5,014,400	2,259,000	3.2	69.8	2.2
2007[e]	7,328,200	5,117,500	2,293,200	3.2	69.8	2.2
Percent change, 2006–07	2.0%	2.1%	1.5%			
Average annual percent change, 2000–07	1.9%	1.7%	2.4%			

Note: Counts of probationers, parolees, and prisoners are for December 31. All jail counts are for June 30. Jail and prison counts include inmates held in private facilities. Estimates were rounded to the nearest 100.

[a]Includes offenders on probation and parole. Because some offenders may have multiple statuses (i.e., held in a prison or jail but remain under the jurisdiction of a probation or parole authority) totals in 2000–04 exclude probationers held in jail or prison; totals in 2005–06 exclude probationers and parolees held in jail or prison; and the total in 2007 excludes probationers and parolees held in jail or prison, probationers who were also under parole supervision, and parolees who were also under probation supervision. For these reasons, details do not sum to total.

[b]Totals include some offenders held in a prison or jail but who remained under the jurisdiction of a probation or parole agency.

[c]Due to changes in reporting, total probation and parole counts include estimated counts for Massachusetts, Pennsylvania, and Washington based on reporting methods comparable to 2004.

[d]Illinois did not provide parole or prison data for 2006; therefore, all parole and prison data for Illinois were estimated.

[e]Oklahoma did not provide community supervision data for 2007; therefore, all data for Oklahoma were estimated. Illinois, Maine, and Nevada did not provide prison data for 2007; therefore, all prison data for these 3 states were estimated.

SOURCE: Lauren E. Glaze and Thomas P. Bonczar, " Table 1. Number of Persons under Adult Correctional Supervision, 2000–07," in *Probation and Parole in the United States, 2007 Statistical Tables*, U.S. Department of Justice, Office of Justice Programs, Bureau of Justice Statistics, December 2008, http://www.ojp .gov/bjs/pub/pdf/ppus07st.pdf (accessed April 7, 2009)

circumstances for 2007 differs little from that reported by Glaze and Bonczar the previous year in *Probation and Parole in the United States, 2006* (December 2007, http:// www.ojp.usdoj.gov/bjs/pub/pdf/ppus06.pdf). More than half (57%) of probation exiters in 2006 left the system because they had completed their probation terms successfully; 4% received a new sentence for committing a new offense, 9% were incarcerated under their original sentence, and 5% were incarcerated under other or unknown circumstances. Another 4% of exiting probationers during 2006 absconded, and 12% left for unsatisfactory reasons.

Jurisdiction and Geographical Distribution of Probationers

A breakdown of probationers by jurisdiction (federal and state), by region, and by state is presented in Table 9.2 as of December 31, 2007. At that time the 4.3 million people on probation represented a rate of 1,873 people on probation per 100,000 adult U.S. residents. Nearly all the probationers (greater than 99%) were under state jurisdiction. Only 23,450 probationers were under federal jurisdiction.

The South had the largest probation population (1,750,300) and the highest regional probation rate (2,091 per 100,000 adult U.S. residents), followed by the Midwest (1,012,378 probationers for a rate of 2,008), the West (805,084 probationers for a rate of 1,528), and the Northeast

(701,951 probationers for a rate of 1,657). The 10 states with the highest probation populations at yearend 2007 were:

- Georgia—435,361 probationers

- Texas—434,309 probationers

- California—353,969 probationers

- Florida—274,079 probationers

- Ohio—254,898 probationers

- Michigan—182,706 probationers

- Pennsylvania—176,987 probationers

- Massachusetts—175,419 probationers

- Illinois—142,790 probationers

- Minnesota—127,797 probationers

The 10 states with the highest probation rates at yearend 2007 were:

- Georgia—6,144 probationers per 100,000 adult residents

- Idaho—4,405 probationers per 100,000 adult residents

- Massachusetts—3,484 probationers per 100,000 adult residents

- Minnesota—3,226 probationers per 100,000 adult residents

TABLE 9.2

Probation population and rate, by jurisdiction, region, and state, December 31, 2007

Region and jurisdiction	Probation population, 12/31/2007	Percent change, 2007	Number on probation per 100,000 adult residents, 12/31/2007
U.S. total[a]	4,293,163	1.8%	1,873
Federal	23,450	−4.1%	10
State[a]	4,269,713	1.9	1,863
Northeast	701,951	0.2%	1,657
Connecticut[b]	57,493	5.9	2,136
Maine	7,853	−0.8	754
Massachusetts[c]	175,419	1.8	3,484
New Hampshire[b]	4,650	1.3	454
New Jersey	126,390	−5.1	1,901
New York	119,963	−2.0	804
Pennsylvania[d]	176,987	2.8	1,829
Rhode Island[b]	26,137	0.5	3,167
Vermont[b, c]	7,059	−7.5	1,436
Midwest	1,012,378	1.4%	2,008
Illinois[b]	142,790	1.3	1,471
Indiana[b]	126,562	−1.6	2,646
Iowa[b]	22,776	0.7	996
Kansas[c]	16,131	4.0	771
Michigan[b, c, d]	182,706	0.9	2,392
Minnesota	127,797	0.9	3,226
Missouri	56,240	2.1	1,256
Nebraska	18,910	1.0	1,417
North Dakota	4,468	3.4	896
Ohio[b, c, d]	254,898	4.2	2,917
South Dakota[c]	5,870	3.7	972
Wisconsin	53,230	−3.2	1,237
South[a]	1,750,300	1.8%	2,091
Alabama[e]	51,745	11.6	1,468
Arkansas	31,676	1.6	1,476
Delaware	16,696	−1.5	2,513
District of Columbia	6,485	−2.8	1,362
Florida[b, c, d]	274,079	0.7	1,917
Georgia[b, f]	435,361	0.7	6,144
Kentucky[b, c, d]	42,510	16.8	1,306
Louisiana	39,006	2.3	1,208
Maryland[b, e]	98,470	4.6	2,301
Mississippi[c]	21,623	−10.3	1,001
North Carolina[b]	111,446	0.9	1,612
Oklahoma[b, g]	**	:	:
South Carolina	42,721	−1.3	1,264
Tennessee[c]	56,179	7.9	1,190
Texas	434,309	0.5	2,485
Virginia[b]	51,954	7.9	877
West Virginia	7,890	2.9	553

- Rhode Island—3,167 probationers per 100,000 adult residents

- Ohio—2,917 probationers per 100,000 adult residents

- Indiana—2,646 probationers per 100,000 adult residents

- Delaware—2,513 probationers per 100,000 adult residents

- Texas—2,485 probationers per 100,000 adult residents

- Michigan—2,392 probationers per 100,000 adult residents

As shown in Table 9.2, most states increased their number of probationers during 2007. The six states with the largest percentage increases were Colorado (23.2%), Kentucky (16.8%), New Mexico (16.2%), Alabama (11.6%), Tennessee (7.9%), and Virginia (7.9%). Mississippi (down

TABLE 9.2

Probation population and rate, by jurisdiction, region, and state, December 31, 2007 [CONTINUED]

Region and jurisdiction	Probation population, 12/31/2007	Percent change, 2007	Number on probation per 100,000 adult residents, 12/31/2007
West	805,084	4.3%	1,528
Alaska[c]	6,416	5.0	1,269
Arizona[b]	76,830	4.9	1,627
California[b]	353,969	2.2	1,295
Colorado[b, c, d]	77,635	23.2	2,094
Hawaii[b]	19,426	4.5	1,934
Idaho[b, d, h]	48,663	0.1	4,405
Montana[b, c]	9,106	3.9	1,223
Nevada	13,461	1.9	697
New Mexico[b, d]	20,774	16.2	1,400
Oregon	43,732	−0.6	1,504
Utah	10,829	4.0	584
Washington[b, c, d, e]	118,885	2.1	2,390
Wyoming	5,358	2.5	1,334

Note: Because of nonresponse or incomplete data, the probation population for some jurisdictions on December 31, 2007, does not equal the population on January 1, plus entries, minus exits. Rates were computed using the estimated adult resident population in each state on January 1, 2008.

**Not known.
:Not calculated.
[a]Includes an estimated 26,000 probationers under supervision in Oklahoma on January 1 and December 31, 2007. Also includes data reported by two local probation agencies in Oklahoma; 1,363 probationers under supervision on January 1, an estimated 2,785 probationers who entered supervision, an estimated 1,998 probationers who exited supervision, and 2,150 probationers under supervision on December 31, 2007.
[b]Some or all detailed data are estimated.
[c]Excludes probationers in one of the following categories: absconder, warrant, supervised out of state, electronic monitoring, or intensive supervision.
[d]Data for entries and exits were estimated for non-reporting agencies.
[e]Due to a change in recordkeeping procedures, data are not comparable to previous reports.
[f]Counts include private agency cases and may overstate the number of persons under supervision.
[g]The state agency did not provide data. Two localities reported 1,363 probationers under supervision on January 1 and 2,150 probationers under supervision on December 31, 2007.
[h]Counts include estimates for misdemeanors based on entries.

SOURCE: Adapted from Lauren E. Glaze and Thomas P. Bonczar, "Table 2. Adults on Probation, 2007," in *Probation and Parole in the United States, 2007 Statistical Tables*, U.S. Department of Justice, Office of Justice Programs, Bureau of Justice Statistics, December 2008, http://www.ojp.gov/bjs/pub/pdf/ppus07st.pdf (accessed April 7, 2009)

10.3%) and Vermont (down 7.5%) reported the largest percentage decreases from 2006 to 2007.

Demographics of Probationers

Table 9.3 provides a breakdown of the probation population in 1995, 2000, and 2007 by gender, race, Hispanic origin, type of probation and supervision, and type and seriousness of offense. In 2007, 77% of probationers were male and 23% were female. The ratio of males to females had changed slightly from 1995, when the population was 79% male and 21% female. In 2007, 55% of probationers were non-Hispanic white, 29% were non-Hispanic African-American, and 13% were Hispanic or Latino. Other races made up 2% of the total. This breakdown had changed little since 1995.

Most probationers (54%) in 2007 were sentenced to probation only (i.e., direct imposition of probation). More

TABLE 9.3

Characteristics of adults on probation, 1995, 2000, and 2007

	1995	2000	2007
Total	100%	100%	100%
Gender			
Male	79%	78%	77%
Female	21	22	23
Race/Hispanic origin			
White[a]	53%	54%	55%
Black[a]	31	31	29
Hispanic or Latino	14	13	13
American Indian/Alaska Native[a]	1	1	1
Asian/Native Hawaiian/ other Pacific Islander[a]	...	1	1
Two or more races[a]	—	—	...
Status of probation			
Direct imposition	48%	56%	54%
Split sentence	15	11	9
Sentence suspended	26	25	27
Imposition suspended	6	7	8
Other	4	1	2
Status of supervision			
Active	79%	76%	70%
Residential/other treatment program	—	—	1
Financial conditions remaining	—	—	2
Inactive	8	9	7
Absconder	9	9	9
Supervised out of state	2	3	3
Warrant status	—	—	7
Other	2	3	2
Type of offense			
Felony	54%	52%	47%
Misdemeanor	44	46	51
Other infractions	2	2	3
Most serious offense			
Violent	—	—	17%
Property	—	—	24
Drug	16	24	27
Public-order[b]	—	24	18
Other[c]	84	52	13

Note: Each characteristic includes persons of unknown type. Detail may not sum to total because of rounding.
...Less than 0.5%.
—Not available.
[a]Excludes persons of Hispanic origin.
[b]Includes driving while intoxicated and other traffic offenses only.
[c]In 1995 and 2000, violent and property offenses were reported among other offenses. In 1995, public-order offenses were also reported among other offenses.

SOURCE: Lauren E. Glaze and Thomas P. Bonczar, "Table 4. Characteristics of Adults on Probation, 1995, 2000, and 2007," in *Probation and Parole in the United States, 2007 Statistical Tables*, U.S. Department of Justice, Office of Justice Programs, Bureau of Justice Statistics, December 2008, http://www.ojp.gov/bjs/pub/pdf/ppus07st.pdf (accessed April 7, 2009).

than a quarter (27%) had their sentence suspended, and 9% were serving a split sentence including probation and incarceration. Seven out of 10 (70%) of the probationers were under active supervision. About half (51%) of probationers in 2007 had been convicted of a misdemeanor; 47% had been convicted of a felony. The ratio of felony offenses to misdemeanor offenses had changed somewhat since 1995, when 54% of probationers had been convicted of a felony, and 44% had been convicted of a misdemeanor. The largest contingent (27%) of probationers in 2007 had been convicted of drug law violations as their most serious crime;

18% were on probation for public order offenses such as driving while intoxicated; 17% were on probation for a violent crime.

PAROLE
Trends in Parole

Discretionary parole is administered by parole boards. Their members examine prisoners' criminal histories and prison records and decide whether to release prisoners from incarceration. Since the mid-1990s several states have abolished discretionary parole in favor of mandatory parole. Mandatory parole is legislatively imposed at the state level and, with some exceptions, takes away parole boards' discretion. Mandatory parole provisions ensure that sentences for the same crime require incarceration for the same length of time. The prisoner can shorten his or her sentence only by good behavior—but time off for good behavior is also prohibited in some states. In some jurisdictions parole can only begin after prisoners have served 100% of their minimum sentences. Jeremy Travis and Sarah Lawrence of the Urban Institute report in *Beyond the Prison Gates: The State of Parole in America* (November 2002, http://www.urban.org/UploadedPDF/310583_Beyond_prison_gates.pdf) that the share of discretionary prison releases decreased from 65% in 1976 to 24% by 1999.

Travis and Lawrence indicate that even though states rely more and more on mandatory release dates to decide when to release prisoners, states have different prison release methods. Some states have cut back on parole supervision, releasing more prisoners directly to the community. Other states have aggressively enforced the conditions of parole, leading to the identification of more parole violations. In these states more parolees are being sent back to prison. States handle different types of offenses differently. Some allow victims or prosecutors to participate in release decisions, whereas others do not. Some states still rely heavily on parole boards to make release decisions, whereas others no longer use parole boards and have mandatory release policies for all their prisoners.

According to Travis and Lawrence, most parole agencies now use drug testing to determine whether a parolee has kept his or her promise to remain drug free. In a number of states parole officers are being permitted to carry weapons. Furthermore, parolees in several jurisdictions are required to wear electronic bracelets so that officials can monitor their movement.

Parole Population

The number of adults on parole at yearend 2007 was 824,365. (See Table 9.4.) The vast majority of these parolees (731,692 or 89%) were under state jurisdiction. The remaining 92,673 parolees were under federal jurisdiction. The number of parolees per 100,000 adult U.S. residents was 360. The 824,365 people on parole at the

TABLE 9.4

Parole population and rate, by jurisdiction, region, and state, December 31, 2007

Region and jurisdiction	Parole population, 12/31/2007	Percent change, 2007	Number on parole per 100,000 adult residents, 12/31/2007
U.S. total[a, b]	824,365	3.2%	360
Federal	92,673	4.1%	40
State[a, b]	731,692	3.0	319
Northeast	155,288	1.7%	367
Connecticut	2,177	−15.2	81
Maine	32	3.2	3
Massachusetts[c]	3,209	−6.6	64
New Hampshire	1,653	2.0	162
New Jersey	15,043	4.4	226
New York	53,669	1.3	360
Pennsylvania[d]	78,107	2.3	807
Rhode Island	462	39.2	56
Vermont[c, e]	936	−3.1	190
Midwest[a]	136,343	4.2%	270
Illinois[c]	33,354	:	344
Indiana	10,362	26.3	217
Iowa	3,546	−0.9	155
Kansas[e]	4,842	−0.9	232
Michigan	21,131	14.3	277
Minnesota	4,744	6.7	120
Missouri	19,849	5.5	443
Nebraska	800	0.4	60
North Dakota	342	−8.1	69
Ohio	17,575	−0.2	201
South Dakota	2,812	1.6	466
Wisconsin	16,986	1.3	395
South[b]	243,512	2.1%	291
Alabama[c, f]	7,790	3.8	221
Arkansas	19,388	7.4	904
Delaware	535	−1.7	81
District of Columbia	5,569	4.3	1,169
Florida[c]	4,654	−2.8	33
Georgia	23,111	0.7	326
Kentucky	12,741	8.4	392
Louisiana	24,085	1.1	746
Maryland	13,856	−3.4	324
Mississippi	2,015	6.1	93
North Carolina[c]	3,311	2.3	48
Oklahoma[c]	—	:	:
South Carolina	2,433	−12.0	72
Tennessee	10,496	9.7	222
Texas[c]	101,748	1.7	582
Virginia[f]	6,850	−4.9	116
West Virginia	1,830	20.2	128

TABLE 9.4

Parole population and rate, by jurisdiction, region, and state, December 31, 2007 [CONTINUED]

Region and jurisdiction	Parole population, 12/31/2007	Percent change, 2007	Number on parole per 100,000 adult residents, 12/31/2007
West	196,549	4.5%	373
Alaska[f]	1,544	1.1	305
Arizona[c]	6,807	5.3	144
California[e]	123,764	4.4	453
Colorado	11,086	16.1	299
Hawaii	2,110	−8.6	210
Idaho	3,114	14.0	282
Montana	966	14.5	130
Nevada	3,653	−4.5	189
New Mexico[c, e, f]	3,527	0.3	238
Oregon	22,658	2.8	779
Utah	3,597	7.6	194
Washington	13,017	3.2	262
Wyoming	706	4.7	176

Note: Because of nonresponse or incomplete data, the parole population for some jurisdictions on December 31, 2007, does not equal the population on January 1, plus entries, minus exits. Rates were computed using the estimated adult resident population in each state on January 1, 2008.
—Not reported.
:Not calculated.
[a]Includes an estimated 34,100 parolees under supervision in Illinois on January 1, 2007.
[b]Includes an estimated 3,100 parolees under supervision in Oklahoma on January 1 and December 31, 2007.
[c]Some or all data were estimated.
[d]Data for entries and exits were estimated for nonreporting county agencies. The December 31, 2007, population includes 25,475 parolees under state parole supervision. Reported entries are parolees who entered state parole supervision through a discretionary release from prison.
[e]Excludes parolees in one of the following categories: absconder, out of state, inactive, or only have financial conditions remaining.
[f]Due to a change in recordkeeping procedures, data are not comparable to previous reports.

SOURCE: Adapted from Lauren E. Glaze and Thomas P. Bonczar, "Table 3. Adults on Parole, 2007," in *Probation and Parole in the United States, 2007 Statistical Tables*, U.S. Department of Justice, Office of Justice Programs, Bureau of Justice Statistics, December 2008, http://www.ojp.gov/bjs/pub/pdf/ppus07st.pdf (accessed April 7, 2009)

end of 2007 represented 16% of the entire population under community supervision (i.e., total probationers and parolees).

Geographical Distribution of Parolees

A geographic distribution of parolees at yearend 2007 is shown in Table 9.4. On a regional basis, the South had the largest number of people on parole, though not the highest rate (243,512 for a rate of 291 per 100,000 adult residents). The West had the highest rate (373) but not the highest number (196,549). The Northeast had 155,288 for a rate of 367, and the Midwest counted 136,343 parolees for a rate of 270.

The 10 states with the highest parolee populations at yearend 2007 were:

- California—123,764 parolees
- Texas—101,748 parolees
- Pennsylvania—78,107 parolees
- New York—53,669 parolees
- Illinois—33,354 parolees
- Louisiana—24,085 parolees
- Georgia—23,111 parolees
- Oregon—22,658 parolees
- Michigan—21,131 parolees
- Missouri—19,849 parolees

The 10 states with the highest parole rates at yearend 2007 were:

- Arkansas—904 parolees per 100,000 adult residents
- Pennsylvania—807 parolees per 100,000 adult residents

- Oregon—779 parolees per 100,000 adult residents
- Louisiana—746 parolees per 100,000 adult residents
- Texas—582 parolees per 100,000 adult residents
- South Dakota—466 parolees per 100,000 adult residents
- California—453 parolees per 100,000 adult residents
- Missouri—443 parolees per 100,000 adult residents
- Wisconsin—395 parolees per 100,000 adult residents
- Kentucky—392 parolees per 100,000 adult residents

The federal system, most states, and the District of Columbia added to their parolee population during 2007. The states with the largest percentage gains were Rhode Island (up 39.2%), Indiana (up 26.3%), West Virginia (up 20.2%), and Colorado (up 16.1%). Connecticut (down 15.2%) and South Carolina (down 12%) experienced the largest percentage decreases.

Characteristics of Parolees

A breakdown of parolees by gender, race, Hispanic origin, types of supervision, sentence length, and type of offense is provided in Table 9.5 for 1995, 2000, and 2007. In 2007 the vast majority of parolees were men (88%), whereas 12% were women. The ratio of males to females had declined very slightly since 1995. The 2007 parolee population contained 42% non-Hispanic whites and 37% non-Hispanic African-Americans; 19% of parolees were Hispanic or Latino.

Most parolees (84%) were under active supervision in 2007, up from 78% in 1995. (See Table 9.5.) In 2007, 7% of the parole population had absconded, up only slightly from 6% in 1995. Nearly all parolees (96%) in 2007 had served a sentence of at least one year, and 4% had served less than a year. More than a third (37%) of parolees in 2007 had been convicted of drug offenses—the largest single crime category. Roughly one-fourth each had served time for violent offenses (26%) or property offenses (24%). Much smaller percentages had been convicted of public-order offenses (7%) or other crimes (6%).

Entries and Exits to the Parole System

In *Parole and Probation in the United States, 2007 Statistical Tables*, Glaze and Bonczar report the distribution of the 505,965 adults who entered parole in 2007 by type of parole. Nearly half (48%; 241,027) of the entries were under mandatory parole, that is, their releases from prison were not the result of parole board decisions but were determined by sentencing statutes. Another 30% (152,018) entered as a result of a parole board decision, and 8% (40,647) were reinstated to parole after serving time in prison for a parole violation. During 2007, 482,180 parolees exited the parole system. Almost half (45%; 214,604) completed their obligation; 38% (183,253) were returned to incarceration—27% (129,609) whose parole was revoked for a technical viola-

TABLE 9.5

Characteristics of adults on parole, 1995, 2000, and 2007

	1995	2000	2007
Total	100%	100%	100%
Gender			
Male	90%	88%	88%
Female	10	12	12
Race			
White*	34%	38%	42%
Black*	45	40	37
Hispanic or Latino	21	21	19
American Indian/Alaska Native*	1	1	1
Asian/Native Hawaiian/other Pacific Islander*	...	...	1
Two or more races*	—	—	...
Status of supervision			
Active	78%	83%	84%
Inactive	11	4	4
Absconder	6	7	7
Supervised out of state	4	5	4
Financial conditions remaining	—	—	...
Other	...	1	2
Sentence length			
Less than 1 year	6%	3%	4%
1 year or more	94	97	96
Type of offense			
Violent	—	—	26%
Property	—	—	24
Drug	—	—	37
Public order	—	—	7
Other	—	—	6

Note: Each characteristic includes persons of unknown type. Detail may not sum to total because of rounding.
...Less than 0.5%.
—Not available.
*Excludes persons of Hispanic origin.

SOURCE: Lauren E. Glaze and Thomas P. Bonczar, "Table 5. Characteristics of Adults on Parole, 1995, 2000, and 2007," in *Probation and Parole in the United States, 2007 Statistical Tables*, U.S. Department of Justice, Office of Justice Programs, Bureau of Justice Statistics, December 2008, http://www.ojp.gov/bjs/pub/pdf/ppus07st.pdf (accessed April 7, 2009)

tion, 10% (47,357) who committed a new offense and received a new sentence, and 1% (6,287) who were incarcerated for other or unknown reasons. Another 15% of parolees officially left the parole system, but under "unsatisfactory" conditions. For example, some still had financial obligations that they had not met. The remaining 2% of parolees who exited the system in 2007 included those who absconded, died, or left for unknown reasons.

Parolees Returned to Incarceration

Table 9.6 provides information about at-risk parolees who were returned to incarceration. "At-risk" parolees simply refers to those adults who were on parole at the beginning of the year and those who entered parole before the end of the year; by virtue of their release status they are considered "at-risk" of re-incarceration. According to statistics reported by the BJS, the total percentage of at-risk parolees that had been returned to incarceration hovered around 15% between 1998 and 2007. In general, just over

TABLE 9.6

Parolees returned to incarceration, by jurisdiction, region, and state, 2007

Region and jurisdiction	Total population at-risk of re-incarceration[a, b]	Returned to incarceration[c]	
		Number	Percent
U.S. total	**1,180,469**	**183,253**	**15.5%**
Federal	132,070	10,573	8.0%
State	1,048,399	172,680	16.5
Northeast	156,866	23,125	14.7%
Connecticut	4,886	1,463	29.9
Maine	33	0	0.0
Massachusetts	8,387	931	11.1
New Hampshire	2,330	569	24.4
New Jersey	23,910	2,757	11.5
New York	78,468	11,880	15.1
Pennsylvania	36,535	5,243	14.4
Rhode Island	847	111	13.1
Vermont	1,470	171	11.6
Midwest	167,826	24,985	14.9%
Indiana	17,422	1,110	6.4
Iowa	6,078	774	12.7
Kansas	10,164	1,494	14.7
Michigan	31,659	4,095	12.9
Minnesota	10,160	2,286	22.5
Missouri	32,929	8,213	24.9
Nebraska	1,812	278	15.3
North Dakota	1,156	168	14.5
Ohio	27,610	1,876	6.8
South Dakota	4,612	870	18.9
Wisconsin	24,224	3,821	15.8
South	332,387	29,780	9.0%
Alabama	9,942	687	6.9
Arkansas	27,139	2,843	10.5
District of Columbia	7,809	920	11.8
Florida	11,826	1,804	15.3
Georgia	34,893	4,491	12.9
Kentucky	17,700	3,101	17.5
Louisiana	37,484	2,688	7.2
Maryland	21,473	1,599	7.4
Mississippi	2,920	209	7.2
North Carolina	6,788	198	2.9
South Carolina	3,365	209	6.2
Tennessee	14,138	1,606	11.4
Texas	133,950	9,009	6.7
West Virginia	2,960	416	14.1

10% of these parolees had their parole revoked and approximately 5% received a new sentence for a new offense.

In 2007, 15.5% of the total at-risk population was returned to incarceration. (See Table 9.6.) This included 16.5% of at-risk parolees under state jurisdiction and 8% of at-risk parolees under federal jurisdiction. On a regional basis, the West had the largest contingent (391,320) of at-risk parolees, and 24.2% of them were re-incarcerated. The South had the next largest contingent (332,387), but only a 9% re-incarceration rate for them. The Midwest had 167,826 at-risk parolees in 2007, and 14.9% of them were returned to incarceration. The Northeast had 156,866 at-risk parolees, and 14.7% of them were re-incarcerated.

The 10 states with the largest percentages of at-risk parolees returned to incarceration in 2007 were:

- Connecticut—29.9% re-incarcerated

- Utah—28.1% re-incarcerated

Region and jurisdiction	Total population at-risk of re-incarceration[a, b]	Returned to incarceration[c]	
		Number	Percent
West	391,320	94,790	24.2%
Arizona	21,325	2,934	13.8
California	296,753	81,431	27.4
Colorado	18,640	4,361	23.4
Hawaii	3,002	313	10.4
Idaho	4,421	501	11.3
Montana	1,613	195	12.1
Nevada	7,477	509	6.8
Oregon	31,241	2,823	9.0
Utah	5,866	1,648	28.1
Wyoming	982	75	7.6

[a]Includes 685,175 adults on parole on January 1 and 495,294 who entered parole between January 1 and December 31, 2007.
[b]Excludes an estimated 174,422 at risk of re-incarceration for which the total returned during 2007 was not reported, including Pennsylvania counties (estimated at 65,851), Illinois (estimated at 68,400), Delaware (910), Oklahoma (estimated at 4,100), Virginia (9,046), Alaska (2,236), New Mexico (5,530), Washington (18,319), and one locality in Alabama (30).
[c]Excludes persons who may have been returned to incarceration but were reported as unsatisfactory (8,834), absconder (53,981), other (9,452), or unknown (4,133). May also exclude some persons reported as having completed parole for whom outstanding warrants were executed immediately upon exit from parole.

SOURCE: Lauren E. Glaze and Thomas P. Bonczar, "Table 6. Parolees Returned to Incarceration, 2007," in *Probation and Parole in the United States, 2007 Statistical Tables*, U.S. Department of Justice, Office of Justice Programs, Bureau of Justice Statistics, December 2008, http://www.ojp.gov/bjs/pub/pdf/ppus07st.pdf (accessed April 7, 2009)

- California—27.4% re-incarcerated

- Missouri—24.9% re-incarcerated

- New Hampshire—24.4% re-incarcerated

- Colorado—23.4% re-incarcerated

- Minnesota—22.5% re-incarcerated

- South Dakota—18.9% re-incarcerated

- Kentucky—17.5% re-incarcerated

- Wisconsin—15.8% re-incarcerated

The five states with highest numbers of at-risk parolees returned to incarceration in 2007 were:

- California—81,431 re-incarcerated

- New York—11,880 re-incarcerated

- Texas—9,009 re-incarcerated

- Missouri—8,213 re-incarcerated

- Pennsylvania—5,243 re-incarcerated

FEDERAL PAROLEES RE-INCARCERATED. In *Compendium of Federal Justice Statistics, 2004* (December 2006, http://www.ojp.usdoj.gov/bjs/pub/pdf/cfjs04.pdf), the BJS notes that the success rate for federal parolees was higher than the national average. In fiscal year (FY) 2004, 49.3% of federal parolees completed their sentences successfully. The success rate for those who had committed violent offenses was 36.6%, whereas for those who had committed property offenses it was 55.1%. About six out of 10 drug offenders (60.4%) successfully completed their parole sentences.

Of those who violated federal parole in FY 2004, most had either violated their parole by committing a new crime (17.3%) or using drugs (10.8%). Male parolees were almost three times as likely as female parolees to terminate parole by committing a new crime, and they were almost twice as likely as female parolees to use drugs. The success rate was 61.9% for white parolees, 39.9% for African-Americans, and 36% for Native Americans or Alaskan natives. The level of education seemed to make a difference in the success rates of parolees. Those with college degrees had a success rate of 82.5%, whereas only 47.8% of those with less than a high school education were successful. Drug use also had a slight effect. Those with no known drug abuse problem had a success rate of 62.5%, whereas those with a known history of drug abuse had a 58% success rate.

Probation Officers

Community corrections has a cost to the community—although it is lower than the cost of housing and feeding prisoners and providing them with health care. A major part of this cost is the employment of skilled probation officers to supervise probationers.

According to Ann L. Pastore and Kathleen Maguire of the Utilization of Criminal Justice Statistics Project, in the *Sourcebook of Criminal Justice Statistics* (2007, http://www.albany.edu/sourcebook/), in 1975 the U.S. government employed 1,377 probation officers to supervise 64,261 federal probationers, a ratio of one officer per 47 probationers. By 2007, 4,932 officers supervised 116,221 probationers, yielding a ratio one officer per 24 probationers. The federal

government has been expending resources to lower the ratio of probationers to officers.

SUPERVISED RELEASE

The Sentencing Reform Act of 1984 created supervised release, an alternative to parole and probation for federal offenders that occurs after an offender's term of imprisonment is completed. Following his or her release, an offender is sentenced to a period of supervision in the community. The act calls for supervised release to follow any term of imprisonment that exceeds one year or if required by a specific statute. The court may also order supervised release to follow imprisonment in any other case. Offenders on supervised release are supervised by probation officers. The BJS notes in *Compendium of Federal Justice Statistics* that in FY 2004, 77,332 (70%) of federal offenders under community supervision were serving a term of supervised release. Most offenders sentenced to supervised release (41,681, or 53.9%) were convicted for drug offenses. Only 4,805 (6.2%) had been convicted of violent offenses.

In FY 2004, 32,930 offenders terminated their supervised release. Most (62.1%) had successfully completed their sentence. Another 13.7% had violated their supervised release by committing a new crime, and 7.2% had used drugs.

The BJS reports that in FY 2004 men were more likely than women to violate the terms of their supervised release; only 59.7% of men successfully completed their supervised release, compared with 74.1% of women. Of those sentenced to supervised release, the youngest (19- and 20-year-olds) and the least educated (less than high school) were the most likely to violate the terms of their sentence.

CHAPTER 10
JUVENILE CRIME

WHO IS A JUVENILE?

Juvenile courts date to the late nineteenth century, when Cook County, Illinois, established the first juvenile court under the Juvenile Court Act of 1899. The underlying concept was that if parents failed to provide children with proper care and supervision, then the state had the right to intervene benevolently. Other states followed Illinois, and by 1925 juvenile courts were in operation in most states. Juvenile courts favored a rehabilitative rather than a punitive philosophy and evolved less formal approaches than those in place in adult courts.

In modern law, juvenile offenses fall into two main categories: delinquency offenses and status offenses. Delinquency offenses are acts that are illegal regardless of the age of the perpetrator. Status offenses are acts that are illegal only for minors, such as truancy (failure to attend school), running away, or curfew violations. Each state defines by legislation the oldest age at which a youth falls under its juvenile court jurisdiction. According to the National Center for Juvenile Justice (NCJJ; 2008, http://www.ncjj.org/stateprofiles/overviews/transfer_state_table.asp), as of 2008 that age was 17 in the vast majority of states. The upper age was set at 16 in 10 states (Georgia, Illinois, Louisiana, Massachusetts, Michigan, Missouri, New Hampshire, South Carolina, Texas, and Wisconsin). Connecticut, New York, and North Carolina use an upper age of 15; however, Connecticut planned to raise the upper age to 17 in July 2009. Many states place certain young offenders in the jurisdiction of the criminal court rather than the juvenile court based on the youth's age, offense, or previous court history.

JUVENILE ARREST STATISTICS

As described in earlier chapters, the Federal Bureau of Investigation (FBI) oversees the Uniform Crime Reports (UCR) Program and summarizes the data in annual reports. The report *Crime in the United States, 2007* (September

2008, http://www.fbi.gov/ucr/cius2007/index.html) includes statistics on crimes reported to law enforcement, arrests, and crimes cleared by arrest or exceptional means through 2007. Crimes cleared by exceptional means are those for which there can be no arrest, such as a murder-suicide, when the perpetrator is known to be deceased. The FBI does provide a partial break down of arrest statistics by age, that is, the age of the arrested offender. However, because the upper age classification for juveniles differs between states, the FBI does not categorize arrested individuals as adults or juveniles.

Every two years the Office of Juvenile Justice and Delinquency Prevention (OJJDP) under the U.S. Department of Justice (DOJ) conducts a detailed examination of UCR data related to people under the age of 18. As of April 2009, the most recent report was *Juvenile Arrests 2006* (November 2008, http://www.ncjrs.gov/pdffiles1/ojjdp/221338.pdf) by Howard N. Snyder of the OJJDP.

Arrests in 2007 of People under the Age of 18

Table 10.1 shows arrest statistics for 2007 for those offenses in which the arrested individuals were under the age of 18. More than 1.6 million people under the age of 18 were arrested. Just over 1.1 million (67%) of them were white, whereas 505,464 (30.8%) were African-American. Much smaller percentages were Native American or Alaskan native (1.2%) or Asian-American or Pacific Islander (1%). The 10 most common specific offenses were:

- Larceny-theft—228,699 arrests

- Assaults other than aggravated assaults—180,615 arrests

- Disorderly conduct—152,817 arrests

- Drug abuse violations—146,785 arrests

- Curfew and loitering law violations—109,575 arrests

- Liquor laws—105,799 arrests

- Vandalism—84,298 arrests

TABLE 10.1

Arrests of juveniles, by offense and race, 2007

[11,929 agencies; 2007 estimated population 225,477,173]

Offense charged	Arrests under 18					Percent distribution[a]				
	Total	White	Black	American Indian or Alaskan Native	Asian or Pacific Islander	Total	White	Black	American Indian or Alaskan Native	Asian or Pacific Islander
Total	1,642,530	1,100,427	505,464	20,504	16,135	100.0	67.0	30.8	1.2	1.0
Murder and nonnegligent manslaughter	1,011	407	580	15	9	100.0	40.3	57.4	1.5	0.9
Forcible rape	2,617	1,610	966	24	17	100.0	61.5	36.9	0.9	0.6
Robbery	26,291	8,119	17,832	122	218	100.0	30.9	67.8	0.5	0.8
Aggravated assault	43,322	24,674	17,773	470	405	100.0	57.0	41.0	1.1	0.9
Burglary	61,523	40,236	20,176	605	506	100.0	65.4	32.8	1.0	0.8
Larceny-theft	228,699	152,143	70,212	2,966	3,378	100.0	66.5	30.7	1.3	1.5
Motor vehicle theft	22,227	12,191	9,426	339	271	100.0	54.8	42.4	1.5	1.2
Arson	5,397	4,123	1,148	49	77	100.0	76.4	21.3	0.9	1.4
Violent crime[b]	73,241	34,810	37,151	631	649	100.0	47.5	50.7	0.9	0.9
Property crime[b]	317,846	208,693	100,962	3,959	4,232	100.0	65.7	31.8	1.2	1.3
Other assaults	180,615	106,119	71,409	1,857	1,230	100.0	58.8	39.5	1.0	0.7
Forgery and counterfeiting	2,341	1,699	596	21	25	100.0	72.6	25.5	0.9	1.1
Fraud	5,649	3,601	1,916	77	55	100.0	63.7	33.9	1.4	1.0
Embezzlement	1,287	753	498	10	26	100.0	58.5	38.7	0.8	2.0
Stolen property; buying, receiving, possessing	16,809	9,203	7,302	127	177	100.0	54.8	43.4	0.8	1.1
Vandalism	84,298	66,406	16,058	1,062	772	100.0	78.8	19.0	1.3	0.9
Weapons; carrying, possessing, etc.	33,040	19,992	12,412	250	386	100.0	60.5	37.6	0.8	1.2
Prostitution and commercialized vice	1,156	473	670	9	4	100.0	40.9	58.0	0.8	0.3
Sex offenses (except forcible rape and prostitution)	11,526	8,139	3,239	77	71	100.0	70.6	28.1	0.7	0.6
Drug abuse violations	146,785	101,152	43,343	1,295	995	100.0	68.9	29.5	0.9	0.7
Gambling	1,584	67	1,511	1	5	100.0	4.2	95.4	0.1	0.3
Offenses against the family and children	4,161	3,029	1,047	60	25	100.0	72.8	25.2	1.4	0.6
Driving under the influence	13,420	12,498	589	238	95	100.0	93.1	4.4	1.8	0.7
Liquor laws	105,799	96,286	5,466	2,965	1,082	100.0	91.0	5.2	2.8	1.0
Drunkenness	12,909	11,532	997	277	103	100.0	89.3	7.7	2.1	0.8
Disorderly conduct	152,817	87,683	62,490	1,602	1,042	100.0	57.4	40.9	1.0	0.7
Vagrancy	2,923	2,267	625	19	12	100.0	77.6	21.4	0.7	0.4
All other offenses (except traffic)	282,244	198,916	77,153	3,313	2,862	100.0	70.5	27.3	1.2	1.0
Suspicion	287	184	100	3	0	100.0	64.1	34.8	1.0	0.0
Curfew and loitering law violations	109,575	69,950	37,532	964	1,129	100.0	63.8	34.3	0.9	1.0
Runaways	82,218	56,975	22,398	1,687	1,158	100.0	69.3	27.2	2.1	1.4

[a]Because of rounding, the percentages may not add to 100.0.
[b]Violent crimes are offenses of murder and nonnegligent manslaughter, forcible rape, robbery, and aggravated assault. Property crimes are offenses of burglary, larceny-theft, motor vehicle theft, and arson.

SOURCE: "Table 43B. Arrests, by Race, 2007," in *Crime in the United States, 2007*, U.S. Department of Justice, Federal Bureau of Investigation, September 2008, http://www.fbi.gov/ucr/cius2007/data/table_43.html (accessed October 3, 2008)

- Running away—82,218 arrests
- Burglary—61,523 arrests
- Aggravated assault—43,322 arrests

Overall, the arrests of people under the age of 18 in 2007 totaled 73,241 for violent crimes and 317,846 for property crimes. The FBI includes four offenses in its definition of violent crimes: murder and nonnegligent manslaughter, forcible rape, robbery, and aggravated assault. All these offenses involve the use or threat of violence by the perpetrator. Property crimes include burglary, larceny-theft, motor vehicle theft, and arson. The FBI counts only the most serious charge for which a single offender is arrested. Violent crimes are considered more serious than property crimes. Thus, a person arrested for rape and burglary would be counted only once in Table 10.1 (for the rape offense).

Juvenile Arrests in 2007

The FBI has collected UCR data for more than a decade; however, not every law enforcement agency has reported data consistently. In *Crime in the United States, 2007*, the FBI used data from 11,936 agencies to calculate the percentage of total arrests in 2007 that were of offenders under the age of 18. Of the nearly 10.7 million arrests that year for which age data were provided, 1.7 million (15.4%) of the arrests were of people under the age of 18. This age group made up 16% of total arrests for violent crimes and 26% of total arrests for property crimes.

The specific delinquency offenses for which this age group made up the largest percentages of total arrests were:

- Arson—47.4% of total arrests
- Vandalism—38.3% of total arrests
- Disorderly conduct—28.4% of total arrests

- Robbery—27.2% of total arrests
- Burglary—27% of total arrests
- Larceny-theft—25.6% of total arrests
- Motor vehicle theft—25% of total arrests
- Weapons violations—23.2% of total arrests
- Liquor laws—22.3% of total arrests
- Suspicion—19.1% of total arrests

However, the OJJDP warns against relying too heavily on these types of data to estimate the proportion of total crime in the United States that is committed by juveniles. Snyder notes that juveniles more often commit crimes in groups than do adults. Thus, a single juvenile-associated crime often results in multiple arrests.

Juvenile Arrest Trends from 1998 to 2007

In *Crime in the United States, 2007*, the FBI uses age data from 7,946 law enforcement agencies to compile 10-year arrest trends for people under the age of 18. Per analysis of arrestee data from these agencies over the period 1998 through 2007, the number of juvenile arrests decreased from approximately 1.5 million in 1998 to 1.2 million in 2007, a 20.4% decline. The decrease was greater among male offenders (23%) than among female offenders (13.5%). Arrests for violent crimes dropped by 14.1%, from 64,755 to 55,651. Arrests for property crimes decreased by 32.9%, from 364,000 to 244,144.

Arrests in 2006 of People under the Age of 18

According to Snyder, approximately 2.2 million people under the age of 18 were arrested in 2006. It should be noted that Snyder does not specify the number of law enforcement agencies that reported any of the arrest data presented in the report. Thus, direct comparisons cannot be made with the 2007 data described earlier in this chapter.

Snyder estimates that the 10 delinquency offenses in 2006 with the most arrests among people under the age of 18 were:

- Larceny-theft—278,100 arrests
- Assaults other than aggravated assaults—249,400 arrests
- Disorderly conduct—207,700 arrests
- Drug abuse violations—196,700 arrests
- Liquor laws—141,400 arrests
- Vandalism—117,500 arrests
- Burglary—83,900 arrests
- Aggravated assault—60,770 arrests
- Weapons violations—47,200 arrests
- Robbery—35,040 arrests

JUVENILE CRIME INDEXES FOR 2006. The OJJDP uses two crime indexes to categorize offenses. The Violent Crime Index covers four crimes: murder and nonnegligent manslaughter, forcible rape, robbery, and aggravated assault. The Property Crime Index includes burglary, larceny-theft, motor vehicle theft, and arson. According to Snyder, 100,700 arrests were made in 2006 of people under the age of 18 for Violent Crime Index offenses. Property Crime Index arrests totaled 404,700 for this age group. The remaining arrests were for what are known as "nonindex" offenses, that is, not included in either index. The nonindex offenses that resulted in the highest number of juvenile arrests in 2006 included assaults other than aggravated assault or rape (249,400), disorderly conduct (207,700), drug violations (196,700), curfew and loitering violations (152,900), and liquor law violations (141,400).

ARRESTS IN 2006 BY GENDER. Snyder notes that male offenders accounted for 71% of arrests of people under the age of 18 in 2006. Females made up 29% of the total. The offenses for which males made up nearly all the arrests were forcible rape (98%), gambling (97%), murder and nonnegligent manslaughter (95%), robbery (91%), weapons violations (90%), and sex offenses other than forcible rape and prostitution (90%). The five offense categories that had the highest proportion of female arrestees included prostitution and commercialized vice (74%), runaways (57%), embezzlement (45%), larceny-theft (41%), and offenses against the family and children (37%).

Overall, male offenders accounted for 83% of those arrested for Violent Crime Index offenses and 68% of those arrested for Property Crime Index offenses.

ARRESTS IN 2006 BY RACE. As with adult arrest rates, minorities are disproportionately represented in juvenile arrests. Snyder reports that in 2006 the breakdown of the U.S. juvenile population (i.e., people under the age of 18) was 78% white, 17% African-American, 5% Asian-American or Pacific Islander, and 1% Native American. The breakdown of juvenile arrests in 2006 for Violent Crime Index offenses was 47% white, 51% African-American, 1% Asian-American or Pacific Islander, and 1% Native American. The breakdown for Property Crime Index offenses was 66% white, 31% African-American, 2% Asian-American or Pacific Islander, and 1% Native American. Thus, white juveniles accounted for 78% of the total U.S. juvenile population, but made up 47% of arrests for violent crimes and 66% of arrests for property crimes. African-American juveniles made up 17% of the total U.S. juvenile population, but accounted for 51% of arrests for violent crimes and 31% of arrests for property crimes.

Table 10.2 shows the African-American proportion of juvenile arrests in 2006 for specific offenses based on the most serious offense charged. African-American juveniles accounted for particularly large percentages of juveniles arrested for robbery (67%), murder (59%), motor vehicle theft (43%), aggravated assault (42%), and simple assault (39%).

TABLE 10.2

Proportion of arrested juveniles that are African-American, by most serious offense, 2006

Most serious offense	Black proportion of juvenile arrests in 2006
Murder	59%
Forcible rape	34
Robbery	67
Aggravated assault	42
Simple assault	39
Burglary	32
Larceny-theft	30
Motor vehicle theft	43
Weapons	37
Drug abuse violations	30
Vandalism	19
Liquor laws	5

SOURCE: Howard N. Snyder, "Black Proportion of Juvenile Arrests in 2006," in *Juvenile Arrests, 2006*, U.S. Department of Justice, Office of Justice Programs, Office of Juvenile Justice and Delinquency Prevention, November 2008, http://www.ncjrs.gov/pdffiles1/ojjdp/221338.pdf (accessed December 5, 2008)

ARRESTS IN 2006 OF JUVENILES UNDER THE AGE OF 15. Snyder also provides statistics on the number of arrests in 2006 of people under the age of 15. These individuals were legally classified as juveniles in every U.S. state. Juveniles under the age of 15 accounted for 29% of the total arrests of people under the age of 18. The younger age group also accounted for 29% of arrests for Violent Crime Index offenses and 33% of arrests for Property Crime Index offenses.

Historical Juvenile Arrest Trends

Table 10.3 shows the percent change in arrests between 1997 and 2006 for juveniles (i.e., people under the age of 18) and adults (i.e., people aged 18 and older). Arrests were down for juveniles for all offenses, except simple assault, which increased by 2%. Adult arrests declined in all categories except burglary, which was unchanged, and drug abuse violations, which increased by 23%.

Among juveniles, the most dramatic arrest declines were for motor vehicle theft (down 53%), larceny-theft (down 45%), and murder (down 42%). (See Table 10.3.) Overall, arrests for offenses within the Violent Crime Index decreased by 20%, and those in the Property Crime Index decreased by 44%. Arrests of juveniles for two nonindex crimes—weapons law violations and drug abuse violations—were down by 10% and 11%, respectively.

JUVENILE ARRESTS BY GENDER, 1997 TO 2006. Table 10.4 shows the percent change in the number of arrests of juveniles (i.e., people under the age of 18) from 1997 to 2006 for the most serious offense charged. Male arrests decreased across the board, and the declines for some crimes were striking—motor vehicle theft down 54%, larceny-theft down 51%, burglary down 38%, and aggravated assault down 24%. By contrast, female arrests declined for some crimes, but

TABLE 10.3

Percent change in juvenile and adult arrests, 1997–2006

Most serious offense	Percent change in arrests 1997–2006	
	Juvenile	Adult
Violent Crime Index	−20%	−11%
Murder	−42	−12
Forcible rape	−31	−8
Robbery	−16	−3
Aggravated assault	−21	−12
Property Crime Index	−44	−14
Burglary	−37	0
Larceny-theft	−45	−18
Motor vehicle theft	−53	−2
Simple assault	2	−6
Weapons law violations	−10	−5
Drug abuse violations	−11	23

SOURCE: Howard N. Snyder, "Percent Change in Arrests, 1997–2006," in *Juvenile Arrests 2006*, U.S. Department of Justice, Office of Justice Programs, Office of Juvenile Justice and Delinquency Prevention, November 2008, http://www.ncjrs.gov/pdffiles1/ojjdp/221338.pdf (accessed December 5, 2008)

TABLE 10.4

Percent change in juvenile arrests, by gender and type of offense, 1997–2006

Most serious offense	Percent change in juvenile arrests 1997–2006	
	Female	Male
Violent Crime Index	−12%	−22%
Aggravated assault	−10%	−24%
Simple assault	19	−4
Property Crime Index	−35	−48
Burglary	−31	−38
Larceny–theft	−34	−51
Motor vehicle theft	−49	−54
Vandalism	−4	−15
Weapons	5	−11
Drug abuse violations	2	−14
Liquor law violations	1	−22
DUI	39	−6
Disorderly conduct	33	−2

SOURCE: Howard N. Snyder, "Percent Change in Juvenile Arrests, 1997–2006," in *Juvenile Arrests, 2006*, U.S. Department of Justice, Office of Justice Programs, Office of Juvenile Justice and Delinquency Prevention, November 2008, http://www.ncjrs.gov/pdffiles1/ojjdp/221338.pdf (accessed December 5, 2008)

increased for other offenses. Notable decreases were recorded for motor vehicle theft (down 49%), larceny-theft (down 34%), and burglary (down 31%). However, female arrests for nonindex crimes increased: driving under the influence (up 39%), disorderly conduct (up 33%), simple assault (up 19%), weapons violations (up 5%), drug abuse violations (up 2%), and liquor law violations (up 1%). Snyder notes that these same trends were evident among adult arrests, in that male arrests have decreased more dramatically than female arrests.

JUVENILE ARRESTS FOR VIOLENT CRIMES BY RACE, 1980 TO 2006. Snyder examines racial differences in the juvenile arrest rate (i.e., the number of arrests of people under the age of 18 per 100,000 U.S. residents aged 10 to 17) for violent crimes from 1980 to 2006. During the 1980s the arrest rate for African-American juveniles charged with Violent Crime Index offenses was six to seven times the arrest rate for white juveniles. The ratio decreased over the following decade. By 1999 the arrest rate for African-American juveniles for violent crimes was four times the arrest rate for white juveniles. However, over the following years the ratio increased. In 2006 the arrest rate for violent crimes for African-American juveniles was five times the arrest rate for white juveniles. The growth in the racial disparity is attributed in large part to two crimes: robbery and aggravated assault. The arrest rate of African-American juveniles between 1999 and 2006 for robbery increased by 38%, whereas the rate for aggravated assault declined by 6%. For white juveniles during this same time period the changes in the arrest rates for these crimes both decreased, with robbery down 16% and aggravated assault down 25%.

VIOLENT CRIME INDEX ARRESTS, 1980 TO 2006. Figure 10.1 illustrates the arrest rate from 1980 to 2006 for crimes within the Violent Crime Index (i.e., murder and nonnegligent manslaughter, forcible rape, robbery, and aggravated assault). The arrest rate is the number of arrests of people under the age of 18 per 100,000 U.S. residents aged 10 to 17. The arrest rate was relatively steady during the early to mid-1980s at around 300. In the late 1980s the rate began a dramatic surge that peaked above 500 in 1994. It then declined after 1995, dropping below 300 by 2004. In 2005 and 2006 the arrest rate increased somewhat, ending at approximately 300 in 2006. The uptick in 2005 and 2006 is blamed on a slight increase in the number of arrests for murder and a more dramatic increase in arrests for robbery. The latter increased by 11% in 2005 and by 19% in 2006.

PROPERTY CRIME INDEX ARRESTS, 1980 TO 2006. The arrest rate from 1980 to 2006 for people under the age of 18 for offenses within the Property Crime Index (i.e., burglary, larceny-theft, motor vehicle theft, and arson) is shown in Figure 10.2. The rate fluctuated near 2,500 for more than a decade, from 1980 to 1995, before beginning a steep decline. By 2006 the rate had fallen to its lowest level ever: near 1,200. The relative steadiness of the rate during the 1980s and early 1990s is particularly striking given that the number of arrests in the Violent Crime Index increased dramatically during this period. Snyder attributes the subsequent rate drop in property crimes to large decreases in arrests from 1994 to 2006 for motor vehicle theft (down 61%), larceny-theft (down 45%), and burglary (down 41%).

HANDLING OF ARRESTED JUVENILES IN 2006. Police have a variety of options when dealing with juvenile offenders. According to Snyder, 21% of all juvenile cases

FIGURE 10.1

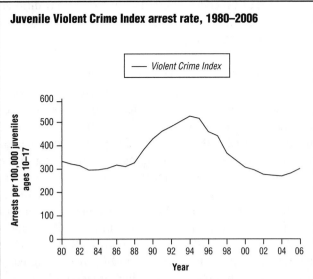

Juvenile Violent Crime Index arrest rate, 1980–2006

SOURCE: Howard N. Snyder, "Following 2004, When It Fell to Its Lowest Level Since at Least 1980, the Juvenile Violent Crime Index Arrest Rate Increased in 2005 and 2006," in *Juvenile Arrests, 2006*, U.S. Department of Justice, Office of Justice Programs, Office of Juvenile Justice and Delinquency Prevention, November 2008, http://www.ncjrs.gov/pdffiles1/ojjdp/221338.pdf (accessed December 5, 2008)

FIGURE 10.2

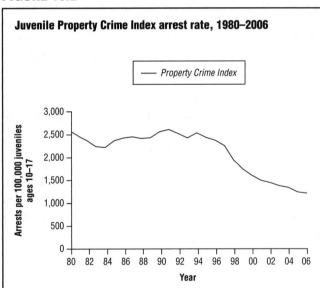

Juvenile Property Crime Index arrest rate, 1980–2006

SOURCE: Howard N. Snyder, "After Years of Relative Stability, the Juvenile Property Crime Index Arrest Rate Began a Decline in the Mid-1990s That Continued through 2006," in *Juvenile Arrests, 2006*, U.S. Department of Justice, Office of Justice Programs, Office of Juvenile Justice and Delinquency Prevention, November 2008, http://www.ncjrs.gov/pdffiles1/ojjdp/221338.pdf (accessed December 5, 2008)

in 2006 were handled within law enforcement agencies, and the offenders were released. Most (69%) were referred to juvenile court, and a small number (8%) were referred to criminal or adult court. The remaining 2% were referred to other police departments or to the welfare system. The percentage of juveniles referred to juvenile court differed little between large cities (i.e., those with populations of more than 250,000) and smaller cities.

Murder: Juvenile Offenders and Victims

In *Juvenile Arrests 2006*, Snyder assesses not only arrest statistics for juveniles but also victimization statistics for murdered juveniles. He notes that in 2006 approximately 17,030 murders occurred in the United States as reported to law enforcement agencies participating in the UCR Program. The vast majority (90%) of the victims were adults, but 1,780 of the victims were under the age of 18. One-third of these young victims were under the age of five. Males made up nearly three-fourths (73%) of murdered juveniles in 2006. Just over two-thirds (68%) of all the murdered juveniles were killed by firearms. Firearm usage was much more prevalent in murders of older juveniles (i.e., those aged 13 and older) than in murders of younger juveniles. Children under the age of five were most commonly murdered by physical assault.

Howard N. Snyder and Melissa Sickmund of the NCJJ report in *Juvenile Offenders and Victims: 2006 National Report* (March 2006, http://www.ojjdp.ncjrs.gov/ojstatbb/nr2006/downloads/NR2006.pdf) that murders involving a juvenile offender increased dramatically from the early 1980s to the early 1990s. In 1984 just over 1,000 murders involved a juvenile offender. By 1994 that number had climbed to more than 3,500. Then, murders by juveniles underwent a steep decline. In 2002 it is estimated that approximately 1,300 murders involved a juvenile offender.

Of known juvenile offenders who committed murder between 1993 and 2002, 74% used a firearm. Snyder and Sickmund report that males (77%) were twice as likely to use a firearm as females (35%). Those aged 17 were more likely than younger juveniles to use a firearm when committing murder; 77% of 17-year-olds used a gun, compared with 74% of 16-year-olds and 70% of those younger than age 16. African-American youth were more likely to use a gun (80%) than white youth (66%).

SCHOOL CRIME

A comprehensive examination of school crime was conducted for the National Center for Education Statistics and the Bureau of Justice Statistics by Rachel Dinkes et al. in *Indicators of School Crime and Safety: 2007* (December 2007, http://nces.ed.gov/pubs2008/2008021.pdf). According to the researchers, students 12 to 18 years of age were the victims of approximately 2.2 million crimes at school during the 2005–06 school year. There were 1.5 million violent crimes including rape, sexual assault, robbery, aggravated assault, and simple assault. Another 242,700 crimes were thefts, and the remaining 458,900 crimes consisted of incidents such as possession of a firearm, distribution of illegal drugs, and the like. Overall, 85.7% of public schools reported experiencing at least one crime. This equates to a rate of 45.8 crimes per 1,000 students enrolled in school in 2005–06.

Among young people aged 5 to 18 years, Dinkes et al. note that there were 14 homicides that occurred at school, on the way to or from school, or at a school-related event during the 2005–06, school year, a slight increase from the 11 counted in 2000–01. However, the 2005–06 number is still lower than the number of homicides of school-aged youth for most years during the 1990s, when the numbers of school-related murders ranged from 28 to 34 per year.

In 2005–06, 25% of students in grades 9 to 12 reported that drugs were readily available on school property, and 8% of students reported that they had been threatened or injured with a weapon while on school property during the previous 12 months. About 28% of students aged 12 to 18 reported that they had been bullied at school during the previous six months.

About 6% of students aged 12 to 18 reported in 2005–06 that they were afraid of being attacked or harmed at school, and 5% were afraid of being attacked or harmed elsewhere. The percentage of students who said they were afraid of being attacked at school (including on the way to or from school) dropped from 12% in 1995 to 6% in 2005. African-American (9%) and Hispanic students (10%) were more likely than white students (4%) to be afraid of being attacked or harmed. Some 6% of students aged 12 to 18 said fear of attack had led them to avoid a school activity or some part of their school during the previous six months; 2% avoided a school activity, and 4% avoided certain places in school. Students in urban areas were more likely (6%) to avoid places in school than suburban (4%) and rural (4%) students.

School Shootings

Despite the relative safety of schools, several school shootings have received national media attention in the past several years:

- February 14, 2008: Armed with a shotgun and three handguns, Steven P. Kazmierczak (1980–2008) entered a lecture hall at Northern Illinois University in Dekalb, Illinois, and without saying a word began shooting at students attending an afternoon geology class. A former student of the school, the 27-year-old Kazmierczak was a graduate student at the University of Illinois–Urbana-Champaign at the time of the incident. Kazmierczak shot randomly at the students, killing five and wounding 18 in addition to taking his own life.

- April 16, 2007: Seung-Hui Cho (1984–2007), a 23-year-old student at Virginia Polytechnic Institute and State University, opened fire at the school and killed 32 people before shooting himself. Considered the worst school shooting in U.S. history, the incident was followed by bomb threats and other threats of violence at various schools across the country, prompting school administrators, politicians, parents, and students to once again review safety procedures and new ways to keep the learning environment safe.

- October 3, 2006: Charles Carl Roberts (1973–2006) shot 10 schoolgirls aged 6 to 13 years old at the one-room West Nickel Mines Amish School in Nickel Mines, Pennsylvania, before shooting himself. Five of the girls and Roberts died.

- March 21, 2005: Sixteen-year-old Jeff Weise (1988–2005) killed his grandfather and a companion. He then went to Red Lake High School in Red Lake, Minnesota, and killed five students, a security guard, a teacher, and finally himself.

- April 14, 2003: A 15-year-old student was killed and three were wounded at John McDonogh High School in New Orleans, Louisiana, by gunfire from four teenagers who attended a different school.

- March 5, 2001: Two were killed and 13 wounded at Santee High School in Santana, California, when Charles A. Williams (1986–), a 15-year-old student at the school, opened fire from a school bathroom.

- February 29, 2000: A 6-year-old student was killed at Theo J. Buell Elementary School near Flint, Michigan, by Dedrick Owens (1993–), a fellow 6-year-old student who brought a handgun to school.

- April 20, 1999: A teacher and 12 students were fatally shot at Columbine High School in Littleton, Colorado, by students Eric Harris (1981–1999) and Dylan Klebold (1982–1999), who eventually killed themselves after an hour-long rampage.

YOUTH GANGS

Even though gangs have been a part of American life since the early 18th century, modern street gangs pose a greater threat to public safety and order than ever before. Many gangs originated as social clubs. In the early 20th century, most were small groups who engaged in delinquent acts or minor crimes, such as fighting with other gangs. By the late 20th century, however, they were frequently involved in violence, intimidation, and the illegal trafficking of drugs and weapons. An increasing number supported themselves by the sale of crack cocaine, heroin, and other illegal drugs, and had easy access to high-powered guns and rifles.

In the fact sheet "Highlights of the 2006 National Youth Gang Survey" (July 2008, http://www.iir.com/nygc/publications/fs200805.pdf), Arlen Egley Jr. and Christina E. Ritz of the National Youth Gang Center summarize results from a 2006 survey of more than 2,500 police and sheriffs' departments around the country. Nearly 2,200 agencies (86% of those contacted) responded to the survey. According to Egley and Ritz, the results indicate that there were approximately 785,000 gang members and 26,500 gangs in the United States in 2006. It should be noted that exact statistics on national gang activity are difficult to compile because local law enforcement agencies may not be aware of gang connections in some cases or may not regularly record offenses as gang-related.

Overall, law enforcement agencies in 14.9% of rural counties, 32.6% of smaller cities (i.e., cities with populations between 2,500 and 49,999), 51% of suburban counties, and 86.4% of larger cities (i.e., cities with populations of 50,000 or more) reported gang problems in 2006. Among the jurisdictions with gang problems, just over half of the agencies reported increases in gang-related aggravated assaults (55% of agencies) and drug sales (52% of agencies) in 2006. Gang-plagued agencies also reported increases in robberies (45% of agencies), larceny-theft and burglary (38% of agencies), and burglary (36% of agencies).

JUVENILE CRIMES—COURT STATISTICS

As noted earlier, most juvenile offenders who enter the court system are handled through juvenile courts. Only a small percentage of juvenile offenders are tried in adult courts.

Juvenile Court Cases

The OJJDP maintains the database Juvenile Court Statistics Databook (http://www.ojjdp.ncjrs.gov/ojstatbb/jcsdb/default.asp), which includes statistics on juvenile court cases from 1985 to 2005. According to the OJJDP, the number of delinquency cases handled in juvenile courts increased from 1.2 million in 1985 to 1.9 million in 1997. The number of cases declined to around 1.7 million by 2000 and remained near that level in 2005. Between 1985 and 2005 the percent of cases involving female juveniles increased from 19% to 27%. The proportion of cases involving offenders under the age of 16 has remained relatively constant at around 60%. The ratio of white to African-American juvenile offenders changed during this period. In 1985, 73% of cases handled by juvenile courts involved white offenders. By 2005 that percentage had dropped to 64%. Meanwhile, the proportion of cases involving African-American offenders increased from 25% in 1985 to 33% in 2005. It should be noted that a case can include more than one charge. For example, a youth brought before a juvenile court on three different robbery charges at the same time is counted as one case.

No nationwide uniform procedure exists for processing juvenile cases, but cases do follow similar paths. An intake department first screens cases. The intake department can be the court itself, a state department of social services, or a prosecutor's office. The intake officer may decide that the case will be dismissed for lack of evidence, handled formally (petitioned), or resolved informally (nonpetitioned). Formal processing can include placement outside the home, probation, a trial in juvenile court, or transfer to an adult court. Informal processing may consist of referral to a social services agency, a fine, some form of restitution, or informal probation. Both formal and informal processing can result in dismissal of the charges and release of the juvenile.

There are two broad types of cases within juvenile court: petitioned and nonpetitioned. Petitioned cases are those in which a petition is filed requesting a hearing. Nonpetitioned cases do not include such a petition and are handled more informally by the courts. In 2005 there were 949,300 petitioned cases, compared with 748,500 nonpetitioned cases. Of the petitioned cases, 623,900 were adjudicated (i.e., tried before a judge), 318,500 were not adjudicated, and 6,900 were waived (i.e., judicially waived to criminal court). Among the nonpetitioned cases, 301,200 were dismissed, 164,000 resulted in probation, and 283,400 had other outcomes.

Juvenile courts may place youths in a detention facility during court processing. Detention may be needed to protect the community from the juvenile, to protect the juvenile, or both. In addition, detention is sometimes necessary to ensure a youth's appearance at scheduled hearings or evaluations.

CHANGING APPROACHES TO JUVENILE DELINQUENCY

Before the 1950s the U.S. juvenile justice system was heavily focused on rehabilitation. This approach began to change as the public judged rehabilitation techniques to be ineffective. A growing number of juveniles were being institutionalized until they reached adulthood because the medical treatment they received did not seem to modify their behavior. Under the impetus of a number of U.S. Supreme Court decisions, juvenile courts became more formal to protect juveniles' rights in waiver situations or if they were to be confined. Congress passed the Juvenile Delinquency Prevention and Control Act in 1968. The act suggested that so-called status offenders (noncriminal offenders such as runaways) no longer be handled inside the court system. The Juvenile Justice and Delinquency Prevention Act of 1974 mandated that juvenile offenders be separated from adult offenders. The act was amended in 1980; part of the amendment required that juveniles be removed from adult jails. During the 1970s the national policy became community-based management of juvenile delinquents.

Prosecuting Juveniles as Adults

Public perception changed again during the 1980s. Juvenile crime was growing, and the systems in place were perceived as being too lenient in dealing with delinquents.

According to Snyder and Sickmund, public opinion was based on a "substantial misperception regarding increases in juvenile crime." Nonetheless, state legislatures responded in various ways:

> Some laws removed certain classes of offenders from the juvenile justice system and handled them as adult criminals in criminal court. Others required the juvenile justice system to be more like the criminal justice system and to treat certain classes of juvenile offenders as criminals but in juvenile court....
>
> As a result, offenders charged with certain offenses now are excluded from juvenile court jurisdiction or face mandatory or automatic waiver to criminal court. In several states, concurrent jurisdiction provisions give prosecutors the discretion to file certain juvenile cases directly in criminal court rather than juvenile court. In some states, certain adjudicated juvenile offenders face mandatory sentences.

The NCJJ (2008, http://www.ncjj.org/stateprofiles/over views/transfer_state_overview.asp) reports that as of 2008 all states allow juveniles to be tried in criminal court under some circumstances. These circumstances include the use of firearms or other weapons and a history of criminality, indicating that the individual has not benefited from previous participation in juvenile justice programs. Juvenile court judges are allowed to determine whether individual suspects are prosecuted in juvenile or adult criminal court in 46 states; 15 states allow prosecutors to determine whether to file cases in juvenile or adult criminal court; and 29 states have laws that determine which court holds jurisdiction over cases, depending on the age of the suspect and the crime committed.

Cases can also be transferred from criminal court to juvenile court under certain circumstances. States that allow prosecutors to file charges directly in criminal court often have provisions for a judicial review hearing once the case is under way in adult court. In some cases the laws require certain types of cases to be waived to criminal court, but juveniles are given an opportunity to appeal the transfer if they can show extraordinary circumstances.

According to the Juvenile Court Statistics Databook, the number of delinquency cases waived to criminal courts increased from 7,200 in 1985 to 13,000 in 1994, before beginning to decline. By 1999 the number was below 10,000. In 2005 only 6,900 cases were waived.

Imprisoning Juveniles and Adults Together

Starting in the 1990s Americans experienced a "moral panic" about juvenile crime that Laurence Steinberg argues in "Introducing the Issue" (*Future of Children*, vol. 18, no. 2, fall 2008) fueled "get tough" on crime policies that treated many juvenile offenders as adults. Several juvenile justice groups and human rights organizations point out the risks associated with incarcerating juveniles with adults. Among the chief concerns is that being held with hardened adult prisoners will likely cause youth offenders to become more violent, more tough, and repeat offenders. Instead of rehabilitation and education, such juveniles will be subjected to more physical and sexual abuse and violence, increasing their likelihood of showing violent tendencies when returning to society one day.

Youth in adult prisons and jails are vulnerable to violence. Amnesty International notes in *Betraying the Young: Human Rights Violations against Children in the U.S. Justice System* (November 20, 1998, http://www.amnesty.org/en/library/info/AMR51/060/1998) that "young people in prison are notoriously a target of sexual and physical assault by adult inmates." Vincent Schiraldi and Jason Zeidenberg of the Center on Juvenile and Criminal Justice echo this sentiment in *The Risks Juveniles Face When They Are Incarcerated with Adults* (July 1997, http://www.cjcj.org/files/the_risks.pdf): "Young people slated to be placed in adult prisons and jails are more likely to be raped, assaulted, and commit suicide." Juvenile justice groups and human rights organizations also point out that juveniles are exposed to attack not only by adult inmates but also by prison guards. Reasons for this can include the juveniles' small stature, lack of confidence, and inexperience at living confined with hardened criminals. Juveniles sometimes resort to suicide because they may give in to despair more quickly.

However, Steinberg suggests that at the end of the first decade of the twenty-first century, get-tough policies were softening "as politicians and the public come to regret the high economic costs and ineffectiveness of the punitive reforms and the harshness of the sanctions." Elizabeth Scott and Laurence Steinberg find in "Adolescent Development and the Regulation of Youth Crime" (*Future of Children*, vol. 18, no. 2, fall 2008) that by 2008 the justice system was once again recognizing that age and maturity level needed to be taken into account when calculating punishment for crimes. They suggest that most juveniles who commit crimes are "adolescence-limited" offenders who will mature out of their criminal tendencies; however, contact with a harsh, adult corrections system can push juveniles into adult criminality. Instead, the authors state, successful programs "seek to provide young offenders with supportive social contexts and authoritative adult figures and to help them acquire the skills necessary to change problem behavior and attain psychosocial maturity."

Other surveys support the idea that get-tough attitudes appear to be changing. The press release "New NCCD Poll Shows Public Strongly Favors Youth Rehabilitation and Treatment" (February 7, 2007, http://www.nccd-crc.org/nccd/pubs/zogbyPR0207.pdf) notes that a survey conducted by the National Council on Crime and Delinquency found that the American public supports rehabilitation and treatment for young people, not prosecution in adult criminal courts or incarceration in adult jails or prisons. Nine out of 10 people surveyed believed this approach might help prevent crime in the future, and seven out of 10 believed

imprisoning juveniles in adult facilities would increase the likelihood that they would commit future crimes. Most people believed that youth should not be automatically transferred to adult court, but that such transfers should be handled on an individual basis.

STATUS OFFENSE CASES

Status offenses are acts that are against the law only because the people who commit them are juveniles. In many communities, social service agencies rather than juvenile courts are responsible for accused status offenders. Because of differences in screening procedures, national estimates of informally handled status offense cases are not calculated. Therefore, the statistics presented in this chapter report only on status offense cases formally handled (petitioned) through the juvenile justice system.

According to Charles Puzzanchera and Melissa Sickmund of the OJJDP, in *Juvenile Court Statistics 2005* (July 2008, http://ojjdp.ncjrs.gov/ojstatbb/njcda/pdf/jcs2005.pdf), the five major status offense categories used by the OJJDP are running away, truancy, alcohol possession, curfew law violations, and ungovernability (also known as incorrigibility or being beyond parental control). According to Puzzanchera and Sickmund, 150,600 status offense cases were petitioned to juvenile courts in 2005. This number was up by 29% from 1995. The following is a breakdown by offenses for 2005:

- Truancy—35% of cases
- Liquor law violations—19% of cases
- Ungovernability—15% of cases
- Running away—14% of cases
- Curfew violations—9% of cases
- Miscellaneous—8% of cases

Age, Sex, and Race

For liquor law violations and curfew violations, Puzzanchera and Sickmund indicate that the case rates (i.e., number of cases per 1,000 juveniles in age group) in 2005 increased with violator age across the age group of 10 to 17. That is, the largest rates were reported for 17-year-olds. Different trends are seen in the age breakdowns for runaways, truancy, and ungovernability. For these offenses the highest case rates were for 15- and 16-year-olds.

In 2005 males accounted for 56% of status offense cases, whereas females accounted for 44%. More than one-third (34%) of the cases involving males were for truancy, 21% were for liquor law violations, 14% were for ungovernability, 11% were for curfew violations, 10% were for miscellaneous offenses, and 10% were for running away. Of the status cases involving females, 36% were for truancy, 20% were for running away, 16% were for liquor violations, 15% were for ungovernability, 7% were for curfew violations, and 6% were for miscellaneous offenses.

Between 1995 and 2005 the number of status cases increased by 25% for males and by 33% for females. The larger increase for female offenders is attributed primarily to large increases in violations of liquor and curfew laws. The caseload for alcohol violations increased by 29% for females during this period, compared with a decrease of 2% for males. Likewise, the caseload for curfew violations increased by 14% for female offenders, but decreased 3% for male offenders.

Between 1995 and 2005 case rates (i.e., the number of cases per 1,000 juveniles aged 10 and up) increased by 17% for whites, 44% for Native Americans, 70% for African-Americans, and 87% for Asian-Americans, native Hawaiians, and other Pacific Islanders. In 2005 the offense profile for each racial group varied somewhat, with white case rates topped by truancy (35% of cases) and liquor violations (23%). The largest groups of African-American status offense cases were brought for truancy (34%) and running away (24%). Among Native Americans the most cases were for liquor violations (45%) and truancy (25%); for Asians, truancy (41%) and running away (22%).

Detention and Case Processing

The handling of status crimes has changed considerably since the mid-1980s. The Juvenile Justice and Delinquency Prevention Act of 1974 offered substantial federal funds to states that tried to reduce the detention of status offenders. The primary responsibility for status offenders was often transferred from the juvenile courts to child welfare agencies. As a result, the character of the juvenile courts' activities changed.

Before this change many juvenile detention centers held a substantial number of young people whose only offense was that their parents could no longer control them. By not routinely institutionalizing these adolescents, the courts demonstrated that children deserved the same rights as adults. A logical extension of this has been that juveniles accused of violent crimes are also now being treated legally as if they were adults.

Those involved in petitioned status offense cases are rarely held in detention. According to Puzzanchera and Sickmund, only 8% of status offenders were detained in 2005. This percentage is virtually unchanged from 7% in 1995. In 2005 the offenders in 23% of liquor law cases were detained. This compares with 19% for ungovernability cases, 18% for miscellaneous cases, 17% for runaways, 15% for truancy violators, and 8% for curfew violation cases.

Puzzanchera and Sickmund explain that in 2005, 88,900 of the 150,600 total juvenile status offense cases were adjudicated. Thus, 59% of the cases resulted in adjudication. Between 1995 and 2005 the number of cases per year that were adjudicated increased 71% for truancy, 69% for curfew violations, 42% for liquor law violations, 32% for ungovernability, and 5% for runaways.

For whites, 44% of runaway, 56% of ungovernability, 58% of truancy, 68% of liquor, and 75% of curfew cases were adjudicated. For African-Americans, the numbers were slightly lower: 42% of runaway, 53% of ungovernability, 56% each of curfew and truancy, and 64% of liquor law cases. In general, males and females were equally likely to have their cases adjudicated. Of the cases that were adjudicated, 52% resulted in formal probation, 16% resulted in out-of-home placement, and the remaining cases involved some other sanction, such as restitution or community service.

HOLDING PARENTS RESPONSIBLE

For many decades, civil liability laws held parents at least partly responsible for damages caused by their children. Also, child welfare laws included actions against those who contributed to the delinquency of a minor. Most researchers recognize that parental involvement is key to juvenile rehabilitation; however, that involvement can be problematic because many parents are seen as contributing to their children's problems rather than helping resolve them. In addition, some parents assume an adversarial role with the juvenile justice system, hoping to protect their children from prosecution. By the 1990s, in response to rising juvenile crime rates, communities and states passed stronger laws about parental responsibility. Several states enacted laws making parents criminally responsible for their children's crimes.

In "From Columbine to Kazaa: Parental Liability in a New World" (*University of Illinois Law Review*, 2005), Amy L. Tomaszewski reports that advocates of parental liability believe the laws motivate adults to become better parents to avoid serious penalties, including jail terms. According to Tomaszewski, even though parental liability laws are not new, states have established a broader range of civil and criminal penalties for parents who do not control their children. However, research shows that juvenile crime rates started declining before most parental liability laws were enacted. For example, between 1994 and 2001 the arrest rates for juvenile murder, rape, robbery, and aggravated assault dropped 44%.

Furthermore, legislators find it very difficult to determine the age when parents are no longer responsible for their children's actions. Parents might be legitimately responsible for a small child's behavior, but teenagers are more independent, so it is more difficult to decide whether teenage crimes are really the result of poor parenting.

JUVENILES IN RESIDENTIAL PLACEMENT

Children who are found guilty of crimes in courts belonging to the juvenile justice system may be sentenced to a residential placement facility. These institutions may be under the administration of the state or be operated by private nonprofit or for-profit corporations or organizations and staffed by employees of the corporation or organization.

TABLE 10.5

Juveniles in public and private residential custody facilities, by sex, race and ethnicity, type of facility, and state, 2006

State	Total	Sex		Race and ethnicity						Type of facility	
		Male	Female	White, Hispanic	Black, Hispanic	Hispanic	American Indian	Asian	Other	Public	Private
United States, total*	92,854	78,911	13,943	32,495	37,337	19,027	1,828	1,155	1,012	64,163	28,558
Alabama	1,752	1,368	384	693	1,017	27	3	0	12	828	924
Alaska	363	288	75	135	39	9	150	15	18	258	105
Arizona	1,737	1,389	348	630	207	762	126	6	3	1,464	270
Arkansas	813	654	159	381	384	39	0	6	6	255	558
California	15,240	13,383	1,854	2,472	4,227	7,824	117	546	51	13,665	1,575
Colorado	2,034	1,761	270	966	327	696	27	18	3	1,071	963
Connecticut	498	381	114	114	219	144	3	0	15	252	243
Delaware	303	273	27	60	219	21	0	0	3	252	51
District of Columbia	339	309	30	12	309	12	0	3	0	240	99
Florida	7,302	6,285	1,014	2,856	3,807	567	12	24	36	2,751	4,551
Georgia	2,631	2,247	384	627	1,875	126	0	3	0	2,175	456
Hawaii	123	81	42	6	3	15	0	36	63	99	24
Idaho	522	414	108	420	6	69	24	3	0	459	66
Illinois	2,631	2,298	333	852	1,239	456	36	30	18	2,391	240
Indiana	2,616	2,052	564	1,623	798	144	3	3	45	1,731	888
Iowa	1,062	714	348	738	198	63	18	12	33	372	693
Kansas	1,053	939	114	507	306	198	15	12	15	711	342
Kentucky	1,242	978	264	804	387	21	0	3	30	900	342
Louisiana	1,200	1,011	189	312	870	9	6	3	0	792	408
Maine	210	183	24	192	9	0	3	3	3	189	21
Maryland	1,104	1,008	93	255	786	48	0	6	9	738	366
Massachusetts	1,164	1,023	138	423	333	315	3	36	51	465	699
Michigan	2,760	2,226	534	1,209	1,299	111	33	9	99	1,275	1,485
Minnesota	1,623	1,359	267	717	537	75	195	78	24	960	663
Mississippi	444	357	90	108	336	0	0	0	0	417	30
Missouri	1,293	1,110	183	603	627	39	3	6	15	1,275	18
Montana	243	180	60	162	9	12	51	0	6	171	69
Nebraska	735	492	243	381	186	111	45	3	9	507	228
Nevada	885	735	150	351	252	234	18	15	15	849	36
New Hampshire	189	153	36	147	21	15	3	0	3	102	87
New Jersey	1,704	1,524	177	267	1,119	291	9	6	9	1,590	114
New Mexico	471	402	72	63	30	339	39	0	0	444	27
New York	4,197	3,321	876	1,017	2,172	876	12	39	81	2,049	2,148
North Carolina	1,029	846	183	327	606	66	15	6	12	726	303
North Dakota	240	201	39	141	3	6	81	0	6	105	135
Ohio	4,149	3,594	555	1,929	2,031	96	0	6	84	3,825	324
Oklahoma	924	810	111	399	318	75	111	9	12	678	246
Oregon	1,254	1,098	156	855	123	177	69	9	21	1,038	219
Pennsylvania	4,323	3,858	462	1,419	2,328	447	6	30	90	1,224	3,099
Rhode Island	348	312	36	132	123	60	12	12	9	234	114
South Carolina	1,320	1,152	168	393	909	15	0	0	3	879	441
South Dakota	597	435	162	264	45	30	240	6	15	279	318
Tennessee	1,419	1,257	162	666	702	33	3	0	18	855	564
Texas	8,247	7,149	1,101	1,980	2,751	3,486	12	18	3	7,197	1,050
Utah	864	696	165	519	87	213	21	18	6	414	450
Vermont	54	51	3	45	3	6	0	0	0	27	27
Virginia	2,310	2,010	300	663	1,461	153	3	27	3	2,265	45
Washington	1,455	1,224	231	849	255	222	78	42	6	1,398	54
West Virginia	579	492	87	471	93	6	0	0	9	357	222
Wisconsin	1,347	1,158	189	609	603	45	51	27	9	849	498
Wyoming	315	219	93	201	30	48	30	0	3	117	198
Tribal facilities	132	96	36	6	3	0	126	0	0	NA	NA

Note: These data are from the Census of Juveniles in Residential Placement, conducted biennially by the U.S. Department of Justice, Office of Juvenile Justice and Delinquency Prevention. Public and private facilities, secure and nonsecure, that hold alleged or adjudicated juvenile delinquents or status offenders are asked to provide information on each juvenile in residence on a specified reference date. Facilities are asked to include all juveniles under 21 years of age assigned a bed in the residential facility on the reference date as a result of being charged or court adjudicated for an offense. The reference date for each census was the last Wednesday in October of each year except for 2006 when the reference date was February 22. The facility response rate for the 1997 census was 96%; for the 1999 census it was 100%; for the 2001 census it was 99%; and for the 2003 and 2006 censuses it was 100%. These data reflect the state where the offense was committed rather than the state in which the holding facility is located.
Detail may not add to total because of rounding.
*Total includes 1,466 juvenile offenders in private facilities for whom the state where the offense was committed was not reported.

SOURCE: Ann L. Pastore and Kathleen Maguire, editors, "Table 6.12.2006. Juveniles in Public and Private Residential Custody Facilities," in *Sourcebook of Criminal Justice Statistics Online*, U.S. Department of Justice, Office of Justice Programs, Bureau of Justice Statistics, undated, http://www.albany.edu/sourcebook/pdf/t6122006.pdf (accessed December 5, 2008)

There were 92,854 juveniles in residential custody facilities in 2006, including 64,163 (69%) juveniles who were in public facilities. (See Table 10.5.)

Males accounted for the largest portion (78,911 or 85%) of those in residential placement. The racial and ethnic breakdown was 37,337 (40%) non-Hispanic African-Americans,

TABLE 10.6

Juveniles in public and private residential custody facilities, by offense and race and ethnicity, 2006

[By race, ethnicity, and offense, United States, 2006[a]]

| Most serious offense | Total | Race and ethnicity | | | | | |
		White, Hispanic	Black, Hispanic	Hispanic	American Indian	Asian	Other
Total	92,854	32,495	37,337	19,027	1,828	1,155	1,012
Delinquency offenses	88,137	30,133	35,766	18,636	1,603	1,109	890
Violent offenses	31,704	10,132	14,061	6,279	521	388	323
Index offenses[b]	21,776	6,425	9,980	4,592	310	304	165
Other violent	9,928	3,707	4,081	1,687	211	84	158
Property offenses	23,177	8,691	8,617	4,863	458	319	229
Index offenses[c]	18,986	7,144	7,214	3,801	380	271	176
Other property	4,191	1,547	1,403	1,062	78	48	53
Drug offenses	7,996	2,521	3,484	1,725	116	82	68
Public-order offenses	9,944	3,423	3,967	2,145	177	146	86
Technical violation[d]	15,316	5,366	5,637	3,624	331	174	184
Status offenses[d]	4,717	2,362	1,571	391	225	46	122

Note: These data are from the Census of Juveniles in Residential Placement, conducted biennially by the U.S. Department of Justice, Office of Juvenile Justice and Delinquency Prevention. Public and private facilities, secure and nonsecure, that hold alleged or adjudicated juvenile delinquents or status offenders are asked to provide information on each juvenile in residence on a specified reference date. Facilities are asked to include all juveniles under 21 years of age assigned a bed in the residential facility on the reference date as a result of being charged or court adjudicated for an offense. The reference date for each census was the last Wednesday in October of each year except for 2006 when the reference date was February 22. The facility response rate for the 1997 census was 96%; for the 1999 census it was 100%; for the 2001 census it was 99%; and for the 2003 and 2006 censuses it was 100%.

[a]Detail may not add to total because of rounding.

[b]Includes criminal homicide, violent sexual assault, robbery, and aggravated assault.

[c]Includes burglary, theft, auto theft, and arson.

[d]Status offenses include running away, underage drinking, truancy, curfew violations, and other offenses that are illegal for juveniles but not adults. Care should be exercised when interpreting status offense data because States differ in what behaviors are classified as adjudicable status offenses.

SOURCE: Ann L. Pastore and Kathleen Maguire, editors, "Table 6.10.2006. Juveniles in Public and Private Residential Custody Facilities, by Race, Ethnicity, and Offense, United States, 2006," in *Sourcebook of Criminal Justice Statistics Online*, U.S. Department of Justice, Office of Justice Programs, Bureau of Justice Statistics, undated, http://www.albany.edu/sourcebook/pdf/t6102006.pdf (accessed December 5, 2008)

32,495 (35%) non-Hispanic whites, 19,027 (20%) Hispanics, 1,828 (2%) Native Americans, 1,155 (1%) Asian-Americans, and 1,012 (1%) other races.

The 10 states with the largest number of juveniles in residential custody facilities in 2006 were:

- California—15,240 juveniles
- Texas—8,247 juveniles
- Florida—7,302 juveniles
- Pennsylvania—4,323 juveniles
- New York—4,197 juveniles
- Ohio—4,149 juveniles
- Michigan—2,760 juveniles
- Georgia—2,631 juveniles
- Illinois—2,631 juveniles
- Indiana—2,616 juveniles

Table 10.6 shows a breakdown by race and ethnicity for the most serious offense for which juveniles had been placed in residential custody facilities. The vast majority of the offenses (88,137 or 95%) were delinquency offenses. The remaining 5% were status offenses. The racial and ethnic breakdown of the juveniles held for delinquency offenses was 35,766 (41%) non-Hispanic African-American offenders, 30,133 (34%) non-Hispanic white offenders, 18,636 (21%) Hispanic offenders, 1,603 (2%) Native American offenders, 1,109 (1%) Asian-American offenders, and 890 (1%) offenders of other races.

There were 31,704 juvenile offenders in residential custody facilities who had committed violent crimes and 23,177 who had committed property offenses. (See Table 10.6.) Additional numbers were held for technical violations (15,316 juveniles), public-order offenses (9,944 juveniles), and drug offenses (7,996 juveniles).

Table 10.7 provides a breakdown of the juveniles in residential custody facilities by age and sex in 2006. The largest contingent (24,646 or 27% of the total) were 16 years old. In descending order, the remaining contingents were 17 years old (23,761 or 26% of the total), 15 years old (17,574 or 19% of the total), 18 years and older (13,115 or 14% of the total), 14 years old (9,127 or 10% of the total), 13 years old (3,424 or 4% of the total), and juveniles less than 13 years old (1,207 or 1% of the total).

The largest proportions of males (26% each) in 2006 were 16 and 17 years old. Together, they accounted for more than half of the males in the facilities. Other age groups made up smaller portions of total males, that is, 15 years old (18% of total males), 18 years and older (15% of total males), 14 years old (9% of total males), 13 years old (3% of total males), and juveniles less than 13 years old

TABLE 10.7

Juveniles in public and private residential custody facilities, by age and sex, 2006

[By age and sex, United States, 2006*]

| | Total | | Sex | | | |
| | | | Male | | Female | |
Age	Number	Percent	Number	Percent	Number	Percent
Total	92,854	100%	78,911	100%	13,943	100%
Less than 13 years	1,207	1	1,011	1	196	1
13 years	3,424	4	2,714	3	710	5
14 years	9,127	10	7,329	9	1,798	13
15 years	17,574	19	14,424	18	3,150	23
16 years	24,646	27	20,769	26	3,877	28
17 years	23,761	26	20,588	26	3,173	23
18 years and older	13,115	14	12,076	15	1,039	7

Note: These data are from the Census of Juveniles in Residential Placement, conducted biennially by the U.S. Department of Justice, Office of Juvenile Justice and Delinquency Prevention. Public and private facilities, secure and nonsecure, that hold alleged or adjudicated juvenile delinquents or status offenders are asked to provide information on each juvenile in residence on a specified reference date. Facilities are asked to include all juveniles under 21 years of age assigned a bed in the residential facility on the reference date as a result of being charged or court adjudicated for an offense. The reference date for each census was the last Wednesday in October of each year except for 2006 when the reference date was February 22. The facility response rate for the 1997 census was 96%; for the 1999 census it was 100%; for the 2001 census it was 99%; and for the 2003 and 2006 censuses it was 100%.
Detail may not add to total because of rounding.

SOURCE: Ann L. Pastore and Kathleen Maguire, editors, "Table 6.11.2006. Juveniles in Public and Private Residential Custody Facilities, by Age and Sex, United States, 2006," in *Sourcebook of Criminal Justice Statistics Online*, U.S. Department of Justice, Office of Justice Programs, Bureau of Justice Statistics, undated, http://www.albany.edu/sourcebook/pdf/t6112006.pdf (accessed December 5, 2008)

(1% of total males). The largest contingents of females were 16 years old (28% of all females), 17 years old (23% of all females), and 15 years old (23% of all females). A breakdown of the other age groups is 14 years old (13% of all females), 18 years and older (7% of all females), 13 years old (5% of all females), and less than 13 years old (1% of all females).

JUVENILE BOOT CAMPS

Boot camps are specialized residential facilities for midrange offenders—those who have failed with lesser sanctions such as probation but are not yet considered hardened criminals. First proposed in the 1980s, juvenile boot camps typically share the 90- to 120-day duration of military boot camps. They employ military customs and have correctional officers acting as uniformed drill instructors who use intense verbal tactics designed to break down inmates' resistance. Boot camps emphasize vigorous physical activity, drill and ceremony, and manual labor. The offenders have little free time, and strictly enforced rules govern all aspects of conduct and appearance. Because of state-mandated education rules, programs spend a minimum of three hours daily on academic education. Most programs also include some vocational education, work-skills training, or job preparation.

The first boot camp for juvenile offenders in the United States was established in Orleans Parish, Louisiana, in 1985. Within a decade similar facilities were operating in about 30 states. Juvenile boot camp programs typically exclude some types of offenders, such as sex offenders, armed robbers, and youths with a record of serious violence.

Definitions for terms such as *nonviolent* vary from program to program. Boot camps operate under the assumption that making a marked, positive change in the life of young offenders can benefit society in the long run by reducing recidivism (relapse into criminal activity), reducing prison populations, and reducing costs.

Are Juvenile Boot Camps Effective?

Several factors have a direct bearing on the success or failure rates for boot camp participants, including the length of the sessions and the amount of postrelease supervision. In *Correctional Boot Camps: Lessons from a Decade of Research* (June 2003, http://www.ncjrs.gov/pdffiles1/nij/197018.pdf), the DOJ states that "participants reported positive short-term changes in attitudes and behaviors; they also had better problem-solving and coping skills.... With few exceptions, these positive changes did not lead to reduced recidivism. The boot camps that did produce lower recidivism rates offered more treatment services, had longer sessions, and included more intensive postrelease supervision. However, not all programs with these features had successful results.... Under a narrow set of conditions, boot camps can lead to small relative reductions in prison populations and correctional costs."

According to the National Mental Health Association (NMHA), in *Mental Health Treatment for Youth in the Juvenile Justice System: A Compendium of Promising Practices* (2004, http://www.nttac.org/views/docs/jabg/mhcurriculum/mh_mht.pdf), juvenile boot camps do not prevent offenders from committing new offenses. Several studies of adult and juvenile boot camps show that graduates of these programs are just as likely to commit new offenses as offenders who were placed in prison or jail and, in some cases, as those sentenced to regular probation supervision.

However, the NMHA notes that many juveniles sentenced to boot camps say that these programs helped them and that they feel more positive about their future. What is not clear is whether these attitudes last once the youths leave the boot camp. It is also not clear if changes in attitude translate into behavioral changes once the juveniles return to their communities.

JUVENILES AND THE DEATH PENALTY

Until 2005 convicted criminals could be executed for crimes they committed as juveniles. Victor L. Streib of Ohio Northern University reports in *The Juvenile Death Penalty Today: Death Sentences and Executions for Juvenile Crimes, January 1, 1973–February 28, 2005* (October 7, 2005, http://www.law.onu.edu/faculty_staff/faculty_profiles/coursematerials/streib/juvdeath.pdf) that between 1973 and 2005, 22 offenders were executed for crimes they committed when they were younger than 18. The U.S. Supreme Court has considered many cases concerning the practice of executing offenders for crimes they committed as children. In *Eddings v. Oklahoma* (455 U.S. 104 [1982]), the court found that a juvenile's mental and emotional development should be considered as a mitigating factor when deciding whether to apply the death penalty, noting that adolescents are less mature and responsible than adults and not as able to consider long-range consequences of their actions. In this case, the court reversed the death sentence of a 16-year-old who had been tried as an adult.

Subsequent Supreme Court rulings have further limited the application of the death penalty in cases involving juveniles. In *Thompson v. Oklahoma* (487 U.S. 815 [1988]), the court found that applying the death sentence to an offender who had been 15 years old at the time of the murder was cruel and unusual punishment, concluding that the death penalty could not be applied to offenders who were younger than 16. However, the following year the court found in *Stanford v. Kentucky* (492 U.S. 361 [1989]) that applying the death penalty to offenders who were aged 16 or 17 at the time of the crime was not cruel and unusual punishment.

The court was asked to reconsider this decision in 2005. In *Roper v. Simmons* (543 U.S. 551), the court set aside the death sentence of Christopher Simmons by a vote of five to four, concluding that the "Eighth and Fourteenth Amendments forbid imposition of the death penalty on offenders who were under the age of 18 when their crimes were committed." Snyder and Sickmund note that few states applied death penalty provisions to juveniles at the time of the *Roper* decision, even though 20 states allowed juveniles to be sentenced to death under the law. Since the 2005 decision, the most severe punishment for juveniles who commit serious crimes is a sentence of life in prison.

IMPORTANT NAMES
AND ADDRESSES

American Bar Association
321 N. Clark St.
Chicago, IL 60654-7598
(312) 988-5000
URL: http://www.abanet.org/

American Civil Liberties Union
125 Broad St., 18th Floor
New York, NY 10004
(212) 607-3300
URL: http://www.aclu.org/

American Correctional Association
206 N. Washington St., Ste. 200
Alexandria, VA 22314
(703) 224-0000
1-800-222-5656
FAX: (703) 224-0179
URL: http://www.aca.org/

American Jail Association
1135 Professional Ct.
Hagerstown, MD 21740-5853
(301) 790-3930
URL: http://www.aja.org/

Anti-Defamation League
1100 Connecticut Ave. NW, Ste. 1020
Washington, DC 20036
(202) 452-8310
URL: http://www.adl.org/

**Bureau of Alcohol, Tobacco, Firearms,
and Explosives
Office of Public and Governmental
Affairs**
99 New York Ave. NE
Mail Stop 5S144
Washington, DC 20226
(202) 927-8500
FAX: (202) 927-1083
E-mail: atfmail@atf.gov
URL: http://www.atf.gov/

**Bureau of Engraving and Printing
U.S. Department of the Treasury**
14th St. and C St. SW
Washington, DC 20228

(202) 874-8888
1-877-874-4114
URL: http://www.moneyfactory.gov/

**Bureau of Justice Statistics
U.S. Department of Justice**
810 Seventh St. NW
Washington, DC 20531
(202) 307-0765
E-mail: askbjs@usdoj.gov
URL: http://www.ojp.usdoj.gov/bjs/

Coalition for Juvenile Justice
1710 Rhode Island Ave. NW, 10th Floor
Washington, DC 20036
(202) 467-0864
FAX: (202) 887-0738
E-mail: info@juvjustice.org
URL: http://www.juvjustice.org/

**Congressional Research Service
Library of Congress**
101 Independence Ave. SE
Washington, DC 20540-7500
URL: http://www.loc.gov/crsinfo/

Federal Bureau of Investigation
J. Edgar Hoover Bldg.
935 Pennsylvania Ave. NW
Washington, DC 20535-0001
(202) 324-3000
URL: http://www.fbi.gov/

Federal Bureau of Prisons
320 First St. NW
Washington, DC 20534
(202) 307-3198
URL: http://www.bop.gov/

Federal Judicial Center
Thurgood Marshall Federal Judiciary Bldg.
One Columbus Circle NE
Washington, DC 20002-8003
(202) 502-4000
FAX: (202)502-4099
URL: http://www.fjc.gov/

Federal Trade Commission
600 Pennsylvania Ave. NW
Washington, DC 20580
(202) 326-2222
URL: http://www.ftc.gov/

**Internal Revenue Service Criminal
Investigation Division**
1111 Constitution Ave. NW, Rm. 2501
Washington, DC 20224
URL: http://www.irs.gov/irs/article/
0,,id=98398,00.html

**Justice Research and Statistics
Association**
777 N. Capitol St. NE, Ste. 801
Washington, DC 20002
(202) 842-9330
FAX: (202) 842-9329
E-mail: cjinfocjinfo@jrsa.org
URL: http://www.jrsa.org/

National Center for Victims of Crime
2000 M St. NW, Ste. 480
Washington, DC 20036
(202) 467-8700
FAX: (202) 467-8701
URL: http://www.ncvc.org/

**National Center on Institutions
and Alternatives**
7222 Ambassador Rd.
Baltimore, MD 21244
(410) 265-1490
URL: http://www.ncianet.org/

National Conference of State Legislatures
7700 E. First Place
Denver, CO 80230
(303) 364-7700
FAX: (303) 364-7800
URL: http://www.ncsl.org/

National Consumers League
1701 K St. NW, Ste. 1200
Washington, DC 20006
(202) 835-3323

FAX: (202) 835-0747
E-mail: info@nclnet.org
URL: http://www.nclnet.org/

National Correctional Industries Association
1202 N. Charles St.
Baltimore, MD 21201
(410) 230-3972
FAX: (410) 230-3981
E-mail: info@nationalcia.org
URL: http://www.nationalcia.org/

National Council on Crime and Delinquency
1970 Broadway, Ste. 500
Oakland, CA 94612
(510) 208-0500
FAX: (510) 208-0511
URL: http://www.nccd-crc.org/

National Crime Prevention Council
2345 Crystal Drive, Ste. 500
Arlington, VA 22202
(202) 466-6272
FAX: (202) 296-1356
URL: http://www.ncpc.org/

National Criminal Justice Association
720 Seventh St., 3rd Floor
Washington, DC 20001
(202) 628-8550
FAX: (202) 448-1723
E-mail: info@ncja.org
URL: http://www.ncja.org/

National Criminal Justice Reference Service
PO Box 6000
Rockville, MD 20849-6000
(301) 519-5500
1-800-851-3420
FAX: (301) 519-5212
URL: http://www.ncjrs.gov/

National Institute of Corrections
320 First St. NW
Washington, DC 20534
(202) 307-3106
1-800-995-6423
URL: http://www.nicic.org/

National Institute of Justice
810 Seventh St. NW
Washington, DC 20531
(202) 307-2942
FAX: (202) 307-6394
URL: http://www.ojp.usdoj.gov/nij/

National Legal Aid and Defender Association
1140 Connecticut Ave. NW, Ste. 900
Washington, DC 20036
(202) 452-0620
FAX: (202) 872-1031
URL: http://www.nlada.org/

National Organization for Victim Assistance
510 King St., Ste. 424
Alexandria, VA 22314
(703) 535-6682
1-800-879-6682 (information hotline)
FAX: (703) 535-5500
URL: http://www.trynova.org/

National White Collar Crime Center
10900 Nuckols Rd., Ste. 325
Glen Allen, VA 23060
(804) 967-6208
URL: http://www.nw3c.org/

National Youth Gang Center
Institute for Intergovernmental Research
PO Box 12729
Tallahassee, FL 32317-2729
(850) 385-0600
FAX: (850) 422-3529
E-mail: nygc@iir.com
URL: http://www.iir.com/nygc/

Office for Victims of Crime
U.S. Department of Justice
810 Seventh St. NW
Washington, DC 20531
(202) 307-5983
FAX: (202) 514-6383
URL: http://www.ojp.usdoj.gov/ovc/

Office of Juvenile Justice and Delinquency Prevention
810 Seventh St. NW
Washington, DC 20531
(202) 307-5911
URL: http://www.ojjdp.ncjrs.org/

Office of National Drug Control Policy
Drug Policy Information Clearinghouse
PO Box 6000
Rockville, MD 20849-6000
1-800-666-3332
FAX: (301) 519-5212
URL: http://
www.whitehousedrugpolicy.gov/

The Sentencing Project
514 Tenth St. NW, Ste. 1000
Washington, DC 20004
(202) 628-0871
FAX: (202) 628-1091
E-mail: staff@sentencingproject.org
URL: http://www.sentencingproject.org/

Southern Poverty Law Center
400 Washington Ave.
Montgomery, AL 36104
(334) 956-8200
URL: http://www.splcenter.org/

Substance Abuse and Mental Health Services Administration
PO Box 2345
Rockville, MD 20847-2345
1-877-726-4727
FAX: (240) 221-4292

E-mail: SHIN@samhsa.hhs.gov
URL: http://www.samhsa.gov/

Supreme Court of the United States
One First St. NE
Washington, DC 20543
(202) 479-3000
URL: http://www.supremecourtus.gov/

UNICOR
Federal Prison Industries, Inc.
1-800-827-3168
URL: http://www.unicor.gov/

Urban Institute
2100 M St. NW
Washington, DC 20037
(202) 833-7200
URL: http://www.urban.org/

U.S. Census Bureau
4600 Silver Hill Rd.
Washington, DC 20233
(301) 763-3030
URL: http://www.census.gov/

U.S. Department of Justice
950 Pennsylvania Ave. NW
Washington, DC 20530-0001
(202) 514-2000
E-mail: askdoj@usdoj.gov
URL: http://www.usdoj.gov/

U.S. Drug Enforcement Administration
U.S. Department of Justice
8701 Morrissette Dr.
Springfield, VA 22152
(202) 307-1000
URL: http://www.usdoj.gov/dea/index.htm

U.S. Parole Commission
5550 Friendship Blvd., Ste. 420
Chevy Chase, MD 20815-7286
(301) 492-5990
URL: http://www.usdoj.gov/uspc/

U.S. Postal Service
Office of the Inspector General
1735 N. Lynn St.
Arlington, VA 22209-2020
1-888-877-7644
(703) 248-2100
FAX: 1-866756-6741
E-mail: hotline@uspsoig.gov
URL: http://www.uspsoig.gov/

U.S. Securities and Exchange Commission
100 F St. NE
Washington, DC 20549
(202) 942-8088
E-mail: help@sec.gov
URL: http://www.sec.gov/

U.S. Sentencing Commission
Office of Public Affairs
One Columbus Circle NE
Washington, DC 20002-8002
(202) 502-4500
E-mail: pubaffairs@ussc.gov
URL: http://www.ussc.gov/

RESOURCES

The various agencies of the U.S. Department of Justice are the major sources of crime and justice data in the United States. The Bureau of Justice Statistics (BJS) compiles statistics on virtually every area of crime and reports those data in a number of publications. The annual BJS *Sourcebook of Criminal Justice Statistics*, prepared by the Hindelang Criminal Justice Research Center, State University of New York at Albany, is a comprehensive compilation of criminal justice statistics. The annual BJS National Crime Victimization Survey provides data for several studies, the most important of which is *Criminal Victimization in the United States.* Other valuable BJS publications include: *Background Checks for Firearm Transfers, 2007—Statistical Tables* (July 2008), *Census of State and Federal Correctional Facilities, 2005* (October 2008), *Compendium of Federal Justice Statistics, 2004* (December 2006), *Criminal Victimization, 2006* (December 2007, Michael Rand and Shannan Catalano), *Drug Use and Dependence, State and Federal Prisoners, 2004* (October 2006, Christopher J. Mumola and Jennifer C. Karberg), *Expenditure Facts at a Glance* (August 2007), *HIV in Prisons, 2006* (April 2008, Laura M. Maruschak), *Homicide Trends in the United States* (July 2007, James Alan Fox and Marianne W. Zawitz), *Identity Theft, 2005* (November 2007, Katrina Baum), *Jail Inmates at Midyear 2007* (June 2008, William J. Sabol and Todd D. Minton), *Justice Expenditure and Employment in the United States 2003* (April 2006, Kristen A. Hughes), *Law Enforcement Officers Killed and Assaulted, 2007* (October 2008), *Medical Problems of Prisoners* (April 2008, Laura M. Maruschak), *Mental Health Problems of Prison and Jail Inmates* (September 2006, Doris J. James and Lauren E. Glaze), *Prison and Jail Inmates at Midyear 2005* (May 2006, Paige M. Harrison and Allen J. Beck), *Prisoners in 2006* (December 2007, William J. Sabol, Heather Couture, and Paige M. Harrison), *Prison Inmates at Midyear 2007* (June 2008, William J. Sabol and Heather Couture), and *Probation and Parole in the United States, 2007 Statistical Tables* (December 2008, Lauren E. Glaze and Thomas P. Bonczar). The BJS Office for Victims of Crime published *Rebuilding*

Lives, Restoring, Hope: OVC Report to the Nation 2007 (2007). The BJS and the National Center for Education Statistics jointly published *Indicators of School Crime and Safety: 2007* (December 2007, Rachel Dinkes et al.).

The Federal Bureau of Investigation (FBI) collects crime data from state and local law enforcement agencies through its Uniform Crime Reports Program. The FBI annual *Crime in the United States* is the most important source of information on crime reported to law enforcement agencies. Information on white-collar crime came from the FBI in *2007 Mortgage Fraud Report* (April 2008) and *Financial Crimes Report to the Public, Fiscal Year 2007 (October 1, 2006–September 30, 2007)* (May 2008). The National White Collar Crime Center published both *IC3 2007 Internet Crime Report* (2008) and the results of a national survey on white-collar crime in *The 2005 National Public Survey on White Collar Crime* (2006, John Kane and April Wall). The U.S. Department of Justice's Computer Crime and Intellectual Property Section provided *Data Breaches: What the Underground World of "Carding" Reveals* (May 2008, Kimberly Kiefer Peretti) and *Prosecuting Computer Crimes* (February 2007).

The Office of Juvenile Justice and Delinquency Prevention published several helpful resources on juvenile crime and justice issues, including *Juvenile Arrests, 2006* (November 2008, Howard N. Snyder), *Juvenile Court Statistics 2005* (July 2008, Charles Puzzanchera and Melissa Sickmund), and *Juvenile Offenders and Victims: 2006 National Report* (March 2006, Howard N. Snyder and Melissa Sickmund).

The Federal Trade Commission, through its Identity Theft Clearinghouse, published *Consumer Fraud and Identity Theft Complaint Data, January–December 2007* (February 2008). The U.S. Sentencing Commission published *Guidelines Manual* (November 2008).

Several sources provide data on hate crimes in the United States. For example, the Anti-Defamation League produces "Map of State Statutes for Hate Crimes" (2009, http://

www.adl.org/learn/hate_crimes_laws/map_frameset.html) as a reference guide on the nation's hate crime legislation. The Southern Poverty Law Center in Montgomery, Alabama, publishes data on hate crimes in its periodical *Intelligence Report*. The FBI discusses it in *Hate Crime Statistics, 2007* (October 2008).

The Sentencing Project conducts research on criminal justice issues and promotes sentencing reform. Key information was also acquired from polling results reported by the Gallup Organization.

Other publications that provided useful information include *2008 Marijuana Sourcebook—Marijuana: The Greatest Cause of Illegal Drug Abuse* (July 2008) from the Executive Office of the President, Office of National Drug Control Policy; *Results from the 2007 National Survey on Drug Use and Health: National Findings* (September 2008) from the U.S. Department of Health and Human Services, Substance Abuse and Mental Health Services Administration; *Drugs of Abuse* (June 2004) from the U.S. Drug Enforcement Administration; *I'd Rather Be Hanged for a Sheep than a Lamb: The Unintended Consequences of "Three-Strikes" Laws* (February 2008, Radha Iyengar) from the National Bureau of Economic Research; and *Methamphetamine: Background, Prevalence, and Federal Drug Control Policies* (January 2007, Celinda Franco) from the Congressional Research Service.

The Urban Institute is a nonpartisan economic and social policy research organization that publishes several reports on crime victims, corrections and prisoners, courts and policing, and juvenile justice. It provided *Beyond the Prison Gates: The State of Parole in America* (November 2002, Jeremy Travis and Sarah Lawrence).

INDEX

Human immunodeficiency virus (HIV), 106
Hurricane Katrina, 57

I